METRICS FOR SUSTAINABLE BUSINESS

Metrics for Sustainable Business is the first book to look comprehensively at the various standards for reporting and evaluating the sustainability of organizations. It presents in detail the two programs for disclosure (the GRI reporting guidelines and the SASB accounting standards) and several standards for corporate ratings and rankings, and for organizational certification.

The chapters on accounting for greenhouse gas emissions, water use, and waste introduce the reader to some of the technical details in sustainability accounting, but it is the comparison and contrast of the standards that takes the reader into questions at the frontiers of sustainability reporting. A chapter on the philosophies of sustainability offers a novel answer to the question, "Why are they asking us—or not—to report *that*?" The book examines the meaning of materiality in sustainability accounting and calls on the profession to re-evaluate how small and medium-size enterprises can report on and manage their sustainability effectively yet economically. The author's examination of the common ESG framework (environment, social, and governance) for sustainability standards reveals that it will not satisfy the current call for an integrated, connected reporting of the triple bottom line of sustainability (people, planet, and profits), and a careful look at the way various standards treat the social category of sustainability reveals questions about the appropriate conceptual framework for reporting the elements of social sustainability.

This book will serve thoughtful students and professionals, who are interested in sustainability and accounting.

Scott R. Herriott is Professor and Dean of the College of Business Administration at Maharishi University of Management, USA. He specializes in the application of quantitative methods to business strategy with a focus on sustainable business. He is the author of a dozen scientific papers and books on economics, organization theory, and business strategy.

"*Metrics for Sustainable Business* is the first book to provide a comprehensive overview and comparison of the frameworks companies can use for reporting on environmental and social issues. It includes a valuable discussion about the use of indicators to measure sustainability performance and offers technical details on the accounting for greenhouse gas emissions, water, and waste. Herriott's writing style makes the material accessible and interesting for readers with varying levels of knowledge about sustainability reporting and related metrics. The book is well-written, well-organized and thorough. This is a must read for anyone interested in learning about this exciting and challenging topic. The book should also serve well as a textbook for college-level courses in sustainability reporting."

Kenton D. Swift, University of Montana, USA

"This is the sustainability accounting text I need for my classes. *Metrics for Sustainable Business* brings together the set of topics needed by accountants engaged in understanding and reporting sustainability issues for organizations. Scott Herriott's book will be foundational for my courses and will be a regularly-consulted reference on my bookshelf."

Darrell Brown, Portland State University, USA

METRICS FOR SUSTAINABLE BUSINESS

Measures and Standards for the Assessment of Organizations

Scott R. Herriott

NEW YORK AND LONDON

First published 2016
by Routledge
711 Third Avenue, New York, NY 10017

and by Routledge
2 Park Square, Milton Park, Abingdon, Oxon OX14 4RN

Routledge is an imprint of the Taylor & Francis Group, an informa business

Library of Congress Cataloging-in-Publication Data
Names: Herriott, Scott R., author.
Title: Metrics for sustainable business : measures and standards for the assessment of organizations / Scott R. Herriott.
Description: New York, NY : Routledge, 2016. | Includes bibliographical references and indexes.
Identifiers: LCCN 2015050448 | ISBN 9781138901711 (hbk) | ISBN 9781138901728 (pbk)
Subjects: LCSH: Sustainable development reporting. | Management—Environmental aspects. | Environmental auditing.
Classification: LCC HD60.3.H47 2016 | DDC 658.4/083—dc23
LC record available at http://lccn.loc.gov/2015050448

ISBN: 978-1-138-90171-1 (hbk)
ISBN: 978-1-138-90172-8 (pbk)
ISBN: 978-1-315-69770-3 (ebk)

Typeset in Bembo
by Apex CoVantage, LLC

For Vicki and Nathaniel

CONTENTS

ACKNOWLEDGMENTS

I would like to thank my MBA students for their helpful questions and for their assistance in the research on sustainability certifications and metrics: Karissa O'Brien, Christina Ring, and Di (Maggie) Zhang on ecolabeling; Zhuowei (Tony) Lai, Cheng (Nathan) Yuan, Fei (Fred) Li, Jonathan MacNamara, and Zhen (Johnny) Tang on the Global Reporting Initiative; Wei (Jocelyn) Chi, Tracy Cui, and Cooper Rose on measures of employee wellness; Guanting (Agnes) Cui, Haiqi (Eric) Mao, and Caleb Prescott on ISO 14001; Avanija Kuntla, Olivia Lopez, and Xin (Jason) Wang on WalMart's supplier certification program; Maartan Schoots and Caspar Jung on the AASHE STARS certification for universities; Lin Long, Peng Jia, Omnia Bekheet, and Guy Hearse-Jones on the various green building standards (LEED, NAHB, ASHRAE, BREEAM, Green Globes); and Maryam Kazemi on water stress. Thanks also to Karen Slowick, Sylvia Richards, and Marianne Barber for their proofreading of the final manuscript.

The four anonymous reviewers of the proposal for this book provided useful suggestions. Darrell Brown and Jean Rogers offered helpful comments on a late draft of the book. A special thank you goes to Wim Bartels of KPMG, who gave many thoughtful comments on the manuscript. The remaining errors are solely mine.

Scott Herriott
Fairfield, Iowa
September 2015

INTRODUCTION

The 21st century is bringing into focus a deeper understanding of the way that business is embedded in society and the natural world. Companies now realize that their owners, the shareholders, are not the sovereign masters of the enterprise. Business leaders now recognize that business relies on forms of natural, human, and social capital, which firms cannot own, as well as on the financial and intellectual capital that firms can own. Relying on natural, human, and social capital, businesses must ensure the preservation of that capital in order to secure their own long-term existence. The focus on the *triple bottom line* of social, environmental, and economic outcomes, or "people, planet, and profit," is the essential theme of sustainable business.

To manage their operations with an eye to these broader responsibilities, companies need a conceptual framework that can suggest which indicators of sustainability to monitor, and they need procedures to measure, summarize, and report on them.

The largest firms in the world are already experimenting with sustainability reporting. A recent report by KPMG showed that by 2013, 93% of the world's 250 largest companies were publishing reports on their corporate responsibility or sustainability. Among the 100 largest companies in 41 countries surveyed by KPMG in 2013, 4,100 firms in all, sustainability reporting had reached a penetration of 71%, up from 64% just two years earlier. On the question of whether firms should issue sustainability reports, KPMG concluded, "the debate is over."[1]

Reporting on sustainability is just the starting point for triple-bottom-line management. Companies need to know how their management of natural, human, and social capitals—and how their engagement with the various stakeholders who do possess those capitals—adds value to the firm. As Yvo de Boer put it, "The questions companies should ask themselves now . . . are 'what should we report on?' and 'how should we report it?' And, most importantly, 'how can we best use the process of reporting to generate maximum value both for our shareholders and for our other stakeholders?'"[2]

The relationship between the management of natural, human, and social capitals and value creation is demonstrated only when sustainability reporting is integrated with financial reporting. Such integrated reporting is now promoted by the International Integrated Reporting Council (IIRC), integrated reporting is required in South Africa, and proposals for its requirement have been put forth in Brazil, India, and the European Union (EU).[3] The natural extension of integrated reporting is *connected reporting*, promoted by the Accounting for Sustainability (A4S) Project of Prince Charles of England, which explicitly draws out the relationships between the environmental and social impacts of a firm and its future financial performance and risk.[4]

Companies need to know how to form composite metrics that reflect a firm's performance in the triple bottom line's environmental, social, and economic categories and in their principal subcategories. Such summative measures permit firms to distill the large volume of information generated by sustainability reports into a manageable set of key performance indicators. To illustrate the potential volume of information, the Global Reporting Initiative's *G4 Sustainability Reporting Guidelines* is a 94-page standard supported by a 266-page implementation manual. Its comprehensive reporting requirement includes 91 indicators on which firms would report specifically about economic, environmental, and social impacts, requiring a total of more than 300 data points.

Identifying indicators of sustainability, measuring them, and assembling the data for a report is only the starting point for an understanding about how to manage a firm for sustainability. The real challenge is to condense the data, rolling indicator scores up into subcategory and category scores (environmental, social, and economic) and into a summative score on the sustainability of a firm and to use this collection of key performance indicators—generically termed *metrics*—to guide business decisions.

Such an undertaking would be well beyond the scope of this book. The science of sustainability is not even near a point where we would have the conceptual frameworks and measurement systems to make fully connected reporting a reality. As a start, this book reviews what is generally known about the essential steps in the development of metrics: (1) how to identify material indicators of sustainability, (2) how to measure those indicators, and (3) how to form composite metrics that reflect a firm's performance in the environmental and social categories and their principal subcategories. The review of these topics will yield insights about how the current practices can be improved.

The state of the art in sustainability reporting is to be found in the standards that exist for sustainability disclosure, rating, and certification. This book features nine such standards. The programs for disclosure are represented in this book by two organizations, the Global Reporting Initiative (GRI), which offers the GRI-G4 reporting guidelines, and the Sustainability Accounting Standards Board (SASB), which publishes a standard for sustainability accounting. These programs for disclosure suggest only what to report, not how to interpret it. The interpretation appears in standards for corporate rating and certification, represented here by the Dow Jones Sustainability Indices, Thompson Reuters' ASSET4 ESG standard, the Financial Times Stock Exchange FTSE4Good metric, and Corporate Knights' Global 100 metric as rating systems and by certifications offered through the Association for the Advancement of Sustainability in Higher Education's STARS metric, Underwriters Laboratories UL 880 standard, and B Labs, Inc.'s B Corporation (benefit corporation) standard.

Chapters 1, 2, and 3 describe these featured standards for disclosure, rating, and certification. They introduce the reader to the vocabulary of sustainability metrics and present the main features of the standards.

Chapters 4 and 5 introduce two conceptual frameworks for understanding the content of standards for sustainability. Chapter 4 is a survey of the ethical perspectives that may account for differences in the operational meaning of "sustainability" across various standards. Chapter 5 is a review of conceptual approaches to the design of systems for measuring and summarizing aspects of sustainability.

Chapters 6, 7, and 8 present the details of measurement and reporting in the three principal subcategories of environmental sustainability (greenhouse gas emissions, water, and waste). Chapter 9 is a discussion of the main components of social sustainability (employees, community, nation-state, and customers and suppliers) as they are represented in the featured standards. Contemporary methods for measuring and summarizing data on greenhouse gases (GHGs), water, and waste are rather well developed, so we do not find controversy there. The social metrics of sustainability are not conceptualized as well, and there is much less standardization of practice in measurement and summation, so Chapter 9 raises many interesting questions for further research.

The book concludes in Chapter 10 with a discussion of issues and questions raised by this examination of the standards for sustainability. We look at whether metrics based on the environmental, social, and governance (ESG) reporting framework truly represent the triple-bottom-line conceptualization of sustainability in environmental, social, and economic categories, which focuses attention on the meaning of governance and "economic." We take a close look at the social category to understand which aspects of sustainability should roll up under it. The final issue is the data-reduction problem, where we consider if and how it would be possible to formulate metrics for sustainability that are not as data intensive as most of the standards featured here. That question will become very important as small and medium-sized enterprises grow in their desire to monitor and manage their sustainability and to publish sustainability reports.

Notes

1 KPMG. 2013. *The KPMG Survey of Corporate Responsibility Reporting 2013*. KPMG International. Available at <www.kpmg.com/Global/en/IssuesAndInsights/Articles Publications/corporate-responsibility/Documents/corporate-responsibility-reporting-survey-2013-exec-summary.pdf> Accessed August 2015.

2 De Boer, Y. 2013. Corporate Responsibility Reporting: Is It Really Worth It? *The KPMG Survey of Corporate Responsibility Reporting 2013*. Available at <www.kpmg.com/Global/en/IssuesAndInsights/ArticlesPublications/corporate-responsibility/Documents/corporate-responsibility-reporting-survey-2013-exec-summary.pdf> Accessed August 2015.

3 Eccles, R., and M. P. Krzus. 2015. *The Integrated Reporting Movement*. Hoboken, NJ: Wiley.

4 Hopwood, A., J. Unerman, and J. Fries, eds. 2010. *Accounting for Sustainability*. London: Earthscan.

1

SYSTEMS FOR DISCLOSURE

In this chapter, we will look in depth at two programs for reporting on sustainability, the "guidelines" of the Global Reporting Initiative and the "standard" published by the Sustainability Accounting Standards Board. We refer to guidelines and standards generically as *systems* or *programs*.

Guidelines and standards have some features in common but also an important difference. At their basis, both guidelines and standards for disclosure identify the variables, called *indicators,* which users of the program may find relevant to an evaluation of sustainability, and they prescribe the procedures for measuring and reporting those indicators. In that way, both guidelines and standards promote consistency in reporting, which permits users to make comparisons within a firm over time and across firms.

Around that basic function, programs for disclosure also convey principles by which reporters should decide which items of information are useful to an evaluation of sustainability and which are not. Borrowing a term from financial accounting, we say that the useful disclosures are *material* to the users and that these principles characterize the *materiality* of the indicators.

Guidelines and standards differ in that standards are designed to be auditable, but guidelines are not. As an example, the ISO 14001:2004 *Environmental Management Systems—Requirements with guidance for use* is a standard against which a firm can be audited and certified, but the ISO 26000:2010 *Guidance on Social Responsibility* is not a program for certification. The Sustainability Accounting Standards Board encourages its users to have their SASB Standard Disclosures audited the using the American Institute of Certified Public Accountants' *Statements on Standards for Attestation Engagements*, which are also used by the Public Company Accounting Oversight Board as an interim standard for attestation engagements with publicly traded companies. As a point of comparison, the Global Reporting Initiative's G4 *Sustainability Reporting Guidelines* is not designed to be auditable, but it offers sufficient detail in its presentation of principles for disclosure and requirements for reporting individual indicators of sustainability that the GRI guidelines recommend that organizations have their reports externally assured in whole or in part, meaning assured by a third party such as an accounting firm.

Programs for disclosure address the fundamental question of what should be reported and how. The standards for sustainability, to be discussed in Chapters 2 and 3, begin with the "what" and "how" of individual indicators and then consolidate that information into subcategory scores, category scores (environmental, social, and economic), and finally summative metrics for the overall sustainability of an organization, which we will discuss in Chapter 5. Thus, the study of standards for disclosure is a good starting point for understanding metrics for sustainable business.

We begin this chapter with a discussion of the concept of materiality. We continue with an examination of programs for disclosure that have been developed by two organizations, the Global Reporting Initiative and the Sustainability Accounting Standards Board. There are many standards for disclosure, most of which have been mandated by government for specific purposes.[1] Our focus in this book is on guidance and standards for the voluntary disclosure of information related to the full scope of sustainability issues—environmental, social, and economic. Notable among these, but not discussed in detail here, is the standard for the disclosure of information related to corporate social responsibility of the Chinese Academy of Social Sciences since 2009 as *Guidelines on Corporate Social Responsibility Reporting for Chinese Enterprises*, published in its third edition in 2014 as CASS-CSR3.0. We will use the GRI as our primary example of voluntary disclosure, but persons interested in CASS-CSR may find a crosswalk of the CASS-CSR3.0 onto the GRI at the GRI website.[2]

The Concept of Materiality

Materiality is the central concept in the analysis of metrics for sustainable business, but its application to sustainability is more complex than its use in accounting. To the Financial Accounting Standards Board (FASB), which governs the practice of financial accounting for nongovernmental organizations in the United States, a fact is material if its omission makes it "probable that the judgment of a *reasonable person* [emphasis added] relying on the [fact] would have been changed or influenced by the inclusion or correction of the item."[3] Facts are material to *users of information,* not to the reporting firm. The user, the person relying on that information, might be taken to be an existing or prospective owner of the shares or debt of the firm, a transactional party (buyer from or seller to) the firm, or a governmental regulator of the firm. In the context of accounting, any of these parties may be interested in the current and future financial status of the reporter, so the information is judged as material to *financial* decisions. The definition of materiality taken from U.S. securities laws and case law is more specific about who the "person" is: information is material if there is "a substantial likelihood that the disclosure of the omitted fact would have been viewed by the *reasonable investor* [emphasis added] as having significantly altered the 'total mix' of the information made available."[4]

In contrast, sustainable business is characterized by an attention to the stakeholders of a firm, not merely to its shareholders. Stakeholders include individuals or companies that have an interest in the firm, where "interest" is not meant only in the financial sense but more broadly as having a relationship to the firm. Yet more broadly, even the natural environment is viewed as a stakeholder. The environment may have a direct impact on organizations, but it is also represented in the social domain by citizens and organizations that have a concern about the effect of business on the environment.

As we consider materiality in the sustainability arena, the user of information may be any stakeholder who has any type of relationship to or interest in the firm. This takes the concept of materiality well beyond its original domain in financial accounting, where the "judgments" in the FASB definition focus in practice on the value of the firm (for investors), its financial stability (for creditors), or the firm's compliance with laws and regulation (for the government). The extension of materiality into accounting for sustainability extends the domain of the interests that persons may have in the business. However, sustainability as a concept is not so well defined that it will always be clear what interests are relevant and what judgments about a firm should reasonably support those interests.

Indeed, in the sustainability domain, materiality may be defined not merely in terms of judgments but by interested parties having *expectations* about the firm. In the Global Reporting Initiative's G4 guidelines on disclosure, which we will examine in detail in this chapter, item G4-2 states that a firm must report on its key impacts, risks, and opportunities. As part of that, reporters are instructed to discuss their

> . . . effects on stakeholders, including rights as defined by national laws and relevant internationally recognized standards. This should take into account the range of reasonable *expectations* and interests of the organization's stakeholders.[5]
>
> *(Emphasis added.)*

That is a qualitative extension of the definition of materiality from the context of financial accounting, because parties may have expectations without having the legal or even ethical grounds for enforcing those expectations. If "reasonable" is meant to mean legal or ethical, then the scope of those interests is constrained somewhat, but as we shall see in Chapter 4, there are many ethical perspectives that may be taken on questions that pertain to sustainability.

As materiality is defined by the FASB (and, as we shall see below, the SASB), the concept pertains to *facts*. Only facts can be material. In the broader use to which the term is put in sustainability accounting and reporting, we will see reference to material *issues* or to material *aspects* of sustainability. We generalize the term by defining issues or aspects to be material if information about the issue or aspect would be material.

The Global Reporting Initiative (GRI)

The Global Reporting Initiative is a not-for-profit organization that promotes guidelines for organizations on how to report their economic and environmental impacts and their policies and practices in relation to social justice and organizational governance. Covering environmental, social, and governance (ESG) elements, the GRI is comprehensive, not targeted to a specific organizational function or process, so we treat it here as an organizational system for disclosure. However, the GRI *does not evaluate* organizations. The GRI promotes a system for *disclosure*, called the *Sustainability Reporting Guidelines*, but it does not offer a summative evaluation of any aspect of sustainability.

In May 2013, the GRI published its fourth-generation program, the G4, which was optional during a transition period of 2013–2015. This section of the chapter reflects on the GRI by comparing the last of the third-generation guidelines, GRI G3.1, with the new G4 guidelines.

History and Organization

The Global Reporting Initiative was formed by the Coalition for Environmentally Responsible Economies (CERES) and the United Nations Environment Programme (UNEP) in 1997, a year after the International Organization for Standardization published its ISO 14001 standard for environmental management systems. The first 20 GRI reports were released in 1999. In 2001, the CERES board separated GRI to form an independent institution, following a recommendation of the GRI Steering Committee. In 2000, the second version of the GRI (G2) was released at the World Summit for Sustainable Development in Johannesburg, South Africa. Over 150 organizations released reports. The third generation (G3) was launched in 2006. In early 2012, 3,500 organizations had filed GRI reports in their database.[6] By mid-2015, there were 25,000 reports from 7,700 organizations, of which 19,000 reports used the GRI standard. The GRI organized working groups in 2012 to formulate aspects of the fourth-generation framework, which came out in 2013 as G4.

Beginning in 2015, the GRI put its standard-setting function under the Global Sustainability Standards Board (GSSB), which has an independent public funding base and directs the GRI's Standards Department in the activities of formulating and updating standards. Distinct from the GSSB are the GRI's organizations for promoting the standard, training individuals and organizations in its use, archiving and distributing sustainability data and reports, and managing government relations.[7]

GRI set up a separate, five-person Due Process Oversight Committee (DPOC) to review the activities of the GSSB in relation to the GRI's policies for standard setting and a five-person Independent Appointments Committee (IAC) to ensure the transparency of the processes of nominating individuals to the GSSB and the DPOC. The members of the IAC are appointed by the nine-person GRI Nominating Committee (GNC), which consists of two members from the Stakeholder Council, two members of the GRI board of directors, the chairs of the GRI board and the Stakeholder Council, and three individuals representing the field of international sustainability standard setters. With the authority for standard setting residing in the GSSB, the GRI Stakeholder Council will be involved in the appointment of members to the GRI Board of Directors, but will provide only "strategic advice" to the Board, and the Board will limit its input on standards to "strategic issues concerning sustainability reporting broadly."[8]

The 50-member GRI Stakeholder Council is the "eyes and ears" of the GRI network, representing the "core constituencies" in GRI's network: for-profit business, civil society organizations, investment institutions, labor, and institutions that provide goods or services associated with the reporting process ("mediating institutions").[9] They meet annually to debate and deliberate key strategic and policy issues. They also approve nominations for the Board of Directors and for two members of the standing GRI Nominating Committee. Seats within the Council have been allocated among stakeholder groups as shown in Table 1.1. These seats are also organized into five major geographic categories with, at minimum, a single representative from each geographic region: Africa, Asia/Pacific, Europe/North America, Latin America/Caribbean, and West Asia.[10]

Sixty percent of the Stakeholder Council members are elected by the Organizational Stakeholders, who are a group of about 600 companies spread across 60 countries and who make annual contributions to the GRI on a sliding scale based on their annual revenues.[11] The remaining 40% of the Stakeholder Council are elected by sitting members of the Council. The expirations of members' three-year terms are staggered so that about one-third of the seats become vacant annually.

TABLE 1.1 GRI Stakeholder Council Membership

Membership Type	*2015 Actual*	*2009 Limit*
Business	14	22
Civil society organizations	5	16
Investment	5	
Mediating institutions	14	16
Labor organizations	4	6
Total	**42**	**60**

The GRI Secretariat is the administrative arm that implements the technical work plan set by the Board of Directors and manages network and institutional communications, outreach, stakeholder relations, and financial administration.[12]

GRI's Governmental Advisory Group was formed in 2008. It is composed of up to 15 people who provide the GRI Board and the GRI executive team with a direct source of advice from governmental stakeholders. Membership is by invitation only and is accepted by the members as voluntary service. Invitation is based upon "experience, a track record of leadership, and an ability to bring independent and innovative thinking to the table."[13]

The governance of the GRI, through a Secretariat, a Board of Directors, a Stakeholder Council, and a standards board, has many similarities with the governance of the International Organization for Standardization, as will be seen in the next chapter, where we consider the ISO 14001 standard for environmental management systems.

Standard Disclosures in the GRI G3.1 and G4

The GRI guidelines consist of disclosures that are either general disclosures, which describe the firm's strategy and structure and the intended boundaries of the GRI report, or disclosures that are specific to an aspect of sustainability. The indicators in the GRI standard are classified by "category" using the familiar triple-bottom-line framework: economic, environmental, and social. The economic and environmental categories are not divided further. The social category has four subcategories: labor practices, product responsibility, society, and human rights. Items related to governance are treated in the GRI as general disclosures.

Information in the GRI report is organized fundamentally in terms of "performance indicators," 126 of which were in G3.1 and 91 are in G4, each labeled with a designation by category or subcategory and number, such as EC1, or EN8, or LA2. If the governance disclosures had been classified as specific to sustainability, rather than as general organizational indicators, that would have added 17 more indicators to GRI-G3.1 and 22 to GRI-G4. These indicators may be direct measures of performance, or they may represent the presence or absence of policies and practices. Each indicator requires the disclosure of one *or more* items of information, some of which may have to be broken down further depending on the number of countries or regions the organization operates in, the number of employee categories it tracks, and so on. Some items are qualitative, calling for summaries of impacts or findings from studies. Some are contingent on the existence of specific types of problem. The scope of reporting therefore depends on the organization, but the number of distinct items of information called for in the entire GRI was at least 500 in GRI-G3.1 and is at least 350 in GRI-G4.

The Global Reporting Initiative recognizes that the material aspects of sustainability vary across industries. The GRI offers specific guidance to some industries through its Sector Supplements for airports, real estate, electric utilities, financial services, oil and gas, mining and metals, food processing, media, NGOs, and event organizers. No other sector supplements were being developed in 2015.

Just as the GRI may be augmented for different economic sectors, it may also be adapted to the different social and political contexts of different nations. GRI's national annexes provide the guidance on how to relate the general GRI guidelines to "local policies, rules, and regulations." The first national annex was formulated for Brazil. A working draft was submitted for public comment in 2011, and by 2012 the working groups were examining the feedback and preparing it for review by GRI's governing body. In 2015, it was still under development, and no other national annexes had been announced.[14]

Sectoral Disclosures in GRI-G4

The GRI has a generic set of guidelines that is supplemented by sector-specific guidance. Between July 2012 and April 2013, the GRI conducted research for what were called Sector Supplements in the GRI-G3 guidelines and are called Sector Disclosures in GRI-G4. GRI wanted to identify the sustainability topics that would be specifically relevant to key industry sectors. They sought the participation of five types of stakeholder group: business associations, labor representatives, civil society organizations, information users, and experts. In the end, according to the GRI, "194 organizations related to the different stakeholder groups either contributed directly or were researched as part of this effort," and the project generated 2,812 topics that were related to 52 industries. Those proposed topics were narrowed to 1,612 by combining topics with similar content. Of the 52 industries, the top 12 had more than 40 sector-specific topics, and the top 33 (63%) had more than 20 topics. Only 10 industries had less than 10 topics.[15]

That master list of sustainability topics provides guidance for companies in their identification of material aspects of sustainability for reporting. Subsequently, the GRI formulated the Sectoral Disclosures for the ten industries listed in Table 1.2. As of late 2015, no further Sectoral Disclosures were under development.

TABLE 1.2 GRI-G4 Sectoral Disclosures

Airport Operators
Construction and Real Estate
Electric Utilities
Event Organizers
Financial Services
Food Processing
Media
Mining and Metals
NGO
Oil and Gas

The GRI Evaluation System (Past and Present)

Under GRI-G3, a reporting entity would assign its own report one of three "application levels," which were designated C, B, and A. These designations identified the scope of the report, meaning the extent to which the various general and specific performance indicators were covered in the report. The C level required a disclosure of 10 indicators, while 20 were needed for B. Out of the total of 126 indicators in the GRI-G3.1, all of the 55 "core" indicators that the reporting firm considers material to sustainability had to be reported for an A-level designation. If the report had been externally assured, it warranted a "+" designation by the letter.

The designations C, B, and A, with optional enhancement by the "+", were reminiscent of the Bronze, Silver, and Gold certification levels that had become popular in the certification marketplace for organizations (see Chapter 3) and for some categories of product certification. There, a Silver or Gold certification level indicated a higher level of demonstrated performance related to sustainability, but in the case of the GRI there was no evaluation of performance, only a disclosure. A company with highly unsustainable practices could, if it disclosed them according to the standard and had the report externally assured, declare itself worthy of an A+ designation under the GRI system.

The potential for misunderstanding was eliminated in GRI-G4, where the focus of analysis shifted to the "material aspects" of sustainability, which are groups of indicators around a particular quality, or aspect, of sustainability. Though these material aspects had been identified in G3.1 as groups of indicators, they took on more importance in G4. GRI-G4 eliminated the three "certification levels" in favor of two "accordance" options. A firm could choose to issue its report "in accordance with" either the GRI-G4 "core" or "comprehensive" reporting guidelines. A core report had to include certain general disclosures and at least one indicator from each of the 46 "material aspects" that constituted subdivisions of the categories and subcategories. A comprehensive report would cover all disclosures.

For each of the material aspects in G4, the disclosure also includes a discussion of Disclosures on Management Approach (DMA), where the reporter may explain its systems and procedures for managing the economic, environmental, and social impacts related to the aspect.

Under G3, though, GRI did not certify reports; it would, if requested, "check" a report and provide a customized GRI Application Level Check Statement. The statement read, in part:

> The Check confirms that the required set and number of disclosures for that Application Level have been addressed in the reporting and that the GRI Content demonstrates a valid representation of the required disclosures as described in the GRI G3 Guidelines.

Under G4, the Application Level Check has been replaced by several "alignment" services. One is a Materiality Matters check, initiated in December 2013, in which GRI verifies that the reporter's treatment of materiality, organizational boundaries, and stakeholder engagement in indicators G4-17 to G4-27 "are located as stated and can easily be found by readers." Reporters that take advantage of this service could receive an acknowledgement via an "official GRI-branded message which reporting organizations can include prominently in their report to communicate to their stakeholders that the report has been checked."[16] In 2015, that check was replaced by the Materiality Disclosures Service, which has the same purpose but results in a GRI Materiality Disclosures Service organizational mark that may be displayed on the report. Another service is the Content Index Service, which helps reporters improve the accuracy and usability of the GRI Content Index, the central navigation tool for the report.[17]

Materiality in the GRI-G4

A consistent theme in the GRI and in the other example (SASB) to be discussed next is that firms must report on what they deem to be material. Material information is relevant to sustainable business, but there is more to materiality than relevance. Material information reflects the impacts of an organization that are significant to stakeholders. The GRI-G4 guidelines remind readers, "Materiality is the threshold at which Aspects [of sustainability] become sufficiently important that they should be reported."

In a firm's report using a guideline or standard, indicators that are not material to the firm may be noted as such, and then the reporting firm is not required to produce the information. The GRI guidelines permit a reporter to omit information in an indicator if the indicator is not applicable to the firm, if the information is subject to confidentiality constraints or legal prohibitions, or if the data are unavailable at the time of the report. However, for the major categories and subcategories of sustainability, the GRI and SASB each require narrative disclosures of any issues that a reporter deems material, and they expect that the reporting firm will provide details on those material impacts even if the details are not called for specifically in the standard. That said, the standards give guidance about what is material and what is not.

The G4 *Reporting Principles and Standard Disclosures* state,

> Material Aspects are those that reflect the organization's significant economic, environmental and social impacts; or substantively influence the assessments and decisions of stakeholders.
>
> *(p. 7)*

In the GRI, stakeholders are defined as

> entities or individuals that can reasonably be expected to be significantly affected by the organization's activities, products, and services; and whose actions can reasonably be expected to affect the ability of the organization to successfully implement its strategies and achieve its objectives. This includes entities or individuals whose rights under law or international conventions provide them with legitimate claims vis-à-vis the organization.
>
> *(p. 92)*

Included in this definition of stakeholders are the types of individuals and organizations who were involved in the development of the standard:

> The Guidelines are developed through a global multi-stakeholder process involving representatives from business, labor, civil society, and financial markets, as well as auditors and experts in various fields; and in close dialogue with regulators and governmental agencies in several countries.
>
> *(p. 5)*

Certification of Organizations and Professionals in GRI-G4

The GRI "guides" organizations, but it does not certify them according to the GRI-G4, nor does it accredit third parties to audit organizations on the GRI-G4. However, it does certify organizations as "training partners" to train individuals to consult with reporting organizations about how to use the GRI guidelines.[18] Correspondingly, for individuals who have taken a training course from one of the certified training partners, the GRI certifies individuals' knowledge of the GRI-G4 by offering the G4 Exam.[19]

Sustainability Accounting Standards Board (SASB)

The Sustainability Accounting Standards Board was established in 2011 as a nonprofit organization. It is independent of all other accounting standards boards. It grew out of research done at the Initiative for Responsible Investment in Harvard's Kennedy School of Government to develop and test a methodology for determining issues that may constitute material information for companies within an industry and the associated performance indicators. Its mission is "to develop and disseminate sustainability accounting standards that help public corporations disclose material, decision-useful information to investors." Corporations may use its standards to disclose material sustainability information in mandatory SEC filings, such as the Form 10-K and 20-F.[20] SASB envisions an integration of financial and sustainability reporting as an outcome of its standards. Included on its website are mock 10-Ks showing how companies can integrate sustainability data, analyses, and discussion topics into the Management Discussion and Analysis section of the 10-K report in compliance with Regulation S-K of the Securities Act of 1933.[21]

SASB's standards development process is overseen by its 12-member Standards Council, which is composed of experts in a variety of fields germane to the development of standards. According to SASB,[22] "In an important independent overseer role, the Council reviews due process and quality of outcomes and ensures compliance of the standards setting process with American National Standards Institute (ANSI) guidance and SASB principles."

SASB is accredited by the American National Standards Institute as a standards developer. This signifies that SASB's procedures to develop standards meet ANSI's requirements for openness, balance, consensus, and due process.[23]

SASB's standards are industry specific. In 2015, SASB had issued standards for 57 industries in eight economic sectors. SASB's target is to develop sustainability accounting standards for more than 80 industries in 10 sectors by 2016.

SASB's Interpretation of Materiality

SASB published a concept paper that presents the essential features of the methodology by which they selected indicators of sustainability to be disclosed under their standards.[24] The intended user of SASB standards is the "reasonable investor" who desires to make informed investment decisions about publicly traded companies. SASB's reasonable investor "invests primarily for economic reasons with a variety of investment horizons—from short-term to long-term—and investment strategies—from income generation to asset valuation."

SASB's characterization of sustainability is consistent with the widely used ESG framework, accounting for environmental, social, and governance issues that bear on a firm's ability to create long-term value. The SASB standards distinguish human capital issues from social issues and add a fifth category for the firm's business model and innovation.[25]

- ***Environment.*** A corporation impacts the environment through its use of nonrenewable natural resources and through the harm it does to natural capital polluting air and water, disposing of waste, and emitting greenhouse gases. These indicators are common to other forms of environmental reporting.
- ***Social Capital.*** This dimension addresses the corporation's management of relationships with key outside stakeholders, which SASB identifies as customers, local communities, the public, and the government. SASB's social indicators relate to access to products and services, affordability, responsible business practices in marketing, and customer privacy.
- ***Leadership and Governance.*** This dimension reflects the common treatment of the governance element of the ESG framework. It identifies aspects of a company's operations that could be in conflict with the interests of stakeholders other than the company's owners, such as the government, community, customers, and employees. SASB's governance dimension includes traditional indicators such as regulatory compliance, lobbying and political contributions, anticompetitive behavior, corruption, and bribery. Compared to the GRI's classification of indicators, SASB's governance category goes outside the familiar boundaries of governance by including risk management, safety management, and supply chain management. It also includes the risk of business complicity with human rights violations, which is treated in the GRI as a subcategory of the social dimension of sustainability.
- ***Human Capital.*** Using this dimension, SASB separates a component that is part of the social dimension in the tripartite ESG framework. This component

addresses the management of a company's human resources—its employees and individual contractors. SASB explains,

> It includes factors that affect the productivity of employees, such as employee engagement, diversity, and incentives and compensation, as well as the attraction and retention of employees in highly competitive or constrained markets for specific talent, skills, or education. It also addresses the management of labor relations in industries that rely on economies of scale and compete on the price of products and services, or in industries with legacy pension liabilities associated with vast workforces. Lastly, it includes the management of the health and safety of employees and the ability to create a safety culture for companies that operate in dangerous working environments.

- ***Business Model and Innovation.*** This category does not address a firm's management of or impact on environmental, social, or human capital directly. However, it reflects SASB's perception that reasonable investors want to know how companies integrate environmental and social factors in their business models through efforts to improve efficiency in the use of natural resources across the life cycle of a product or to develop products that address the world's need to manage environmental and social impacts.

Figure 1.1 illustrates the generic sustainability issues that are included in SASB's five-factor model.

Narrowing The Focus

SASB's prioritization starts with a comprehensive set of sustainability issues

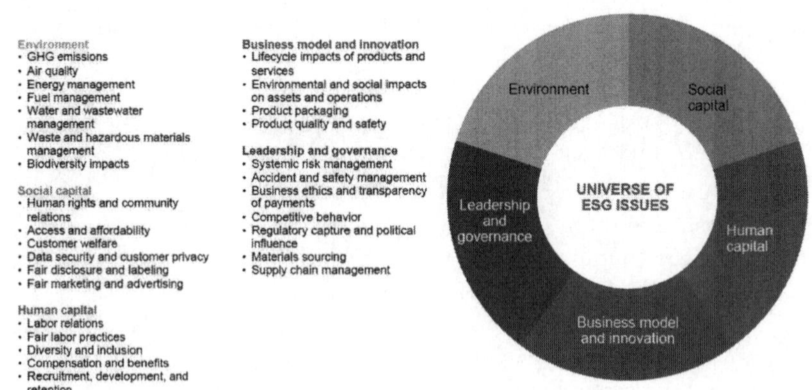

FIGURE 1.1 SASB Universe of Sustainability Issues

SASB's documents emphasize that each firm bears the final responsibility to determine which information is material to their investors and which, therefore, should be revealed in its Form 10-K and other public disclosures. However, each industry standard developed by SASB is intended to highlight the issues related to sustainability that are likely to constitute material information to investors in that industry. To that end, SASB uses the definition of materiality taken from U.S. securities laws and case law, which is that information is material if there is "a substantial likelihood that the disclosure of the omitted fact would have been viewed by the reasonable investor as having significantly altered the 'total mix' of the information made available."[26]

SASB anticipates that the users of its standards will summarize their key sustainability data in the Management Discussion and Analysis (MD&A) section of a 10-K report. SASB points to Item 303 of Regulation S-K in the Code of Federal Regulations (17 CFR 229.303(a)(3)), which requires companies to disclose, "any known trends or uncertainties that have had or that the registrant reasonably expects will have a material favorable or unfavorable impact on net sales or revenues or income from continuing operations. If the registrant knows of events that will cause a material change in the relationship between costs and revenues (such as known future increases in costs of labor or materials or price increases or inventory adjustments), the change in the relationship shall be disclosed." Instructions to Item 303 also state that the MD&A "shall focus specifically on material events and uncertainties known to management that would cause reported financial information not to be necessarily indicative of future operating results or of future financial condition." Thus, sustainability indicators that may have a significant impact on financial outcomes and risks warrant discussion in the MD&A section of the 10-K report.

SASB Disclosure Topics

As of 2015, SASB had published standards for 56 industries within eight economic sectors, and at least 22 more standards were under development in the three sectors designated by an asterisk (*) in Table 1.3.

SASB's standards attempt to identify environmental, social, and governance topics for disclosure that constitute material information to investors in specific

TABLE 1.3 SASB Industry Counts by Sector

Health Care (5)
Financials (7)
Technology and Communications (6)
Nonrenewable Resources (8)
Transportation (8)
Services (10)
Resource Transformation (5)
Consumption I (7)
*Consumption II (8)
*Renewable Resources and Alternative Energy (6)
*Infrastructure (8)

industries. Material aspects are common within economic sectors and industries owing to firms' similar business models and types of operation, meaning their use of similar resources and technologies and their similar exposure to environmental, social, and legal conditions. Table 1.4 summarizes the topics required for disclosure in a few of SASB's industries.

TABLE 1.4 Disclosure Topics in Selected Industries

Sector:	*Technology & Communications*	*Nonrenewables*	*Services*	*Services*
Industry:	*Semiconductors*	*Metals & Mining*	*Media Prod'n & Distribution*	*Education*
Environment	• GHG emissions • Energy management • Water and waste management	• GHG emissions • Air quality • Energy management • Water management • Water and hazardous materials management • Biodiversity impacts		
Social Capital		• Community relations • Security, human rights, and rights of indigenous peoples	• Journalistic integrity and sponsorship identification • Media pluralism	• Quality of education and gainful employment • Marketing and recruiting practices
Leadership and Governance	• Supply chain management and materials sourcing • Intellectual property protection and competitive behavior	• Business ethics and payments transparency	• Intellectual property protection and media piracy	
Human Capital	• Recruiting and managing a global skilled workforce • Employee health and safety	• Workforce health safety, and well-being • Labor relations		
Business Model and Innovation	• Product life-cycle management			

Table 1.4 shows that, in any industry, the topics on which firms must report do not necessarily cover all five categories of sustainability issues, and even when a category is covered, not all of the issues in that category are required. Clearly, not all of the 43 items in SASB's universe of sustainability issues (Figure 1.1) are required in any particular report. In fact, SASB reports can be very limited, as the examples of education and media show. Among the 57 industries for which SASB has issued standards, the median number of topics per industry is 5. The range is 2 to 11 topics.

To illustrate the variety of reporting requirements across industries, we now take a deeper look at Metals and Mining and at Education, using SASB's accounting standard for each industry.

The SASB Standard for Metals and Mining

The 11 topics listed above in the SASB standard for the Metals and Mining industry consists of 22 labeled indicators that are formed from 32 items of quantitative data, 5 textual responses concerning management processes and policies, and 2 items that have variable data requirements depending on the number of minerals processed or business units of the company. The breakdown of the 32 quantitative items by topic is shown in Table 1.5.

This count of 32 items across 22 sustainability indicators stands in contrast to the 350 items in 91 labeled indicators of the GRI-G4. SASB's standard for educational organizations brings out this point even more clearly.

TABLE 1.5 SASB Metals and Mining Standard (Quantitative Data)

Category	*Indicator Description*	*Items*
Environment	Air Quality	2
Environment	Biodiversity Impacts	3
Environment	Energy Management	1
Environment	GHG emissions	6
Environment	Waste and Hazardous Materials Management	3
Environment	Water Management	2
Governance	Business Ethics and Payments Transparency	2
Human Capital	Labor Relations	2
Human Capital	Workforce Health, Safety, and Well-Being	1
Society	Community Relations	7
Society	Security, Human Rights, and Rights of Indigenous Peoples	3
	Total of Items	**32**

The SASB Standard for Education

Education is one of three SASB industries that use only two topics. In education, those topics are broken down into nine indicators calling for eleven items of quantitative information, one textual response about policies, and one item that depends on the number of relevant academic programs. The quantitative indicators concern graduation rate, program completion rate, job placement rate, graduates' debt load, program loan default rates, fines, budget data, and revenue by source. As Table 1.4 shows, there are no indicators relating to governance, environmental or human capital impacts, or business model. The required indicators are all categorized as having social impacts. These are data that the U.S. Department of Education use to evaluate institutions of higher education.

This count of 9 indicators and 11 items of information stands in contrast not only to the extent of reporting required in the GRI, but also to the 70 indicators in the STARS 2.0 standard for sustainable universities. One of the central purposes of this book is to understand better the reasons why standards differ in these ways.

Comparing GRI-G4 and SASB in Two Industries: Media and Mining

SASB has standards issued or in development that are specific to 77 industry sectors. The GRI has a generic program that is supplemented by sector-specific guidance for ten industries. The industry sectors for which both programs offer guidance are media, mining and metals, and oil and gas. The GRI Sector Disclosure for financial service firms is covered by SASB's separate standards for commercial banking, investment banking, and consumer finance. GRI's Sector Disclosure for food processors is covered by SASB's separate standards for agricultural production, meat-poultry-dairy, processed foods, and nonalcoholic beverages.

GRI and SASB on Media

In December 2014, SASB issued a provisional standard for Media Production and Distribution.[27] Table 1.4 shows that it covers three aspects of sustainability. Those aspects are reported in eight indicators, designated SV0302–01 to SV0302–08. These are listed in Table 1.6 together with a sustainability subcategory classification that will be used in the comparison with GRI-G4 in Table 1.7.

Table 1.7 summarizes the SASB disclosures numerically in relation to the GRI-G4 standard disclosures taken together with the GRI-G4 Media Sector Disclosures. The numbers of indicators are illustrative but not definitive, because both the GRI and SASB leave it to the reporting organization to determine which of the indicators are material. Table 1.7 accounts for the supplemental indicators that are defined in the GRI sectoral disclosure standard, but it does not show the 13 indicators in the general standard for which additional items of information must be disclosed under the sectoral standard.

TABLE 1.6 SASB Indicators for the Media Industry

Label	*Description*	*Subcategory Classification*
SV0302–01	Amount of legal and regulatory fines for libel or slander	Governance: Ethics and Integrity
SV0302–02	Fact-checking expenses as a percentage of news production costs	Economic Performance
SV0302–03	Revenue from embedded advertising (advertorials, product placement, sponsored content)	Economic Performance
SV0302–04	Management approach to assuring journalistic integrity of news: factual, independence of or transparency of bias, protection of privacy and limitation of harm	Governance: Ethics and Integrity
SV0302–05	Percentage of gender and racial/ethnic group representation among executives, professionals, and others	Labor: Diversity and Equal Opportunity
SV0302–06	Policies and practices ensuring pluralism in news content	Content Creation and Dissemination
SV0302–07	Number of copyright infringement cases, number successful, number as copyright owner	Intellectual Property
SV0302–08	Policies and practices for assuring protection of intellectual property	Intellectual Property

TABLE 1.7 GRI-G4 and SASB on Media Disclosure Requirements

Sustainability Category	*Sustainability Subcategory*	*GRI Indicators*	*SASB Indicators*
General	Governance (G4 34–41, 44–45, 49–55, 57–58)	19	
General	Governance: Ethics and Integrity. G4-56	1	2
Economic	Economic performance	4 standard 1 sectoral	2
Economic	Economic: other	5	
Environmental	Materials, energy, water, biodiversity, emissions, waste, products, compliance	34	
Social	Human Rights	12	
Social	Labor: Diversity and Equal Opportunity	1	1

(Continued)

TABLE 1.7 (Continued)

Sustainability Category	*Sustainability Subcategory*	*GRI Indicators*	*SASB Indicators*
Social	Labor: other	15	
Social	Products	9	
Social	Society or Community	11	
Sectoral	Intellectual Property	1 sectoral	2
Sectoral	Privacy	1 sectoral	
Sectoral	Freedom of expression, portrayal of human rights and cultural rights	3 sectoral	
Sectoral	Content creation and dissemination	6 sectoral	1
Sectoral	Audience interaction and media literacy	4 sectoral	
	Totals	127	8

A comparison of these two systems reveals the parsimony of the SASB approach to disclosure in relation to that of GRI. The GRI disclosure requirement ("comprehensive" scope) has 127 possible indicators, while SASB calls for only 8. We simply note the numbers here for future reference without evaluating either GRI as excessively voluminous nor SASB as excessively parsimonious. In Chapter 10, we will reflect on the appropriate amount of disclosure in light of SASB and a few other standards that stand out as parsimonious.

GRI and SASB on Mining & Metals

A similar analysis using the GRI-G4 sectoral requirements for Mining and Metals and the SASB's standard for that industry appears in Table 1.8, which shows that the GRI disclosure requirement ("comprehensive" scope) has 122 possible indicators, while SASB calls for 22. The table does not show the 7 indicators in the standard disclosures that call for additional items of information under the sectoral standard for Mining and Metals.

Metrics for Sustainability Disclosure

Before leaving the topic of sustainability reporting, we note that a few systems rate firms on their disclosure of information related to sustainability, a task that requires the formulation of a summative measure of disclosure. One metric evaluating environmental reporting is the UNEP/SustainAbility rating, developed in 1994, which evolved into the Engaging Stakeholders rating system undertaken jointly by UNEP

TABLE 1.8 GRI-G4 and SASB on Mining Disclosure Requirements

Sustainability Category	*Sustainability Subcategory*	*GRI Indicators*	*SASB Indicators*
General	Governance (G4 34–41, 44–45, 49–55, 57–58)	19	
General	Governance: Ethics and Integrity. G4-56	1	2
Economic	Economic, all subcategories	9	
Environmental	Materials, energy, water, emissions, products, compliance	25	6
Environmental	Biodiversity	4 standard 2 sectoral	3
Environmental	Waste	5 standard 1 sectoral	3
Social	Human Rights	12 standard 1 sectoral	3
Social	Labor	16 standard 1 sectoral	3
Social	Products	9 standard	
Social	Society or Community	11 standard 5 sectoral	2
	Totals	121	22

and SustainAbility. That rating system consisted of 50 indicators, mostly equally weighted, covering the disclosure of management policies and systems, inputs and outputs, investments, stakeholder relations and partnerships, sustainable development, and report design and accessibility. There was a shorter version for small and medium-sized enterprises. A second example was the environmental report "score card" published by Deloitte Touche Tohmatsu, which likewise evaluated firms in a summative measure.[28] Other summative measures have been developed for academic research, as summarized by Morhardt in 2009.[29]

Discussion

The contrast between the GRI-G4 and SASB systems, in terms of the extent of reporting required, introduces an important question that will continue as a theme in this book: *How much information is really necessary for a company's sustainability report?* This is a question about materiality, so the answer, by definition, turns on the concept of materiality that is implemented in a standard. We will return to this question in Chapter 10, but here we may look for an explanation in terms of the ways that GRI and SASB characterize materiality. Can that explain, for example, why SASB would not require a media firm or a university to report any environmental impacts?

SASB frames its disclosure standard around the requirement of Regulation S-K,[30] which calls on public companies to discuss, in the Management Disclosure and Analysis section of 10-K and 20-F reports, "any known trends or uncertainties that have had or that the registrant reasonably expects will have a material favorable or unfavorable impact on net sales or revenues or income from continuing operations." This discussion is specifically forward looking. It "shall focus specifically on material events and uncertainties known to management that would cause reported financial information not to be necessarily indicative of future operating results or of future financial condition." Case law and guidance from the Securities and Exchange Commission further establish a two-pronged characterization of material information in terms of (1) the probability that the trends or events will occur and (2) the magnitude of the financial impact of the trends or events.

In the GRI, "Materiality is the threshold at which Aspects [of sustainability] become sufficiently important that they should be reported." The SEC's two-pronged characterization of materiality captures that idea but with details about the probability and magnitude of impact. The difference between the GRI and SASB centers on the questions, "important for whom?" and "why?"

The GRI characterizes materiality in relation to the interests of "stakeholders," who are entities and individuals who can be reasonably expected to be significantly affected by the organization's activities *and* who can affect the ability of the organization to implement its strategies. The GRI characterizes material aspects of sustainability as the firm's economic, environmental, and social impacts on stakeholders, including rights under national law and internationally recognized standards, that affect the "reasonable expectations and interests" of the stakeholders or substantively influence the "assessments and decisions" of stakeholders.

SASB's characterization of materiality draws more closely from the FASB's definition and case law used in the context of financial reporting. SASB's intended audience for sustainability disclosure is the "reasonable investor" who desires to make informed investment decisions about publicly traded companies. SASB's focus on the investor as the stakeholder for sustainability reporting is consistent with the approach to materiality taken by RobecoSAM, which collects the data used in the Dow Jones Sustainability Indices (DJSI).[31] SASB's reasonable investor "invests primarily for economic reasons with a variety of investment horizons—from short-term to long-term—and investment strategies—from income generation to asset valuation." SASB's outside stakeholders include a firm's customers, local communities, the public, the government, and employees. Their interests are addressed in the SASB standards if a firm's impacts on these stakeholders would affect the long-term value or financial performance of the firm or otherwise have economic implications for investors.

SASB's process for developing standards reflects its characterization of materiality. The process begins with in-house research, characterizing material sustainability issues (disclosure topics) as those for which there is "evidence of interest" as seen by the presence of key words related to 43 general sustainability issues in industry-related documents such as 10-Ks, shareholder resolutions, CSR reports, media, and SEC comment letters. The result is "a 'heat map' that indicates interest in certain issues by investors and other stakeholders." Likely, materiality is also determined by evidence of financial impact as seen in "sell-side research, investor call transcripts, third party case studies, anecdotal evidence, and news articles."[32] In the second phase of development, SASB convenes an industry working group, first by online survey and then by direct outreach, to provide feedback on the indicators proposed from the first phase. The working groups have balanced representation from corporations, investors and analysts, and intermediaries. A disclosure topic would advance in the standard-setting process only if the working group participants reached 75% agreement on its materiality to investors. In total across all standards, SASB had 2,800 participants—representing $23.4 trillion in assets under management and $11 trillion in market capitalization—participate in its industry working groups.[33]

The difference in materiality between the GRI and SASB could have several explanations. An obvious factor is the difference in their primary stakeholder(s), SASB being focused on the informational needs of investors and the GRI looking at the impacts on an organization emanating from the environment and from political and social groups. However, that explanation loses force when we recognize that both systems take into consideration the trends and events that have evidence of impact on an organization's long-term value. In SASB, the focus on shareholder value is obvious, but the GRI-G4 framework also includes such a consideration. Its item G4-2 calls on reporters to account for their impacts that affect "the long-term prospects and financial performance of the organization." The GRI-G4 appears to go a step farther than SASB in its requirement to account for the "reasonable expectations and interests of the organization's stakeholders," but the GRI characterizes stakeholders as individuals or entities "whose actions can reasonably be expected to affect the ability of the organization to successfully implement its strategies and achieve its objectives." These corporate strategies and objectives may indeed be focused, in the long term, on the creation of shareholder value, so the GRI's characterization of stakeholders brings our attention back, ultimately, to indicators that have a long-term impact on traditional financial measures of corporate performance. SASB's explicit focus on the shareholder does not distance that standard greatly from the GRI's system.

Another explanation for the differences between the SASB and GRI systems could be about the purpose of the disclosure. SASB standards are designed for use in SEC filings (the 10-K and 20-F) in compliance with the SEC's Regulation S-K. The GRI is explicitly a standard for sustainability reporting. Would a standard for disclosure in SEC reports differ substantially from a standard for sustainability reporting? Two considerations help us analyze this question, one focusing on the meaning of materiality in each context and another focusing on the audience of the report. We consider each in turn.

Regulation S-K calls on firms to disclose "trends or uncertainties that have had or that the registrant reasonably expects will have a material favorable or unfavorable impact on net sales or revenues or income from continuing operations." That appears to indicate a short-term focus for materiality, but we noted above that the instructions to Item 303 in Regulation S-K state that management's discussion and analysis of a financial report should focus on issues that would cause the reported *financial* information to give a misleading picture "of future operating results or of future financial condition." Thus, Regulation S-K has an open-ended view of the future over which trends may have their effects, and that appears to be consistent with the GRI's characterization of materiality at G4-2 in terms of impacts on the "long-term prospects and financial performance of the organization."

Are SEC filings and stand-alone sustainability reports designed to be written for different audiences, and would that impact their content? The audience for the SEC filings consists of participants in the financial markets. We note in passing that as financial and sustainability reporting become integrated,[34] the audiences will merge, but even in the interim, it would be a mistake to assume that a GRI-G4 report has content that is intended exclusively for a noninvestor audience. The GRI-G4 guidelines do not contain the word "audience." The guidelines define materiality in terms of the impacts that stakeholders have on the reporting organization in the near and long term. Any such impacts are likely to be material to investors.

Another explanation for the differences between the SASB and GRI systems might be the processes they used to develop their guidelines or standard. Both systems used committees or working groups, though SASB's working groups represented corporations, investors and analysts, and financial intermediaries, while the GRI's committees included representation from business, labor, civil society (including consumer organizations), and financial markets in "close dialogue" with regulators and governmental agencies in several countries.[35] Added to that, the two systems may have had different procedures for group decision-making. SASB used a consensus threshold of 75% to include an indicator in its standard. GRI does not report the decision rules used by its working groups, but if its groups were more heterogeneous than SASB's and if they used a simple majority rule or handled their diversity by tending to accommodate varied opinions through the inclusion of minority-sponsored indicators, then one would expect the GRI system to have many more indicators than SASB's.

The differences in the composition of the SASB and GRI working groups also raises the possibility that the participants could have had quite different beliefs about the relationship between sustainability indicators and the long-term prospects and financial performance of an organization. In Chapter 4, we will refer to such beliefs as worldviews, the cause-and-effect chains that describe a person's understanding about their world. Science informs a person's worldview, but when scientific results are not conclusive or are controversial in relation to social values and ethics, worldviews may come to differ substantially among people. People may also differ in how far back up a causal chain they are able to look, and that would result in differences in the range of primary indicators considered in a system for disclosure related to sustainability.

This chapter began a presentation, to be continued in the next two chapters, that reveals the variety of approaches to measuring and reporting on sustainability. All systems take the *materiality* of information as their conceptual starting point. However, as we have seen in comparing the GRI-G4 framework with that of the Sustainability Accounting Standards Board, there can be substantial differences among systems for reporting on sustainability. In Chapter 4, we will analyze these differences using ideas from philosophy, ethics, and measurement theory. However, before we can do that, there are two more classes of standard to look at, the involuntary corporate ratings (Chapter 2) and the voluntary certification systems (Chapter 3).

Notes

1 GRI. 2013e. Carrots and Sticks. Available at <www.globalreporting.org/reporting/reporting-support/publications/research-anddevelopment-publications/Pages/default.aspx> Accessed June 2015.
2 GRI. 2014b. Linking CASS-CSR 3.0 and GRI's G4 Sustainability Reporting Guidelines. Available at <www.globalreporting.org/resourcelibrary/Linking-CASS-CSR-3.0-and-GRI's-G4-Sustainability Reporting-Guidelines.pdf> Accessed June 2015.
3 FASB. 2015. Statement of Financial Accounting Concepts No. 2: Qualitative Characteristics of Accounting Information, Paragraph 132. Available at <www.fasb.org/cs/BlobServer?blobcol=urldata&blobtable=MungoBlobs&blobkey=id&blobwhere=1175820900526&blobheader=application%2Fpdf> Accessed June 2015.
4 TSC Indus. v. Northway, Inc., 426 U.S. 438, 449 (1976).
5 GRI. 2013a. G4 Sustainability Reporting Guidelines: Reporting Principles and Standard Disclosures. Global Reporting Initiative. Available at <www.globalreporting.org/standards/g4/Pages/default.aspx> Accessed July 2015.
6 GRI. 2015a. Sustainability Disclosure Database. Global Reporting Initiative. Available at <http://database.globalreporting.org/> Accessed June 2015.
7 GRI. 2015b. GRI's Governance Bodies. Available at <www.globalreporting.org/network/network-structure/governance-bodies/Pages/default.aspx> Accessed June 20, 2015.
8 GRI. 2015c. An Introduction to GRI's New Governance Structure. Available at <www.globalreporting.org/SiteCollectionDocuments/2014/GRIs-new-governance-structure.pdf> Accessed August 2015.
9 GRI. 2015d. Stakeholder Council. Available at <www.globalreporting.org/network/network-structure/stakeholder-council/Pages/default.aspx> Accessed August 2015.
10 GRI. 2009. Rules and Procedures for the GRI Stakeholder Council. Available at <www.globalreporting.org/SiteCollectionDocuments/SC_RulesProcedures2009.pdf> Accessed August 2015.
11 GRI. 2015e. Organizational Stakeholders. Available at <www.globalreporting.org/network/organizational-stakeholders/Pages/default.aspx> Accessed June 2015.

12 GRI. 2015f. GRI Secretariat. Available at <www.globalreporting.org/network/network-structure/secretariat/Pages/default.aspx> Accessed June 2015.
13 GRI. 2015g. Governmental Advisory Group. <www.globalreporting.org/network/network-structure/governmental-advisory-group/Pages/default.aspx> Accessed June 2015.
14 GRI. 2015h. National Annexes. Global Reporting Initiative. Available at <www.globalreporting.org/standards/reporting-framework-overview/national-annexes/Pages/default.aspx> Accessed June 2015.
15 GRI. 2013c. Sustainability Topics for Sectors: What Do Stakeholders Want to Know? Global Reporting Initiative. Available at <www.globalreporting.org/resourcelibrary/sustainability-topics.pdf> Accessed July 2015.
16 GRI. 2013d. Materiality Matters-GRI's New Check Service. December 11, 2013. Available at <www.globalreporting.org/information/news-and-press-center/Pages/Materiality-Matters-GRIs-new-check-service-.aspx> Accessed August 2015.
17 GRI. 2015i. Content Index Service. Available at <www.globalreporting.org/services/alignment/Content_Index_Service/Pages/default.aspx> Accessed August 2015.
18 GRI. 2015j. Become a Certified Training Partner. Global Reporting Initiative. Available at <www.globalreporting.org/services/preparation/certified-training-partners/certified-training-program/Pages/default.aspx> Accessed June 20, 2015.
19 GRI. 2015k. G4 Exam. Global Reporting Initiative. Available at <www.globalreporting.org/reporting/Pages/GRI-G4-Exam.aspx> Accessed June 20, 2015.
20 SASB. 2015a. Vision and Mission. Sustainability Accounting Standards Board. Available at <http://www.sasb.org/sasb/vision-mission/> Accessed July 2015.
21 Park, D. 2015. Putting the 'A' Back in MD&A. Sustainability Accounting Standards Board. Available at <www.sasb.org/putting-a-mda/> Accessed June 2015.
22 SASB. 2015b. Standards Council. Sustainability Accounting Standards Board. Available at <http://www.sasb.org/sasb/standards-council/> Accessed June 2015.
23 SASB. 2015a. Vision and Mission. Sustainability Accounting Standards Board.
24 SASB. 2013. Conceptual Framework. Sustainability Accounting Standards Board. Available at <www.sasb.org/wp-content/uploads/2013/10/SASB-Conceptual-Framework-Final-Formatted-10-22-13.pdf> Accessed June August 2015.
25 Ibid.
26 TSC Indus. v. Northway, Inc., 426 U.S. 438, 449 (1976).
27 SASB. 2014. Media Production & Distribution: Provisional Standard. Sustainability Accounting Standards Board. Available at <www.sasb.org/standards/download/services/> Accessed July 2015.
28 Kolk. A. 1999. Evaluating Corporate Environmental Reporting. *Business Strategy and the Environment*, 8, 225–237.
29 Morhardt, J. E. 2010. Corporate Social Responsibility and Sustainability Reporting on the Internet. *Business Strategy and the Environment*, 19:7, 436–452.
30 17 CFR 229.303(a)(3) (Item 303)
31 GRI and RobecoSAM. 2015. Defining Materiality: What Matters to Reporters and Investors. Global Reporting Initiative and RobecoSAM. Available at <http://www.robecosam.com/images/Defining-Materiality-What-Matters-to-Reporters-and-Investors.pdf> Accessed August 2015.
32 SASB. 2013. Conceptual Framework. Sustainability Accounting Standards Board.
33 Personal communication from SASB, September 2015.
34 Eccles, R. G., and M. P. Krzus. 2015. *The Integrated Reporting Movement.* Hoboken, NJ: Wiley.
35 GRI. 2013a. G4 Sustainability Reporting Guidelines, p. 5.

2

CORPORATE RATINGS AND RANKINGS

The information disclosed by companies about their sustainability is used by consumers, policy makers, and investors. Within the investment community, attention to sustainability has increased markedly in recent years. At first, the only advisers who paid attention to sustainability data were investment funds screening on corporate social responsibility. Now, investment firms are using nonfinancial disclosures to assess firms' financial risks related to environmental and social trends and to evaluate firms' abilities to take advantage of business opportunities presented by these trends.

The response of the investment banks and financial advisory services has been to develop systems to rate or rank corporations on matters related to sustainability. In 2010, SustainAbility inventoried 108 systems that rate, rank, or otherwise evaluate firms according to one or more of the principal attributes of sustainability—environmental or social policies and impacts, and governance.[1] Among the better known of these from the United States are the Dow Jones Sustainability Index series and *Newsweek*'s Green Rankings. Goldman Sachs has a GS Sustain Focus List, which functions like a sustainability stock index, but less information is available about it, so it will not be used as an example here. From the United Kingdom come Thomson Reuters' ASSET4 ESG Ratings and the FTSE4Good Index series. Corporate Knights' Global 100 Most Sustainable Corporations, from Canada, has had high credibility on its own and is the basis of the *Newsweek* Green Rankings.

These are a type of standard radically different from the standards for disclosure that were discussed in Chapter 1. These rating and ranking systems form a *summative evaluation* of firms' sustainability using the data that firms disclose about specific indicators. In this chapter and the next, we continue the theme of Chapter 1 by describing the essential features of these standards as a basis for the conceptual analysis of standards in Chapters 4 and 5 of the book and for the recommendations and reflections that appear in Chapter 10.

The Dow Jones Sustainability Indices

The Dow Jones Sustainability Indices (DJSI) are stock indices, meaning that the value of the index is a composite of the prices of the shares of the firms that meet the criteria to be in the index. Sustainability is the criterion for membership in the index set. It is not measured by the value of the index.

The World Index tracks the financial performance of the "top 10%" of the 2,500 largest companies in the S&P Global BMI who submit sustainability information or for which the information can be located publicly. The DJSI North America, Europe, and Asia Pacific indices use the top 20% of those large companies. In these indices, all firms must have revenues of at least $500 million per year. The DJSI series also includes national indices for Australia, Canada, and Korea.[2]

DJSI Blue Chip indices have selection and weighting criteria different from those of the world, regional, and national indices. The DJSI series also includes indices that use ethical filters that eliminate firms in one or more of the following industries: alcohol, gambling, tobacco, armaments and firearms, nuclear power, and adult entertainment.

The "top" companies are selected based on their Total Sustainability Score (TSS), which is calculated using data from the RobecoSAM Corporate Sustainability Assessment (CSA).[3] The content of the Corporate Sustainability Assessment and the calculation of the Total Sustainability Score vary by industry. RobecoSAM uses the 59 industries of the Global Industry Classification Standard (GICS). Depending on the industry, the CSA questionnaire consists of 80–120 indicators of sustainability (referred to in the CSA as "questions.") Indicators roll up into subcategories of sustainability ("criteria"), and the subcategories roll up into the broad categories ("dimensions") of the familiar three-P model of sustainability: social (people), environmental (planet), and economic (profits).

Due to the industry specificity of the CSA and the TSS, there is no single formula, no single set of weights, that describes the priorities given to various indicators or even to the indicators and subcategories that constitute the Total Sustainability Score. RobecoSAM illustrates the variation of the TSS across industries by showing the weights given to each of the three dimensions across three industries in the 2011 CSA. Those weights are summarized in Table 2.1. It shows

TABLE 2.1 RobecoSAM Sustainability Weights by Industry (2011)

Industry	*Social*	*Environmental*	*Economic*	*Total*
Banking	38%	24%	38%	100%
Electric Utilities	30%	35%	35%	100%
Pharmaceuticals	50%	10%	40%	100%

that there can be significant differences across industries in the weights assigned to a dimension. The weights were determined from a "fundamental bottom-up analysis of each industry" by RobecoSAM's analysts.

Each indicator in the CSA is evaluated in points, and the maximum sum of the points in the assessment is 100, so the TSS ends up as a value in the range of 0–100. Within an industry, the Total Sustainability Score is used to rank companies for inclusion within the Dow Jones Sustainability Index.

The CSA uses some indicators that are generic across industries and some that are specific to an industry. According to RobecoSAM, the general criteria account for approximately 40%–50% of the assessment, depending on the sector. The remainder are industry specific.

The subcategories ("criteria") within each of the CSA categories ("dimensions") for banks, utilities, and pharmaceutical firms are shown in Table 2.2 to illustrate the range of subcategories that are evaluated in the TSS. Their weights within the dimension may vary by industry sector. The RobecoSAM "economic" dimension appears to include subcategories that in other systems are treated as governance aspects. To facilitate comparison with ESG metrics such as

TABLE 2.2 Categories and Subcategories in the RobecoSAM Total Sustainability Score (TSS)

Environmental	*Social*	*Economic-Governance*	*Economic-Financial*
biodiversity	addressing cost burden	anticrime policy/ measures	brand management
business opportunities	bioethics	codes of conduct, compliance, anticorruption, and bribery	customer relationship management
business risks large projects	controversial issues, dilemmas in lending and financing	corporate governance	innovation management
climate change governance	corporate citizenship and philanthropy		market opportunities
climate strategy	financial inclusion, capacity building		marketing practices
environmental footprint	health outcome contribution		price risk management
environmental policy and management system	human capital development		privacy protection
environmental reporting	labor practice and human rights		research and development

(Continued)

TABLE 2.2 (Continued)

Environmental	*Social*	*Economic-Governance*	*Economic-Financial*
	occupational health and safety		risk and crisis management
	social reporting		stakeholder engagement
	stakeholder engagement		supply chain management
	standards for suppliers		
	strategy to improve access to products		
	talent attraction and retention		

Thomson Reuters' ASSET4ESG, we separate RobecoSAM's "economic" indicators into those related to governance and those related more directly to financial performance.

A unique feature of the RobecoSAM CSA is its use of a subjective rating called "Media and Stakeholder Analysis" (MSA), which reflects RobecoSAM's analysts' interpretation of news about the company pertinent to each of the subcategories listed above. Specific subcategories have been identified as potentially affected by the media and stakeholder analysis. Analysts evaluate the company's response to any news event that is material to the firm's sustainability and give the response a score in the range 0–100, which flows into each affected subcategory. If there is no news in the year of evaluation, the firm gets a full 100 points for MSA, so the MSA effectively is a negative score for imperfect handling of material news events.

ASSET4 ESG and the Thomson Reuters Corporate Responsibility Indices

ASSET4 ESG is a Thomson Reuters database that in 2015 contained corporate social responsibility data on 4,600 public companies worldwide, including some of the largest companies in the U.S. ASSET4 ESG does not apply preliminary screens to determine the constituents of its universe of firms. As its efforts to secure data continue, ASSET4 is adding about 300 companies per year. ASSET4 has at least six years of data for most companies.

The ASSET4 ESG system breaks the three ESG categories (their "pillars") down into subcategories (their "categories" or "factors") whose scores are derived from 226 key performance indicators (KPIs) computed from more than 500 data items. A breakdown of the KPIs in ASSET4 ESG, by ESG category and subcategory, is shown in Table 2.3.

TABLE 2.3 ASSET4 ESG Data Categories, Subcategories, and Indicators

Environmental	*Social*	*Governance*
Emission reduction, policies (4) and practices (14)	Employment Quality (17)	Board Structure (17)
Product innovation, policies (4) and practices (16)	Health and Safety (9)	Board Functions (15)
Resource reduction policies (4) and practices (6)	Training and Development (10)	Compensation Policy (13)
Controversies (4)	Diversity and Opportunity (10)	Shareholder Rights (11)
Emission reduction vs revenue (6)	Human Rights (8)	Vision and Strategy (12)
Resource reduction vs revenue (4)	Community (14)	
Leadership (8)	Product Responsibility (19)	
	Effective tax rate (1)	
Total 70 indicators	***Total 88 indicators***	***Total 68 indicators***

On each of the three ESG categories, a firm's "rating" is determined by comparing its raw values against other firms in a comparison group. The raw values are transformed to fit a bell curve to derive an indicator score in a range of 0–100, the mean and median reasonably close to 50.[4]

The comparison group that is used to calculate an indicator score depends on the category of the indicator. Environmental scores are calculated by comparison within one of 52 industry groups. Social scores are calculated either by comparison within industry (for 38 of the 88 component indicators) or by geography (for 41) in 9 regions consisting of U.S./Canada, Latin America, Africa, Oceania, Asia, Europe, and the Middle East, with separate consideration for Russia/Ukraine and Japan, or the indicator is considered universal and thus compared with all firms in the ASSET4 ESG universe (for 9 indicators). Governance scores are calculated by comparison within the stated regions.

The indicator scores, calculated to have a common range of 0–1 based on minima and maxima in the comparison group, roll up into subcategory scores using indicator weights that are determined by ASSET4's analysis of several attributes of the indicator and data including:

- relevance to the comparison group (more weight)
- wide reporting within the comparison group (more weight, with break points at 0.5% and 15% of the group)
- the distribution of the raw scores (less weight to narrowly distributed indicators)

- correlation with other indicators (less weight to highly correlated ones)
- type of indicator: policy variables getting less weight than activity variables and activity variables getting less weight than outcome measures
- consistency with the academic literature (more weight).

Subcategory scores roll up to ESG category scores based on the indicators' weights within the subcategory. Each of the three ESG categories is weighted equally in the total sustainability score for a firm.

FTSE4Good Indices

The *Financial Times* and the London Stock Exchange Group own the trademark to the FTSE4Good index series. The FTSE4Good rating system and methodology is overseen by an independent committee representing the investment community, firms, NGOs, unions, and academia.[5]

FTSE4Good indices are stock-price indices, so they track the financial performance of the included firms, but a firm's inclusion in an index is a mark of distinction in sustainability performance. FTSE publishes stock-price indices that are differentiated geographically: the All-World Developed, the USA, the Developed Europe, the Japan, and the All-Share index for the UK. The FTSE4Good *benchmark* indices consist of all firms in the FTSE whose "universe indices" meet the FTSE4Good criteria. The *tradable* indices are the FTSE4 Good Global 100, US 100, Europe 50, UK 50, Australia 30, and Japan Benchmark, which consist of a specific number of the largest firms that qualify for inclusion in the corresponding FTSE4Good benchmark index. There are related indices for Spain and Malaysia, and there is an Environmental Leaders Europe 40 index.[6]

FTSE4Good indices use explicit criteria for excluding companies. Excluded firms produce tobacco, whole weapons systems, and components of controversial weapons. Also excluded are companies that have been identified as having significant controversies. There are also specific criteria for companies producing breast milk substitutes or nuclear power.[7]

The selection of a firm for inclusion in the benchmark index is based on an analysis of up to 300 indicators that cover 14 "themes" (subcategories) within the three "pillars" (categories) of environmental, social, and governance practices. More than 100 of the 300 indicators are sector specific, and about 60 are quantitative or performance indicators. On average, about 125 indicators are relevant to a particular firm.[8] The high-level summary of indicators in FTSE4Good lists 180 indicators across the 14 themes and 3 pillars that may be interpreted as neither sector specific nor location specific. Within each theme, there are qualitative indicators related to a firm's "strategy and practice," quantitative indicators of a firm's actions and performance, and sector-specific indicators. These 180 nonspecific indicators are summarized in Table 2.4.

TABLE 2.4 Pillars, Themes, and Common Indicators in FTSE4Good

Environmental	*Social*	*Governance*
Climate change (10,3)	Human rights and community (10,5)	Corporate governance (11,11)
Water use (6,3)	Labor standards (9,3)	Anticorruption (8,3)
Biodiversity (7,0)	Health and safety (12,6)	Risk management (10,9)
Pollution and resources (7,5)	Customer responsibility (7,1)	Tax transparency (4,2)
Environmental supply chain (8,7)	Social supply chain (9,4)	
= 38 strategy & policy	= 47 strategy & policy	= 33 strategy & policy
= 18 quant/performance	= 19 quant/performance	= 25 quant/performance
= 56 both types	= 66 both types	= 58 both types

The numbers in parentheses with each theme are, in order, the numbers of indicators of type "strategy & policy" and "quantitative/performance."

For each theme, FTSE evaluates a firm's "exposure" to the theme, reflecting the relevance and materiality of the theme to the firm, based primarily on the firm's FTSE Industry Classification Benchmark (ICB)[9] industry subsectors and the countries in which the firm operates. Theme exposures are evaluated as High, Medium, Low, or Negligible, using a rules-based methodology and publicly available information.

As an example, for environmental management, companies are classified by 41 industry supersectors, of which 19 are deemed high impact, 13 medium impact, and 9 low impact. For climate change, 12 industries are designated high-impact, and 18 are medium-impact. For human rights and community, the high-risk companies are in the Global Resource Sector (oil, gas, and mining); medium-risk companies have significant operations in 44 "Countries of Concern," and all other companies are low risk. For social supply chain, high-risk companies are those that have significant operations in high-risk products (8 agricultural products and 10 consumer products) or high-risk countries (the non-high-income OECD countries) or high exposure to high-risk products (33% of revenue or GBP 100 million revenues). For anticorruption, 20 industries and 125 countries are identified as high risk. For corporate governance, FTSE treats all companies as medium risk, because this area of corporate evaluation is still evolving.

Data for the indicators used in the calculation of FTSE4Good's theme, pillar, and overall ESG scores are taken only from publicly available sources. Though companies are given a chance to verify the public information, to enhance transparency, FTSE4Good does not accept information that is provided privately by the companies, which sets it apart from the Dow Jones Sustainability Index.

Within each theme (subcategory), a firm earns points on each applicable indicator. Firms with higher "exposure" to a theme are assessed using tougher standards: there are sector-specific indicators for firms in sectors with high exposure, and the percentage of indicator points a firm must get for a particular theme score (1–5) is higher for companies with higher exposure.[10] The aggregation of indicator scores into a theme score for a firm results in a measure on a 0–5 scale that is calibrated, based on a firm's percentile ranking within its industry supersector, so that a 3 is considered "good practice" and 5 is "best practice."[11]

The theme scores are used to calculate a pillar (category) score on a 0–5 scale graded in increments of 0.1. Each firm's theme score is weighted by the firm's exposure score for the theme (0–1–2–3 for Negligible–Low–Medium–High) and then rolled up into the pillar score. The weighting of 0 for negligible exposure means that the firm is not evaluated on the indicators for that theme. At the pillar level, firms are ranked relative to other firms in their ICB supersector, and the result is reported in increments of 10% on a 0%–100% scale.

The final, composite ESG score for a firm is calculated in an analogous manner. A firm's 14 theme scores on the 0–5 scale are weighted by their respective exposure scores and rolled up, resulting in a composite score on a 0–5 scale. A firm is brought into the relevant benchmark indices if its overall ESG score is at least 3.5 on the 0–5 scale, and it must maintain a score of 2.5 in subsequent years to remain in the index.

FTSE4Good also calculates a relative composite ESG score, on a 0–100 percentile scale, to show the standing of a firm in relation to others in its industry supersector, the result being reported in deciles as it is for the relative scores within pillars.

Global 100 Most Sustainable Companies in the World

The *Global 100* list is published by Corporate Knights (CK), a Toronto-based media, research, and investment research company. Corporate Knights uses a rules-based methodology[12] that begins with a universe of all companies having a market capitalization of at least US $2 billion. It then applies four screens to those companies:

1. Disclosure practices: disclose at least 75% of the (12) key performance indicators used in CK's research model that are disclosed by at least 10% of all companies in a Global Industry Classification System industry group.
2. Financial health: have a Piotrosky F-score[13] of at least 5.
3. Product category: exclude producers of tobacco products and firearms.

4. Financial sanctions: exclude the bottom quartile performers in the CK Financial Sanctions screen, which measures the amount of money that companies have paid out in qualifying fines, penalties, or settlements.

Then it assigns points to the shortlisted companies in 12 indicators using data sourced from Bloomberg.[14] Each of the key performance indicators (Table 2.5) is scored on a 0–100 scale, and each has equal weight in the total. Companies are scored only on the "priority KPIs" for their respective GICS industry groups. In industry groups where all 12 KPIs are deemed to be priority KPIs, each KPI will have a weight of (100% / 12) ≅ 8.3%. The 12 indicators are summarized in Table 2.5, which also shows a classification of each indicator in terms of the ESG framework augmented by a Financial and a General category.

The final Global 100 list is made up of the top performing companies in the 10 sectors of the Global Industry Classification Standard.[15] The number of positions in the Global 100 given to each GICS sector is determined by the sector's relative market capitalization in the Global 100's financial benchmark, the MSCI All Country World Index (ACWI).

The Global 100 metric has 12 indicators, of which 4 are clearly environmental, 6 are clearly social, one (#12) is general, and one (#5, R&D intensity) is related to future revenues and competitive advantage and thus treated here as a financial indicator. None of the Global 100 indicators is specifically related to governance.

TABLE 2.5 The Global 100 Sustainability Metric

Name of KPI	*Measurement*	*Weight*	*Category*
1. Energy Productivity	Based on Revenue ($US) / Total Energy Use (GJ). This measure is a weighted average of the firm's percentile in its industry for energy productivity (75%) and for the two-year change in energy productivity (25%).	8.3%	Env
2. Carbon Productivity	Based on Revenue ($US) / kgCO2e using Scope 1 and Scope 2 emissions. This measure is a weighted average of the firm's percentile in its industry for carbon productivity (75%) and for the two-year change in carbon productivity (25%).	8.3%	Env
3. Water Productivity	Based on Revenue ($US) / Total Water ($m^3$). This measure is a weighted average of the firm's percentile in its industry for water productivity (75%) and for the two-year change in water productivity (25%).	8.3%	Env
4. Waste Productivity	Based on Revenue ($US) / Total Waste Generated (metric tons). This measure is a weighted average of the firm's percentile in its industry for waste productivity (75%) and for the two-year change in waste productivity (25%).	8.3%	Env

(Continued)

TABLE 2.5 (Continued)

Name of KPI	*Measurement*	*Weight*	*Category*
5. Innovation Capacity	Based on R&D expenditures to total revenue averaged over a trailing three-year period, percentile ranked against that of all same-industry group peers.	8.3%	Fin
6. Percentage Tax Paid	Based on the amount of taxes paid in cash over a trailing five-year period (2007–2011) divided by total EBITDA over the same period, percentile ranked against that of all same-industry group peers. Companies score 0% in the event that their total EBITDA or taxes paid in cash is zero or lower over the period.	8.3%	Soc
7. CEO to Average Employee Pay	Based on total CEO compensation divided by average employee compensation, excess percentile ranked against that of all same-industry group peers within the CK coverage universe. (The lower the ratio, the higher the rank.)	8.3%	Soc
8. Pension Fund Status	Companies are not scored on this indicator if the total liability of a company's defined benefit pension plan divided by the total number of employees is less than $US 50,000. Based on unfunded liabilities at year end divided by market capitalization at year end, percentile ranked against that of all same-industry group peers within the CK coverage universe.	8.3%	Soc
9. Safety Performance	Comprising the Lost Time Injury Score (50% weight) and the Fatality Score (50% weight). The Lost Time Injury rate (lost time incidents per 200,000 employee hours) percentile ranked against that of all same-industry group peers within the CK coverage universe. The Fatality rate (defined as the number of fatalities divided by the total number of employees) is percentile ranked against that of all same-industry group peers within the CK coverage universe. The "priority KPI" test described above will be performed on both lost time incidents and fatalities. Accordingly, companies in industry groups that do not prevalently disclose fatalities will only be scored on their Lost Time Injury Score.	8.3%	Soc
10. Employee Turnover	Based on annual Employee Turnover calculated as (1—retention rate), excess percentile ranked against that of all same industry group peers within the CK coverage universe. (The lower the ratio, the higher the rank.)	8.3%	Soc

Name of KPI	*Measurement*	*Weight*	*Category*
11. Leadership Diversity	Comprising the Board Diversity Score (50% weight; percentile ranking in the industry group of the proportion of female directors) and Leadership Diversity Score (50% weight; percentile ranking in the industry group of the proportion of females in the senior executive team).	8.3%	Soc
12. Clean Capitalism Pay Link	The Clean Capitalism Pay Link indicator rewards companies for linking executive compensation to the achievement of "clean capitalism" goals such as GHG emissions, energy efficiency, and safety and health. It is scored in three levels only. A score of 100% is given to companies that describe such a linkage in detail, e.g., specifying the proportion of a particular named executive's compensation that is linked to the achievement of a corporate clean capitalism target. A firm earns a 50% score by providing a high-level description of such a mechanism, e.g., mentioning the existence of such a link but does not specify the proportion of compensation that is linked, the criteria, etc. If a firm reports no linking mechanisms, it gets a score of 0%. Notice that this is the only Global 100 indicator that does not use a percentile ranking.	8.3%	Gen

Newsweek's Green Rankings

Newsweek's contribution to the analysis of corporate sustainability is a ranking, not a stock index. The *Newsweek* Green Rankings U.S. 500 ranking evaluates the environmental performance of the largest 500 publicly traded companies in the United States, sized by market capitalization, and the Global 500 evaluates the 500 largest public companies worldwide.

The *Newsweek* Green Rankings (NGR) are derived from eight key performance indicators (Table 2.6). The first four and the sixth of these eight are taken from the 12 indicators used in Corporate Knights' Global 100 index. As noted by *Newsweek*, these items can be calculated from data disclosed under the Global Reporting Initiative's G4 guidelines. Table 2.6 shows the indicators and their GRI-G4 sources.

The Global 100 indicators that are *not* used in the *Newsweek* Green Rankings are innovation capacity, percentage of tax paid, the ratio of CEO pay to average employee pay, pension fund status, safety performance, employee turnover, and leadership diversity. Indicators in the NGR but not in the Global 100 are #5, #7, and #8 above: green revenue score, sustainability board committee, and audited environmental metrics.

TABLE 2.6 *Newsweek* Green Rankings Metric

Name of KPI	*Measurement*	*Weight*	*GRI-G4*
1. Energy Productivity	Based on Revenue ($US)/Total Energy Use (GJ). This measure is a weighted average of the firm's percentile in its GICS industry group for energy productivity (75%) and for the two-year change in energy productivity (25%) measured by quartiles.	15%	EN3
2. Carbon Productivity	Based on Revenue ($US)/kgCO2e using Scope 1 and Scope 2 emissions. This measure is a weighted average of the firm's percentile in its GICS industry group for carbon productivity (75%) and for the two-year change in carbon productivity (25%) measured by quartiles. Departing from the Global 100, the NGR weights that result by 90% and gives 10% weight to a binary measure of whether (1) or not (0) the company discloses Scope 3 emissions.	15%	EN 15, EN 16, EN 17
3. Water Productivity	Based on Revenue ($US)/Total Water ($m^3$). This measure is a weighted average of the firm's percentile in its GICS industry for water productivity (75%) and for the two-year change in water productivity (25%) measured by quartiles.	15%	EN8, EN10
4. Waste Productivity	Based on Revenue ($US) / Total Waste Generated (metric tons). This measure is a weighted average of the firm's percentile in its GICS industry for waste productivity (75%) and for the two-year change in waste productivity (25%) measured by quartiles.	15%	EN24
5. Green Revenue Score	Calculated by HIP Investor, Inc., this measure breaks the firm's revenues down by ICB industry subsectors[i] to evaluate the percentage of the firm's revenues that are "green," meaning "derived from products and services that contribute positively to environmental sustainability and social health."[ii] The Green Revenue Score for a subsector is scaled 0%–100%, so this composite measure is also scaled 0%–100%, as are the other indicators in this metric.	20%	
6. Sustainability Pay Link	This indicator gives a score of 100% to companies that publicly disclose a policy that compensates any member of a firm's senior executive team based on the achievement of an environmental performance target. The Global 100 metric measures this indicator in three levels (0%, 50%, 100%), but NGR makes it a binary measure, disclosed (100%) or not (0%).	10%	G4-51

Name of KPI	*Measurement*	*Weight*	*GRI-G4*
7. Sustainability Board Committee	A binary indicator scoring 100% if the firm's Board of Directors has a committee whose mandate is related to the sustainability of the company, including environmental matters; 0% otherwise.	5%	G4-54
8. Audited Environmental Metrics	A binary indicator scoring 100% if the firm's most recently reported environmental metrics were audited by a third party; 0% otherwise.	5%	G4-33

i ICB, 2015. Industry Classification Benchmark. Available at <www.icbenchmark.com> Accessed July 2015.

ii Corporate Knights Capital, 2015a. *Newsweek* Green Rankings Methodology 2015. Available at <www.newsweek.com/sites/www.newsweek.com/files/newsweek-green-rankings-final-methodology_2015.pdf> Accessed August 2015.

Discussion

In Chapters 6–9, we will undertake a detailed conceptual analysis of how all types of sustainability metric may differ, but it is worth noting here a few observations about the corporate ratings and rankings. We focus on the difference between two categories of rating and ranking systems: the stock indices and the corporate rankings.

The sustainability stock indices described here are DJSI and FTSE4Good. These metrics use a large number of variables as indicators of sustainability: 80–120 in DJSI and an average of 125 indicators per firm (out of 300 available) in FTSE4Good. They produce an overall sustainability measure that is broken down into category measures that correspond to familiar trichotomizations of sustainability: environmental, social, and economic (the three P's) for the DJSI and environmental, social, and governance (ESG) in FTSE4Good. These categories are further subdivided into subcategories ("criteria" in DJSI and "themes" in FTSE4Good), for which sustainability measures are calculated using the constituent indicators.

In both the DJSI and FTSE4Good, factors are weighted according to their relevance to sustainability and thus to their materiality to investors; the weights on a particular indicator (in DJSI) or theme (FTSE4Good) may therefore differ according to the firm's industry. The number of firms used in the index set is a point of difference between these metrics. The DJSI takes the "top 10%" of the firms in the applicable universes for its indices. FSTE4Good's tradable indices have a fixed number of members. Membership in both cases depends on a firm's standing relative to others in its industry and geographic region, so the absolute measures of sustainability that are constructed from the data on indicators get transformed into relative measures. This is worth noting, because in the following chapter, where we consider certification systems for sustainability, we will see standards that do not consider a firm's relative performance in its industry.

In contrast to the stock indices are the rating programs, Global 100 and *Newsweek* Green Rankings. These use a small number of indicators, 12 for the Global 100 and only 8 for the NGR. *Newsweek* uses its Green Rankings as valuable content that attracts a readership. Corporate Knights is a publisher of information about sustainability; it uses its Global 100 ranking as a pillar among its informational offerings and as an aid to investors, selling its entire historical dataset to individuals for $99. The sale of its data and analysis to *Newsweek* for use in the NGR also demonstrates value added.

Thompson Reuters' ASSET4 ESG product is a hybrid of these two. The metric is based on a large amount of data, 226 indicators built from more than 500 data points, and it yields an overall evaluation of the sustainability of firms, but it is not used to compose an index. Rather, Thompson Reuters sells its data, fully disaggregated to the indicator level, as well as aggregated to subcategories and categories. Investors my use the indicator-level data for their own analyses, and they may rely on the aggregated measures for a simpler approach to sustainability investing.

The key question presented by these examples is, *How much data on sustainability is necessary for investment decisions, and of what type?* At this stage in the development of the markets for information about sustainability, it is still an open question. We will reflect on it in the final chapter of this book.

Notes

1 SustainAbility. 2010. Rate the Raters Phase Two: Taking Inventory of the Ratings Universe. Available at <www.sustainability.com/library/rate-the-raters-phase-two#.VYmUr1aWsVo> Accessed June 2015.
2 S&P Dow Jones Indices. 2015. Dow Jones Sustainability Indices Methodology (June 2015). Click on "Methodology" at <http://eu.spindices.com/indices/equity/dow-jones-sustainability-world-index> Accessed July 2015.
3 RobecoSAM. 2014. Measuring Intangibles: RobecoSAM's Corporate Sustainability Assessment Methodology (March 2014). Available at <www.robecosam.com/images/CSA_methodology_en.pdf> Accessed July 2015.
4 Thomson Reuters. 2014. Thomson Reuters Corporate Responsibility Ratings: Rating and Ranking Rules and Methodologies (August 2014). Available at <www.trcri.com/images/pdf/TRCRR_Rule_Book_8–14–2014.pdf> Accessed July 2015.
5 FTSE. 2015a. Index Inclusion Rules for the FTSE4Good Index Series, Version 1.6, June 2015. Available at <www.ftse.com/products/downloads/F4G-Index-Inclusion-Rules.pdf> Accessed July 2015.
6 FTSE. 2015b. Ground Rules for the FTSE4Good Index Series, Version 2.2, April 2015. Available at <www.ftse.com/products/downloads/FTSE4Good_Index_Series.pdf?95> Accessed July 2015.
7 FTSE. 2015a. Index Inclusion Rules for the FTSE4Good Index Series.
8 Ibid.
9 ICB. 2015. Industry Classification Benchmark. Available at <www.icbenchmark.com> Accessed July 2015.
10 FTSE. 2014a. FTSE ESG Ratings: Integrating ESG Into Investments and Stewardship. Available at <www.ftse.com/products/indices/F4G-ESG-Ratings> Accessed August

2015. A short summary is available at that site. With a free registration at <www.ftse.com/Analytics/ftse4good-esgratings/RegisterEmail.aspx>, users may log in to access resources such as the full summary referenced here.

11 FTSE. 2014b. FTSE ESG Ratings and FTSE4Good. Available at <www.ftse.com/products/indices/F4G-ESG-Ratings> Accessed August 2015. Access requires free registration at <www.ftse.com/Analytics/ftse4good-esgratings/RegisterEmail.aspx>

12 Corporate Knights. 2015b. 2015 Global 100 Methodology. Corporate Knights. Posted January 21, 2015. Available at <www.corporateknights.com/reports/global-100/methodology/overview.html/> Accessed June 2015.

13 The Piotrosky F-score is explained at <www.global100.org/methodology/criteria-a-weights.html>

14 Corporate Knights. 2014. Key Performance Indicators. Corporate Knights. Posted January 22, 2014. Available at <www.corporateknights.com/reports/2015-global-100/key-performance-indicators/> Accessed June 2015.

15 Standard and Poors. 2015. Global Industry Classification Standard Methodology. Available at <www.spindices.com/documents/index-policies/methodology-gics.pdf> Accessed June 2015.

3

ORGANIZATIONAL CERTIFICATIONS

Corporate certifications for sustainability designate an organization as having met the requirements of a standard. In that respect, they are similar to the corporate sustainability indices, where a listing in the index represents a level of achievement that sets the firm apart from those that did not make the index. The logic of certifications, however, differs from that of the ratings. In the examples that we will study in this chapter, the certifications emphasize how much a firm has improved on specific aspects of sustainability in relation to a prior year baseline. In contrast, ratings indicate how a firm compares to its industry peers. Thus, even for a firm that improves, a rating can go down in a year when the peers do much better. A focus on organizational improvement is also the motivation for companies to assess their own sustainability, formulate key performance indicators around sustainability, and to issue a sustainability report. Therefore, what we learn about certifications may help organizations in their planning and management of sustainability.

We begin this chapter with a description of the grandfather of all certifications for sustainability, the ISO 14001 standard for environmental management systems. Then, we look at three standards that use a summative sustainability score to assess a firm's performance on environmental, social, and governance issues: the STARS system for higher education, the B Corporation standard, and Underwriters Laboratories UL 880 standard for the sustainability of manufacturing firms. We omit a treatment of Green Seal's GS-C1 standard for product manufacturers, because the UL 880 represents that market. We also omit ICLEI's STAR standard for certifying municipalities,[1] more due to lack of space than lack of interest.

ISO 14001 Environmental Management Systems

The ISO 14001 standard for environmental management systems is not an organizational standard, in the sense that it evaluates the sustainability of an organization as a whole. Rather, it is a standard for one specific process in a business, that of managing environmental impacts. We discuss it along with the truly organizational standards, because ISO 14001 is commonly perceived to be an "organizational" standard, and its limiting features frame some important elements of contrast with the genuine organizational standards.

ISO 14001 was first published in 1996. It was revised in 1999 and 2004, and another revision was expected in late 2015. ISO 14001:2004 is not broad enough to be a sustainability standard, because it covers only one-third of the "triple bottom line" concern for environmental, social, and economic outcomes. More to the point, however, it is not a standard for environmental outcomes. It is a standard for management systems; as such, it has its intellectual origin in the well-known ISO 9001 standard for *quality* management systems. The value of a firm having ISO 14001 certification is based on the assumption that having a management system for a process produces better outcomes of that process.

We discuss ISO 14001 here briefly, because it seems to be the intellectual predecessor of the corporate certifications for sustainability that are the main subject of this chapter: the STARS system for universities, Underwriters Laboratories' UL 880 standard for manufacturing firms, and B Lab, Inc.'s B Corporation standard for companies and organizations.

The ISO 14001:2004 standard is set by the International Organization for Standardization (abbreviated ISO), based in Geneva, Switzerland. The ISO's procedure for setting a standard and updating it is defined in its statutory documents. ISO's members are the governmental units that set standards for their respective countries around the world. An ISO standard has to be developed by a technical committee composed of ISO members and is ratified by a two-thirds vote of the members.[2]

The decision to certify or not certify is based on an evaluation of 18 elements of the firm's environmental management system, each of which is described in the ISO 14001:2004 manual,[3] which the ISO sells at its website. A useful summary of these 18 elements is published by the U.S. Forest Service and is outlined in Table 3.1.[4]

TABLE 3.1 Elements of an ISO 14001 Report

4.1 General Requirements
4.2 Environmental Policy
4.3 Environmental Planning
4.3.1 Environmental Aspects
4.3.2 Legal and Other Requirements
4.3.3 Objectives, Targets, and Programs

(Continued)

TABLE 3.1 (Continued)

4.4 Implementation and Operation of the EMS
- 4.4.1 Structure and Responsibility
- 4.4.2 Competence, Training, and Awareness
- 4.4.3 Communications
- 4.4.4 EMS Documentation
- 4.4.5 Control of Documents
- 4.4.6 Operational Control
- 4.4.7 Emergency Preparedness and Response

4.5 Performance of the EMS
- 4.5.1 Monitoring and Measurement
- 4.5.2 Evaluation of Compliance
- 4.5.3 Non-conformances, Corrective and Preventive Action
- 4.5.4 Control of Records
- 4.5.5 Internal Audit

4.6 Management Review

In 2010, the ISO put forward its ISO 26000 Guidance on Social Responsibility, which we will discuss in more detail in Chapter 9. ISO 26000 takes the organization as its unit of analysis, but it is only "guidance." It is not a standard against which an organization can be certified.

AASHE's STARS Program for Universities

Since 2008, the Association for the Advancement of Sustainability in Higher Education (AASHE) has promoted its Sustainability Tracking, Assessment, and Rating System (STARS) as a way for higher education institutions to account for their activities that relate to sustainability. The beta version of STARS was tested in 2008 and 2009, and STARS 1.0 was officially introduced in January 2010. Further refinements were brought out as STARS 1.1 in February 2011, STARS 1.2 in February 2012, and STARS 2.0 in January 2014.

As of 2015, 715 colleges and universities in 21 countries had registered for STARS, and, of those, more than 340 had completed the submission of data to earn recognition through the system.

STARS is designed uniquely for higher education. In the introduction to the STARS 2.0 technical manual, the chair of the board of directors of AASHE and the chair of the STARS Steering Committee explain,

> STARS was developed by and for higher education, and recognizes the unique missions, challenges, obligations, constraints, and opportunities of

> colleges and universities. It provides a tool for looking at all facets of our institutions—curriculum and research, campus operations, planning and institutional capacity—with the goal of aiding strategic planning, fostering cross-sector dialogue about sustainability on campus, and stimulating conversations and learning between institutions.[5]

Thus, STARS is a tool for teaching sustainability through which universities may better "model the behaviors that contribute to a just and more civil society."

STARS calls on reporting organizations to report their achievement of sustainability outcomes in a manner that permits comparisons over time and across organizations. It has that in common with the corporate rating systems that will be considered in the next section of this chapter. However, as we shall see, STARS also rewards reporters for promoting sustainability as a concept and for building a stronger, more diverse community of adherents to sustainability, which sets it apart from the corporate rating systems.

STARS yields a numerical summative measure, so universities can measure their progress toward sustainability year-to-year in fine grain. Based on the numerical summary, reporters can earn Bronze, Silver, Gold and Platinum grades of recognition and compare themselves to other institutions.

STARS reporters publish self-evaluations on the STARS website, which presents the reporter's summative evaluation (Bronze, Silver, etc.) based on the points claimed. AASHE publishes a technical manual on its website,[6] which reporters use to guide their data collection and analysis. AASHE does not certify against its standard, and there are no third party evaluators that certify the campuses or verify that their information is true. Each university must attest to its declared points. For each indicator in the standard, a person from the institution must provide a statement that the information submitted is accurate. Also, the institution's president or chancellor must write a letter stating that all the information submitted is true.

AASHE sets the standard. However, the standard develops through feedback from experts in the sustainability community. AASHE uses a Steering Committee, a Strategic Advisory Committee, and a Technical Advisory Committee to develop the standard. The STARS Steering Committee has eight campus representatives, four members of the AASHE Board of Directors, and two AASHE staff. Steering Committee members advise on program policy, finances, and strategic positioning, and they review and approve updates and revisions to the technical content of STARS. AASHE continually works with STARS participants and the campus sustainability community to improve the system. Prior to releasing a new version of STARS, AASHE holds a public comment period to allow stakeholders an opportunity to comment on proposed changes.

AASHE has technical advisors whose role is to answer technical questions about the STARS ratings. Consulting groups such as Affinity have already developed practices to help universities conduct their STARS assessments.

The STARS system takes the university as the unit of analysis in a measurement of overall sustainability. STARS assigns weights or "points" to various indicators ("credits") of sustainability that a university must measure.

The STARS 1.2 Technical Manual explained that each item in the STARS assessment system was vetted using the following "gatekeeper questions":

- Does the credit speak to improved environmental, social, and/or financial impacts?
- Is the credit relevant and meaningful for diverse institutions?
- If the credit is based on the presence of a strategy, is a performance-based indicator not available or appropriate?
- Is the credit measurable, objective, and actionable?

That explanation does not appear in the STARS 2.0 manual, which addresses only the rationale for the magnitude of the points awarded for each indicator ("the impact, not the difficulty"), not the choice of the indicator itself. However, STARS 2.0 has an evident focus on environmental and social impacts that are measurable, objective, and actionable and, ideally, are indicators of performance rather than of strategies.

The STARS 2.0 system consists of 70 indicators ranging in value from 1 point to 14 points and grouped into four major categories—academics, engagement, operations, and planning and administration. A total of 204 points is available across the 70 indicators. No indicator is specifically required to be reported. Some indicators do not apply to all institutions of higher education. A reporter's preliminary total score is calculated as the number of points earned as a percentage of applicable points (0–100). To that preliminary score is added up to 4 points for "innovation," so the maximum score is 104. For a Bronze designation, 25 points are required, 45 gets Silver, 65 gets Gold, and 85 achieves Platinum.

STARS is not meant to be a comprehensive sustainability standard, meaning that it does not cover all of the "three P's" of sustainability: people, planet, and profit. For nonprofit organizations, the third P is best interpreted in terms of financial sustainability and financial risk. STARS is therefore better described as an ESG metric, focusing on environmental, social, and governance indicators.

Table 3.2 summarizes the points allocated in STARS across the three ESG categories. A fourth category, General, counts points for indicators that are not specific to environment, social, or governance issues; such indicators pertain to sustainability in general, such as having training courses for staff on "sustainability."

The fact that more than half of the points in STARS are associated with sustainability in general reflects the purpose of the standard, which is to foster dialogue and stimulate conversations and learning—in short, to teach sustainability.

TABLE 3.2 STARS Points

Aspect	*Points (%)*
Environmental	62 (30%)
Social	26 (13%)
Governance	3 (1.5%)
General	113 (55.5%)
Total	*204 (100%)*

Underwriters Laboratories UL 880 for Manufacturing Firms

Arising from a partnership between GreenBiz Group and Underwriters Laboratories' UL/Environment division in 2009, the UL 880 standard seeks

> to encourage organizations to develop performance data and reporting, such that over time these requirements will better enable organizations to link their organizational practices and performance to environmental, social, and financial objectives pertinent to not only their organization, but to broader objectives. In other words, UL 880 seeks to build a bridge between an organization's immediate needs and the needs of future generations.[7]

The UL 880 indicators are divided into five areas: governance for sustainability, environment, workforce, customers and suppliers, and community engagement and human rights. Reporters may be certified on all five areas (full certification) or in specific focus areas: environment alone, or on governance plus one of the social areas (workforce, customers and suppliers, and community).

UL 880 certification is based on a system of points allocated to indicators. In total, there are 1,008 points across 95 indicators. Certification requires fulfilling the requirements of eight required, zero-point, prerequisite indicators across the five focus areas and earning a minimum of 149 points out of 240 across 22 *core* indicators. The standard has a maximum of 1,008 points. The UL 880 technical manual refers to "higher levels of achievement under the certification program" that may be recognized by earning points from the noncore indicators, but those levels of achievement are not specified. The UL 880 program results in certification or not.

Like STARS, the UL 880 does not give weight to financial performance. That is deliberate according to the UL 880 technical manual (page 14), "This Standard does not include financial indicators, the third leg of the triple bottom line. Such issues are covered by sources of financial data that do not bear repeating in this Standard." The UL 880, like STARS, is essentially an ESG metric. A breakdown of the 1,008 points in the UL 880 standard in terms of the ESG categories appears in Table 3.3.

TABLE 3.3 UL 880 Points Allocation

Aspect	*Points (%)*	*Points (%)*
Environmental	461 (45.7%)	461 (45.7%)
Social—Workforce	140 (13.9%)	
Social—Customers & Suppliers	235 (23.3%)	440 (43.7%)
Social—Community	65 (6.4%)	
Governance	0 (0%)	
General	107 (10.6%)	107 (10.6%)
Total	*1,008 (100%)*	*1,008 (100%)*

The UL 880 standard is a remarkable effort by an organization that has been active in the standard-setting domain for many decades. Though the standard was piloted in 2011 by LG, Intuit, and Igefa,[8] and the Director of Sustainability at Westinghouse used the UL 880 in 2013 as a basis for evaluating the firm's own sustainability program,[9] a Google search in 2015 did not reveal any firms that publicize their certification under UL 880. Despite this response from the marketplace, we will continue to use examples from this standard to illustrate concepts that help us to understand metrics for sustainable business.

B Corporations

B Lab, Inc., is a not-for-profit organization that certifies companies as B Corporations.[10] As of mid-2015, more than 1,300 organizations in 40 countries and 120 industries had undergone certification.

The essential characteristic of a B Corporation is that, according to its articles of incorporation or bylaws, when members or directors are acting in the interest of the organization, they "shall not be required to regard any interest, or the interests of any particular group affected by such action, as a dominant or controlling interest or factor."[11] The B Corporation must give due consideration to the interests of shareholders, current and retired employees, customers and suppliers, its community and society, and the environment and economy of the state, region, and nation. B Corporations may be corporations, LLCs, or sole proprietorships.

The "benefit corporation" concept, modeled on the B Corporation concept, has been recognized as a legal form of organization in 27 states of the United States. Any organization that is recognized by its state of incorporation as a benefit corporation does not need to change its articles of incorporation to meet the requirements for B-Corp certification.

Certification by B Lab, Inc., as a B Corporation requires a demonstration of social and environmental performance standards through the achievement of 80 out of 140 points across 100 indicators on the B Impact Assessment questionnaire.

TABLE 3.4 B-Corp Points

Aspect	*Points (%)*
Environmental	20 (14%)
Social	86 (62%)
Governance	15 (11%)
General	19 (13%)
Total	*140 (100%)*

Organizations receive 30 to 60 points toward the required 80 if their business model is primarily in health, social, or cultural services, poverty alleviation, renewable energy, environmental services, or environmental conservation, or if its business practices emphasize worker ownership (40%) or significant charitable contributions (20% of profits).

B-Corp certification is meant to be interpreted in terms of sustainability. According to B Labs, the certification "bakes sustainability into the DNA of your company." Like STARS and the UL 880, the B-Corp standard does not award points for *financial* sustainability directly, but it does cover governance.

For comparison with STARS, the distribution of its 140 general points over the ESG categories is shown in Table 3.4 for the case of a university (service sector) with up to 1,000 employees. Not surprisingly, the B-Corp standard is weighted more heavily than STARS on governance and social issues. It is much lighter than STARS on environmental matters. Interestingly, it is much more focused on specific ESG matters, giving much less credit than STARS for matters generally related to sustainability.

The applicable indicators and their weights in the standard's B Impact Assessment are tailored to a firm's industry sector and size. The 72 variations on the B Impact Assessment are derived from specialization across industry, market type, and size categories.

Applicants for B-Corp certification complete an online survey, submit documentation showing that they fulfill legal requirements appropriate to their corporate structure and state of incorporation, and pay a fee that depends on sales revenue (0.5% or less). B Labs certification is good for two years. Each year, B Labs randomly selects 10% of the certified B-Corps for an on-site review of their B Impact Assessment. The reviewer randomly selects 8–12 credit-bearing questions and asks the company to document the practices on which the points are claimed.

Discussion

The organizational standards for sustainability have their intellectual origin in the ISO 14001 certification of environmental management systems. UL 880 and the B-Corp evaluations yield a yes/no result that either certifies the applicant or does not, as in ISO 14001, but the evaluation is based on an accumulation of points to a threshold level, whereas the summative evaluation in ISO 14001 is a checklist: pass all components or fail. Importantly, the STARS and UL 880 certifications have a strong orientation toward institutional improvement, which is also the main theme of ISO 14001. These two standards allocate points for having management systems and goals or for improvement from baseline measures in environmental aspects such as greenhouse gas emissions, waste, and water and energy usage. The B-Corp standard has less of a focus on those environmental variables, so it seems to capture more of a static picture of the organization.

AASHE's STARS 2.0 standard for universities is distinctive in several respects. Its summative evaluation is not yes/no but graduated in levels designated Bronze, Silver, Gold, and Platinum, an idea that is probably inherited from the LEED standard for buildings. It is focused on one industry, higher education, which enables it to be more specific in its expectations for applicants than is the case for the UL 880 standard for manufacturing organizations and the B-Corp standard for socially conscious organizations. For example, STARS has specific expectations for universities' greenhouse gas emissions, energy, and waste ratios in the present (as thresholds at which an organization begins to earn points) and as limits that express genuinely sustainable levels of carbon footprint (zero), building energy consumption (net zero), waste (90% reduction from threshold), and water (30% reduction from baseline).

STARS and B-Corp have been received well in the marketplace. Underwriters Laboratories' UL 880 and a similar standard for manufacturing organizations offered by Green Seal, the GS-C1 standard, have not gotten traction in the market. The difference may lie in their extent of industry-specific customization, choice of clientele, and institutional support. STARS is a standard for universities that was developed by universities through a widely collaborative process, so STARS has a built-in clientele. Also, that clientele, like the customers of B-Corp, is internally predisposed to socially responsible business practices, whereas the manufacturing organizations served by the UL 880 are likely responding to external pressures. Nevertheless, we will continue to take examples from the UL 880 standard in this book, because it represents a serious effort at organizational certification by a well-reputed standards organization.

Notes

1 The International Organization for Standardization, in its ISO series, publishes standards for product certification (the ISO 14020 series standards for product ecolabeling) and for specific business processes related to sustainability (ISO 14001 for environmental management systems and others related to occupational safety and health, product safety, and so forth), but ISO does not have a standard for certifying organizations as sustainable. The ISO 26000 guidance on social responsibility includes environmental measures and therefore is comprehensive in its treatment of organizational sustainability, but ISO states clearly that ISO 26000 is merely guidance, not a certifiable standard.

2 The composition of the technical committee and the ratification process are somewhat more complex than what is represented here. See the details in Chapter 4's section about the Community of Practice.

3 ISO. 2004. ISO 14001:2004 Requirements With Guidance for Use. Available at <www.iso.org/iso/iso_catalogue/catalogue_tc/catalogue_detail.htm%3Fcsnumber=31807> Accessed June 2015.

4 US Forest Service. 2005. Summary of Requirements for ISO 14001:2004 <www.fs.fed.us/ems/includes/sum_ems_elements.pdf> Accessed June 2015.

5 AASHE. 2014. STARS Technical Manual Version 2.0. Association for the Advancement of Sustainability in Higher Education, p. 3.

6 AASHE. 2015. STARS 2.0 Technical Manual. Available at <https://stars.aashe.org/pages/about/technical-manual.html> Accessed June 2015.

7 Underwriters Laboratories. 2015. UL 880 Standard for Sustainability for Manufacturing Organizations. Available at <http://ulstandards.ul.com/standard/?id=880&edition=1&doctype=ule> Accessed June 2015.

8 Herrera, T. 2011. LG, Intuit, Igefa Pilot New UL 880 Sustainability Standard. GreenBiz.com (December 6, 2011). Available at <http://www.greenbiz.com/blog/2011/12/06/lg-intuit-igefa-pilot-new-ul-sustainability-standard> Accessed June 2015.

9 Spence, C. 2013. Sustainability Assessment & Evaluations—How To Get Started & Pitfalls To Avoid. Presentation at the 2013 Meeting of the Manufacturers Alliance for Productivity and Innovation (MAPI). Available at <www.mapi.net/events/sustainability-council-meeting-fall-2013> Accessed June 2015.

10 B Lab, Inc. 2015a. B Corporation. Available at <www.bcorporation.net> Accessed June 2015.

11 B Lab, Inc. 2015b. Corporation Legal Roadmap. Available at <http://www.bcorporation.net/become-a-b-corp/how-to-become-a-b-corp/legal-roadmap/corporation-legal-roadmap> Accessed June 2015.

4

PHILOSOPHIES OF SUSTAINABILITY

The Values and Worldview Behind a Standard

The previous three chapters illustrated the ways that standards for sustainability may differ. In Chapters 4 and 5, we develop two conceptual frameworks for analyzing those differences. Here, we take up a question that companies attempting to get a product or firm certified to a sustainability standard often wonder about when writing their sustainability report: *Why are they asking for that information?* We take a philosophical perspective on that matter, looking at the meaning of sustainability and delving into the issues about ethics and worldviews that underlie the demand for specific types of information in standards. Following that, in Chapter 5, we will use measurement theory to look at the different ways by which indicators of sustainability can be measured and, in particular, how a summative judgment about sustainability can be formed from the measures of various indicators.

The collection of indicators in a standard defines the requirements for certification or for obtaining a high standing in a rating system. Any *requirement* makes a statement that the indicator is important to the standard setter. This chapter addresses the question that a reporting organization might ask about any indicator in the standard, "Why is the standard requiring me to report this?" and the question that an advocate of sustainability might ask, "Why is the standard NOT requiring them to report . . . ?"

There are basically two answers to the "why" question. One is that the indicator is either an outcome directly related to sustainability or an action that is reasonably expected to lead to an outcome that is directly related to sustainability, whatever "sustainability" means to the standard setter. The other answer is that the action or outcome is valued inherently by the standard setter as an essential characteristic of "sustainability." The first of these answers describes a *worldview*, which is a set of beliefs about cause-and-effect relationships in the world. The second is a statement about values, which are the components of an *ethical system*. The set of assertions that follow logically from a consistent ethical system and a consistent worldview constitute a *philosophy* of sustainability.[1]

Do we need to define sustainability in order to evaluate a worldview or an ethical system? Not necessarily. Sustainability is about good human life in the long term. The "good" part reflects an ethical system at the basis of sustainability. The "long term" part invokes a worldview that links present actions to present or future outcomes. In our philosophical analysis of standards in this chapter, we will not presuppose a worldview or an ethical system. Rather, in our analysis of standards, we take the perspective that *sustainability is whatever is measured in a standard for sustainability*. Different standards may be derived from different concepts of sustainability, which we may infer are derived from either different worldviews about sustainability or different ethical systems defining what is good in human life, or both. Even more significantly, in light of what is commonly known about the nature of decision-making in committees, it is possible for a single standard to call for the report of data that reflect different, perhaps even contradictory, philosophies of sustainability. Thus, the analytic question addressed in this chapter is, "What philosophy, or philosophies, of sustainability is (are) implied by the indicators in a standard?"

We approach this question by looking at the individual indicators required by the standard and attempting to infer the ethic and/or worldview that would call for such an indicator. To illustrate the concepts and the analysis, we will draw on indicators that are called for in the GRI-G4 system for disclosure.

The fundamental logic is that an ethic implies, possibly through a worldview, a requirement for the reporter to perform actions or to achieve outcomes that the indicator reveals. Thus, the choice of the indicator is a consequence of the ethic. However, our goal is to infer an ethic from the indicator. For that, the indicator would have to be *uniquely* identified with the ethic. Put another way, if there are two ethics that each imply the use of the same indicator, the presence of the indicator in a standard would point back to either the one ethic or the other rather than to a single ethic. We will be watchful for that indeterminate case as we look at indicators in this chapter, but we will learn the most from indicators that are uniquely implied by specific ethics.

A standard consists of many indicators, each of which weighs positively or negatively in the standard's summative measure(s) of sustainability. Each indicator will point back to one (or more) ethics, and there is no guarantee *a priori* that the ethics implied by all the indicators together will form a coherent ethical system. A good standard is ethically consistent, but if a standard has been created by a committee of individuals having diverse ethical perspectives, it is quite possible that the standard might include indicators that reflect inconsistent ethics.

Sustainability is generally categorized in terms of the three P's—people, planet, and profits. Indicators in sustainability metrics relate to one of these categories or to the general category of sustainability itself. We will see in Chapter 5 that some standards give sustainability points for promoting the general concept of sustainability. Such indicators do not point back to specific ethics. However, indicators in each of the three specific categories may point toward specific ethical perspectives, as we shall see in the examples of this chapter.

The chain of logic that takes us backward from an indicator to an ethical premise usually draws on assumptions about cause-and-effect relationships, which are components of a worldview. Thus, it is not only the ethic that may be implied by an indicator; a worldview may be implied as well. For example, some indicators related to the environment may be derived from a value placed on the conservation of scarce resources, such as nonrenewable energy sources, clean water, clean air, and a protective ozone layer in the atmosphere. Modern environmental science gives us a worldview by which we can link some actions in the present (e.g., the production of the chemical CFC-11) to consequences for these scarce resources (depletion of the ozone layer). Thus, that worldview is implied by the presence of an indicator about those actions (CFC-11 emissions) in a standard if there are no other reasons to require disclosure of that information.

The social sciences are not generally as strong as environmental science in establishing an undisputed worldview. Thus, the social indicators in a standard may not be tightly related, through a cause-and-effect logic worked backwards, to one or more ethical values. In the absence of a tight cause-and-effect link between a social indicator and its consequences, the presence or absence of a social indicator may reflect primarily its direct relationship to a concept of the "good" in human life, rather than to a value judgment made on the known consequences of the indicator. As Underwriters Laboratories explains in its manual for the UL 880 standard, in the theory of sustainability, "there is often an enormous gap in understanding how an organization's business decisions and operations translate into positive or negative social and environmental impacts."[2] By implication, the presence or absence of social and environmental indicators in a standard may reflect ethical imperatives associated directly with the indicator rather than with its consequences.

The Ethics of Sustainability

Some philosophers, such as Michael Boylan, have sought to identify a few philosophical assumptions, in the form of imperatives or principles, from which a wide range of ethical obligations may be deduced.[3] That is not our task here. We will be content to identify a variety of ethical statements that are implicated by various sustainability indicators and to look at a standard as the expression of a set of ethical perspectives. We will find intellectual value in this analysis as we examine the consistency or inconsistency of those perspectives and as we observe the breadth or limits on the ethics implicated by a standard.

The debates about sustainability that boil down to questions of value center on ethical questions about our responsibilities toward people we transact business with and people we live with and about the status of humankind in the natural world. We now look to these ethics as a way to understand the design of standards for sustainability. For specific examples, we use the 91 indicators of the GRI-G4 guidelines for disclosure and, for each indicator, seek to answer the question, "Why is the GRI-G4 asking for *that*?"

Transactional Ethics

A transactional ethic puts limits on a person's responsibilities to others with whom the person is in a transactional, or exchange, relationship. Transactions are the essence of business, so transactional ethics are foundational to the conduct of business. We may distinguish four transactional ethics, or perspectives, that answer the question of what responsibility an actor has to others.

The Null Responsibility Ethic

The null responsibility ethic imposes on an actor no responsibility to others. This perspective is characterized by the Law of the Jungle. There are no rules. Only the fittest survive.[4] This ethic holds that there are no constraints on behavior, moral or otherwise.

The Legal Perspective

The most elementary of the ethics that impose responsibility on an actor is the ethic that we might call the *Law of the Concrete Jungle*.[5] The actor is subject to laws that impose responsibilities irrespective of one's will, such as responsibility for actions that damage others. Beyond that, the actor is subject to responsibilities of his or her own choosing. In law, this is the perspective of neoclassical contracting. It holds that an individual becomes responsible to others by having mutually agreed to specific conditions and behaviors, including contingencies.[6] Under this ethic, a person should obey the law and hold to their agreements. We may therefore call it a *legal perspective* on the responsibility ethic. This ethical perspective alone implies the use of sustainability indicators that call on a reporter to account for their compliance with contracts (GRI G4-EC03, obligations under defined benefit retirement plans) and with laws (G4-PR02, product health and safety; G4-PR04, product labeling; G4-PR06 to PR09, business practices; G4-SO7 monopolistic practices and SO8 general violations).

The Relational Perspective

In the legal perspective, one is not responsible for other people's expectations about one, nor for the effects of one's actions that are conditioned by other people's actions to which one has not explicitly agreed. Under the *relational perspective*, an actor must accept responsibility for behaviors that are expected by others as individuals. (In the section on social philosophy, below, we deal with societal expectations.) In law, the responsibility that accrues out of the history of interactions between individuals, even in the absence of a formal agreement, is called a relational contract.[7] A formal agreement, if one exists, is only the starting point for an ongoing relationship. Expectations that arise from the history of interactions between the parties constitute a responsibility. For example, a landlord who habitually allows a tenant to pay rent after the due date or in amounts short of the contracted rent has a responsibility, owing to the pattern established, to permit the tenant to continue to pay late or short until a new history of attempts to enforce the contracted date and amount has established new expectations.

This relational perspective acknowledges a person's responsibilities for the consequences of their actions within an exchange relation, whether those actions were subject to specific, formal agreement or not. The focus of this perspective is on the consequences of actions that are not covered by law. A firm has ongoing exchange relationships with its employees, customers, suppliers, and the local community. A direct indication of obligations to these stakeholders that arise from a relational perspective is data on the presence of mechanisms for noncontractual, ongoing engagement with the stakeholders. Even formal grievance mechanisms (G4-EN34, HR12, and LA16) indicate a relational perspective, because they acknowledge the incompleteness of the underlying contract and attempt to resolve disputes internally rather than through the judicial system. Indicators of community engagement (G4-SO1), local hiring (G4-EC6), corporate investments in local infrastructure (G4-EC7) and indirect economic impacts (G4-EC8), and local purchasing (G4-EC9) likely reflect a relational perspective on corporate responsibility.

The Reactive Perspective

Broader yet than the relational perspective is a perspective that holds one responsible for the reactions of others to one's own actions. This *reactive perspective*, to be workable in practice, must condition the responsibility upon the reasonableness or predictability of others' reactions. In that context, a person becomes responsible for knowing what a reasonable or predictable reaction to one's actions would be, and one bears responsibility, at least in part, for those reactions.

As an example in sustainability reporting, the expectation that a firm will report Scope 2 and Scope 3 greenhouse gas emissions (GRI-G4 EN16 and EN17) reflects this reactive responsibility ethic. Scope 2 and Scope 3 emissions, as we will see in Chapter 7, are emissions *by a firm's suppliers*, not the direct emissions of the firm. The firm is held to account for those emissions, though the firm may not have any control over the supplier's operations, because the supplier's productive activities and emissions are a reaction to the firm's decision to purchase from that supplier. Likewise, a requirement to report *suppliers'* negative impacts on society (G4-SO9, SO10), their human rights practices (G4-HR10, HR11), or their labor practices (G4-LA14, LA15) reflects the reactive perspective on the relationship ethic.

The ethic of sustainability expressed generally in the Global Reporting Initiative is at least relational, because it envisions a responsibility of the sustainable firm that is broader than the terms of its contracts. In item G4-2, the GRI calls upon reporters to disclose "the organization's key impacts on sustainability and effects on stakeholders. . . . This should take into account the range of reasonable expectations and interests of the organization's stakeholders." The *reasonable expectations and interests* of stakeholders establish responsibilities of the firm that go beyond what the corporation is contractually responsible for. That these expectations must be "reasonable" suggests that the rationale for the responsibility is based on reasoning from evidence or logic or both. If that evidence were drawn from the history of an exchange relationship, the ethic would be relational.

If the GRI had required reporters to take into account the range of *customary* expectations and interests, irrespective of a history of exchange, the ethic would not be one of responsibility in the sense presented here, where responsibility derives from the actions of the actor. Responsiveness to the customary expectations of others is a matter of duty, which we will consider later in this chapter. Before we do that, we consider the ethical perspective that defines right action in relation to its effects on others.

The Consequential Perspective on Transactions

Also broader than the relational perspective is one that holds an actor responsible for the consequences of their behavior on others who are not directly a party to a transaction. Under this *consequential perspective*, an actor is responsible for the effects of his or her transactions on people who are not primary parties to the transaction. Such people may be called related or secondary parties or implicit parties to the transaction. The familiar example is pollution, which affects people who are neither the buyer nor seller of the product whose production creates the pollution. Another example is an actor's use of a common resource, such as public grazing land or fishing grounds, which impacts other users of the resource. Under this perspective, an actor is responsible for the consequences of his or her actions on these related parties.

In the sustainability arena, an example of pollution is the direct production of greenhouse gases (called Scope 1 emissions) by an organization. A worldview that relates CO2 concentration in the atmosphere to global warming or climate change, together with the consequential relational ethic, would condemn a firm's production of greenhouse gases. In the GRI, indicator G4-EN15 calls for the disclosure of direct emissions by the firm, and the disclosure of polluted waste products is called for in items G4-EN15, EN19-EN27, and EN29-EN31. Other requirements for disclosure in the GRI are situated similarly from an ethical point of view.

The GRI calls for data on the negative impacts of a firm on its local community (G4-SO2).

Consequential Ethics (Utilitarianism)

The ethics of responsibility extend beyond the consequences of an action on parties to a transaction. It is instructive to examine the general concept of corporate responsibility expressed in the Global Reporting Initiative. In indicator G4-2, organizations are called on to disclose their "key *impacts* on sustainability and effects on stakeholders . . . [accounting for] the range of reasonable expectations and interests of the organization's *stakeholders*" (emphasis added). Here, we focus on the terms "impact" and "stakeholder." The point of the GRI is to disclose impacts on stakeholders. Presumably, those impacts impose obligations on the corporation in relation to those stakeholders. This general view of ethics, defining obligations in relation to the consequences of action, is called *utilitarianism.* Thus, in this section, we investigate the utilitarian perspective on corporate responsibility.

The transactional ethics presented in the previous section all assume that the actor is in a business relationship with another person or organization. A utilitarian ethic puts limits on the behavior of the actor according to the effects of that behavior on others. Those "others" may be transactional parties or they may be individuals or organizations who are not directly in business with the actor.

The starting point for a utilitarian analysis is to identify the effects, called "impacts" in the Global Reporting Initiative, and the affected parties, the "stakeholders." The analysis itself requires a principle for evaluating the collective welfare of the stakeholders, to which we now turn.

The Measurement of Impact in Terms of Human Happiness

The theory of ethics seeks grounds for determining actions that are "right." The utilitarian theory of ethics defines "right" as actions that lead to greater *happiness* in human society.

The entire marketing research industry grew from a desire of businesses to evaluate the happiness that their products and services brought to their customers. Satisfaction surveys are now used even for employees, suppliers, and community members. In a typical survey, respondents are asked to rate their satisfaction with a product or service on a seven-point scale with "neutral" as a central point and "satisfied," "very satisfied," or "extremely satisfied" on one end of the spectrum and corresponding entries for "not satisfied" on the other.

A general feeling of happiness is related to other experiences that might be measured. It seems reasonable to measure as correlates of happiness qualities such as health, safety, and personal development. The GRI calls for disclosures on each of these: G4-PR1 and PR3 on customer health and safety, G4-LA6 to LA8 on employee health and safety, and LA9 to LA11 on employee training and education.

Increased happiness is the ultimate ethical objective in utilitarianism, so using correlates such as these as proxy measures of happiness implies the assumption of a worldview, a cause-and-effect relation between the correlate and happiness itself. We note for the record that the use of measures of health, safety, or personal development in a standard for sustainability would be derived from a utilitarian ethic together with a particular worldview, and worldviews need to be evaluated for their truth.

The Concept and Measurement of Collective Happiness

In the early formulation of utilitarianism by Bentham and Mill, the principle for evaluating an action was to consider its impact on the sum of human happiness. As Bentham put it in 1776, "The said truth is that it is the greatest happiness of the greatest number that is the measure of right and wrong."[8]

The customer survey approach appears to be a well-defined method to evaluate human happiness, but it has a major flaw if the goal is to evaluate the happiness of a group of people. There is no way to know whether one person's "very satisfied" implies more or less happiness than another person's "very satisfied." One might even doubt that a cranky customer's "satisfied" is worse than a normal customer's "very satisfied." This is a problem that economists call the *interpersonal comparison of utility*. There is no absolute measure of a single person's happiness, so there is no meaningful way to measure the sum of people's happiness.

Satisfaction may be difficult to define in its gradations, but it seems to be meaningful in a binary metric: satisfied or unsatisfied. Observations of human behavior indicate that people act more like *satisficers* than like utility maximizers.[9] People have goals or expectations, and they know when those goals or expectations are met and when they are not. They seek satisfaction relative to their expectations. In a world of satisficers, it would be possible to calculate the *percentage of people* that are satisfied with a particular experience, phenomenon, or organization, and that would be a valid measure of collective happiness.

The Global Reporting Initiative calls on organizations to report the use of customer surveys (G4-PR5) and to report measures of customer satisfaction (G4-LA1, LA3). The practice of surveying customers might be a survey for organizational engagement with customers as stakeholders, but by itself it is not an indication of human happiness. The direct measurement of customer satisfaction would be an indication of human happiness, if it were expressed in terms of the percentage of satisfied customers and if the satisficing worldview were valid.

The Pareto Ethic

The fallback strategy in economics—one that does give us some help in the ethics of sustainability—is to let each person evaluate their own happiness and evaluate a proposed action in terms of whether it makes him or her better off. The *Pareto ethic* states that an action is right if it makes at least one person better off and *no person worse off*. In effect, the Pareto rule gives a veto to every person in the society.

The Pareto ethic does not approve any action that makes some people better off at the expense of others, even if it would seem that a large number of people are greatly better off and only a few are weakly worsened. As a result, it is not very useful for decision-making, but it does help us work toward an ethical rationale for one class of indicators of sustainability, those related to pollution.

Pollution, in its various forms, violates the Pareto ethic. Pollution negatively affects one class of people in society while benefitting (through lower costs of production) the owners of the company that is creating the pollution, so the act of pollution can be evaluated (unfavorably) using the Pareto ethic.

To use the Pareto ethic, the subgroup of society that benefits from the action must be completely separate from the subgroup of society that is injured by the action. However, in the case of industrial pollution, the reporting organization is not the only beneficiary of the emissions. Consumers who use the emitter's products and suppliers who profit from sales to the emitter each benefit economically from the emissions, even while they suffer the effect of the pollution. In such a case, the society's ethical problem is to balance the costs and benefits of the pollution across several subgroups of the society, and the Pareto ethic cannot do that. Only if we were to ignore the benefits to consumers and suppliers, who also suffer the effects of the pollution, can we frame the evaluation of the polluter in terms that permit us to invoke the Pareto ethic to call for the polluter to halt the pollution. Therefore, the more fundamental grounds for a call to stop pollution is the consequential transactional ethic described in the previous section.

Other requirements for disclosure in the GRI are situated similarly from an ethical point of view. The GRI calls for data on the negative impacts of a firm on its local community (G4-SO2), but that would be condemned under the Pareto ethic only if the community provides no employees nor customers to the firm. The GRI calls for data on firm behavior that could be considered exploitative even if it is legal, such as child labor in G4-HR5 and compulsory labor in G4-HR6, but employees also are paid.

Health and safety are reasonable surrogates for human happiness, and the GRI has indicators for these as employee safety and health (LA6-LA8) and consumer safety and health (PR01). However, while employees might be injured or get sick from their work, they also get paid, and likewise consumers get the benefit of using the product, so it is not clear that the firm is the only beneficiary and the employees or customers are the only disadvantaged party, to which the Pareto ethic would apply. The employee or consumer has to decide if the net benefit from their transaction with the company is positive or not. If it is positive, presumably the employee would stay in employment and the consumer would continue to buy, so the employee and consumer effectively vote for or against the company by their own behavior, and in that case there should be no ethical grounds for requiring a firm to disclose health and safety data.

However, that argument assumes that the employee has many alternatives in the labor market and that the consumer has perfect knowledge of the consequences of consumption (even before buying the product) and many alternatives in the product market. Markets in the real world are not perfect, so consumers can be fooled by unscrupulous organizations and employees can be trapped in jobs they would rather leave. The requirement to disclose information about the safety and health of employees and consumers and of other situations where a firm might exploit its informational or economic advantages must have a different ethical rationale (a duty of forbearance, discussed further below).

Ethics of Distributive Justice

The give-and-take in a marriage involves a balancing over time of one person's happiness with another's. That is difficult enough when the assessment involves only two people who are in a long-term relationship in which an ultimate balance is possible. A more difficult task for any practical ethicist would be to formulate the trade-off between one group's happiness and another's, especially when economic, social, and political forces are divisive rather than unifying.

The simplest measure of the *sum* of human happiness has been formulated by economists in terms of the happiness derived from consuming or using a product or service. In that context, it is possible to define the amount of money a person would be willing and able to pay for a product, and it is possible to see how much they actually pay, so one can define the *consumer surplus* experienced by the individual as the difference between the willingness to pay and amount paid.[10] This amount is measured in units of money, so it can be summed across all the consumers in the market for the product, and as such it represents the surplus of all consumers. By a similar analysis, one can see the amount of revenue received by a producer in selling a unit of the product, and one can calculate the producer's cost to produce that one extra unit of the product. The difference between revenue and cost is the producer's surplus (profit), and summed across all producers of the product, it yields a measure of the total producer's surplus in the market for that product. In economics, the sum of consumer surplus and producer's surplus is called *total welfare*.

This approach to understanding the sum of human happiness is limited first by the assumption that happiness comes only from consumption and second by the definition of consumer surplus in terms of what people are willing *and able* to pay. As Lisa Newton observes in her book *Ethics and Sustainability*, this gives the poor less influence than the rich in determining the sum of human happiness.[11] Even within the domain of consumptive happiness, to use total welfare as a measure of happiness, additional assumptions are needed about how important some people are relative to others, and it may be very difficult for a society to reach agreement on those.

Questions about distributive justice are implied by the indicators in the Global Reporting Initiative, but specific ethics are not. The GRI is a standard for reporting, not a metric for sustainability, so it has no summative measure that might reveal weights given to the happiness, or even just the economic benefits received by an organization's various stakeholder groups. The GRI implies an attention to distributive justice, because the information required in disclosure can be used by stakeholder groups to make their own evaluation of how fairly they are treated by the company. Indicator G4-EC1 calls for an accounting of economic value generated *and distributed* to suppliers as operating costs, to employees as wages, to owners as dividends, to government as taxes, and to communities as donations. The GRI also calls for disclosure of the ratio of the highest paid individual's compensation to the median compensation of employees, broken out for every country having significant operations, in absolute terms (G4-54) and in terms of percentage increase (G4-55). The ratio of pay between men and women, across employment categories, must be disclosed under item G4-LA13.

Questions about the fair allocation of common resources also call for a distributive ethic. In G4-EN9, reporters are asked to disclose their sources of water that are significantly affected by the withdrawal of water and to state in particular the "value or importance of water source to local communities and indigenous peoples." This clearly reflects an attention to the fair distribution of water between the local people and the company's owners and consumers. G4-EC4 calls for a disclosure of financial assistance received from government, which also reflects attention to the fairness of the organization's use of a common resource.

Ethics of Duty (Deontology)

Deontological ethics are obligations that derive from an actor's sense of duty (Greek *deon*) to others. Duty in turn derives from a person's *role* in a societal *context*. Whereas utilitarianism is an economic perspective on ethics, deontology is sociological. Utilitarianism follows what James March and Johan Olsen identify with economics as the *logic of consequence*, while deontology follows the sociological nature of their *logic of appropriateness*.[12]

Implicit or explicit in a duty ethic is an actor's role and the boundaries of the society to which that role applies. For example, a father or mother has duties within a nuclear family. An elder has duties within a clan. A member has duties within a church or fraternal organization. A person has duties within a state (nation). A corporation has duties within a local community.

These duties are the customary expectations placed on the actor within that particular unit of society. As such, duties are cultural. They will change over time as culture changes. They are not necessarily clear. They may be ambiguous, particularly during times of cultural change and in societies that have subgroups with their own subcultures.

Recall that the Global Reporting Initiative calls upon organizations to disclose their impacts, taking into account "the range of reasonable expectations and interests of the organization's stakeholders." If we were to interpret *reasonable* expectations and interests of stakeholders as the *customary* expectations and interests of stakeholders, then we would have a deontological interpretation of the basic intent of the GRI.

Duties can appear to be arbitrary, if their purposes are obscure. Or, they may be clearly purposed in relation to an ethical value or sense of the good. Thus, duties can be formulated from a utilitarian consideration of the consequences of action,[13] but the duty derives primarily from an assessment of an actor's role in a social context.

The Social Perspective on Responsibility (Duty)

In the section on transactional ethics, we discussed various perspectives on responsibility. All of them were based on a transactional relationship between two parties. Broader than that as a responsibility ethic is the *social perspective* under which an actor incurs responsibility to others by virtue of the society to which the actor and others belong. Put another way, a person incurs the responsibility that is appropriate to one's membership or class.

The motive that enforces this responsibility is loyalty. Under loyalty to one's friends, neighbors, church, community, or nation, an actor should accept responsibility for the expectations that they have of the actor irrespective of individual agreement, irrespective of a history of actions that would imply such expectations, and irrespective of what the actor has done. The responsibility arises out of the person's societal relationship to the actor. A firm's presence in a local community, when such presence is interpreted as membership, establishes a responsibility to be a "good corporate citizen," according to the expectations of the citizenry about what is appropriate for a corporate citizen.

The Forbearance Ethic

Forbearance is the restraint of self-interest. In the context of corporate responsibility, forbearance is the restraint of actions that would benefit the corporation's owners at the expense of other stakeholders. As such, the action of forbearance admits interpretation in favor of an ethic of distributional justice, but if the actor's *motive* for forbearance is a sense of duty, rather than the specific outcome of the action, then the forbearance is deontological.

Several disclosures in the GRI can be interpreted as indicators of forbearance or the lack thereof. G4-EC5 calls for disclosure of the ratio of standard entry-level wage to local minimum wage, giving evidence of the extent to which an organization presses its economic advantage to the limits of the law. Indications of an organization's willingness to take advantage of imperfections in labor markets are disclosures about constraints to collective bargaining (G4-HR4), child labor (HR5), and forced or compulsory labor (HR6), benefits given to full-time employees that are not given to part-time employees (LA2), minimum notice periods (LA4), and wage differentials between men and women (LA13). An example related to imperfections in product markets is the disclosure of product information on labels (G4-PR3). The GRI used a definition of corruption as "the abuse of entrusted power for private gain," so disclosures related to corruption (G4-SO3 to SO5 and SO6 on political contributions) seem difficult to justify without an ethic of forbearance.

Naturohomic Ethics

An ethic that defines the position of humankind in relation to the natural world may be called *naturohomic.* In the classical treatment of this topic, three perspectives give different answers to the naturohomic question. The *anthropocentric perspective* holds that humankind is unique in the universe, standing apart from it yet acting in it. In that view, nature, both animate and inanimate, is valued for its utility to humankind. In religious terms, this perspective gives humans "dominion" over all of nature.[14]

In contrast, the *biocentric perspective* values humankind on the same terms as other individual living beings. It holds that all organisms pursue their own good in their own way and that humans are not inherently superior to other living things.[15]

The *ecocentric perspective* is broader yet than the biocentric perspective. Ecocentrism takes the ecosystem, the biotic community, as the unit to which moral questions are referred, not individual beings as in the biocentric perspective.[16] It holds that humans, as an integral part of nature and interdependent with other living beings, must respect the integrity of the system as a whole. Newton (2003: 21–23) offers, as an example of the distinctively ecocentric perspective, Aldo Leopold's land ethic,[17] "A thing is right when it tends to preserve the integrity, stability, and beauty of the biotic community. It is wrong when it tends otherwise."

Calls for the conservation of land and other natural resources, to support a broader or subsequent use by humans, are anthropocentric. Calls for animal rights are biocentric. Calls for the preservation of large tracts of land without the intent to exploit them in the future and laws against harvesting rare plants even on "private" property reflect an ecocentric perspective.

The GRI-G4 framework has ten indicators that address the conservation of materials, energy and water (G4-EN1 to EN10), which reflects the anthropocentric perspective. GRI-G4 also has four items (G4-EN11 to EN14) that relate to areas of high biodiversity, protected habitats, and species subject to a risk of extinction, which reflect an ecocentric perspective.

The Social Philosophy of Sustainability

The philosophy of sustainability addresses several issues that go beyond the questions of transaction, fair distribution, and duty discussed in the previous sections. The manner in which a person or organization practices sustainability is also guided by a *life ethic,* which defines the value of one life in relation to the life of the species or system of which it is a part. It needs a *sovereignty ethic* to guide the balance of freedom with authority, and it needs an *identity ethic* to value one's own traits, history, and culture in relation to those of others.

Life Ethics: Darwinism Versus Humanitarianism

The law of nature that governed the evolution, and the perpetuation, of species over millions of years was Darwinism. The fundamental value in Darwinism is that the survival of the species is more important than the survival of a specific individual. The Darwinian worldview is the law of the survival of the fittest: if an organism is fit for its environment, it will survive, grow, and reproduce; the unfit do not.

In the modern era, scholars and policy makers apply the Darwinist ethic freely to economic systems and to organizations. Corporations that do not serve a need in the economy, as evidenced by success in the marketplace, deserve to fail and be replaced by those that do. Under this ethic, even the largest and oldest firms should enjoy no favoritism through financial support from the government. Such an ethic is consistent with the Global Reporting Initiative's call for data on a firm's receipt of significant financial assistance from government (G4-EC4). Likewise, the Darwinist ethic is applied to the employment relation to yield a policy under which people who cannot do their job should be removed from the job and either transferred to a job that they can do or be fired from the organization.

In contrast, humanitarianism values each person individually. This value implies that every person should be given the opportunity to live, grow, and reproduce. The Quakers express the logic or worldview in religious terms, "There is that of God in every man."[18] Hindus believe that only with a human body can a soul reach enlightenment, the ultimate value of spiritual evolution, so a human incarnation is especially precious. A less religious, and more utilitarian, worldview that reaches the same result holds that every person has within himself or herself the ability to grow into someone who can make a contribution to society. That is the developmental worldview. The humanitarian ethic is rarely endorsed as a guide to industrial policy, though during the financial crisis of 2008 there were those who argued that some companies were too large and too important to be allowed to fail.[19] As applied to the employment relation, the humanitarian ethic would call for a treatment of the poor performance of an employee using the tools of training, supervision, and compensation, so the person could stay in the job.

The Darwinian perspective will likely be repugnant to many people in some contexts of sustainability, particularly in matters related to social justice. The B Corporation standard treats inequality of income across jobs in an organization as a reportable item. Most treatments of ecotourism view the elimination of local poverty through support from tourist operations as a fundamental tenet. In a discussion of any aspect of sustainability, it will help the analyst, scholar, or practitioner to surface their values and worldview by asking, "Why should we *not* look at this matter from a Darwinian perspective?"

Sovereignty Ethics and the Authoritarian Worldview

A *sovereignty ethic* defines the scope of acceptable limits to action. The *individualistic* perspective values individual freedom and rejects subjugation to authority. The *authoritarian* perspective on the sovereignty ethic values control and order.

Bundled with a perspective on the sovereignty ethic is a worldview about the human response to power. The *authoritarian* worldview holds that people in positions of authority can be trusted to behave lawfully and uphold their duties. The worldview that goes with the individualistic ethic is *antiauthoritarian*. It holds that people lack forbearance, so the concentration of power leads to particularly bad outcomes in human life. It is famously captured in the statement of Lord Acton, "Power tends to corrupt, and absolute power corrupts absolutely."[20] As applied to business, the antiauthoritarian worldview locates employment and slavery at their respective points along a single continuum that has authority at one end and freedom at the other. In the antiauthoritarian worldview, corporate power is only weakly constrained by consumers in the market. Therefore, power over others, seen especially in the power of owners, executives and managers, should be constrained formally through the engagement of other stakeholders in corporate governance.

The extensive disclosure of information about the internal governance of the reporting organization called for in the GRI implicates a distrust of concentrated power. The GRI-G4 has items that ask about the separation of control between the directors and the executive (G4-39), the presence of independent directors (G4-38, 40), compensation of managers and executives (G4-51, 52), conflicts of interest (G4-41), selection of board members (G4-40), participation in joint management–worker committees (G4-LA5), the percentage of employees covered by collective bargaining agreements (G4-11), association with suppliers in whom the right to collective bargaining may be at risk (G4-HR4), and an array of items about stakeholder engagement (G4-37, 38, 40, 45, 49, 50, 53).

Identity Ethics: Homogeneity Versus Diversity

The identity ethic specifies the value of one's own traits, history, and culture in relation to those of others. The *homogeneity perspective* on this ethic values the integrity of one's own race or culture. The *diversity perspective* values heterogeneity and seeks to integrate different values in a larger wholeness.

We may call this an identity ethic, because it relates fundamentally to a person's view about how far their sense of self extends into the environment. The identity ethic puts bounds on the scope of the society to which a deontological ethic applies. In what respects does one's duty go beyond one's stomach to one's family? To one's tribe? To one's race or language group? To one's nation? To the family of nations? To the animate and inanimate world?

The Global Reporting Initiative has numerous indicators that disclose the diversity of the reporting organization and the effects of its actions on societal groups.

Discrimination in general is addressed in G4-HR3. The GRI requires extensive disclosure related to gender: employment contract type, employment type, and supervisory status (G4-10), composition of the governing board (G4-38, LA12) wage rates (EC5, LA13), wage differential (LA13), employee hires and turnover (LA1), return to work after parental leave (LA3), work-related injury and disease (LA6), training (LA9), and performance reviews (LA11). The GRI shows less attention to racial and ethnic distinctions, breaking out reported information in this way only for the composition of the governing body and employment categories (G4-38 and LA12) and criteria for selecting board members (G4-40). Age is distinguished only in employee hires and turnover (LA1) and the composition of the governing body and employment categories (G4-LA12 but not G4-38).

Derivative Ethics

The preceding list of ethical issues was meant to be a set of questions about value that are independent of each other, meaning that actors may take a position on each of the major questions—about responsibility in transactions, about balancing the interests of different stakeholders, about duty to others, about humans' relationship to nature, about the value of life, about sovereignty and authority, and about identity—without fear of inconsistency. Some familiar ethical perspectives may be derived from combinations of the perspectives discussed in the preceding sections, as we see here.

Intergenerational Ethics

The Brundtland Commission's definition of sustainable development extends the concept of fair allocation across time, treating unborn generations as stakeholders in the present: "Sustainable development is development that meets the needs of the present without compromising the ability of future generations to meet their own needs."[21]

The intergenerational ethic is derived from an identity ethic, which extends the concept of personal responsibility beyond the self to others who might benefit from assets in the future, and a form of distributive justice that allocates benefits between stakeholders in the present and those in the future.

Attention to an intergenerational ethic is implicated in the GRI's call for disclosure of an organization's consumption of nonrenewable resources, such as fossil energy (as greenhouse gas emissions in G4-EN15 to EN17), and more specifically of common nonrenewable resources, such as water in aquifers (G4-EN9) and land for waste disposal (proxied by the amount of waste in EN23), and in the emission of hazardous wastes (G4-EN25), particularly those that are long-lived.

Possession Ethics: Ownership and Stewardship

Possession refers to the use of property. For example, a tenant has possession of an apartment even though he or she does not own it. However, there are different perspectives about what rights come with the possession of property.

Under the *ownership perspective*, a person has a right of ownership in property, which permits the owner to do whatever he or she wants to do with their "private" property. Ownership includes the right to use, trade, or destroy the owned property. In the Western version of the ownership ethic, the ownership of land extends from the surface of the land to the center of the earth. The owner may drill the land to extract water or oil as their personal property. Under this ethic, a company that owns land may strip-mine it or fill it with trash as they wish, as long as they bear all consequences of its use. Here we avoid transactional issues by assuming that the owner of the strip mine is required to operate the land without affecting his or her neighbors' watersheds or air quality. Ownership in private property extends even to the living beings on the land, except humans and any legally protected species, which permits the owner to hunt and harvest at will on private property.

The *stewardship perspective* takes a different view of what it means to possess property. The steward acts as the caretaker of property, knowing that at some time in the future this property will pass to others who deserve to enjoy its benefits as well. The stewardship perspective has a weak form and a strong form. Its weak form values property for the service that it can provide to humankind. In this view, the possessor of property is the custodian of the property and has a duty to any other potential owner to uphold the quality of service provided by the property, subject perhaps to reductions in service due to ordinary wear and tear.

The weak form of the stewardship perspective is derived from a naturohomic ethic together with an identity ethic. The weak form values property for the service that it can provide to humankind and thus takes the anthropocentric perspective on the naturohomic question about the relationship between humans and nature. Anthropocentrism is utilitarian in regarding property for the service it provides. The extension of the benefits of that use beyond the owner calls for an identity ethic that values others, even those living now, who might come to possess the property in the future. A semi-strong version of the stewardship ethic would justify the stewardship of resources using an intergenerational perspective.

A strong form of the stewardship perspective holds that natural property should be preserved because it has inherent value. This form of stewardship is ecocentric.

An implication of the stewardship ethic in its semi-strong form if not the strong form is the requirement of the Surface Mining Control and Reclamation Act of 1977, that owners restore land to a viable state after strip mining.

Not all constraints on the use of "private" property are consequences of a stewardship ethic. One example is the public management of ecosystems. Restricting hunting to specific seasons, even on private property, limits an owner's ability to kill certain mobile animals, because the animals live in an ecosystem that extends beyond the boundaries of the private property. Thus, they "belong" not to the owner of the property on which they are standing, but to a system that is bigger than the individual property owner's. The mobile animals are a type of common resource, and the allocation of that resource among people is governed by the consequential transactional ethic.

Human Rights

The GRI calls for disclosure of information related to human rights in several of its indicators. G4-HR1 looks at investment agreements that have undergone a human rights screening. G4-HR2 and HR7 are about training employees and security personnel in human rights matters as they apply to a firm's operations. G4-HR8 is about violation of the rights of indigenous peoples, and G4-HR9 is about human rights reviews and impact assessments of operations.

The scope of human rights issues spans the issues presented previously in this chapter under specific ethics. Human rights issues are ethical issues. The disregard of human rights, according to the United Nations' Universal Declaration of Human Rights (UDHR), "outrage[s] the conscience of mankind."[22]

Organized in terms of the ethical issues to which they are responses, the human rights issues raised in the Universal Declaration on Human Rights deal with questions of *identity*: the equality of rights of men and women; nondiscrimination on the basis of race, color, gender, language, religion, political or other opinion, national or social origin, property, or birth; and equality before the law; they call for special care and assistance to mothers and children. They also deal with *sovereignty*: the right to life, liberty, and security of person; freedom of movement with each state; the right to leave or enter one's country and to own property; freedom of thought and religion; the freedom to peaceably assemble; and prohibitions of slavery, servitude, torture, arbitrary arrest, detention, and exile. They address *transactional* issues: free choice of employment, protection against unemployment, and the right to join a trade union; a reasonable limitation on working hours and periodic holidays with pay; and the right to free education, at least at the elementary stages, and, indeed, make elementary education compulsory and higher education equally accessible to all on the basis of merit.

The United Nations Guiding Principles on Business and Human Rights (UNGP), adopted in 2011, applies the UDHR specifically to business. Also known as the Ruggie Framework, the UNGP establishes the responsibility of business organizations to respect human rights actively by being aware of human rights issues that arise in their work, identify the impacts of their work on human rights, and to remediate any infringements of human rights. The UNGP holds that "business can affect virtually all internationally recognized rights,"[23] so it does not seek to define specific human rights to be respected by business. The commentary above on the philosophical issues raised by the UDHR therefore applies to business under the UNGP.

Discussion

Of the 91 specific indicators in the Global Reporting Initiative G4 guidelines for disclosure, we found an ethical justification for 90. The only indicator that appears to be ethically neutral is G4-EC2, "Financial implications and other risks and opportunities for the organization's activities due to climate change."

We looked at each indicator and asked, "What ethical perspective would call for the disclosure of this information?" We showed that an ethical perspective is sufficient to account for 90 of the 91 disclosures of the GRI-G4. Does that prove that ethics are necessary to understand the GRI, that an ethical perspective is implied by the presence of an indicator? It does not, unless it can be proved that there is no other rationale for demanding the disclosure of the indicator, and that task is beyond the scope of this work. However, the present analysis makes a plausible case for the value of such an investigation. We studied only the GRI here, but in light of our discussion of the liberal and conservative perspectives on sustainability, it is reasonable to hypothesize that different standards for sustainability might reflect different ethical perspectives and thus, in practice, different concepts of sustainability. A philosophical analysis of standards is therefore useful and warranted.

Notes

1 This characterization differs from that of Boylan (2014b:3), to whom a worldview includes an understanding of facts and values. See Boylan, M. 2014b. Ethical Reasoning. In Michael Boylan (ed.). *Environmental Ethics*, 2nd ed. Malden, MA: Wiley-Blackwell, pp. 3–13.

2 UL Environment. 2011. UL 880 Standard for Sustainability: Manufacturing Organizations, 1st ed. (November 2, 2011), p. 9. Available at <http://ulstandards.ul.com/standard/?id=880&edition=1&doctype=ule> Accessed April 2015.

3 Boylan, M. 2014a. Worldview and the Value-Duty Link to Environmental Ethics. In Michael Boylan (ed.) *Environmental Ethics*, 2nd ed. Chichester, West Sussex: Wiley Blackwell, pp. 95–109.

4 Below, we treat the responsibility to family members, common even under the law of the jungle, as an implication of an identity ethic, not a responsibility ethic.

5 Huang, A., and S. Herriott. 2013. Relational Governance: The Normative Element in Technology Licensing Contracts. *Journal of Management Policy and Practice*, 14:4, 137–151.

6 Williamson, O. E. 1979. Transaction-Cost Economics: The Governance of Contractual Relations. *Journal of Law and Economics*, 22:2, 233–261.

7 See Macaulay, S. 1963. Non-Contractual Relations in Business: A Preliminary Study. *American Sociological Review*, 28:1, 55–67. Also see Macneil, I. R. 1974. The Many Futures of Contracts. *Southern California Law Review*, 147, 691–816.

8 Andrews, R. 1993. *Columbia Dictionary of Quotations*, New York: Columbia University Press, p. 392.

9 March, J. G., and H. A. Simon. 1958. *Organizations*. New York: Wiley.

10 Black, J., N. Hashimzade, and G. Myles. 2012. *Oxford Dictionary of Economics*. Oxford: Oxford University Press.

11 Newton, L. H. 2003. *Ethics and Sustainability*. Upper Saddle River, NJ: Addison-Wesley.

12 March, J. G., and J. P. Olsen. 1998. The Institutional Dynamics of International Political Orders. *International Organization*, 52:4, 943–969.

13 Newton, L. H. 2003. *Ethics and Sustainability*.

14 White, L. 1967. The Historical Roots of Our Ecological Crisis. *Science* 155, 1203–1207.

15 Taylor, P. W. 1986. *Respect for Nature: A Theory of Environmental Ethics*. Princeton, NJ: Princeton University Press.

16 Newton, L. H. 2003. *Ethics and Sustainability.*

17 Leopold, A. 1949. *A Sand County Almanac and Sketches Here and There.* New York: Oxford University Press.

18 Benson, L. 1970. That of God in Every Man–What Did George Fox Mean By It? *Quaker Religious Thought,* 12:2 (Spring). Available at <www.qhpress.org/essays/togiem.html>

19 Dash, E. 2009. If It's Too Big To Fail, Is It Too Big To Exist? *New York Times* (June 20, 2009). Available at <www.nytimes.com/2009/06/21/weekinreview/21dash.html?partner=rss&emc=rss> Accessed July 2015.

20 Phrase Finder. 2015. Power Corrupts; Absolute Power Corrupts Absolutely. Available at <www.phrases.org.uk/meanings/absolute-power-corrupts-absolutely.html> Accessed July 2015.

21 World Commission on Environment and Development. 1987. *Our Common Future.* Oxford: Oxford University Press.

22 United Nations. 1948. Universal Declaration of Human Rights. Available at <www.ohchr.org/EN/UDHR/Pages/UDHRIndex.aspx> Accessed July 2015.

23 Ruggie, J. 2008. Protect, Respect and Remedy: A Framework for Business and Human Rights. *Innovations,* 3:2, 189–212, paragraphs 6 and 52. Also available at <www.reports-and-materials.org/sites/default/files/reports-and-materials/Ruggie-report-7-Apr-2008.pdf> Accessed July 2015.

5

INDICATORS AND MEASUREMENT SYSTEMS

In this chapter, we look "under the hood" of a measurement system, identifying the types of indicators that may be used in a certification or rating system, how those indicators are measured, and how they are aggregated into component scores and into a summative evaluation of the sustainability of an organization. This will yield useful insights both for users who are evaluating different standards and for companies that might design their own systems for measuring and reporting their sustainability.

Existing standards for certification and for rating provide the best collection of examples of how specific aspects of sustainability may be defined, measured, and aggregated. The standard setter for a voluntary standard typically publishes a reference guide or technical manual that tells applicants how to prepare the self-study report required for certification. The involuntary standards—the rating systems and indices used by investors—vary in how much they reveal about the ingredients of their ratings, but many publish enough information that analysts can evaluate the what and the how of the standard and speculate about the why.

The technical manual for a certification standard will describe the data that must be collected and reported in the application for certification. There are various names in use for the basic units of data that are evaluated by the certifier. The terminology has not stabilized in this field, so words like attribute, criterion, item, or indicator may be used in the technical manual to indicate these basic units of evaluation. In general scientific terminology, it would be called a variable. We have used the term "indicator" in this book. An **indicator** is the smallest unit of information *that is evaluated* under the standard. Look for any item of information on which the certifier must make an evaluation of compliance/noncompliance or must assign points. Those are the indicators used in the standard. A **measure** is a specific way to quantify or evaluate an indicator.

A single indicator may require the use or reporting of several **items** of information. An item is the smallest unit of information *that is reported* under the standard. For example, a standard might ask for two years' of data on GHG emissions in order to calculate the percentage change in GHG emissions. The individual years' data would be items, and the percentage would be the indicator.

Groupings of indicators, and their corresponding aggregations of measures, are called by various names; the terminology is not standardized. In the GRI, the term **aspect** may describe a single indicator (G4-EC9 Procurement Practices) or a group of indicators that reflect a particular theme, an "aspect of sustainability" that is material to the reporting organization, such as Energy (G4-EN3 through EN7).[1] The term **category** is commonly used to refer to the largest grouping of indicators that is less than the whole of the standard, such as according to the three P's (people, planet, profit: social, environmental, economic) or ESG (environmental, social, governance). We will use the term "category" in that sense throughout this book. Where a category is broken down further, we will call the components **subcategories** or occasionally "aspects" or "attributes."

It is important to be clear about the entity that is being described by a measured indicator. In general, we may think of the measurement as being taken on an entity such as a product, process, or a company. In the social sciences, where people are the object of study, the entity being analyzed is called a **subject**. The general scientific term in the context of data analysis is **case**, and scientists measure a particular *variable* for a specific *case*. In the context of certifications and ratings, the object of study is the **reporting unit**.

Types of Indicators

The naïve reader might think that a standard for the sustainability of an organization would measure the sustainability of the organization. In other words, one would expect that the indicators in the standard would be the various *outcomes* that comprise the concept of sustainability, such as the number of metric tons of greenhouse gases emitted or the number of tons of waste recycled, number of dollars donated to charity, and so on. That turns out not to be the case. We begin this section by reviewing the categories in which the direct indictors of sustainability are grouped. Then we look at the other types of indicators for which credit is often given organizational metrics for sustainability to find out what is really being measured in a sustainability metric.

Categories of Sustainability (PPP or ESGF)

The outcomes of sustainability are commonly distinguished according to the three P's of the triple bottom line—people, planet, and profit.[2] A parallel development of the concept of sustainability, coming out of the literature on the social responsibility of business, resulted in the ESG framework—environmental, social, and governance.

The typical direct environmental indicators are greenhouse gas emissions, which we will discuss fully in Chapter 6, water usage and water quality (Chapter 7), and waste in its material and pollutive forms, such as the emissions of smog-forming gases, ozone-depleting gases, and gases that contribute to acid rain, and other measures of toxicity (Chapter 8). Biodiversity is an environmental outcome that is mentioned in the Global Reporting Initiative.

Direct measures of the social component of sustainability have been coming into focus as the work of the Global Reporting Initiative has been incorporated into or influenced formal organizational metrics for sustainability, such as the UL 880, SA8000, and B Corporation, and investor-oriented ratings, such as the Global 100 and Dow Jones Sustainability Index. These typically concern the treatment of employees, customers, the local community, and the nation as stakeholders of the organization. We will discuss these in detail in Chapter 9, but as examples of social outcome measures we may cite employee-oriented measures such as employee satisfaction, employee health and wellness, the diversity of an organization (by gender, race, or nationality), instances of human rights violations, and equity in compensation. An example of a customer-oriented outcome measure is employee satisfaction. Outcome measures related to community relations include the amount of donations to local charities or public works, the number of employees' hours given in community service, and the percentage of managers who are hired locally. Indicators of corporate citizenship outcomes at the national level include taxes paid (+) and fines paid (–).

Good governance is not an end in itself. The outcomes of good governance are its impacts on the financial, social, and environmental performance of an organization through the effective engagement of investors, employees, the local community, and nongovernmental organizations that represent environmental concerns. We will return to this idea in Chapter 10.

Outcome measures related to long-term financial performance and risk should be a part of any organizational metric for sustainability, if sustainability refers to the long-term performance of the organization. The familiar metrics identified by accountants are profitability ratios, leverage ratios, solvency ratios, sustainable growth rate, and activity ratios such as asset turnover. Indicators of longer-term performance include Tobin's q, which is similar to the market/book ratio, and the percentage of profits invested in research and development.

Those are examples of measures of financial, social, and environmental *outcomes*, but that is not the only type of indicator that is reported in firms' CSR or sustainability reports nor called for by the standards for corporate ratings and certification. It will be useful to look at what else is reported and to understand why it is reported.

Saying, Doing, and Achieving

An ideal metric for sustainability would—one might expect—define the outcomes that directly measure sustainability and would award a certification or rating based on those outcomes. That expectation may be fulfilled in standards for products, but for all of the organizational metrics reviewed in this book, it is met only partially. The difference is that organizational metrics for sustainability also give consideration, sometimes substantial consideration, to what an organization says and what it does, as well as what it achieves in terms of sustainability. The rationale for including "saying" and "doing" in a metric for sustainability is the expectation that such measures are leading indicators of sustainability—they predict the level of sustainability that the company will have in the future or the direction of change in the sustainability of the company. One may question whether it is appropriate to award a certification or rating for what a company might be in the future rather than for what the company is in the present. For our purposes here, we simply acknowledge the practice of awarding credit for saying and doing as well as for achievements in terms of sustainability.

Saying

Measures that indicate what a firm "says" include the *disclosure* of sustainability outcomes (awarding points for the disclosure irrespective of the outcome), *publicity* given to sustainability initiatives, and the *training* of employees in the concepts and methods of sustainability. *Saying* conveys a corporate intent in relation to sustainability, but it does not assure action, much less the achievement of outcomes.

Some of the organizational metrics give credit for what the organization reveals in its corporate reports—not for the content of the reporting but for the mere fact of reporting itself. That practice essentially gives credit for transparency, not for sustainability. For example, Underwriters Laboratories' UL 880 standard for the sustainability of manufacturing firms gives points to an organization that discloses its political contributions, issues a habitat and ecosystem conservation report, or issues reports on diversity and inclusion, occupational safety and health, or human rights. It also gives points for merely reporting GHG emissions, water use, and waste. In the case of GHG emissions, water, and waste, the firm can earn *other* points that depend on how much emissions or waste is produced or how much water is consumed, but the mere fact of reporting is sufficient to earn at least some credit in the UL 880 system.

Training can be targeted specifically to certain outcomes, but when a metric awards credit to a firm merely for training in "sustainability," without further specificity as to the category of outcomes intended from the training, a critic might say fairly that such a practice is giving credit to a firm merely for its cheerleading in the sustainability movement.

Another form of saying is *policy-making*. Some metrics give credit to a firm that merely has policies related to sustainability without confirming that those policies translate into actions or outcomes. This type of indicator likely has its intellectual roots in the ISO 14001, which is a standard for environmental management systems where certification is awarded based on the presence and operation of a system, not on the outcomes of the system. A heavily polluting firm can be certified to

ISO 14001 as long as the firm has policies in relation to the pollution and is putting those policies into practice. Examples of credit for the existence of policies related to sustainability abound in AASHE's STARS system for the sustainability of colleges and universities and indicators of policies, as well as of disclosure, are common in Underwriters Laboratories' UL 880 standard.

Doing

Doing means action. The firm earns points for taking some action, presumably for actions that are plausibly related to the direct measures of the sustainability of the firm in the future. Enforcing an existing policy by staffing a job or creating a management system is a type of doing. A stronger form of doing consists in actions that have an almost immediate relationship to the achievement of sustainability outcomes for the reporting organization. Creating the position of sustainability director is a form of doing. Examples from AASHE's STARS system are the construction of environmentally certified buildings, the purchase of EnergyStar certified appliances and low-power lighting, and paying incentives to employees who carpool.

Achieving (Outcomes)

The distinction between measures of organizational actions and measures of the achievement of organizational outcomes is important, because the public perception of sustainability metrics is arguably that they certify the *current* sustainability of a company, not its anticipated future sustainability.

The distinction between doing and achieving is blurry in the case of purchasing. The purchase of low-VOC paints for an office building is a proxy for indoor air quality and employee health, which are the ultimate achievements of the purchase. Such purchases impact the firm, so they are indicators of "doing" that are related to the current or future sustainability of the organization. However, the purchase of products from *sources that are certified* for the sustainability of *their* practices and management is a different matter. Examples are Fair Trade certification of products, Forest Stewardship Council certification of wood products, organic food, and many others. There, the impact of the purchase, the purchaser's achievement, is on the social and environmental *outcomes of the supplier.* The purchaser achieves sustainability outcomes upward in the supply chain, so in some sense, the purchaser inherits a part of the environmental and social outcomes of the suppliers. Those outcomes would be very difficult to quantify in a sustainability metric for the purchaser, so the purchase stands as a proxy for those outcomes. It would seem reasonable to classify such purchasing as an achievement in sustainability.

Doing-type indicators, as proxies for current or future sustainability, may be necessary if the corresponding direct measures of current outcomes are difficult or costly to measure. Tracking the disposal of electronics that are ePEAT certified (or not) is less costly than trying to measure the quantity of heavy metals sent to landfills. Nevertheless, in all cases the scholar of sustainability should ask, "Why don't they just measure the direct outcome?" We illustrate this point with some examples.

- Having a LEED-certified building is an action. The reduced use of energy, water, and waste resulting from the quality of that building is the direct outcome.
- Buying hybrid vehicles is an action. The reduction in CO2 emissions is the direct outcome.
- Purchasing food locally for a campus dining hall is an action. The stimulation of the local economy and the reduction in CO2 emissions from the shorter transportation of food are achievements.
- Having a policy of trayless dining is an action. Reduced production of grey water from dishwashing is the direct achievement.
- Operating a program of electronic waste recycling is an action. Reduced emissions of heavy metals is the direct outcome.

The word *performance* is frequently used in standards for sustainability, in relation to what is measured by an indicator, but "performance" is ambiguous. If a "performance measure" refers to the performance of an action, then that measure is an indicator of doing, not of achieving. If it refers to the performance of the organization, as in the phrase "financial performance," or perhaps even "social performance," then it likely refers to an outcome achieved by the organization. For this reason, it is better to use the term *outcome measure* than "performance measure."

Saying, Doing, and Achieving in the STARS Standard

The STARS 2.0 (January 2014) metric for colleges and universities consists of 70 distinct indicators that contribute between 1 and 14 points each in a standard that totals 204 points, with 4 points as credit for "innovation." The four broad categories of STARS 2.0 are academics (28%), engagement (21%), operations (35%), and planning and administration (16%). By comparison, the UL 880 (November 2011) standard for manufacturing firms consists of 108 distinct indicators contributing anywhere between 1 and 25 points in a total of 1,008 points.

Table 5.1 shows the distribution of points within STARS 2.0 by category of sustainability and by type of indicator (disclosure, action, outcome). In that table, we treated indicators about the amount of sustainability content in teaching and research as direct sustainability outcomes rather than as actions, because the context of academia would seem to make such activities directly relevant to a "sustainable university." This is only loosely analogous to a manufacturing firm producing sustainable products, so in Table 5.1, STARS benefits from a liberal interpretation of the meaning of "outcome."

TABLE 5.1 Points Distribution in STARS 2.0

Type	*Env*	*Soc*	*Gov*	*Fin*	*Gen*	*Grand Total*	*Row Pct*
Saying					88	88	**43%**
Doing	34	19	3		25	81	**40%**
Achieving	28	7				35	**17%**
Grand Total	62	26	3		113	204	
Column Pct	**30%**	**13%**	**1%**	**0%**	**55%**	100%	

The categories of E, S, G, and F (financial) had to be supplemented by a General category that includes indicators that refer only to sustainability as a whole, such as "offers training in sustainability."

This table shows that more than half of the points in the STARS system are for general (nonspecific) qualities of sustainability, which means for sustainability itself, and among those are two-thirds that are for publications or planning in favor of sustainability, not for actions or outcomes.

Leading, Lagging, and Coincident Indicators

Indicators differ in how they relate to the sustainability of an organization in time. Coincident indicators are measures of the sustainability of the organization at the point in time when the measurement was taken. Lagging indicators show what the sustainability was at some time prior to the measurement. Leading indicators are predictors of future sustainability.

The choice to use leading, lagging, or coincident indicators in a standard depends on the purpose of the standard. If a standard is meant to describe the sustainability of an organization at a point in time, the way a grade represents a student's knowledge at the end of a semester, then the standard should consist only of coincident indicators. If the standard is meant to predict an organization's future sustainability—including its exposure to risks associate with future carbon prices, water shortages, landfill availability, and workforce norms—then leading indicators are appropriate.

"Doing" leads achievement, and "saying" leads "doing," so these types of indicators have a role in future-oriented standards. So, too, would measures of change in coincident indicators, which we will consider later in this chapter.

Proxy Indicators

In corporate governance, your proxy is a person who stands in for you at the annual meeting of the corporation to cast your votes. For our purposes, a **proxy indicator** is one that stands in for another indicator, the primary indicator, to reflect the primary indicator's quality of sustainability.

In the design of a corporate sustainability report or a corporate standard for sustainability rating or certification, a balance must be struck between the availability or the cost of acquiring the information, on the one hand, and its value to users of the report, rating, or certification, on the other. Some indicators that may be ideal as outcome measures may be too difficult or expensive to measure, or they may not be reliably measured.

This point is especially salient to small and medium-sized enterprises that design their own corporate sustainability report. They tend to have limited budgets for sustainability reporting. It would be easier to report, echoing an example from earlier in this chapter, that the firm uses low-VOC paints than to perform an analysis of indoor air quality, though air quality is the desired outcome. The type of paint is only one factor affecting indoor air quality. The choice of carpeting and the type of materials used in cabinetry are also factors, as are certain aspects in the operation of the heating and air conditioning system. So, the use of low-VOC paints is at best a moderate proxy for the desired outcome of good indoor air quality.

The Global Initiative for Sustainability Ratings raises the point about proxy indicators explicitly in the context of making comparisons among companies:

> Comparability of evaluations of peer companies within a single time period requires a high level of uniformity and quality of data across evaluated companies. Where uneven and/or incomplete data is in play, sound comparisons are not possible. Where data deficiencies severely compromise comparability, a rating should seek reasonable proxy issues and/or indicators to maximize analytically defensible comparisons.[3]

Scales of Measurement

To appreciate how an indicator might be reported in an analysis of sustainability, we must understand the various "scales of measurement" by which information can be reported.

Ratio-Scaled Measures

A ratio scale has a meaningful "zero" point, which makes it possible to calculate meaningful ratios and proportions. Using a ratio-scaled indicator, one may say that a company has made a 15% improvement from one year to the next or that one company scored 20% lower than another company.

GHG is a numerical (CO2e) and single-dimensioned ratio scale. A company that is responsible for the release of 2,000 metric tons of CO2-equivalent per year would be producing twice as much as another company that is only releasing 1,000 metric tons.

Interval-Scaled Measures

An interval scale has no meaningful zero point, but differences between scores are still meaningful. The textbook example of a ratio scale is temperature. Neither the Fahrenheit scale nor the Celsius scale has a meaningful zero point, because in neither case can you say that a 20 degree temperature is twice as hot as 10 degrees. However, the difference between 10° and 20° represents the same increase in heat as the difference between 50° and 60°, so *intervals* of measurement have meaning.

Ordinal-Scaled Measures

An ordinal scale of measurement consists of categories that are sequenced in value, but there is no meaningful concept of distance between categories. A Gold-level certification is better than Silver, and Silver is better than Bronze, but this much information alone is not sufficient to determine whether the transition from Bronze to Silver is easier or harder or the same level of difficulty as the transition from Silver to Gold. An ordinal scale shows only that one value is more or less than another.

Corporate rankings, rating firms as #1, #2, #3, and so on in their industry, form an ordinal scale. Expressing the ranking as a percentile within the industry is likewise an ordinal-scaled indicator. The Global 100 corporate rating system makes extensive use of percentile rankings within a firm's industry, basing 11 of its 12 indicators on percentile rankings (Table 2.5 in Chapter 2).

Categorical Measures

A categorical measurement system does no more than place an entity into one of several defined categories. The categories are not related to each other along any continuum; otherwise, they would represent an ordinal scale. Examples of variables that are assessed categorically are gender (M/F), race, and occupation. A question that is answered Yes/No results in a categorical measure, so categorical variables might appear in a sustainability assessment if the standard awards points to one answer but not to the other.

Categorical Measures With Weights Become Interval Measures

By itself, the presence or absence (a categorical measure) of a corporate policy does not convey information about the achievement of sustainability outcomes. For example, having an environmental management plan does not by itself make a company more sustainable than one that does not have an environmental management plan; the plan has to be implemented and monitored to demonstrate specific outcomes. However, categorical indicators of this type get upgraded to interval-scaled indicators in a sustainability standard when they are assigned specific numbers of points that contribute to a summative score on which a certificate or rating is based. In the UL 880, having a sustainability training program (Item 15.3) is worth 10 points. Disclosing water use (Item 19.6) is worth 5 points. This does not mean that a 10-point item is twice as good as a 5-point item (which would be true for a ratio scale), but this assignment of points does mean that a 10-point item *adds twice as much* to the firm's score as a 5-point item does (interval scale).

AASHE's STARS 2.0 standard for the sustainability of colleges and universities has a maximum of 204 points allocated across 70 items. The items vary in their point count from 1 to 14, so the number of points given to an item expresses the item's weight in calculating the total score. The items themselves fall into groups, and the subtotal of points within a group tells how important that group is within the entire STARS evaluation system.

What Difference Does the Measurement Scale Make?

In broad terms, the scale of measurement affects the amount and type of information that is conveyed by the data. The "amount" of information refers to the granularity of the measurement system. A more *fine-grained* measurement system yields finer distinctions than a *coarse-grained* system. For example, a record of employees' race as Black or White tells less about the employees than would a record that had more categories—White, Hispanic, Native American, African American, and Asian American.

Up the scale from categorical to ordinal, new information is revealed. Ordinal data permit *direct comparisons* among cases, because the value measured for one case (product or company) can be interpreted to be more than or less than another. Farther up the scale to interval data, we can make *comparisons of changes or differences* as being greater or less in one case than in another case. It is only possible to say that one company has improved more than another has if you are measuring their performance using a system that is at least interval scaled. Moreover, a meaningful summative score, created by summing or averaging across a set of indicators, is possible only if the indicators are measured at the interval scale or higher. Farther up the scale from interval to ratio, more information is revealed. Comparisons among cases can be expressed in percentages and ratios. One product can be 20% more sustainable than another can only if the indicator being measured is ratio scaled.

The Choice to Lose Information and Gain Simplicity

Some variables have only one scale of measurement, and it is the obvious one. One example is biological gender. It is described as a binary categorical indicator—male or female. For some variables, however, the scale of measurement is a matter of choice. That choice will affect the granularity under which information is recorded, and it may affect the interpretation of the variable itself.

An example familiar to students is a quiz grade. In the finest level of granularity and the most informationally rich, the professor would grade a quiz on a

0–100 scale, corresponding to the percentage of correct answers among the questions. A student who earned 75 points had answered 50% more questions correctly than the student who earned 50 points. The zero point of no correct answers has an absolute meaning. This is the essential feature of a ratio scale of measurement.

Suppose instead that the professor chose to report students' grades using a **grade-point scale**, where 4.0 is an A, 3.0 is a B, 2.0 a C, 1.0 a D, and 0 is no credit (NC). Mathematically, this looks like a ratio scale, because 2.0 is twice as much as a 1.0, but what does this scale really convey? It conveys only the professor's sense of excellence (A, 4.0), good (B, 3.0), fair (C, 2.0), poor (D, 1.0) and failing (NC, 0). The professor would likely establish those grade points as corresponding to specific scores on the quiz, such as 90 for the A/B boundary (3.5), 80 for the B/C boundary (2.5), 70 for the C/D boundary (1.5), and 60 for the D/F boundary (0.5). By that measure, the zero grade point would correspond to 56.6% correct on the quiz, and by convention any quiz score below that would get the same 0.0 grade-point measure.

If a student's performance on the quiz is meant to indicate their knowledge of the subject matter, then the grade-point measure has a rather arbitrary zero. It would make no sense to say that the student who scored 56.6% correct on the quiz knows nothing about the subject. Indeed, the zero point on a grading scale is largely arbitrary. The 90–80–70–60 scheme is purely conventional. Another professor might choose to use 85–70–65–50, in which case 45% correct would be the 0.0 mark in grade points. Thus, if we know only the student's grade point but not their quiz score, we cannot really say that one student knows twice as much about the subject if they got a B (2.0) than if they got a C (1.0). However, knowing that the professor followed some type of rule that gave equal score intervals to the grades, such as 10 points per grade in the first example and 15 points per grade in the second, the grade-point scheme would have an interval scale of measurement, and we could make meaningful statements about whether one student's improvement from Quiz 1 to Quiz 2 was greater or less than another student's improvement.

A yet weaker measurement system for the quiz would be a **letter-grade scale**. Reporting grades only as A+, A, A–, B+, B, B–, and so on would enable us to say that one student knows more about the subject than another, according to the higher grade, but we could not say for certain that the professor's difference between an A+ and an A is the same as their difference between a B and a B–. The letter grade is the preferred method of measurement for essay exams, where a student's performance is not easily reducible to points. The grade is the professor's subjective assessment. It recognizes that the professor can tell if one essay is better than another, but it does not assume that the gain in quality from an A to an A+ is the same as the difference in quality between a B– and a B. Thus, the letter grade scale is ordinal, not interval. It conveys less information.

The next weakest measurement system for the quiz is the **pass/fail** scale. It is a two-category system of measurement, hence binary, but a pass indicates more knowledge learned than a fail, so we have to call it a binary ordinal scale, not a binary categorical scale. Its low granularity, however, makes it the weakest way to represent a student's knowledge of a subject as demonstrated on a quiz.

An example of a purely categorical scale for the quiz would be a **present/absent scale**, indicating whether the student took the quiz or not. That scale conveys no information about the student's performance on the quiz.

When a ratio-scaled measure like GHG emissions or carbon intensity is converted to an industry-normed percentile ranking (ordinal scaled), as in the Global 100 rating system, information about the relative sustainability of the firms gets lost. A firm with 10 kgCO2e per $1,000 revenue has half the carbon intensity of a firm with 20 kgCO2e per $1,000, but they may end up within their industry as the 20th and 30th percentiles, depending on the distribution of carbon intensity values among all the other firms. The percentile measure captures only which firms are better than others, not by how much. In the Global 100 rankings, that is not a problem, because the objective of the Global 100 is to identify which firms are better than others, not to say by how much. But for investors who want to know *how much more to pay* for the shares of a more-sustainable firm than a less-sustainable firm, the sustainability measure would have to be at least interval scaled, not ordinal. A metric like the Global 100 only gives readers a sense of the position of a firm in its industry, not of how sustainable it is.

Measures for Indicators

The ability to compare one firm with another on sustainability indicators is central to the purposes of investors, and it is relevant to other stakeholders such as employees, business-to-business buyers, and the community. However, not all corporate sustainability metrics call for the reporting of data in a manner that permits a useful comparison across firms. It will be interesting to see how data are reported in these less useful ways and to speculate on the reasons for such practices. We begin with a look at how the construction of a sustainability indicator affects its usefulness in comparisons.

Absolute Measures

Indicators that have an **absolute** meaning can be reported on their own and still permit a meaningful evaluation of the sustainability of the reporting unit. The total amount of a pollutant emitted by a firm, or the amount of water or materials used by a firm, are one type of example; they may be usefully compared between firms and within a firm over time. However, as we shall see immediately below, the comparison of pollution or resource utilization across firms usually requires a statement of the measure *relative to* the size of the firm, as what is called an intensity or productivity measure. An example that does not require such framing, taken from the UL 880 standard, is the *percentage* of a firm's purchases, by value, that are "environmentally preferred." In the UL 880, environmental preference has a specific meaning: consumable purchases must have at least 30% post-consumer content or 20% post-industrial content (UL 880 item 23.3.2a), and durable purchases must meet energy efficiency standards such as the EnergyStar label or the IEEE 1680.1 standard for personal computer products (UL 880 item 23.3.2b).

Normalized Measures (Intensity and Productivity Measures)

Not all measures are meaningful for comparison in an absolute sense. For example, total greenhouse gas emission is an absolute measure, and it is ratio scaled to permit a comparison across firms. However, it is not useful as a measure of the relative sustainability among firms, because large firms would reasonably be expected to produce more GHG emissions than small firms would. It is not the GHG emissions *per se* that are relevant to the sustainability of the firm, but its emissions relative to its level of business activity. Dividing the GHG emissions quantity by a measure of the size of the business would be **normalizing** the GHG emissions by size. That way of presenting GHG emissions, in a ratio with a size variable, yields a measure that permits meaningful comparisons among firms.

The best choice of the normalizing variable may depend on the indicator and the firm's industry. Where the industry produces a homogeneous product, the total quantity of the product produced during a year would be an obvious choice for normalization by size. Thus, the GHG emissions could be expressed as mtCO2e per 1,000 gallons of milk or per 1,000 board-feet of lumber.

If the industry produces many products or services, then a normalization by sales revenue or by the number of employees might be used. Neither of these is perfect. The measure mtCO2e per $1,000 revenue would go down if the firm were to raise its price even with steady output, resulting in the appearance of an improved sustainability measure when the reality of GHG emissions relative to physical output would be unchanged. GHG emissions per employee might be a better measure, as it would be independent of price fluctuations, but even the number of employees is not a perfect proxy for the aggregate output of a firm.

The **polarity** of a measure, a term coming from ASSET4 ESG,[4] shows whether the measure is positively or negatively related to sustainability. In a list of indicators in a standard, those that are related positively to sustainability should be indicated by a "+" sign, and those that are negatively related should be indicated by "–". The GISR's Principle of Comparability calls for a standard to declare the polarity of its indicators whenever there could be doubt about their meaning, and it identifies normalized measures as particularly vulnerable to such misunderstanding,

> Comparability is enhanced when the rating provides clarity and consistency as to whether increases or decreases in numerical values reflect higher or lower levels of performance. Ratings that rely on ratios to measure performance need adequate explication. Only through full and understandable disclosure of ratio

data can users properly interpret shifts in company performance that are expressed in ratio forms.[5]

Measures of a sustainability variable normalized by an activity variable are called **intensity measures**, examples being GHG intensity, water intensity, energy intensity, waste intensity, and so on. GHG and other types of waste emission and the use of water energy are negatively related to sustainability in absolute terms, so as intensity measures, their lower values indicate greater sustainability, giving measures of pollutant or resource intensity a negative polarity in a sustainability metric.

When an intensity measure is inverted, it becomes a **productivity measure**. For example, the Global 100 corporate rating system calculates *carbon productivity* as a ratio of revenue to carbon emissions, often measured in thousands of dollars (or euros, etc.) of revenue per kilogram of CO2e emitted. Like the intensity measure, it can be used to compare one firm with another. However, if one firm has a higher ratio of revenue to GHG emissions than another has, the one is more sustainable than the other is. As odd as it may sound, *waste productivity* and *resource productivity* indicators have a *positive* relationship to sustainability and thus a positive polarity in a sustainability metric, validating the GISR call for explicit notation of the polarity of indicators in a standard.

Normed Measures (Percentile Rankings and Z-scores)

A measure is **normed** when it is calculated in relation to the scores among many reporting units. The two types of normed measure are percentile rankings and z-scores.

Eleven of the twelve indicators in the Global 100, a corporate rating system, are percentile ranked against a comparison group of companies in the firm's industry. Thus, a firm's score on an indicator such as carbon productivity is not based on the firm's carbon productivity *per se* but on the *percentile ranking* that its carbon productivity figure achieves when compared to a specific group of firms in its industry. A percentile ranking results in a measure between 0% and 100%, usually written in decimals on a 0-to-1 range.

An alternative measure for a normed indicator is the z-score, which is the position of the firm in the referent group's distribution on the measured indicator, expressed in standard-deviation units. This measure ranges theoretically from minus infinity to plus infinity, but in 99.7% of the cases it will lie between –3 and +3.

Norming causes a loss of information in the metric, because a firm at the 90th percentile of its industry is not necessarily twice as sustainable as a firm at the 45th percentile of its industry. If most firms had nearly the same carbon productivity, there might be relatively little distinction, meaning a relatively small ratio in their carbon productivities, between the 45th percentile and the 90th percentile.

That is not a problem for corporate rating systems, such as the Global 100 and the *Newsweek* Green Rankings, whose purpose is achieved just by *ranking* firms within their industry. Ranking only attempts to show which firm is better than another (an ordinal measure), not better by how much (an interval or ratio measure).

Thresholds, Benchmarks, and Other Judgmental Standards

In specific contexts, it may be possible to establish numerical standards that characterize exemplary, good, acceptable, and poor performance on an indicator, or perhaps just acceptable and unacceptable. Examples include the FTSE4Good corporate sustainability metric discussed in Chapter 2 and the Aqueduct water risk measure to be discussed in Chapter 7. Even in the presence of an obviously desirable zero point, as exists for GHG emissions and waste, the delimitation of ranges of values corresponding to different levels of desirability would require personal judgment or a consensus of expert opinion. In industries that have had enough time to evaluate what levels of achievement are possible, a standard setter may be able to set specific benchmarks of performance on an indicator of sustainability.

Example: STARS on Carbon Emissions, Energy, and Waste

The STARS standard for universities has several examples of threshold measures for indicators. STARS gives points for a university's progress toward carbon neutrality, but it gives extra points for universities that have beaten their carbon footprint below a threshold of 0.020 metric tons of carbon dioxide equivalent (mtCO2e) per gross square foot of floor area per year (1.86 kgCO2e per gross square meter.)

For energy consumption, STARS assigns extra points to organizations that can beat a threshold of 28 BTU per gross square foot of energy-use-intensity adjusted floor area per degree-day per year (2.6 BTU/m^2/d-d/y). STARS' steering committee or technical advisors evidently determined that this threshold represents a distinctive achievement in energy consumption.

For waste generation, STARS does not even begin to award points to universities until they do better than a threshold of 0.45 tons (410 kg) of materials diverted and disposed per weighted campus user per year.

Example: WRI's Indicators for Water Risk

The World Resources Institute's Aqueduct project assesses water risk around the world. WRI set out to establish a summative measure of water risk that could be expressed numerically in a range of 0 to 5 and whose one-unit intervals would correspond subjectively to five levels of water risk: Low, Low-to-Medium, Medium-to-High, High, and Extremely High. Each of the 12 indicators in the WRI water risk metric therefore needed to be expressed on this 0–5 range using a scale that suitably matched the interpretations that are ascribed to each one-unit interval.

Observing the range and distribution of indicator values in their natural units, Gassert and colleagues used the existing scientific literature and expert judgment to identify the four thresholds or benchmarks that would separate the raw data into the five subjectively meaningful categories of water risk (Low, Low-to-Medium, etc.)[6] Each indicator was then transformed mathematically by a linear or logarithmic function so that its range of natural values would come to fit between 0 and 5, with priority given to matching well the lowest and highest benchmarks, which define Low and Extremely High risk, to the values of 1 and 4.

Example: FTSE4Good

The FTSE4Good metric uses a similar approach in calculating its overall score for corporate sustainability. Each of its indicators (about 125 for a firm, depending on the industry) has to be transformed from its natural units of measurement onto a 0–5 scale in which 5 designates "Best Practice" and 3 is "Good Practice," essentially producing an interval-scaled measure. As with Aqueduct, the mathematical formulas for those transformations have to be determined by expert opinion as to what is "good" and "best" for each indicator.

The examples of WRI's indicators for water risk and of FTSE4Good show that it may indeed be possible to ascribe different subjective levels of sustainability to the values of an indicator variable. The STARS examples show that a team of experts can come to agreement about the meaning of specific levels of performance on some indicators (GHG emissions, energy, waste, and water), in terms of sustainability for organizations in the higher education industry.

It is an open question whether a given indicator can be ascribed a universal interpretation in terms of sustainability, or whether the interpretations of indictor values must depend on the industry or other contexts. The Global Reporting Initiative has responded to a demand for industry-specific reporting guidelines by issuing supplements for selected industries.[7] The Sustainability Accounting Standards Board has likewise issued industry-specific standards for disclosing material sustainability information.[8] These two examples of systems for reporting do not address the question of how to interpret the reported data in terms of sustainability, but the very fact that they recognize differences in reporting requirements across industries suggests that the relevance of some indicators varies by line of business. Underwriters Laboratories issued its UL 880 standard specifically for manufacturing firms, as did Green Seal with its GS-C1 standard. Their restriction of the applicability of their standard makes the same point.

Baselined Change Measures

A common managerial practice within firms is to set targets for future performance in relation to current performance. Managers may then be evaluated according to the absolute change in performance or the percentage change. For example, the award of stock options to managers establishes a baseline (the exercise price of the option) above which the manager is rewarded in absolute terms. A marketing manager might be incentivized by compensation based on the percentage increase in sales from a specific point in time.

When should a sustainability indicator be measured as a change rather than as an absolute value? Greenhouse gas emissions offer an illustration. A firm's incremental contribution to global warming and climate change is determined by the *absolute level* of its annual GHG emissions (metric tons of CO2-equivalent). However, to compare one firm's GHG emissions with another's, it makes sense to *normalize* the absolute measure by the size of the firm. Taken one step further, a firm's competitive advantage in dealing with carbon risk might better be captured by its *percentile ranking* in carbon productivity among firms in its industry. Yet further, for a firm that must buy carbon permits in an emissions trading system, its exposure to the economic risks associated with GHG emissions, relative to others in its industry, may be better captured by its progress in reducing GHG emissions percentagewise *relative to its baseline* in the base year that the system uses to determine the number of emission permits available in a given year.

The concept of change relative to a baseline level of performance appears in many corporate standards for sustainability, but practices differ in how the baseline is established, whether there is a long-term target for change from the baseline, and if there is, who sets the target and how.

Example: STARS on GHG and Waste Diversion

AASHE's STARS standard for universities uses an organization's change relative to a baseline to award points for reductions in GHG emissions, water use, and waste. Each variable is normalized by an indicator of size (weighted campus users) for reporting and is calculated as a percentage reduction from a standard base year, 2005. STARS gives points proportionally for the reduction of the baseline value to zero. The maxima of 4 points for GHG and 3 points for waste diversion establish the relative priorities of these two components of sustainability.

Example: UL 880 on Waste Diversion

Underwriters Laboratories' UL 880 standard gives full credit (25 points of 1,003) to a firm that has a zero-waste goal and has eliminated 95% of the waste generated relative to the baseline value in a standard base year of 2005.

The goal of GHG emissions policies is carbon neutrality, meaning zero net GHG emissions. The goal of waste management policies is zero waste to landfills and incinerators, meaning a reuse, repair, repurposing, or recycling of all purchased items. GHG emissions and waste diversion have obvious zero points as their targets in a sustainable world, but that is not the case with energy and water consumption, which are also important indicators of sustainability.

What *would* be the energy and water consumption of a perfectly sustainable organization? That is a matter of judgment according to the geographic and industrial context of the organization. Voluntary standards can use their technical advisors to establish thresholds that define in absolute terms the levels of acceptable performance and the targets that characterize sustainability. Involuntary standards, the corporate rating systems, either will do the same or, by having access to the data on many firms in an industry, will fall back on measures of one firm relative to its industry peers. The example of the AASHE's STARS metric for colleges and universities illustrates this point.

Example: STARS on Energy Consumption and Waste Generation

STARS awards points for reductions in energy consumption and waste generation based on an organization's change relative to its baseline and a target, a benchmark standard, that represents STARS' expectation of the sustainable level of the variable.

For building energy consumption, the target is 2.8 BTU per gross square foot of energy-use-intensity adjusted floor area per degree-day per year, which is 10% of the threshold at which an organization begins to earn points. For waste generation, the target is 0.045 tons of waste per weighted campus user. This is likewise 10% of the threshold at which an organization begins to earn points related to waste generation.

The fact that the target is set equal to 10% of the threshold value for both energy consumption and waste generation suggests that the standard for the target was a matter for judgment by the STARS steering committee and its technical advisors. The science of sustainability in business is not as exact as the statement of the standard would imply.

Example: STARS on Water Consumption

STARS is not as specific about a benchmark for water consumption as it is for energy consumption and waste generation. STARS awards a maximum of 2–6 points (out of 208 in the summative measure) for indicators pertaining to water consumption. The maximum number of points goes to organizations that have reduced their potable water use by 30% relative to their baseline, with a proportional allocation of points rewarding performance short of the 30% target reduction. STARS uses three separate indicators for water use, normalizing gross water use by weighted campus user, by area of building space, and by area of vegetated land. Notice that the target of a 30% reduction is not stated in absolute terms, only relative to the organization's own baseline value.

The maximum number of points varies between 2 and 6 depending on the level of water stress in the region where the university is located, as indicated by the World Resources Institute's Aqueduct Water Risk Index.[9]

Baselined Change Measures in the UL 880

In Underwriters Laboratories' 880 corporate sustainability standard and AASHE's STARS 2.0 standard, several environmental indicators are measured as the *percentage reduction* in a quantity (e.g., GHG emissions, waste, water usage) from a "base year."

However, the UL 880 allows the reporting organization to choose the target for reduction against which the metric awards points. The UL 880 basically asks, "How well did your actual reductions conform to your planned reductions?" That self-defined reference point does not result in an allocation of points that permits a comparison of one firm with another on the environmental metrics.

STARS uses a standardized base year (2005) for comparison against the reporting year, but since STARS is specific to academia, the metric was written with specific targets that seemed reasonable for all colleges or universities to aim at.

Some sustainability indicators have a meaningful zero point, so while some degree of comparison is lost by allowing firms to have different starting points as their baselines, if they are all targeting the same outcome, such as zero GHG emissions or zero net waste, there is some value in knowing how much, percentagewise, a firm has advanced toward its goal.

Other sustainability indicators have no meaningful zero. Water usage is an example. The long-term sustainable level of water usage, even normalized by some size variable as water intensity, will be some positive number. Thus, if firms were allowed to set their own targets and earn points as they advance toward those targets, the points earned for water intensity would not be comparable across firms even in the same industry.

Comparability would be possible only if experts in the industry agree on a long-term target for the indicator, common to all firms, and if points are awarded based on a firm's progress from a common threshold point to the target point, as in the example of STARS on energy consumption and waste generation.

Why Do Some Standards Use Baselined Measures?

A baseline is a point of reference specific to the organization. Progress from that baseline is a measure of achievement for the organization, even if it does not permit comparison across organizations even in the same industry. Thus, baselined measures have internal motivational properties, even if they do not mean much to outside observers. This suggests the speculation that organizational metrics that use baselined measures, such as the Underwriters Labs UL 880 or Green Seal's C-1 corporate standard or AASHE's STARS system for universities, may have been developed in the spirit of the ISO 14001 environmental management standard. ISO 14001 is awarded to firms that have a well-designed and functioning environmental management system irrespective of the firm's absolute level of environmental impacts. ISO 14001 permits the applicant firms to set their own targets. As a voluntary standard with self-defined goals, it guides the reporting firm to higher levels of environmental achievement. The voluntary sustainability metrics for organizations likewise have elements that appear to be meant for internal use, to help the organization improve its sustainability, rather than for external comparison.

Rolling Change Measures

Is the sustainability of a firm better indicated by its absolute level of performance on a sustainability indicator or by the *trend of recent changes* to that indicator? Corporate Knights' Global 100 corporate rating system takes both into consideration. Each of its productivity indicators (carbon productivity, energy productivity, water productivity, and so on) has two components. One, weighted 75% in the indicator, is the percentile ranking of the firm within its industry on an absolute measure of that indicator. The other, weighted 25%, is a two-year percentage change in the productivity measure. Being a percentage change against a baseline that is always two years behind the reporting year, we call this a *rolling change* measure.

Unlike the absolute measures, rolling change measures are forward looking. They express the momentum of the firm on the indicator. Even a percentage change from a baseline cannot capture the momentum of an indicator, especially if the baseline has receded some distance into the past.

With this understanding of how indicators can be measured and transformed, we turn to how standards aggregate data about several indicators to form subcategory scores or category scores and even to create a summative evaluation of the sustainability of a company.

Methods of Aggregation for Subcategories, Categories, and Summative Measures

We distinguish five methods of aggregation, based on whether each item is evaluated on a continuous scale (e.g., 0–100) or on a Yes/No basis (called *binary*) and whether the summative evaluation across all items is based on a system of "points" for the various items or not.

Absolute Binary

The absolute binary system results in a pass/fail decision. The decision is based on an evaluation of several indicators, but each indicator is evaluated pass/fail, and a failure on any of the indicators results in a summative evaluation of "Fail." This type of system leaves no room for weakness in one indicator to compensate for strength in another indicator. Thus, the criteria for the pass/fail decisions on the various indicators are the subject of intense debate when the standard is being created or being reviewed.

Example: ISO 14001

The ISO 14001:2004 certification for environmental management systems applies to a process within a company, possibly restricted to a particular plant or location within the company. Thus, it is not an organization-wide certification but is specific to the process of environmental management and, possibly, to location.

The ISO 14001:2004 is an example of a binary standard, where the outcome of the evaluation is a decision to certify or not certify the applicant. More specifically, the decision to certify or not certify is based on an evaluation of 18 elements of the firm's environmental management system, each of which is described in the ISO 14001:2004 manual.[10]

An ISO registrar evaluates an applicant against each of the 18 elements of the standard. Within each element, the registrar makes a judgment to determine whether the applicant is compliant with the expectations of the standard, compliant with minor nonconformities, or not compliant. Any instance of noncompliance across the items in the standard results in a decision not to certify the applicant.

The ISO 14001 evaluation is a matter of professional judgment by the registrar's audit staff. The proper training and experience of auditors ensures consistency in the application of the standard.

Nested Binary

The nested binary method of summative evaluation results in an assignment of the case to one of three or more levels. The summative evaluation is therefore of ordinal scale, but it is formed from an evaluation of compliance or noncompliance (binary) on many indicators. The indicators are organized in nested sets as illustrated by the Venn diagram in Figure 5.1, where we show three levels of summative evaluation and name them Bronze, Silver, and Gold.

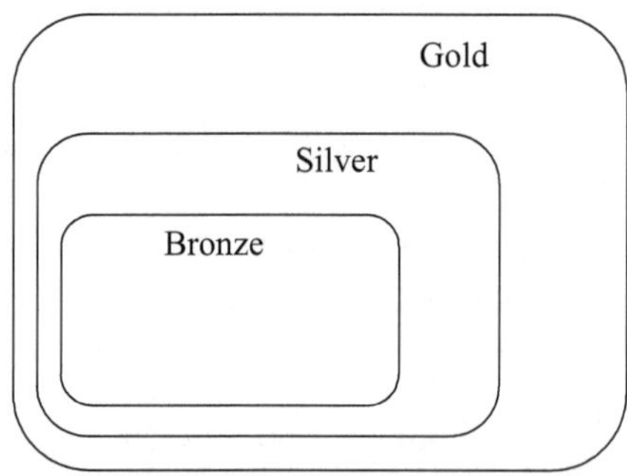

FIGURE 5.1 Venn Diagram for a Nested Binary Evaluation

If the case is compliant on all the Bronze items, it earns that level of summative evaluation. If it is compliant on the Bronze and on the extra items that comprise the remainder of the Silver set, it earns the next level of evaluation. If it is compliant on the Silver set and the remainder of the Gold set, it earns that level.

This system can be used for any number of levels, but the key point is that the higher level of evaluation implies compliance with all the requirements of the lower levels.

Example: Green Seal GS-C1 for Manufacturing Firms

Green Seal's 2009 GS-C1 standard is a nested binary system with slight modification. It awards a Bronze, Silver, or Gold rating. The Bronze level specifies the indicators needed to get a "passing" grade and earn the certification. The Silver level includes all the Bronze indicators and more, but some of the new indicators at the Silver level can be selected from among a list. The Gold level of certification requires a pass on all indicators.

Weighted Binary (Points)

In the weighted binary system, all indicators are evaluated in a pass/fail manner (binary), but each indicator is weighted by a specific number of "points." The aggregate measure for the case is the total number of points earned, so the summative measure is compensatory. The summative measure used in reporting could be a pass or fail as determined by some threshold number of points; a series of levels each earned by a higher number of points and given names such as Bronze, Silver, and Gold; or the point score itself.

This system is similar to the nested binary method in that each indicator is evaluated on a pass/fail basis. However, it differs from the nested binary in how those pass/fail evaluations are aggregated. In the nested binary method, if one case has a higher summative evaluation than another case, the first case must be compliant with all of the items that the second complies with but also with some others. However, in the weighted binary method, the award of a Gold, Silver, or Bronze level of achievement depends only on the total number of points earned, not on which items earned those points. Thus, a case that gets a Gold evaluation may not have complied with all of the items that a Silver case complied with, but the Gold case earned more points on other items that the Silver did not comply with.

The relative number of points given to one indicator versus another expresses the relative importance of the indicators in the summative evaluation.

Weighted Averages and "Points" Systems

The weighted-average method appears in two forms, one that varies the weights across indicators and one that varies the maximum number of "points" awarded for each indicator.

In the first method, all indicators are measured on a scale having the same range, but different indicators may be given different weights in the calculation of the summative measure. A familiar example of an unequal weighting of common-range indicators is a student's grade in a college course, where the professor grades each quiz, exam, or assignment on the same 0–100 point scale, but gives different weights to certain items, such as 20% for a quiz and 40% for a final exam. There, the student's course grade is a weighted average of the grades earned on the individual items, and the weights reflect the relative importance of each item in the course grade.

Example: Global 100

Another example is the Global 100 corporate rating system, where the productivity measures for energy, water, carbon, and waste are all normed against the firm's industry and expressed as a percentile ranking (0%–100%), thus putting all indicators on a 0-to-1 scale. The Global 100 summative measure is an equal weighting of the 12 indicators in the standard, rescaled to result in a measure with a 0–100 range.

The second of the weighted average systems is a generalization of the weighted binary system discussed in the previous section, where each indicator was assigned one of two scores, either 0 or the maximum number of "points" available for the indicator, and the summative measure was the sum of the points across all indicators. There, the maximum number of points indicated the relative importance of the indicator in the overall measure of sustainability. The same mathematical effect is achieved if indicators can take on values within ranges that have different maximum values, but the summative measure is a simple sum of the indicators' values. As with the weighted binary system, the indicators' values are usually called "points," and the maximum number of points available for an indicator reflects the relative weight of the indicator in the summative measure.

Example: ASSET4 ESG

Like the Global 100, Thomson Reuters' ASSET4 ESG metric uses indicators that are ranked in percentiles relative to other firms in a comparison group, so indicators get scores on a 0–100 scale. The weights applied to these commonly scaled indicators therefore reflect the relative importance of the indicator in a subcategory or category. Depending on the indicator, those weights may be universal, or they may depend on the industry or the region of a firm's operation. A differential weighting by industry might reflect the relative significance of various stakeholders. A differential weighting by region could also reflect cultural differences, including ethical sensibilities.

ASSET4 ESG equally weights its main categories ("pillars") when forming its summative score. However, ASSET4 ESG publishes its category scores for each company, so users of the information may apply weights that reflect their own priorities.

Example: STARS

AASHE's STARS 2.0 standard for college and university sustainability uses such a system. Each indicator has a specific maximum number of "points," some of which are binary and others of which are scaled on a range from zero to the maximum. A university's overall sustainability score is the sum of all the points earned. The maximum number of points assigned to an indicator, and to groups of indicators (aspects), reveals the relative importance of the indicator or aspect in the STARS system.[11] The 208 points in STARS are allocated across five major aspects of a university's activity: curriculum (58 pts, 28%), engagement (42 pts, 20%) operations (72 pts, 35%), planning and administration (32 pts, 15%), and innovation (4 pts, 2%), which disaggregate into 18 minor aspects formed from 74 distinct indicators. The percentage of each aspect in the summative measure indicates the importance of that aspect in the opinion of the people who designed the STARS standard.

Publicly, STARS reporters reduce their summative measure from a ratio scale (the number of points earned) to an ordinal scale and report only a Bronze, Silver, Gold, or Platinum evaluation, using as cut-off points 25%, 45%, 65%, and 85% of the number of points applicable to the reporting college or university.

Example: LEED for New Construction

The Leadership in Energy and Environmental Design (LEED) system for buildings is similar to STARS in that the standard permits four levels of evaluation, those being Certified, Silver, Gold, and Platinum, based on the number of points earned, as seen in Table 5.2. The LEED system for new buildings awards a total of 136 points across eight categories as shown in Table 5.3. As such, LEED is a compensatory system using weights on the various attributes.

TABLE 5.2 LEED Points

LEED level	*Points needed*
Platinum	90–136
Gold	75–89
Silver	60–74
Certified	45–59

TABLE 5.3 LEED Criteria and Points

LEED Criteria	*Points*	*Percent*
Innovation and design process	11	8%
Location and linkage	10	7%
Sustainable sites	22	16%
Water efficiency	15	11%
Energy and atmosphere	38	28%
Materials and resources	16	12%
Indoor environmental quality	21	15%
Awareness and education	3	2%
Totals	**136**	**100%**

Example: B Corporations

The B Corporation assessment is, like STARS, a compensatory scheme calculated using points, but there is only one outcome, pass or fail. To pass, a corporation must get a minimum of 80 points out of 240 on the B Impact Assessment.

Mathematically, in the weighted arithmetic average, each attribute A_i is scored on the same range of values, each attribute is given a positive weight w_i, and the weights must sum to 1 (100%). The summative score is the sum of each attribute value multiplied by its weight,

$$T = w_1A_1 + w_2A_2 + \ldots + w_nA_n \text{ (weighted arithmetic average).}$$

In the weighted binary system and its generalization, all weights w_i are 1, and each indicator has its own range of values. In the second type, the weights w_i are positive percentages summing to one 1, and each indicator takes on values in the range of 0 to 1.

Weighted Geometric Average

One problem with the **weighted-average** approach described above is that a product or company can get a zero score on one attribute but still get a high overall rating if other attributes are scored high. For example, if reductions in GHG emissions count for 10% of a company's sustainability rating, then a company that has a serious rise in emissions, thereby getting zero points on the GHG item, could still get 90 points out of 100 by scoring at the top on all other attributes. It may seem inappropriate to give as high as a 90% score to a company that fails miserably on GHG emission reductions, but the alternative of using an absolute binary system, where a failure on any one attribute results in a failure overall, seems unduly harsh as well.

The aggregation method that finds a middle ground between the weighted average and the absolute binary method is the weighted geometric average. The method works as follows. Each of the attributes of a reporting unit should be graded on the same scale, like 0–10 or as on a grading scale where "excellent" A = 4.0, "good" B = 3.0, "fair" C = 2.0, "poor" D = 1.0, and "fail" F = 0. As in the simple weighted average above, each attribute score or grade A_i is given a positive weight w_i, and the weights must sum to 1. The overall score is the product of each attribute grade raised to the power of its weight,

$$T = A_1^{W_1} * A_2^{W_2} * A_3^{W_3} \ldots * A_n^{W_n} \text{ (weighted geometric average)}$$

For example, suppose that a company is graded separately on its environmental performance (E), its social performance (S), and its governance (G), all on a 0–4 scale. Suppose furthermore that the weights of these three attributes are 0.40, 0.35, and 0.25 respectively. Compare two companies that have the scores shown in Table 5.4. What overall grade would each one get?

Our formula for the total score of any firm will be

$$T = E^{0.40} * S^{0.35} * G^{0.25}$$

Firm A: $T = 3.0^{0.40} * 3.0^{0.35} * 3.0^{0.25} = 3.0^{(.40+.35+.25)} = 3.0^1 = \mathbf{3.00, B}$

Firm B: $T = 1.0^{0.40} * 4.0^{0.35} * 4.0^{0.25} = 1 * 1.62 * 1.41 = \mathbf{2.28, C+}$

Notice how this weighted geometric average compares to a simpler weighted arithmetic average:

Firm A: T = 3.0*40% + 3.0*35% + 3.0*25% = 3.0*(100%) = **3.00, B**

Firm B: T = 1.0*40% + 4.0*35% + 4.0*25% = 0.4 + 1.4 + 1.0 = **2.80, B–**

The geometric average gives the same answer as the arithmetic average when all the component scores are the same. But when the components differ, the geometric average penalizes the firm more for bad performance on even one attribute.

The weights in the geometric average have an interpretation that is known in economics as an *elasticity*. They represent the percentage change in the total score

TABLE 5.4 Example of Scores

	E	*S*	G
Firm A	3.0	3.0	3.0
Firm B	1.0	4.0	4.0

that would result from a 1% increase in the component score. So, in the example above, no matter what a company's environmental score (E) might be, if they can raise that score by 1%, they will increase their total score by 0.40%.

In the FTSE4Good index series, companies that are assigned a High risk exposure on a particular ESG theme but score 0 (on a 5-point scale) for that theme, due to their performance on that theme's indicators, are excluded from the index. In this way, FTSE4Good penalizes poor performance more than proportionally. No sustainability metric for organizations uses the weighted geometric average, probably because the arithmetic average is easier to compute with a basic calculator. An Excel spreadsheet can easily perform the weighted geometric average's calculations using exponents, so this method is clearly possible. An example of the use of a geometric average is found in the United Nations Development Program's Human Development Index (HDI). Since 2010, its summative measure has been the equally weighted geometric average of its three components—health, education, and standard of living.[12] UNDP justifies this type of summative measure along the lines explained in this section,

> The geometric mean reduces the level of substitutability between dimensions and at the same time ensures that a 1% decline in index of say life expectancy at birth has the same impact on the HDI as a 1% decline in education or income index. Thus, as a basis for comparisons of achievements, this method is also more respectful of the intrinsic differences across the dimensions than a simple average.[13]

The Quality of Data for Indicators and Summative Measures

This chapter has focused on the ways that indicators of sustainability can be measured, transformed, and aggregated, concentrating on the mathematical aspects of their representation. The users of sustainability information should also attend to the quality of the data that go into the indicators and the choice of indicators for the summative measure or evaluation.

Accountants have developed standards for the quality of data that go into financial reports, and to a large extent those standards carry over to the accounting for sustainability. Beyond the quality of data is the consideration of the quality of the report as a whole, and there the sustainability metrics have had to break new ground, because the concept of materiality is more complex in sustainability reporting than it is in financial reporting.

Principles for Data Quality in Indicators

Several principles from data management and accounting apply to the measurement of indicators of sustainability. The goal of these principles is that the resulting measures of sustainability can be assured by third parties and that the measures will be usefully comparable within a company over time and across companies.[14]

Clarity

The verbal description of an indicator is the starting point for measurement, but words can be ambiguous and descriptions can be incomplete. When a firm develops its own standard for reporting on sustainability and when public standards are revised, indicators must be described clearly and completely.

Validity

The measurement of an indicator should represent faithfully the concept of sustainability that is expressed in the verbal presentation and interpretation of the indicator. The verbal description of an indicator is just the starting point for measurement, because concepts of sustainability must be operationalized by the collection of data. A valid measure corresponds faithfully to its concept. It is "on target." A less valid measure represents only part of the concept or is weakly related to the concept and is thus skewed away from the target concept. Validity is a crucial issue when a reporter must select a proxy variable to stand in for the ideal measure. For example, if the concept is indoor air quality, the use (or not) of low-VOC paints is a poor proxy for that concept, because there could be other factors that impact indoor air quality.

Reliability

The measurement of an indicator should be the same no matter who does the measuring. Reliability is essential for the assurance of sustainability reports by auditors. The GRI's presentation of the principle of reliability makes this point well, "The organization should gather, record, compile, analyze and disclose information and processes used in the preparation of a report in a way that they can be subject to examination."[15]

Precision

Measurements may result in focused images or fuzzy images of an indicator. A precise measurement is focused and detailed. The precision of a measurement process becomes an issue when firms must use statistical sampling techniques to make an inference about the value of an indicator. Larger sample sizes produce more-precise estimates of a value, but they are also more expensive. A good standard balances the cost of data collection with the benefits of precision as perceived by the stakeholders to whom the indicator is material.

Timeliness

Measurements of indicators should be either current at the time of publication or labeled as to the period from which they are taken. Current measures are preferred, because they will be more useful to the decisions of stakeholders.

Consistency

Measurements should use the same definitions and methods of data collection over time.

Indicators that are both valid (on target) and precise (focused) will fulfill the principle of accuracy, which is one of the standards for report quality promulgated by the GRI. Indicators that are measured consistently over time will permit the comparison of an organization's performance from one year to the next, fulfilling one aspect of the GRI's principle of comparability. Indicators that are clear, accurate, and reliable will fulfill the GISR's principle of assessability.

Principles for Summative Measures

In standards for sustainability, the values of indicators commonly are rolled up into subcategory scores and then to category scores and then to a summative metric for the sustainability (or ranking) of an organization. The GRI's principles of comparability and balance in report quality and the GISR's principle of inclusiveness apply to this process of data aggregation.

Comparability

The GRI's principle of comparability, as an aspect of report quality, requires that reported information should be presented in a manner that "could support analysis relative to other organizations."[16] The GISR puts this in further perspective, seeking comparability among standards, not just across companies within a standard or over time within a standard: "Comparability across ratings, as opposed to across companies or within peer groups, is a separate but equally critical challenge. Users understandably seek multiple ratings to guide decision-making."[17] A call for the comparability of companies within a standard implies that measures should be normalized whenever the size of an organization would affect the interpretation of the measure. In such cases, intensity or productivity measures are preferred to absolute measures.

The call for comparability across standards focuses attention on the definitions used for subcategories and categories of sustainability in different standards. For subcategory and category scores to be comparable, the definitions must be consistent across standards.

Balance

As applied to aggregated scores, the principle of balance calls for a proper weighting of the components. The choice of indicators for subcategories and categories is determined by the principle of materiality, which is applied in relation to the informational needs of the stakeholders identified by the organization. However, only the principle of balance can assure that the material indicators are aggregated in a manner that represents stakeholders' interpretation of the meaning of the subcategories ("aspects of sustainability") and categories (PPP, ESG, or another framework.)

The GISR's interpretation of balance in standards focuses on the variety of types of indicators used in a standard: "A rating should utilize a mix of measurement techniques to capture historical and prospective performance."[18] The variety of measures listed by the GISR include leading versus lagging, process versus outcome (our "doing versus achieving"), absolute versus relative (normalized), and quantitative versus qualitative (numerical versus categorical). GISR's commentary on the application of this principle is instructive:

> A rigorous rating contains a mix of the above. Users seek insights into the mindset, culture and quality of a company's management, as well as the hard, quantitative evidence of the company's capacity to achieve its performance objectives. In some instances, quantitative indicators may serve as proxies for qualitative aspects of the organization.[19]

Discussion

We began this chapter with the observation that a naïve reader might think that a standard for the sustainability of an organization would measure the sustainability of the organization. The standards for the disclosure of sustainability and standards for certifying or rating organizations on sustainability prove that standards call for much more than data about outcomes. Data on "saying" and "doing" figure prominently in all but the most parsimonious standards (the Global 100 and the *Newsweek* Green Rankings derived largely from it). Why would a good standard for sustainability, or a good template for a corporate sustainability report, not just focus on how sustainable the firm is at present, using outcome metrics such as pollution, waste, and resource productivities, employee and customer satisfaction, community satisfaction, taxes and fines paid, and financial profitability and risk?

Part of the answer is that the world still has a little time to restructure business and society toward sustainability, so stakeholders should evaluate what a firm will look like in the near future, not just now. Indeed, the GISR explains its horizon principle by saying that ratings "routinely should favor outcomes associated with stewardship and enrichment of the multiple capitals [human, intellectual, natural, and social] that materialize in the 3–5 year time horizon and beyond."[20] Saying is a leading indicator of doing, and doing is a leading indicator of achieving outcomes. Put another way, organizational commitments to goals and their present actions in progress toward those goals do have some predictive value about the future sustainability of the organization.

The deep details of a standard are in the design of its indicators and the methods for aggregating indicators to subcategories, categories, and a summative metric.

Those details are what set corporate rating systems apart from each other and thereby confer their respective competitive advantages, so the ratings standards tend to publish only enough information about those details to satisfy investors that the standard is what it claims to be. The DJSI publishes two examples of the questionnaire used to gather its data (one for services, another for mining), but it does not publish the weights on its indicators. ASSET4 ESG publishes its indicators and their weights for various industries and regions. FTSE4Good lists its indicators that are common to all industries and some of the industry-specific indicators but not their weights.

The rating standards are based on measures of firms' relative sustainability performance within their industries. The standing of a firm relative to others does not indicate its sustainability in an absolute sense, because all firms could be performing poorly. The one exception among the rating systems discussed here is FTSE4Good, which establishes thresholds for "good" performance (the score of 3 on a 0–5 range) on each of its indicators. FTSE does not publish the details of that evaluation, but if it is based on expert analysis and judgment, it would set that standard apart from others.

The voluntary (certification) standards make significant use of measures baselined against a past level of performance. STARS establishes targets using a consensus of industry experts about what levels of environmental indicators are thresholds for credit and what are reasonable long-term goals consistent with sustainability. That approach is consistent with the GISR's Principle #8 Sustainability Context, which states, "A rating should assess performance in the context of science-based thresholds and limits or, if unavailable, widely-accepted norms pertaining to long-term human and ecological well-being."[21] The UL 880 standard uses self-defined targets, which limits its comparability across reporting firms.

The final noteworthy issue of this chapter is the principle of comparability as it applies to subcategories and categories of sustainability. There is divergence of practice among standards, especially in how the social category is defined and even in its subcategories. We will return to this issue in Chapter 10.

Notes

1 GRI. 2013b. G4 Sustainability Reporting Guidelines: Implementation Manual. Global Reporting Initiative, p. 20. Available at <www.globalreporting.org/resourcelibrary/GRIG4-Part2-Implementation-Manual.pdf> Accessed June 2015.
2 Elkington, J. 1998. Partnerships From *Cannibals With Forks: The Triple Bottom Line of 21st-Century Business. Environmental Quality Management,* 8:1, 37–51.
3 GISR. 2015a. Global Initiative for Sustainability Ratings: Principles Version 1.1, p. 15. Available at <http://ratesustainability.org/core/principles/> Accessed August 2015.
4 Blank, H. 2012. The ESG Decision Tree. Thompson Reuters Corporate Responsibility Ratings. Available at <www.trcri.com/images/TRCRI_Precis_Herb_Blank.pdf> Accessed August 2015.
5 GISR. 2015a. Global Initiative for Sustainability Ratings.

6 Gassert, F., M. Luck, M. Landis, P. Reig, and T. Shiao. 2015. Aqueduct Global Maps 2.1: Constructing Decision-Relevant Global Water Risk Indicators. Working Paper. Washington, DC: World Resources Institute. Available at <http://www.wri.org/publication/aqueduct-global-maps-21-indicators> Accessed June 2015.

7 GRI. 2012. Sector Guidance for G4. Available at <www.globalreporting.org/information/news-and-press-center/Pages/Sector-guidance-for-G4.aspx> Accessed July 2015.

8 SASB. 2015c. Industry Briefs. Available at <www.sasb.org/approach/our-process/industry-briefs/> Accessed July 2015.

9 WRI. 2015. AQUEDUCT: Measuring and Mapping Water Risk. World Resources Institute. Available at <www.wri.org/our-work/project/aqueduct> Accessed June 2015.

10 ISO. 2004. ISO 14001:2004 Requirements With Guidance for Use.

11 STARS is a little more complex than that. Not all indicators apply to any university. A university's summative score is adjusted in relation to the number of *applicable* points in the total of 204 available in the first four major aspects, plus the number of points earned in the last aspect, innovation.

12 UNDP, 2015a. Human Development Index (HDI). United Nations Development Program. Available at <http://hdr.undp.org/en/content/human-development-index-hdi>. Accessed August 2015.

13 UNDP, 2015b. FAQ: Why is geometric mean better suited for the HDI than the arithmetic mean? United Nations Development Program. Available at <http://hdr.undp.org/en/faq-page/human-development-index-hdi#t292n50>. Accessed August 2015.

14 These higher-level goals reflect the principles of Assurability and Comparability as expressed by the GISR. See GISR. 2015a. Global Initiative for Sustainability Ratings

15 GRI. 2013a. G4 Sustainability Reporting Guidelines, pp. 17–18.

16 Ibid., p. 18.

17 GISR. 2015a. Global Initiative for Sustainability Ratings, p. 15.

18 Ibid., p. 14.

19 Ibid.

20 GISR, 2015a, p. 13

21 Ibid., p. 12.

6

GREENHOUSE GAS ASSESSMENT AND ENERGY ACCOUNTING

The first three chapters of this book demonstrated the variety of approaches that have been taken to measuring sustainability, through standards for disclosure, rating, and certification. Chapters 4 and 5 introduced conceptual frameworks from philosophy and measurement theory to help us understand what should be measured and how it might be measured. In this and the next three chapters, we take a deeper look at the assessment methods that standards tend to use to measure environmental and social attributes, specifically greenhouse gas emissions, water, waste, and social responsibility.

The "greenhouse gases" (GHGs) are those that trap infrared radiation onto the earth, which causes the earth to become warmer. Global warming from the emission of GHGs is a global problem, because these gases mix readily in the atmosphere, and local emissions from the combustion of carbon-based fuels and other industrial processes are transported widely by the jet stream and global wind patterns. Thus, one company's pollution becomes everybody's problem, and an ethic of responsibility calls for companies to be held accountable for those emissions. Due to the universality of this atmospheric effect, well-standardized methods have been developed to account for the emission of greenhouse gases. Those are the subject of the first part of this chapter.

Energy use is also a global problem. It can create pollution, as GHG emissions and other forms of waste, and it impacts biodiversity and human rights, particularly at the development stage. But those impacts have their own general metrics. What makes energy accountable in its own right is the dependence of contemporary society on nonrenewable sources of energy, the so-called "fossil fuels" of coal, oil, and underground natural gas. The world has to share a dwindling supply of these fuels. That sharing of a finite resource raises issues of equitable distribution both among the present people and nations and between the present and future generations. As with GHG accounting, the methods for reporting energy usage are well standardized. They will be discussed at the end of this chapter.

The Greenhouse Effect

A greenhouse is a building made entirely of glass or clear plastic, which lets the sun's rays pass through to plants growing inside. The heat of the sun is absorbed there inside the greenhouse, rather than on a conventional roof where it would be lost to the air above, and it is kept inside the house by the glass walls. The "greenhouse effect" refers to the capture of heat rather than its loss by reflection.

Sunlight in the visible spectrum passes through the earth's atmospheric gases and is absorbed on the surface, where some of it is radiated back into the atmosphere as infrared light. Carbon dioxide in the atmosphere acts like a glass wall. It allows the visible light to pass through to the surface of the earth, but it reflects back the infrared light that comes up from the surface. When that reflected infrared light is reabsorbed at the surface of the earth, it creates heat. This is the greenhouse effect.

The Seven Kyoto Gases

The Kyoto Protocol is a part of the United Nations Framework Convention on Climate Change. It was signed in 1997, became effective in 2005, and has been ratified by 190 nations, including all UN members, except Afghanistan, Andorra, South Sudan, and the United States. Canada withdrew in 2011. The Kyoto Protocol, for its second commitment period that began in 2012, identified seven gases that contribute to global warming. The seven "Kyoto gases" or groups of gases are carbon dioxide (CO2), methane (CH4), nitrous oxide (N2O), the 19 hydrofluorocarbons (HFCs), the 7 perfluorocarbons (PFCs), nitrogen trifluoride (NF_3), and sulfur hexafluoride (SF6).

If we define the global warming potential (GWP) of carbon dioxide to be 1, then the warming potential of all other Kyoto gases can be expressed as a multiple of CO2's warming potential. The estimates of those multiples, published by the Intergovernmental Panel on Climate Change (IPCC) in 2014 are shown in Table 6.1.[1] In that table and in the remainder of this book, we use full-script abbreviations for the chemical compounds, not their subscripted chemical notations. The table shows, for example, that methane (CH4) is 28 times as powerful as CO2 in creating a greenhouse effect.

TABLE 6.1 GWP

Kyoto Gas	*100-yr GWP*
CO2	1
CH4	28
N2O	265
HFCs	*2,200* ±
PFCs	*8,600* ±
NF3	16,100
SF6	23,500

The HFCs vary greatly in their global warming potentials, from 4 to 12,400. The PFCs are a more homogeneous group, with GWP clustered in the range of 6,600–11,100. For each of these groups, the table presents in italic type an approximation of the average of the group.

Industrial Processes That Release Greenhouse Gases Into the Atmosphere

When coal, which is almost purely carbon, is burned, the carbon (C) unites with atmospheric oxygen (O2) to become carbon dioxide (CO2). Coal-burning electric power plants release such CO2 into the atmosphere. Likewise, when natural gas (methane, CH4) is burned, the output gases are one molecule of CO2 and two molecules water, H2O. Furnaces that burn natural gas release this CO2 into the atmosphere. The burning of other hydrocarbons, such as ethane C2H6, propane C3H8, butane C4H10, and so on, release even more CO2 into the atmosphere.

Methane CH4 is released directly into the atmosphere by bacterial action on organic compounds in the absence of oxygen (anaerobic metabolism). This occurs in the guts of ruminant livestock such as cattle, in garbage left in landfills, and in some forms of wastewater treatment.

Nitrous oxide N2O is released as a result of fertilizer use (15% of anthropogenic sources), livestock waste (65%), and industrial production (20%).[2]

Sulfur hexafluoride SF6 is released in the production of magnesium and by electrical utilities and electronics manufacturers, but its production is very low in comparison with that of CO2 and CH4, so its overall contribution to global warming is estimated to be less than 0.2 percent.[3]

The hydrofluorocarbons (HFCs) and the perfluorocarbons (PFCs) are used chemically in pharmaceuticals and agrochemicals.

The Regulation of GHG Emissions Drives the Need for Accurate GHG Assessment

Governments have the power to regulate the production of greenhouse gases within their jurisdictions. The two principal regulatory methods are the taxation of "carbon" and a cap-and-trade system of permits for the production of greenhouse gases. With a carbon tax, such as that used in British Columbia and proposed in Australia and South Africa, the government places a tax on activities that directly involve the production of greenhouse gases, such as the purchase of fuel for vehicles or for industrial use, including electric energy production. The revenues from the carbon tax can then be used for any governmental purpose or distributed to individuals and firms who are particularly disadvantaged by the tax.

Contrasted to the carbon tax is the cap-and-trade system, such as that used in the European Union, Switzerland, California, and Quebec and at national or subnational levels in Australia, New Zealand, and Japan. Cap-and-trade systems are planned for China and South Korea. In such systems, the government sets a criterion to define which firms must participate in the system, and its sets a limit to the total amount of CO2-equivalent (CO2e) emissions that may be produced within the government's jurisdiction (state, nation, or alliance of nations) and prepares a specific number of permits corresponding to that limit. Usually, one permit is for permission to emit one metric ton of CO2e. The government then distributes the permits according to specific rules and/or runs an auction to sell the permits to the participants. The government may use money from the sale of the permits to promote GHG-reducing programs and activities within their jurisdiction or for any other governmental purpose.

Under the carbon tax, the government needs to monitor the sale of GHG-producing fuels or substances. The amount of the tax *per unit of fuel* is calculated based on technical data about the emission factor of the fuel, expressed as kgCO2 per unit of the fuel, and on some economic assumptions about how much consumers of the fuel would reduce their purchases based on a higher total price for the fuel. Thus, taxation does not assure a specific reduction in the total emission of GHGs. The cap-and-trade system, in contrast, does assure a specific reduction in total GHG emissions, because the permits are denominated in metric tons of CO2e and the government decides on a specific limit to the number of permits that may be sold. Therefore, in the cap-and-trade system, every participant in the system must have their GHG emissions measured and reported reliably to the government. For that reason, a formal system for GHG assessment is essential to the operation of the cap-and-trade regulation of greenhouse gas emissions.

Mandatory Reporting in the European Union Emissions Trading System (EU ETS)

In the European Union, companies that emit CO2 in sufficiently large quantities are required to buy permits for CO2 emissions and must therefore account annually for their emissions of CO2 and have that accounting audited. "Carbon" permits are issued by the European Union Emissions Trading System (EU ETS) and trade on the ICE Futures Europe exchange.

The EU ETS operates in the 28 EU countries and the three EEA-EFTA states (Iceland, Liechtenstein, and Norway). Its participants include all airlines operating in the EU and EFTA countries and more than 11,000 power stations and industrial plants, in total accounting for 45% of the EU's greenhouse gas emissions. The requirement for manufacturing firms to participate in the EU ETS and to report GHG emissions is based in most cases on a rated thermal input of 20 megawatts or more, which means a total energy usage rate of 20 MW. The requirement is based on production capacity for a few industries: pig iron or steel, cement clinker, lime, glass, ceramics, mineral wool, paper or cardboard, and bulk organic chemicals that use oxidation or reformation processes.[4]

funds from the auction of permits and to provide the framework for administering those funds. The auctions began for the 2013 emissions year.

California's goal is to reduce GHG emissions to 1990 levels by the year 2020 and to only 20% of the 1990 level by 2050. The number of permits to be issued for each year by the Air Resources Board is set to meet these targets.

The California Cap-and-Trade Program sets forth standards that define which firms are required to *participate* in the program.[5] Some firms must participate regardless of their emissions level. These include operators of facilities in California in cement, lime, nitric acid, and petroleum refining industries and firms that geologically sequester carbon dioxide or inject carbon dioxide. In general, firms are required to participate if their total GHG emissions rate is at least 25,000 metric tons (MT) per year.

The state of California has a separate requirement for mandatory GHG *reporting*.[6] As in the requirement for participation in the cap-and-trade program, there is mandatory reporting by firms in the cement, lime, nitric acid, petroleum refining, and CO2 sequestration and injection industries. The threshold for reporting in general is 10,000 MT of emissions per year.

In January 2014, California linked its cap-and-trade program with that of Quebec, Canada, creating an integrated market for GHG permits.

Mandatory Reporting in the RGGI

The Regional Greenhouse Gas Initiative (RGGI) began in the northeastern states in 2009 as the United States' first mandatory cap-and-trade program to limit CO2 emissions.[7] It operates CO2 budget trading programs for Connecticut, Delaware, Maine, Maryland, Massachusetts, New Hampshire, New York, Rhode Island, and Vermont. All regulated power producers with plants in these states are required to participate and report their emissions. According to the RGGI, "Regulated power plants can use a CO2 allowance issued by any participating state to demonstrate compliance with an individual state program. In this manner, the state programs, in aggregate, function as a single regional compliance market for CO2 emissions."[8]

Mandatory Reporting of GHG Emissions in the United States

The United States does not have either a carbon tax or a cap-and-trade system, but with an eye to the future, the Environmental Protection Agency is administering a system of mandatory reporting of GHG emissions "to collect accurate and timely

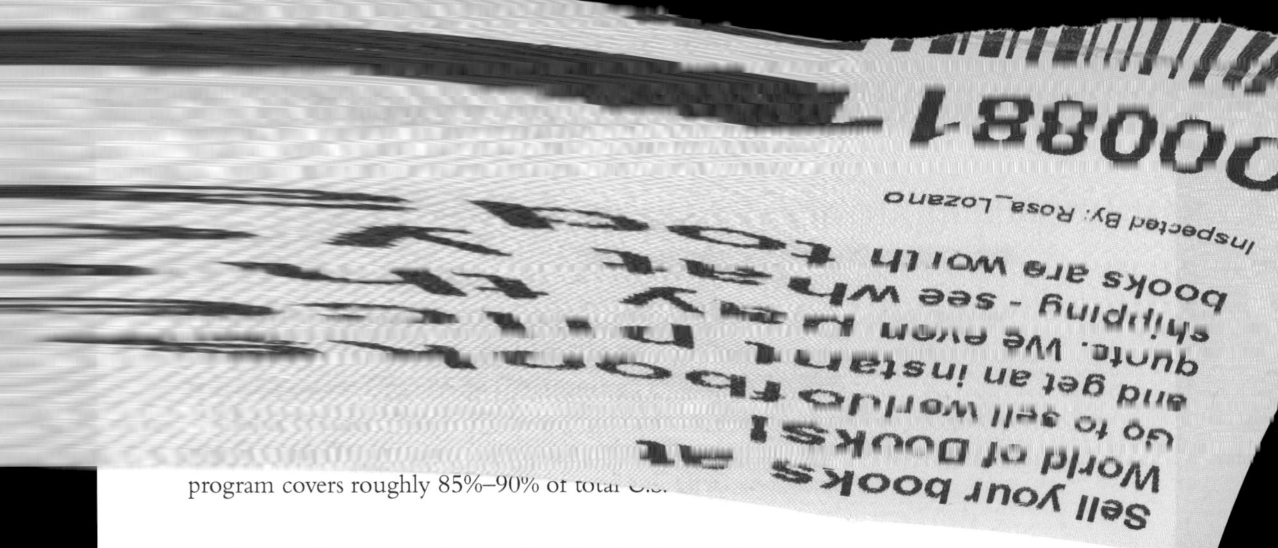

program covers roughly 85%–90% of total U.S.

Carbon Offsets and the Market for GHG Permits

In regions where firms are required to have permits that account for their releases of greenhouse gases, the market for GHG permits is called a *compliance market*, and the market price of the GHG permits is driven by the supply of permits and the demand for permits. The supply in a given year is dictated by the governmental organization that administers the emissions trading system (ETS) and reflects how lenient or aggressive the government's goals are for reducing total GHG emissions in its region. The demand for permits is determined by the quantity of greenhouse gases being produced, which reflects both the general level of economic activity (expansion or recession) and the sustainability of the production methods being used by industry.

Individuals and companies that want to offset their own GHG emissions may purchase carbon certificates in the voluntary market from firms that participate in the retail segment of this industry. A list of such firms is published as the Carbon Catalog.[11]

A special feature of the carbon emissions trading systems is that they do not just issue carbon allowances, which permit firms to emit CO2-equivalent quantities. They also validate *carbon credits*, or "offsets," that are issued to companies whose activities reverse the effect of CO2 emissions by sequestering carbon or by generating energy using renewable methods. The companies that receive the offsets may then sell them to firms that need to buy carbon permits. In this way, the ETS financially rewards firms that directly mitigate climate change.

Carbon certificates that trade in an ETS must all be equivalent to a one metric ton reduction in CO2e, so all such certificates are equivalent to each other and therefore must trade at the same price. This requirement in the compliance markets determines the need for precise standards by which carbon certificates are validated, so the firms that certify and issue carbon offsets follow standards that are substantially equivalent. One such standard is the Kyoto Protocol's Clean Development Mechanism (CDM), which provides details about the principles and practices for calculating the reductions in GHG attributable to specific projects. According to the Carbon Trade Exchange,

> In the compliance market, carbon credits are generated by projects that operate under one of the United Nations Framework Convention on Climate Change (UNFCCC) approved mechanisms, such as the Clean Development

> Mechanism (CDM). Credits generated under this mechanism are known as Certified Emissions Reductions (CERs).[12]

According to the United Nations Framework Convention on Climate Change, CERs originate from projects in *developing countries* under the CDM. Credits that originate in *developed countries* are called Emissions Reduction Units (ERUs) and operate under a mechanism known as Joint Implementation.

There is also a demand for GHG contracts in a *voluntary market*, where individuals or companies choose to pay for contracts representing activities that offset their own emissions of greenhouse gases. In the United States, the Chicago Climate Exchange operates such a voluntary market. According to the Carbon Trade Exchange, credits in the voluntary market

> are generated by projects that are accredited to independent international standards such as the Verified Carbon Standard (VCS). These credits are known as Verified Emission Reductions (VERs).[13]

In the voluntary market, carbon offsets may trade at different prices, depending on the reliability and validity of the methods used by the issuers of the certificate to certify the offset. Various firms compete in the business of certifying carbon offsets, which makes the offset more attractive in the compliance and voluntary markets. These firms include APX Verified Carbon Standard (VCS), The Gold Standard, American Carbon Registry (ACR), and Climate Action Reserve (CAR).

Ecosystem Marketplace and Bloomberg New Energy Finance publish an annual report, *State of the Voluntary Carbon Markets*,[14] that accounted for 131,200 metric tons of CO2e carbon certificates traded in 2011 for a total of $424 million. Voluntary carbon certificates were trading on the Chicago Climate Exchange (CCX) in the U.S., the Chicago Climate Futures Exchange (CCFE), the Carbon Trade Exchange (CTX) in Australia, and China Beijing Environmental Exchange (CBEEX). The CCX nearly collapsed in 2010 due to slow progress by the U.S. government on climate policy, so its prices were around $0.10, but in over-the-counter trading elsewhere certificates had an average price of $6 in 2010. Even in 2012, renewable energy certificates were selling on the CCX for only $0.10 to $0.15 per metric ton of avoided CO2e.

Later in this chapter, we will see how to calculate the amount of CO2 offset by a project or program.

The GHG Protocol

The Carbon Disclosure Project's climate change Guidance document lists 70 standards, protocols, or methods that reporters might use to calculate their GHG emissions.[15] Some are industry specific. Others come from national standards organizations, such as the U.S. EPA's Climate Leaders program. Among the

Protocol, with the following caveat from the GHG Protocol:

> GHG trading programs are likely to impose additional layers of accounting specificity relating to which approach is used for setting organizational boundaries; which GHGs and sources are addressed; how base years are established; the type of calculation methodology used; the choice of emission factors; and the monitoring and verification approaches employed.

Global Warming Potential of the Greenhouse Gases

The various Kyoto gases have different effects on global warming. The standard of comparison is CO2, which is defined to have a global warming potential of 1. The greenhouse-inducing powers of these gases are all expressed as multiples of the greenhouse-inducing power of carbon dioxide. The estimates of the global warming potentials of the Kyoto gases, published by the IPCC in 2007, are shown in Table 6.1 (page 103).[16]

Using the GWP multipliers, the effect of any combination of gases emitted by a reporting unit can be reduced to a single number, the **CO2-equivalent** emission, which is also called the **carbon footprint** of the reporting unit. Thus, the GHG emissions of any product, company, nation, or region are expressed in tonnes of CO2-equivalent (CO2e). "Tonnes" means metric tons, 1,000 kilograms, not the English (short) ton of 2,000 pounds; the metric system is commonly used to measure GHG emissions.

Example: Agriculture

A farm has taken an inventory of its greenhouse gases using CO2, CH4, and N2O as the focus of analysis. The inventory of each type of emission is shown in Table 6.2. What is the farm's carbon footprint?

TABLE 6.2 Agriculture Example

Type of Emission	*Inventory (kg)*
CO2 carbon dioxide	45,000
CH4 methane	2,500
N2O nitrous oxide	200

TABLE 6.3 Solution to the Agriculture Example

Type	*Inventory (kg)*	*GWP*	*CO2e (kg)*
CO2 carbon dioxide	45,000	1	45,000
CH4 methane	2,500	28	70,000
N2O nitrous oxide	200	265	53,000
Total CO2-e			**168,000**

Solution to the Example

The carbon footprint is the total mass of CO2-equivalents in the inventory. To calculate that, we multiply the mass of each type by its global warming potential (GWP) to get the CO2-equivalent mass, then add the CO2-equivalents from all of the gas types, as shown in Table 6.3.

Overview of the GHG Assessment Methodology

The methodology to inventory a company's greenhouse gas emissions consists of three steps:

1. Define the boundaries of the reporting organization. This should include a parent company and all subsidiaries that are majority owned.
2. Identify the greenhouse gases for study. Rarely would all seven Kyoto gases be included in a GHG study. Manufacturing companies may have significant ("material") releases of N2O, SF6, HFCs, or PFCs. Farms typically have significant releases of N2O, CH4, and CO2. However, most service organizations will only conduct a carbon inventory (CO2).
3. Identify the sources of GHG production that are related to the activities of the organization. The **Scope 1** emissions are those generated by directly activities of the reporting organization. They include stationary sources, such as furnaces and boilers, as well as nonstationary sources, such as company-owned vehicles. The **Scope 2** or "indirect" emissions result from the generation of electricity and steam by the utility companies from which the reporting organization buys its energy. **Scope 3** emissions are those generated by all other suppliers to the reporting organization.

In this simple introduction to GHG accounting, we will focus on how to conduct a GHG inventory for a service organization.

Principles for GHG Accounting and Reporting

The GHG Protocol is based on five principles that guide greenhouse gas accounting and reporting: [17]

Consistency. Use consistent methodologies to allow for meaningful comparisons of emissions over time. Transparently document any changes to the data, inventory boundary, methods, or any other relevant factors in the time series.

Transparency. Address all relevant issues in a factual and coherent manner, based on a clear audit trail. Disclose any relevant assumptions and make appropriate references to the accounting and calculation methodologies and data sources used.

Accuracy. Ensure that the quantification of GHG emissions is not systematically over or under actual emissions, as far as can be judged, and that uncertainties are reduced as far as practicable. Achieve sufficient accuracy to enable users to make decisions with reasonable assurance as to the integrity of the reported information.

GHG accounting begins with a definition of the boundaries of the reporting organization and then defines Scope 1, Scope 2, and Scope 3 emissions. In what follows, we illustrate this for a service organization.

The Boundaries of a Service Organization

In the GHG Protocol, the organizational boundary identifies the "businesses and operations that constitute the company for the purpose of accounting and reporting GHG emissions."[18]

One standard is to account for 100% of the GHG emissions of any entity over which the reporting organization has operational control. Usually this means that the reporting organization owns at least 50% of the shares of the entity.

Scope 1 Emissions (Direct Emissions)

Scope 1 emissions are the emissions under the direct control of the reporting organization. The GHG Protocol explains,

> Direct GHG emissions occur from sources that are owned or controlled by the company, for example, emissions from combustion in owned or controlled boilers, furnaces, vehicles, etc.; emissions from chemical production in owned or controlled process equipment.[19]

The Scope 1 sources are typically broken down as stationary or nonstationary. The **stationary sources** are furnaces, boilers, and power generation equipment owned or controlled by the reporting unit. The **nonstationary sources** of GHG emissions include all vehicles (e.g., cars, vans, trucks, buses, trains, ships, and airplanes) owned or controlled by the reporting unit.

The GHG protocol describes fugitive emissions as yet another class

> These emissions result from intentional or unintentional releases, e.g., equipment leaks from joints, seals, packing, and gaskets; methane emissions from coal mines and venting; hydrofluorocarbon (HFC) emissions during the use of refrigeration and air conditioning equipment; and methane leakages from gas transport.[20]

How to Calculate Emissions From Activity Data Using Emission Factors

A reporting unit must account for all activities that generate GHG emissions. The easiest way to understand the method is to see how it applies to an inventory of CO2 only. Carbon dioxide is produced by burning fuels, so the reporter should account for all fuels purchased. The amount of fuel used is the "activity" related to that source of CO2. The measure of activity is converted to a measure of CO2 emission by multiplying the activity level by the appropriate **emission factor**. An emission factor is therefore expressed as the number of kilograms of CO2 per unit of the activity. For example, the emissions factor for gasoline, when gasoline usage is measured in gallons, is 8.78 kgCO2/gal. Emissions factors for all sources of CO2 have been estimated through engineering analyses and have been published by the GHG Protocol, the Climate Registry,[21] the U.S. Department of Energy,[22] and others.

Emission factors will differ depending on the unit of measurement of the source activity, so the analyst who prepares a GHG must be ready to convert activity measures into the appropriate units when using a GHG software package or spreadsheet.

Example: A Personal Annual Carbon Footprint

A private individual who owns a home and a car has Scope 1 emissions coming from burning fuel to heat the home and burning fuel in the engine of a car. A few emission factors (EF) for such sources are shown in Table 6.4 using 2015 Climate Registry data. Biodiesel, when burned, emits 9.45 kgCO2e/gal, but that carbon was extracted from the atmosphere when the biosource synthesized its hydrocarbons, so in carbon footprint calculations, biodiesel is considered to have a 0 *net* carbon footprint.

For this example, let's assume that the individual has a furnace that burns natural gas and one car that uses gasoline. To calculate a person's annual carbon footprint, one would have to determine the individual's use of these fuels. The quantity of home heating fuel used would appear on the individual's utility bills. For this example, say it is 900 therms.

[illegible] (gal)	10.2
Propane (gallon)	5.72
Gasoline (gal)	8.78
E85 ethanol (gal)	1.33
Diesel fuel (gal)	10.2
B100 biodiesel	0

TABLE 6.5 Solution to the Personal Example

Source	*Unit of Measurement*	*Usage*	*x Emissions Factor for kgCO2*	*x GWP Factor*	*= CO2-Equivalent (kg)*
Natural gas	therms	900	5.31	1	4,779
Gasoline	gallons	500	8.78	1	4,390
Total					**9,169**

To calculate the quantity of gasoline purchased, a reasonable method is to look at the number of miles driven in the year and divide that by the (known or approximated) fuel efficiency of the vehicle. Suppose that the individual owns a Toyota Prius hybrid that averages 40 mpg. The odometer reading at the start of the year was 43,000 and at the end of the year was 63,000. The annual usage of gasoline is 20,000miles/40mpg = 500 gal. We use the usage data for natural gas and gasoline in a table with the emissions factors and GWP factor to calculate the total CO2e as shown in Table 6.5.

Scope 2 Indirect Emissions

Scope 2 emissions are the emissions that are induced by a firm's purchase of electric energy and steam. Because the energy company is outside the control of the firm, these emissions are called indirect.

> Scope 2 accounts for GHG emissions from the generation of purchased electricity consumed by the company. Purchased electricity is defined as electricity that is purchased or otherwise brought into the organizational boundary of the company. Scope 2 emissions physically occur at the facility where electricity is generated.[23]

Many electric utilities publish an environmental report in which they calculate their emissions of CO2, CH4, and N2O from the generation of electricity and report it on a per-kWh basis as an emission factor. However, most utilities buy energy from other utilities and sell their own-generated energy to other utilities, so the power company's emission factor from owned generation will not reflect all the emissions attributable to the energy that reaches a particular customer. For this reason, the Climate Registry's annual *Default Emission Factors* document[24] publishes emissions factors for the various regions (electric reliability councils) of the United States in which utilities buy and sell their power.

Notice that Scope 2 emissions are based on the power company's process of generation alone. The GHG Protocol treats the losses of electric energy in transmission and distribution to the end user as Scope 3 emissions. In this way, the reporter of Scope 2 emissions does not have to estimate transmission and distribution losses but can work directly with the published emission factors.

Example: A Personal Annual Carbon Footprint (continued)

A private home in Iowa is located in the MRO East regional electric reliability council. The home has an annual usage of electric energy equal to 11,000 kilowatt-hours (kWh). How much Scope 2 emission does this account for?

Solution to the Example

Though the Scope 1 calculations for this example looked only at CO2, here for purposes of illustration we will examine CO2, CH4, and N2O. In the MRO East region, which includes Iowa, Wisconsin, and Minnesota, the Climate Registry's 2013 emission factors are 1,592 lb CO2/MWh, 24 lb CH4/GWh and 27 lb N2O /GWh (1 MWh = 1,000 kWh and 1 GWh = 1,000,000 kWh). However, these emission factors must be converted to kg per kWh, which is the common unit of measurement for CO2-equivalents. Convert pounds to kg by multiplying by 0.4536. Convert MWh to kWh by multiplying by 1,000 and GWh to kWh by multiplying by 1,000,000. Thus, we get the new emission factors shown in Table 6.6.

TABLE 6.6 Original and Converted Emission Factors

Type	*Original EF*	*Converted EF*
CO2	1,592 lb/MWh	0.722 kg/kWh
CH4	24 lb/GWh	0.000,011 kg/kWh
N2O	27 lb/GWh	0.000,012 kg/kWh

	CH4	0.000,011	28	3
	N2O	0.000,012	265	35
Total				**7,980**

We set these data up in a table that includes the GWP factors for these three gases (Table 6.7).

Table 6.7 shows that the CH4 and N2O emissions are very small, even in terms of CO2-equivalent, in relation to the CO2 emissions. That is why the World Resources Institute permits small service business to ignore CH4 and N2O emissions.[25]

In the first part of this example, the household's Scope 1 emissions were about 9,000 kg CO2. Here we see that the Scope 2 emissions for the same household are about 8,000 kg CO2. This illustrates the point made by the GHG Protocol that for many businesses, the Scope 2 emissions are about the same or greater than the Scope 1 emissions.

Purchased Steam

If a business purchases steam for heating or for running equipment, the emissions from the production of that steam should be accounted for in Scope 2.

Scope 3 Emissions

Scope 3 emissions are all indirect emissions, other than those from purchased electric energy and steam (Scope 2).

> Scope 3 is an optional reporting category that allows for the treatment of all other indirect emissions. Scope 3 emissions are a consequence of the activities of the company, but occur from sources not owned or controlled by the company.
>
> *(GHG Protocol, p. 25)*

Scope 3 is optional, but it provides an opportunity to be innovative in GHG management. Companies may want to focus on accounting for and reporting those activities that are relevant to their business and goals and for which they have reliable information. Since companies have discretion over which categories they choose to report, Scope 3 may not lend itself well to comparisons across companies (GHG Protocol, p. 29).

Scope 3 typically includes the following types of activity.

- Extraction and production of purchased materials and fuels
- Transport-related activities
- Transportation of purchased materials or goods
- Transportation of purchased fuels
- Employee business travel
- Employees commuting to and from work
- Transportation of sold products
- Transportation of waste
- Use of sold products and services (life-cycle emissions of products)

Accounting for Carbon Offsets: The Alternative to Buying Carbon Permits

The U.S. government's Environmental Protection Agency has a GHG Equivalency Calculator[26] that translates activity measures into CO2-equivalents and shows what remediation would neutralize the GHG production from an emissions-generating activity. Below are the activities that would reduce a carbon footprint by one metric ton of CO2.

- Planting 25.6 tree seedlings and letting them grow for 10 years.
- Owning 0.82 acres (0.33 hectares) of an average U.S. forest for one year.
- Recycling 750 pounds of waste rather than sending it to a landfill.

When an organization's activities *reduce* the amount of carbon in the atmosphere, and thus *offset* the effect of GHG emissions by other firms, that organization deserves credit for slowing down the process of global warming, whether or not it occurs within the boundaries of a mandated emissions cap-and-trade program. If it occurs within the boundaries of the program, it reduces the number of allowances or permits that the organization must acquire, so the organization internalizes the benefit of the activity. However, most emissions trading programs allow participants, to some degree, to apply the benefit of emissions-reduction activities outside the physical boundaries of the program. For example, the Kyoto Protocol permits its member nations to undertake emissions-reduction projects in developing countries and apply the benefits of those projects to their requirements under the Protocol. Likewise, the California Air Resources Board (CARB) permits Californian firms to use emissions-reducing activities outside of California to account for up to 8% of the firm's requirement under CARB's cap-and-trade system.

ited to do so for the emissions trading program following standards set down by the program. For example, emissions-reduction activities that are authenticated under the United Nations' Clean Development Mechanism (CDM) may be counted toward a nation's obligations under the Kyoto Protocol and may be sold in a compliance market as equivalent to the carbon allowances that are sold by the government that operates the market.

Various firms compete in the business of setting standards for or certifying carbon offsets for the compliance and voluntary markets. Especially in the voluntary markets, their standards for certification may differ. These standards include the APX Verified Carbon Standard, Gold Standard, American Carbon Registry, and Climate Action Reserve.

The GHG Project Protocol: Basic Considerations

Emissions offsets occur due to three processes: reductions in emissions, destruction of CO2 by chemical or biological means, and the storage of CO2. The UNEP DTU Partnership at the Danish Technical University lists many types of project eligible for carbon credits, most of which fall into the following types:[27]

- Renewable energy generation (wind, hydro, solar, biomass, geothermal, tidal, waste)
- Biofuel production (ethanol, biodiesel)
- Methane avoidance (composting, manure digestion, wastewater treatment)
- Displacement of one fossil fuel for another (e.g., to natural gas)
- Reforestation
- CO2 recycling
- Energy efficiency (lighting, buildings)
- Industry-specific emissions reduction
- Reduction of fugitive emissions
- Destruction of the industrial pollutants HFCs, PFCs, SF6, and N2O

According to the UNEP DTU, projects to destroy the industrial pollutants represented 58% of the CERs issued in 2012.

In this section, we review the GHG Protocol's Project Protocol, which "provides specific principles, concepts, and methods for quantifying and reporting GHG reductions—i.e., the decreases in GHG emissions, or increases in removals and/or storage from climate change mitigation projects."[28] The accounting for emissions offsets in the GHG Project Protocol addresses the following elements:

Assessment Boundary. The assessment boundary defines all sources of GHG emissions and sinks of emissions that must be examined to quantify a project's GHG reductions.

Baseline Scenario and Time Horizon. The project description must state a baseline scenario that accounts for the GHG emissions that would be expected to result, over a specified period, *if the project activity were not implemented*. The baseline may be static, representing the emissions level previous to a replacement of the emitting technology, or the baseline may be dynamic, changing from year to year, as when the baseline is determined by reference to emissions from purchased electric energy, which may be expected to change over time.

Project Effects Over the Time Horizon. The effects of the project must be compared to the baseline over a specific time horizon. The article on carbon offsets at Wikipedia notes a few special considerations about the effects over time,

> Are some benefits of the reductions reversible? (For example, trees may be harvested to burn the wood, and does growing trees for fuel wood decrease the need for fossil fuel?) If woodlands are increasing in area or density, then carbon is being sequestered. After roughly 50 years, newly planted forests will reach maturity and remove carbon dioxide more slowly.[29]

Additionality. The project activity must reduce emissions relative to the baseline scenario. Carbon offsets are not given for activities that "would have happened anyway." For example, a project that must be undertaken to comply with environmental laws or regulations will not have emissions that differ from the baseline scenario and thus will not exhibit "additionality." A project would be considered "additional" if it uses technology that would not likely have been used but for its effect in reducing emissions, would not be economically feasible without the benefit of selling GHG offsets, or reduces GHG emissions below levels associated with "common practice" technologies that produce the same products and services as the GHG project.

Primary and Secondary Effects. The primary effects of the project will be its impacts on the designated sources and sinks of GHG emissions. There may be secondary effects that are felt outside the assessment boundary, and if these are significant, they must be accounted for, especially if the project might cause higher emissions outside its boundary.

Monitoring and Verification of Effects. A distinct feature of GHG offsets is that they are based on projected effects in the future, but they are issued as certificates in the present. Certificates sold in the compliance markets must therefore be verified at the end of their vintage year, and if the projected GHG emission reductions were not achieved, the then-owner of the certificate would have to make up the difference by purchasing more certificates. For example, the California Air Resources Board has the right to invalidate improper offsets. This is one reason cap-and-trade system.[30]

The GHG Project Protocol: Accounting Principles

Six principles guide the GHG Protocol's standard for accounting for GHG projects.

1. **Relevance**. Use data, methods, criteria, and assumptions that are appropriate for the intended use of reported information.
2. **Completeness**. Consider all relevant information that may affect the accounting and quantification of GHG reductions and complete all requirements.
3. **Consistency**. Use data, methods, criteria, and assumptions that allow meaningful and valid comparisons.
4. **Transparency**. Provide clear and sufficient information for reviewers to assess the credibility and reliability of GHG reduction claims.
5. **Accuracy**. Reduce uncertainties as much as is practical.
6. **Conservativeness**. Use conservative assumptions, values, and procedures when uncertainty is high.

Accounting for Carbon Offsets

The *GHG Protocol for Project Accounting* includes two excellent case studies, one about GHG emissions reduction in cement manufacturing and one about improving the energy efficiency of compressor stations in a natural gas pipeline, which provide details about project accounting.[31]

Renewable Energy Certificates in the United States

The U.S. Environmental Protection Agency has established a system of renewable energy certificates (RECs) that accrue to producers of electric energy from renewable sources. The EPA explains RECs by noting that a renewable energy producer actually produces two products, the energy and a REC, and each can be sold separately:

> As renewable generators produce electricity, they create one REC for every 1000 kilowatt-hours (or 1 megawatt-hour) of electricity placed on the grid. If the physical electricity and the associated RECs are sold to separate buyers, the electricity is no longer considered "renewable" or "green." The REC product is what conveys the attributes and benefits of the renewable electricity, not the electricity itself. RECs serve the role of

laying claim to and accounting for the associated attributes of renewable-based generation.[32]

RECs are defined in relation to the energy produced (MWh), not its CO2-equivalent (kgCO2e), so they translate into GHG offsets only with an additional assumption about the efficiency factor (kgCO2e/MWh) of the electric utility producing the nonrenewable energy that is purchased by the consumer. However, by this means, RECs are suitable to the offset of Scope 2 emissions.[33]

GHG Calculators and Guides

Several organizations publish online calculators to help consumers estimate their GHG emissions.

- U.S. Environmental Protection Agency's *Household GHG Emissions Calculator.* <http://www.epa.gov/climatechange/ghgemissions/individual.html>
- World Resource Institute's *Working 9 to 5 on Climate Change: An Office Guide.* <www.ghgprotocol.org/files/ghgp/tools/working9–5.pdf>
- WRI's *Hot Climate, Cool Commerce: A Service Sector Guide to Greenhouse Gas Management.* <http://www.ghgprotocol.org/files/ghgp/tools/HotClimateCool Commerce_lowrez.pdf>
- The Association for the Advancement of Sustainability in Higher Education's STARS metric for sustainable colleges and universities has published a *Campus Carbon Calculator.*

A full set of emissions factors and calculation tools is found in the GHG Protocol's 2012 *Cross-Sector Tools* spreadsheet.

The U.S. EPA has a *Waste Reduction Model* (WARM) in spreadsheet form, which enables a company to estimate the GHG emissions resulting from its waste management practices. That tool is available at <http://epa.gov/epawaste/conserve/tools/warm/index.html>.

Energy Accounting

The immediate environmental impact of corporate energy use is the emission of greenhouse gases, and we have seen in this chapter how to account for them. Therefore, a separate reporting of energy use may seem to be redundant. A requirement to report energy use, in addition to the GHG accounting, can only be justified on grounds other than the ethic against pollution that justifies the reporting of GHG emissions. The most likely candidate for that other ethic is distributive justice in the allocation of the world's nonrenewable energy resources. We will see a similar ethic invoked to account for the corporate use of water in Chapter 9, but water is derived from rainfall, which is a common resource in a region, and report their use of nonrenewable energy? The ethical perspective of distributive justice would be appropriate only if those property rights may come into question as the supply of those nonrenewable resources diminishes over the next century.

In the Global Reporting Initiative G4 system, corporations are called on to report their total energy consumption in terms of the energy content of fuels consumed, expressed in the standard scientific unit of joules or its multiples, kJ, MJ, or GJ. GRI-G4 item EN3 calls for the total energy consumed within (by) the reporting organization to be broken down as nonrenewable fuel consumed; renewable fuel consumed; purchased electric energy, heating, cooling, and steam; and self-generated electric energy, heating, cooling, and steam; with a subtraction of electric energy, heating, cooling, and steam that is sold.

The energy content of various types of fuels has been well established in prior research and is published in numerous sources. As an example, the Engineering Toolbox has pages for fossil fuels[34] and for biofuels.[35] Unfortunately for almost everyone, the United States has not converted to the use of metric units for energy, so some sources may report the energy content of fuels in units such as BTUs[36] or calories. The standard metric unit is the joule (J), which is so small that in practice energy is measured in megajoules (MJ) or gigajoules (GJ). In Europe, it is common to measure all energy in the units of electric energy: watt-hour, kilowatt-hour (kWh), or megawatt-hour (MWh). Table 6.8 shows the conversion factors among these four units of energy. The table gives the number of column-units per row-unit. Thus, in the first line, 3412.14 is the number of BTUs per kWh. In other words, 1 kWh (row) = 3412.14 BTU (col).

For illustration, not for completeness, Table 6.9 gives the energy content of some familiar fossil fuels and biofuels in a variety of units. The energy content of fuels is often stated in both a lower heating value (LHV) and a higher heating value (HHV). The LHV represents the energy recovered when burning the fuel and exhausting the resulting carbon dioxide and water vapor. The HHV represents the energy recovered if additional energy is captured by converting the water vapor to

TABLE 6.8 Conversion Factors for Units of Energy

Col/Row	*kWh*	*BTU*	*kCal*	*MJ*
kWh	1	3412.14	860.44	3.6
BTU	0.00029307	1	0.25217	.001055
kCal	0.0011622	3.9657	1	.0041868
MJ	0.27778	947.82	239.01	1

TABLE 6.9 Energy Content of Some Fuels

Ethanol	11,500 BTU/lb = 75,700 BTU/gallon = 26.7 GJ/tonne* = 21.1 MJ/liter
Biodiesel	approx. 37.8 GJ/tonne (33.3 to 35.7 MJ/liter)
Natural gas LHV	930 BTU/ft^3 = 34.6 MJ/m^3
Barrel of oil equivalent (boe)	approx. 6.1 GJ = 5.8 million BTU = 1,700 kWh
Gasoline LHV	115,000 BTU/gallon = 121 MJ/gallon = 32 MJ/liter
Petro-diesel	130,500 BTU/gallon = 36.4 MJ/liter = 43.8 GJ/tonne
Coal bituminous/anthracite**	27–30 GJ/tonne = 11,500–13,000 BTU/lb
Coal lignite/sub-bituminous	15–19 GJ/tonne, 6,500–8,200 BTU/lb

* one (metric) "tonne" is 1,000 kg. One U.S. "ton" is 2,000 lb.

** "Typical" coal (rank not specified) usually means bituminous, common for power plants (27 GJ/tonne)

liquid form and letting it cool to the original temperature of the fuel. Because most combustive technologies release the water byproduct as vapor, the LHV parameter is the fuel content to use in most applications.

In item G4-EN4, the GRI-G4 system also calls for reporting of energy consumed in activities upstream and downstream from (outside of) the reporting organization on the grounds that this accounting "provides a basis for calculating some of the relevant other indirect (Scope 3) GHG emissions" in item G4-EN17.[37] Indicator G4-EN5 calls for the calculation of an energy intensity ratio using an activity measure of the reporter's choosing, such as sales revenues, units of product, number of employees, or floor space. In indicator G4-EN6, the GRI also calls for an accounting of reductions in energy consumption that result from conservation or efficiency initiatives (not from reduced production or outsourcing) undertaken subsequent to a specified base year, and in G4-EN7 reporters disclose the reductions in the energy requirements of products or services subsequent to a base year and the resulting reductions in energy consumption attributed to those more efficient products and services.

Among the corporate rating systems, the DJSI (via the RobecoSAM Corporate Sustainability Assessment) calls for reporters to disclose their total energy consumption (in MWh, following the European convention) along with the cost of the energy and a measure of activity (sales or units produced). With the amount of energy used and the activity measure, the ratio of energy used per unit of activity yields a measure of energy intensity. The DJSI questionnaire does not ask for a breakdown of energy used by type or source, but reporters must show a four-year time series of energy consumption from which readers can infer a trend in energy intensity.

ASSET4 ESG takes data on energy use, both total and renewable, and takes note of whether the company has introduced innovations that reduce the energy footprint of products, produce renewable or clean-energy products, or constitute energy efficiency initiatives.

universities allocates 10 points (about 5% of the total) as credit for building energy consumption and clean/renewable energy. STARS focuses on energy intensity, measured in millions of BTUs per square foot (or square meter) of building space. Consistent with its approach to related subjects such as GHG emissions, water, and waste, in indicator OP-8, STARS gives points for a reduction in building energy intensity relative to a baseline year (maximum points for a 50% reduction), and it gives points for absolute levels of energy intensity below a threshold of 28 BTU/sq.ft. or 2.6 BTU/sq.m., with maximum points being awarded for an energy intensity 90% less than that threshold. In indicator OP-9, STARS gives the maximum number of points to organizations that use clean or renewable energy for 100% of their energy requirements. That energy may be produced locally, purchased as energy, or purchased as renewable energy certificates.

Underwriters Laboratories, in its UL 880 standard, gives credit for organizations having a program to manage energy and GHG emissions, for having targets for energy and GHG reduction, and for making progress toward those goals, though the targets and amount of progress may be determined by the reporting organization. UL 880 also gives points either for having targets and progress in the use of renewable energy or for using renewable energy (up to 100% of its energy requirement) directly or via the purchase of renewable energy certificates.

The B-Corp standard takes data on energy use, both in total and from renewable sources, and uses that to award points for the percentage of renewable energy and for an increasing trend in that percentage. It gives points for having management systems that monitor the usage of energy and for reducing energy use relative to a base year.

Discussion

There is general agreement about the methods to account for greenhouse gas emissions by organizations. The GHG Protocol is widely used and is the foundation for the other familiar standards for GHG accounting, the Climate Registry and the ISO 14064.[38] Work is ongoing to create tools that help users apply these principles and standards to specific circumstances, but the science of emissions and the principles for accounting are now well established.

For people who are new to GHG accounting, the main point is that the seven Kyoto gases each have a potential to create global warming, but carbon dioxide (CO2) is the one among those gases that serves as a point of reference for all the others. The global warming potential of each of the Kyoto gases is expressed as a multiple of the effect of CO2. Any quantity of emission, multiplied by its GWP factor, yields an emission quantity in "CO2-equivalents" and is usually measured in pounds or tons, kilograms, or metric tons. The GWP factors have been modified slightly over the past decade or two as the science of global warming has advanced, so depending on the age of the source one reads, the GWP for methane, as an example, might be 21 (from 1995) or 25 (more recently) or 28 (most recent, from 2014). Despite these updates, the basic conclusion is not changed greatly—business and industry generate a lot of greenhouse gas.

Every fuel that creates GHG emissions when burned has an emission factor, which is the mass of CO2 emitted per unit of the fuel. Those emission factors are crucial in the calculation of emissions. Their numerical values are based on the chemistry of combustion, so they have not changed noticeably in recent decades.

A central feature of the cap-and-trade policy for GHG emissions reduction is the measurement of corporate GHG emissions. In California, which runs a statewide cap-and-trade program, firms that generate more than 25,000 metric tons of CO2-equivalent per year must participate in the program and account for their emissions. Firms with as little as 10,000 metric tons per year must measure and disclose their emissions. The message is clear: the threshold for participation is likely to decrease over time so that more and more of the state's emissions will be included in the system. The alternative policy instrument is a tax on carbon, meaning a tax on all fuels that generate CO2 emissions. A carbon tax would be applied "at the pump," so it would not require firms to account for their emissions, but a tax does not guarantee specific reductions in emissions. However, even if a nation chooses a carbon tax over a cap-and-trade system, companies that issue sustainability reports will be called on to account for their GHG emissions, so it is a skill worth developing.

Carbon offsets, and related concepts such as renewable energy certificates, are a very interesting aspect of this subject. A firm's carbon footprint is the *net* of its emissions less carbon sequestered or emissions avoided through investments in low-carbon technologies. The accounting for carbon offsets is more subtle and difficult than the accounting for emissions, and its details are beyond the scope of this book, but it is an important subject for the professional in sustainability accounting to master. The renewable energy certificates also involve a subtle and novel concept—that you can buy the "environmental attributes" of a renewable power source *separately from* the energy and thus that the purchase of a one megawatt-hour REC from a distant renewable energy producer can offset the (Scope 2) emissions created when the energy your company uses was produced by your local electric utility. With the correct use of carbon credits and RECs, a company can achieve carbon neutrality even though it has some fossil fuel emissions.

The accounting for energy use is likewise well understood and standardized, but one has to question its relevance to sustainability accounting. If its use as a sustainability measure is driven by the desire to reduce GHG emissions, an accounting for energy use (getting points in a standard for reducing energy use) duplicates what is already accounted for in a firm's carbon footprint. However, if the interest

Notes

1 GHG Protocol. 2015c. Global Warming Potentials (May 2015). Available at <http://ghgprotocol.org/sites/default/files/ghgp/Global-Warming-Potential-Values.pdf> Accessed August 2015.

2 Wikipedia. 2015e. Nitrous Oxide. Available at <http://en.wikipedia.org/wiki/Nitrous_oxide> Accessed July 2015.

3 Wikipedia. 2015c. Sulphur Hexafluoride. Available at <http://en.wikipedia.org/wiki/Sulphur_hexafluoride#Greenhouse_gas> Accessed July 2015.

4 EC. 2010. Guidance on Interpretation of Annex I of the EU ETS Directive. European Commission, March 18, 2010. Available at <http://ec.europa.eu/clima/policies/ets/docs/guidance_interpretation_en.pdf> Accessed August 2015.

5 ARB. 2015a. Cap-and-Trade Program. California Environmental Protection Agency Air Resources Board. Available at <www.arb.ca.gov/cc/capandtrade/capandtrade.htm> Accessed August 2015.

6 ARB. 2015b. Mandatory Greenhouse Gas Reporting Regulation. California Environmental Protection Agency Air Resources Board. Available at <www.arb.ca.gov/cc/reporting/ghg-rep/regulation/mrr-regulation.htm> Accessed August 2015.

7 RGGI. 2015a. Regional Greenhouse Gas Initiative. Available at <http://www.rggi.org>

8 RGGI. 2015b. Program Design. Regional Greenhouse Gas Initiative. Available at <www.rggi.org/design> Accessed August 2015.

9 U.S. EPA. 2014. Basic Information: GHG Reporting Program. U.S. Environmental Protection Agency. (Updated July 31, 2014). Available at <www.epa.gov/ghgreporting/basic-info/> Accessed May 2013.

10 U.S. EPA. 2013b. GHG Data and Publication. Q413. What Percentage of Total U.S. GHG Emissions is Covered in the GHG Reporting Program? (Updated February 6, 2013). Available at <www.ccdsupport.com/confluence/pages/viewpage.action?pageId=141983792> Accessed August 2015.

11 Carbon Catalog. 2015. Carbon Catalog. Available at <www.carboncatalog.org/> Accessed August 2015.

12 CTX. 2015. How Are Carbon Credits Created? Carbon Trade Exchange. Available at <http://ctxglobal.com/faqs/how-are-carbon-credits-created/> Accessed August 2015.

13 Ibid.

14 Peters-Stanley, M., K. Hamilton, T. Marcello, and M. Sjardin. 2011. State of the Voluntary Carbon Markets. 2011. The Ecosystem Marketplace. Available at <www.ecosystemmarketplace.com/pages/dynamic/resources.library.page.php?page_id=8351§ion=our_publications&eod=1> Accessed August 2015.

15 CDP. 2015c. Climate Change Program Guidance. Carbon Disclosure Project. Available at <www.cdproject.net/en-US/Pages/guidance-climate-change.aspx> Accessed August 2015.

16 U.S. Energy Information Administration. 2015. Voluntary Reporting of Greenhouse Gases Program / Emissions Factors and Global Warming Potentials. Available at <http://www.eia.gov/survey/form/eia_1605/emission_factors.html> Accessed August 2015.

17 GHG Protocol. 2013. The Greenhouse Gas Protocol: A Corporate Accounting and Reporting Standard, Revised ed. Available at <www.ghgprotocol.org/files/ghgp/public/ghg-protocol-revised.pdf> Accessed August 2015.

18 Ibid., p. 16.

19 Ibid., p. 25.

20 Ibid., p. 27.

21 The Climate Registry. 2015. 2015 Default Emissions Factors. Available at <www.theclimateregistry.org/wp-content/uploads/2015/04/2015-TCR-Default-EF-April-2015-FINAL.pdf> Accessed August 2015.

22 U.S. Energy Information Administration. 2015. Voluntary Reporting of Greenhouse Gases Program. Available at <http://www.eia.gov/survey/form/eia_1605/emission_factors.html> Accessed August 2015.

23 GHG Protocol. 2013. The Greenhouse Gas Protocol, p. 25.

24 The Climate Registry. 2015. 2015 Default Emissions Factors.

25 Putt del Pino, S., and P. Bhatia. 2002. Working 9 to 5 on Climate Change: An Office Guide. World Resources Institute. Available at <http://www.wri.org/publication/working-9-to-5-on-climate-change> Accessed August 2015.

26 EPA. 2015i. Greenhouse Gas Equivalencies Calculator. U.S. Environmental Protection Agency. Available at <www.epa.gov/cleanenergy/energy-resources/calculator.html> Accessed August 2015.

27 UNEP DTU. 2015. CDM Projects by Type. Centre on Energy, Climate and Sustainable Development. Available at <http://cdmpipeline.org/cdm-projects-type.htm> Accessed August 2015.

28 GHG Protocol. 2015a. Project Protocol. Greenhouse Gas Protocol. Available at <http://www.ghgprotocol.org/standards/project-protocol> Accessed August 2015.

29 Wikipedia. 2015a. Carbon Offsets. Available at <http://en.wikipedia.org/wiki/Carbon_offset> Accessed August 2015.

30 EON. 2013. Buyer Liability Insurance Now Available for California's Cap-and-Trade Offset Program. Enhanced Online News. May 22, 2013. Available at <http://eon.businesswire.com/news/eon/20130522006404/en/Climate-Action-Reserve/cap-and-trade/carbon-offsets> Accessed August 2015.

31 GHG Protocol. 2015b. GHG Protocol for Project Accounting. Greenhouse Gas Protocol. Available at <www.ghgprotocol.org/standards/project-protocol> Accessed August 2015.

32 EPA. 2015h. Renewable Energy Certificates. U.S. Environmental Protection Agency. Available at <http://www.epa.gov/greenpower/gpmarket/rec.htm> Accessed August 2015.

33 EERE. 2015. Green Power Markets. U.S. Department of Energy, Office of Energy Efficiency and Renewable Energy. Available at <http://apps3.eere.energy.gov/greenpower/markets/carbon.shtml?page=0> Accessed August 2015.

34 Engineering Toolbox. 2015a. Fossil Fuels-Energy Content. The Engineering Toolbox. Available at <www.engineeringtoolbox.com/fossil-fuels-energy-content-d_1298.html> Accessed July 2015.

35 Engineering Toolbox. 2015b. Fossil Fuels-Energy Content. The Engineering Toolbox. Available at <www.engineeringtoolbox.com/biofuel-energy-content-d_1356.html>. Accessed July 2015.

36 BTU stands for British Thermal Unit. It is no longer used in Great Britain, but it remains in use in the United States.

37 GRI. 2013b. G4 Sustainability Reporting Guidelines.

38 GHG Protocol. 2015d. What Is the GHG Protocol? GHG Protocol. Available at <www.ghgprotocol.org/about-ghgp> Accessed August 2015.

7

WATER

The issues of sustainability that pertain to water and waste have some similarities to, but also important differences from, the issues that drive the accounting for greenhouse gases. Greenhouse gas emissions readily mix with atmospheric gases, so every emitter of GHGs increases the concentration of GHGs in the atmosphere worldwide. As a result, the whole world feels the effects of each polluter's emissions. Furthermore, the world has a finite capacity to absorb GHG emissions, so access to that capacity must be shared among the polluters. A consequential perspective of the transactional ethic would call for GHG emitters to take responsibility for the deleterious effects of their actions on others, and a distributional ethic must guide the allocation of access to the world's absorptive capacity. Carbon taxes and cap-and-trade systems, where they exist, use financial incentives (prices) and limits (caps) to drive emitters to reduce their pollution to acceptable levels. Investors care about the financial risk implied by prices on GHG emissions, and other stakeholders care about the consequences to human life of climate change resulting from GHG emissions.

The water problem is different from the GHG problem in that water is a local problem. Different regions of the world have different water resources and different demands on those resources. However, in both the GHG and the water problem, there is a common resource that must be shared, whether the sharing is global or local. In the GHG problem, the common resource is the earth's atmosphere and the photosynthetic plants worldwide that absorb carbon dioxide from the atmosphere and release oxygen into it. In the water problem, the common resource is the amount of annual rainfall available to human use and the amount of groundwater. As with any common-resource problem, a transactional ethic must hold each actor accountable for the effects of his or her claim on the commons, but it is a distributional ethic that guides the way those claims are allocated. As in the GHG problem, investors in water-dependent companies care about the financial risk implied by future pricing of and access to the common resource, and other stakeholders—other users of water—care about the consequences to their lives of depleting or damaging the common resource.

For the purposes of reporting on water use, the materiality of a firm's water consumption depends on the likelihood of future water shortages in the regions where the firm operates. This makes water accounting much more complex and difficult than GHG accounting. The authors of the 2010 CEO Water Mandate manual expressed this point,

> Collecting and disseminating meaningful water-related information is a complicated and difficult undertaking. And while corporate water accounting methods and tools have been under development for the past decade, there is still near universal agreement that current methods—though a good start—are inadequate and need to be refined.[1]

By 2014, the CEO Water Mandate manual had not moderated the concern by much, "Current practice in corporate water disclosure (even among the most advanced reporters) typically does not adequately capture the incredibly complex and location-specific nature of water resource dynamics and corporate action on water."[2]

Our goal in this chapter is to understand the issues of accounting for water use and water risk at an introductory level and to see the implementation of these ideas in various standards and metrics. We therefore begin our consideration of water accounting by considering the water cycle in nature and then looking at measures that describe the geographical context in which a firm uses water.

The Water Cycle

Fresh water rains onto the land in annual quantities that depend on the region. Some of that water runs into rivers, lakes, and reservoirs as surface freshwater, where it can be accessed for human use. Some of it seeps into the land to recharge groundwater bodies called aquifers. The rest of it evaporates back into the atmosphere or is transpired through plants and released as water vapor, or it is absorbed by plants and used chemically in the production of carbohydrates.

Humans' consumptive use of water consists of all quantities drawn from surface and groundwater resources (rivers, lakes, and aquifers), as well as from anthropogenic sources such as desalination plants, minus the amount of water returned to the environment through leakage and evaporation.

The main problem in water resource planning at the regional level is caused by the annual variability of rainfall in the context of a relatively stable per capita consumptive use. Thus, human populations can only be sustained securely by having surface and groundwater bodies and anthropogenic capacity (desalination and water recycling) sufficient to make up the deficit in rainwater supply during dry periods. The concepts of water scarcity and water stress derive from this need to balance the supply of and demand for water at the regional level.

scarce. Thus, measures of water scarcity, water stress, and water risk are essential as a context in which to evaluate a firm's use of water. These measures are regional, not firm specific, so in the construction of a sustainability report, a company's analyst will find these measures from external sources. Even so, it will be instructive to review a sampling of the methods that have been proposed to assess water scarcity.

The simplest measure, and perhaps the most widely used,[3] is the 1989 **Falkenmark indicator,**[4] also known as the **water stress index**. For a given country, it is calculated as the amount of renewable freshwater that is available per person per year. The labels used for varying levels of this index are shown in Table 7.1.

The weaknesses of the Falkenmark indicator, according to Chris White of Australian National University,[5] are that it does not account for the accessibility of the freshwater resources (in lakes versus deep aquifers), nor for water quality or human-made sources such as desalination plants, and it attempts to establish a global standard though there are regional differences in how much water people need, driven in particular by local industrial and agricultural use.

Falkenmark's indicator also mixes the terms "water scarcity" and "water stress" as different levels in one metric, though contemporary usage distinguishes these two concepts. Water scarcity is a physical measure of the amount of water present in relation to the human population but typically not considering its usefulness for humans due, for example, to pollution or depth of groundwater. Water stress in contemporary usage evaluates the available water in relation to human and ecological needs.

Ohlsson's **social water stress index**[6] in 2000 adapted the Falkenmark indicator, using the UNDP Human Development Index, to account for the different abilities of countries to adapt to water stress by economic, technological, and other means.

The contribution of Raskin and colleagues in 1997 was to define a country's water scarcity as total annual withdrawals of water relative to its available water supply.[7] This ratio has been called the **criticality ratio**[8] or the **water resources vulnerability index**[9] and is one of a class of measures called water-to-availability (WTA) ratios. Raskin et al. labeled *water scarcity* as demand in the range of

TABLE 7.1 Falkenmark's Country Water Stress Index

Level Descriptor	*Available Freshwater ($m^3/p/y$)*
No water stress	1,700+
Water stress	1,000–1,700
Water scarcity	500–1,000
Absolute water scarcity	0–500

20%–40% of the annual supply and *severe water scarcity* as demand at more than 40%. As White points out, this measure ignores human-made sources of fresh water, and it does not account for water withdrawals that are recycled. Like the Falkenmark indicator, while it may be useful as a measure of water scarcity, it is not a predictor of future scarcity, because it does not account for the ability of people to change their consumptive behavior nor develop technologies that conserve water or produce fresh water,[10] as the Ohlsson index does.

Seckler's measure of water scarcity,[11] developed in 1998 with the International Water Management Institute (IWMI), is essentially a criticality ratio, but it includes human-made sources of fresh water, as from desalination plants, and recycled water by measuring water demand in terms of consumptive use rather than total withdrawals.

A more complex measure, proposed in 2002, is Sullivan's water poverty index, which evaluates physical measures of water availability in the context of two socioeconomic variables that reflect poverty, the percentage of the population having access to safe water and sanitation and the proportion of the population having access to water in or near the home.[12] In a review of measures of water stress, White comments, "The complexity of this approach, however, means that it is more suited for analysis at a local scale, where data is more readily available, than on a national level."[13] Brown and Matlock note the conceptual challenges in finding appropriate weights for the three main variables in Sullivan's index.[14]

Smakhtin's **water stress indicator**[15] in 2004 accounted for the environmental requirements of water, not only for the human uses, and thus modified the total water availability into an account of mean annual runoff. The result was that some areas of the world are more stressed for water than had previously been estimated.

A measure of water scarcity gives information about the condition of human water consumption in a region at a point in time. It compares available water with the demand for water. The concept of *water stress* goes further, taking into account the usefulness of the available water for human life. Available water may be polluted or inaccessible due to its presence deep underground. Water stress measures the supply–demand imbalance, considering only the available and useful water supply.[16]

Beyond that, a *water risk* measure conveys information about the current state relative to the historical trends. One example is Asheesh's **water scarcity index**,[17] which considers the population growth rate, water availability, and domestic, industrial, and ecological water usage to calculate the water deficit, the difference between available water and sustainable water demand.[18]

The watershed sustainability index (WSI) proposed in 2007 by Chaves and Alipaz[19] is a composite of four variables, equally weighted and scaled on the interval between 0 and 1. The components are hydrological, environmental, human development, and policy. The innovation of the WSI is its use of five-year changes in the key variables or current data relative to long-term averages and its incorporation of sociological variables in addition to water-related variables. The hydrological component is derived from both the five-year water availability relative to its long-term average and the water's biochemical oxygen demand in a five-year average and changes in expenditures on water resource management (WRM).

The water supply sustainability index (WSSI), developed by Shi and colleagues at the Columbia Water Center and published in 2013,[20] is innovative in its use of precipitation as the supply to a location, which they note exposes the reliance on imported river water or mined groundwater in other analyses. Their index continues in the theme of demand/supply ratios, but it looks at water supply and demand over a long historical period both within a year and across years. Their normalized deficit index (NDI) measures the "maximum cumulated water shortage each year during the dry period that needs to be provided for from ground water or from surface water storage or transfers from other areas," while their normalized deficit cumulated (NDC) represents "the largest cumulative deficit between renewable supply and water use over an historical period of analysis." The two measures reflect "the stress associated with multi-year and within-year drought impacts at a location." Using the county as the unit of analysis for data from the United States, these two indices answer the question, "How sustainable are the water resources in this [county], if we consider only the renewable endogenous supply as defined by the rainfall?" In this formulation, water stress is associated with the need for water storage. They found that much of the agricultural belt in the Midwest is severely stressed, and in California and Arizona, "many locations requiring greater than 2 times to greater than 5 times the average annual rainfall in the location in storage or to be transferred from other locations." Their comparison of the cumulated deficit (NDC) with the largest annual deficit (max NDI) revealed that some parts of the United States are particularly at risk during multi-year droughts.

WRI's Aqueduct Water Risk Measure

The World Resources Institute's Aqueduct™ Water Risk Atlas[21] deserves special attention, because it was recently developed and is extensive in its consideration of variables related to water risk. Moreover, it is available as a public, Web-based, interactive tool. AASHE's STARS 2.0 standard for sustainable universities uses the Aqueduct measure of water risk as a basis for weighting a university's water use relative to other indicators.

The Aqueduct atlas reveals the results of a water risk assessment down to the level of one-square-mile cells in the United States, though its measures are "intended for comparative analysis across large geographies to identify regions or assets deserving of closer attention, and are not appropriate for local or site-specific analyses."[22] The end result is a report of water risk on a 0–5 scale, where 0–1 is Low risk, 1–2 is Low-to-Medium, 2–3 is Medium, 3–4 is High, and 4–5 is Extremely

High. These risk levels are color-coded in their online atlas. Future projection maps extend the forecast to 2020, 2030, and 2040.

Aqueduct is a complex model that calculates water risk for a particular location based on 12 factors. One is the basic measure of relative water demand, like Raskin's criticality ratio, which in Aqueduct is called baseline water stress: the ratio of total annual water withdrawal to average annual available blue water. They also consider the total volume of upstream storage and the percentage of withdrawn water that is returned to the water system. They consider the ratio of groundwater withdrawal relative to its sustainable recharge rate over a given aquifer. They account for the amount of protected land upstream from the location, media coverage of water issues at the national level, the proportion of population without access to improved drinking water sources, and the percentage of amphibian species classified by the International Union for Conservation of Nature (IUCN) as threatened in each water catchment area.

In addition to those static variables, they consider variables that relate to trends and uncertainties around water availability. For a particular location, they consider the severity of drought events between 1901 and 2008, the number of floods recorded between 1985 and 2011, the within-year variation of water supply, and the variation in natural water supply between years.

Each of those 12 indicators is measured in its natural units and then transformed onto a 0–5 scale that corresponds subjectively to the meanings presented above: 0–1 as low risk, etc. The thresholds of the natural units that correspond to those categories were determined "using existing literature, the range and distribution of indicator values, and expert judgment."

The 12 indicators were then weighted and averaged to form the composite water risk measure. The online atlas uses a default set of indicator weights, which were derived using input from six staff water experts using the Delphi technique. Recognizing that the water risk of different industrial sectors is affected differently by these 12 indicators, Aqueduct is set up with preset weighting schemes for nine industry sectors that were developed with input from industry experts and based on information disclosed by companies on their exposure to, and losses from, water-related risks. The nine industries are listed in Table 7.2.

TABLE 7.2 Aqueduct Industries

Agriculture
Food and beverage
Chemicals
Electric power
Semiconductors
Oil and gas
Mining
Construction materials
Textiles & Apparel

Contemporary Metrics for Water Use

Water risk must be reported as the context in which stakeholders will evaluate an organization's use of water, but the specific indicators of water use needed by stakeholders will depend on the ethical perspectives that stakeholders use when evaluating water use. Investors who are interested only in the financial risk implied by water use in the context of water risk might need to know only the current economic value of water impounded in the firm's product revenue stream, in order to calculate the firm's water intensity and evaluate that in the context of local water stress.

Other stakeholders may intend to use distributional ethics to evaluate the firm's usage of water relative to other users in the region, or they may use a biocentric perspective to focus on the impact of the firm's operations on both aquatic and terrestrial beings and ecosystems. A specification of measures suitable to those uses is beyond the scope of the present work. Here, we review the data on water that are called for in various rating and certification systems and speculate on how that information might be used.

Water Indicators in the GRI-G4

The Global Reporting Initiative's approach to water reporting is focused on the environmental and social impacts of water use, reflecting biocentric and social ethics. The GRI Guidance document justifies the relevance of water reporting as an indicator of an organization's "relative size and importance as a user of water," and adds that water discharge practices can impact the surrounding environment and affect the firm's "relationship with communities and other water users." The GRI-G4 system has four indicators that are primarily related to water.

- EN8: Total water withdrawal broken down by source (rainwater, surface water, groundwater, wastewater from another organization, and municipal water)
- EN9: Water sources significantly affected by withdrawal of water, meaning that the annual withdrawal is 5% or more of the volume of the water body or that the body is a listed wetland or has high biodiversity value. Items required are the size of the water source, whether or not it is in a protected area, its biodiversity, and the importance of the source to local communities.
- EN10: Total volume of water recycled and reused, to calculate that as a percentage of the total water withdrawn.
- EN22: Total water discharge by quality and destination. Quality is measured by biochemical oxygen demand (BOD) and total suspended solids (TSS). Destination distinguishes water treatment facilities from natural water bodies.

The GRI-G4 does not call for a specific accounting of the local context of water use as measured by any form of water stress, though presumably firms consider water stress when determining the materiality of water use and water management.

Standards Specific to Reporting on Water

The Carbon Disclosure Project's Water Disclosure Project questionnaire and the Water Footprint Network's guidelines are two standards specific to water reporting.

CDP Water Disclosure Project

The Carbon Disclosure Project (CDP) launched its Water Disclosure Project in 2010. The goal of the WDP is to promote "corporate water stewardship."[23] The CDP restructured its WDP questionnaire substantially in 2014–15 with input from other participants in the water disclosure arena: the UN Global Compact's CEO Water Mandate, the Global Reporting Initiative, the World Resources Institute, and the World Business Council for Sustainable Development. It also initiated a scoring system to evaluate water stewardship in four sequential categories or levels: disclosure, awareness, management, and leadership. The 64 scorable items requested in the WDP questionnaire each relate to one or more of these levels.

Participation is voluntary. Firms submit their data via an online response system available at the WDP website.[24] A 133-page technical manual supports reporters' disclosure.[25]

Most of the 64 indicators in the WDP related to the levels of assessment, management, and leadership are qualitative. They express respectively how a firm assesses the significance of the firm's use of water for its business, community, and ecosystems; how well a firm practices good water management; and whether the firm's actions represent best practices in water stewardship. These items relate to water-related risks as well as impacts across stakeholders.

Firms must account for the location of their facilities, operations, and financial value by water basin. Water accounting is requested by facility. The quantitative data in the WDP may be summarized as follows:

- Total water withdrawal data by source, using the GRI sources rain, surface, ground, municipal, and wastewater, as well as sources not used in the GRI: brackish surface water or seawater, nonrenewable groundwater, and produced water
- Water discharge by destination: fresh surface water, municipal treatment, seawater, and groundwater
- Water consumption
- Annual change in water-related capital expenditure and operating expenditure.

Measures of water scarcity are not reported directly in the WDP, though firms may report that they use such measures in assessing water risks and opportunities.

Reporters earn points at a level only if they have achieved 50% of the maximum number of points at the previous level. The WDP calculates summary scores for the four categories or levels—disclosure, assessment, management, and leadership—but not an overall score.

UN Global Compact's CEO Water Mandate Corporate Water Disclosure Guidelines

The United Nations Global Compact's CEO Water Mandate Corporate Water Disclosure Guidelines [illegible] in corporate water management, as well as disclosure. For example, it identifies seven broad categories, or levels, of corporate water management activities, which are believed to track generally from basic to more advanced practice (Table 7.3).

Likewise, the Guidelines suggest a range of disclosure practices that are typically associated with basic and more advanced water management and reporting (Table 7.4).

The Guidelines point out that the aspects of water that are material to a particular company will depend on its industry and on the geographic, social, and political context of the company's operations. Water quantity can be an issue, on the side of surplus, if floods are becoming more frequent or more severe in a basin. Water quality may be an issue even in locations where water is abundant if the firm's production processes have low tolerances for pollutants. Water scarcity, which reflects only the imbalance of availability and supply in a region, may be the relevant aspect if the firm has the ability to purify polluted water or to reach deep groundwater (both considered "available" in the definition of scarcity), or to create missing infrastructure, and the regulatory context is stable. Water stress is the relevant aspect where a firm's legal and social "license to operate" may be at risk due to its consumption of potable water that is also needed for domestic or ecological use in a location where the social and regulatory conditions are in flux.

For basic reporting on water issues, the Guidelines suggest the following "profile metrics" that summarize companywide water performance and risk with a focus on regulatory compliance and overall water use:

- Percent of facilities with a water-related compliance violation
- Percent of facilities adhering to relevant water-quality standards
- Total and percentage of withdrawals located in water-stressed or water-scarce areas
- Average water intensity in water-stressed areas (as appropriate)
- Percent of facilities with WASH services for all workers.

TABLE 7.3 Levels of Strategic Water Management

1. Provide water, sanitation, and hygiene (WASH) services in the workplace.
2. Measure and monitor water management practices.
3. Drive operational efficiency and reduce pollution.
4. Identify and understand water-stressed and high-risk basins.
5. Integrate water management into business strategy.
6. Leverage improved performance throughout the value chain.
7. Advance sustainable water management and engage in collective action.

Source: CEO Water Mandate Corporate Water Disclosure Guidelines

TABLE 7.4 CEO Water Mandate Basic and Advanced Disclosures

Category	*Basic Level*	*Advanced Level*
Context	• High-level assessment of basins	• Detailed assessment of basins where water challenges are significant • High-level assessment of water basins of key suppliers
Performance	• Withdrawals in water-scarce and -stressed areas • Percent of facilities adhering to water quality standards • Average water intensity in water-scarce or -stressed areas • Percent of facilities with WASH services for workers	• Location-specific performance data: –Water withdrawals by source –Water intensity –Water consumption –Water discharge by destination –Water performance in the value chain
Compliance	• Percent of facilities with a water-related regulatory compliance violation	• Adoption of sustainability standards • Water-related compliance violations in the value chain
Business risks	• High-level assessment of risks at a portfolio level	• Detailed assessment of risks, location-specific analysis at the facility level • Value chain risks
Business opportunities	• High-level assessment of opportunities	• Detailed assessment of opportunities • Value chain opportunities
External impacts	• N/A (legal compliance used as proxy)	• Water availability, water quality, and access to water resources and WASH services • Prioritizing impacts
Policies, governance, and targets	• Commitment to water stewardship and human rights to water and sanitation • Goals and targets	• Policies, strategies, and governance • Respecting the human rights to water and sanitation
Internal actions	• Improvements in direct operations	• Product innovation • Value chain prioritization, engagement, and improvements
External engagement	• Participation in global initiatives	• Consumer/public engagement and awareness building • Policy advocacy • Place-based collective action

Source: Adapted from the CEO Water Mandate *Corporate Water Disclosure Guidelines,* Table 3, and used with permission.

Advanced reporting provides details about water withdrawals by source type, water consumption, water discharge by destination type, and water intensity at the basin or facility level. It also focuses on the "hot spot" basins where the relevant water aspects are potential risk factors for the business. The analysis begins analysis of water-related issues in the locations of key value-chain actors, such as suppliers.

Water Footprint

The Water Footprint Network (WFN) published its Global Water Footprint Assessment Standard in 2009, revised it with the publication of its Assessment Manual in 2011, and extended the concept to a Grey Water Footprint Assessment in 2013.[27] The water footprint of an organization can be calculated in terms of direct (operational) use of water and indirect (supply chain) use. The water footprint of an organization is the sum of the direct and indirect footprints, so the water footprint concept focuses an organization on water use in its supply chain. For both direct and indirect, the total water footprint is an annual volume of freshwater consumed or polluted. This is equal to water withdrawn from all sources minus water consumed, minus water returned in an ecologically acceptable state, *plus* water polluted.

The water footprint concept is not meant to measure the severity of the local environmental impact of water pollution, but the grey water footprint does this indirectly via a special interpretation of the concept of "water polluted." The **grey water footprint** of an organization is "the volume of freshwater that is required to assimilate the load of pollutants given natural background concentrations and existing ambient water quality standards."[28] Thus, the grey water footprint is not the annual quantity of grey water emitted by an organization, but the annual quantity of freshwater needed to assimilate the grey water emissions, effectively the amount of freshwater that must be devoted to the restoration of polluted water.

Water scarcity, in this framework, is equal to the water footprint of a region in relation to the water availability. An "environmental hotspot" is a region where this ratio exceeds 100%.

ISO Standard for Water Footprint Accounting

In 2014, the International Organization for Standardization (ISO) published a standard for water accounting using the water footprint concept. *ISO 14046:2014 Environmental management—Water footprint—Principles, requirements and guidelines*[29] "specifies principles, requirements and guidelines related to water footprint assessment of products, processes and organizations based on life cycle assessment." Air and soil emissions that impact water quality are included in the assessment.

Water Indicators in the Corporate Ratings

To illustrate the variety of practices in water reporting for the corporate rating and ranking systems, we review the requirements of the DJSI, FTSE4Good, ASSET4 ESG, Global 100, and *Newsweek* Green Rankings.

Dow Jones Sustainability Index

Information for the Dow Jones Sustainability Indices comes from the RobecoSAM Corporate Sustainability Assessment (CSA) questionnaire. According to the two sample questionnaires provided to the public,[30] reporters are asked, at the least, to provide data on total water withdrawal, identified also as GRI indicator G4-EN8. For firms in industries that depend more on water, that figure is broken down in three categories: municipal, brackish-salt, and other. Firms also report the amount of water returned to its source at similar or better quality.

For water-dependent firms, the RobecoSAM CSA uses the Falkenmark indicator ($< 1{,}700\ m^3/p/y$) to define local water stress and calls for data on the percentage of production plants located in water-stressed areas and the percentage of cost of goods sold (COGS) associated with production from those plants in aggregate. The CSA also calls for the plant-level freshwater consumption and water intensity (m^3/COGS) from the three plants with the highest levels of freshwater consumption and the water-related targets and methods to achieve targets for those plants. It also calls for companies to identify the tools, management systems, standards, or frameworks used to record, analyze, and report various aspects of water use and water risk, how the company manages risks associated with water availability and quality, and water regulation and pricing, and potential stakeholder conflicts over water.

Thompson Reuters ASSET4 ESG

The ASSET4 ESG scores are derived from 226 key performance indicators computed from more than 500 data items, but the quantitative data on water use and risk appear to consist of total water withdrawn, water recycled, and wastewater discharged,[31] which are the GRI's indicators G4-EN8, EN10, and EN22.

FTSE4Good

FTSE4Good has nine indicators of water use that are common to firms of all industries and locations. Firms earn points for having a policy to address water use, assessing risks in water-stressed regions, taking action to reduce water use, making progress against targets, collaborating with others to improve water efficiency, and having an independent audit of water-related data. The quantitative performance measures used by FTSE4Good are the total water usage (interpreted as water withdrawn) and the percentage of water recycled, which are familiar as equivalent

general screening of suppliers on environmental criteria (G4-EN32).

Global 100 and Newsweek *Green Rankings*

The single item on water among the 12 indicators in the Global 100 is water productivity, which is the reciprocal of water intensity and measured as revenue per cubic meter of water withdrawn. The Global 100 water indicator is calculated as a composite that gives 75% weight to the current-year water productivity and 25% weight to the two-year change in water productivity. The water indicator carries a weight of 1/12th (8.3%) in the Global 100 sustainability metric.

The *Newsweek* Green Rankings uses the same measure, taken from the Global 100.

Bloomberg ESG

The Bloomberg Finance ESG data are available only by subscription, and their indicators and methodology are not made public. However, the World Business Council for Sustainable Development (WBCSD) Global Water Tool manual reports its consistency with the Bloomberg water reporting system on the following indicators:

- Total Water Consumption
- Water Consumption per production unit
- Percent Recycled/Reused (G4-EN10)
- Total Water Discharge (G4-EN22)

These indicators enable the calculation of a fifth Bloomberg indicator, the Water Discharge Percentage (total water discharge/total water consumption).

Water Indicators in the Sustainability Standards

To illustrate further the variety of approaches to reporting and weighting water-related issues, we look at the STARS 2.0, UL 880, and B-Corp standards.

AASHE STARS 2.0

The Association for the Advancement of Sustainability in Higher Education STARS 2.0 metric for universities allocates between 5 and 9 points out of approximately 205 (2.5%–4.5%), depending on the level of local water risk as indicated by the WRI's Aqueduct's water risk atlas. Universities earn a maximum of 2–6 points for reducing their potable water use by 30%, compared to a baseline year, as indicated by water use normalized by weighted campus user, by gross square foot/meter of floor area, and by acre/hectare of vegetated grounds. The maximum of 6 points is available for universities in areas of extremely high water risk. Universities may earn another 2 points by practicing Low Impact Development to reduce rainwater and stormwater runoff and 1 point by using natural wastewater systems.

UL 880

Underwriters Laboratories, in its UL 880 standard for manufacturing firms, allocates a maximum of 59 points (5.9%) out of the total 1,008 points for items related to water or wastewater. Reporters earn up to 5 points for providing written documentation of an enterprise-wide commitment to water conservation. They may get another 14 points for documenting water and wastewater use, consumption, efficiency, and risks using standard reporting frameworks such as the WBCSD Global Water Tool, the CDP's Water Disclosure Project questionnaire, or the Water Footprint Network guidelines, and/or an internal data collection system that covers consumption, efficiency, and risk factors.

They get up to 10 more points for developing a plan for water and wastewater efficiency and reduction, using the plan to reduce production-related wastewater discharge toward a goal of zero, and having a plan to reduce nonpoint source pollution that could affect water supplies. They get up to 25 more points for meeting or exceeding previously established targets for water use and for establishing new targets and making progress toward them. A final 5 points is available for evidence of participation in a voluntary public reporting program such as the CDP's Water Disclosure initiative.

B-Corp

The B-Corp standard of B Labs, Inc., weights indicators differently according to the reporter's industry sector, size, and business model. The water-related items earning points in the B-Corp metric are the practices of monitoring and reporting of the usage of water and of using water conservation methods. Total annual water use is reported but not weighted.

Tools for Reporting on Water

Water accounting is complicated by regional differences in water stress as the context that determines the materiality of a firm's use of water and its practices of water management. It is further complicated by the relationships between water withdrawal, water use, water recycling, and the discharge of polluted water (grey water) into the environment. Thus, several tools have been developed and published to help firms analyze their use of water and the consequent risks.

World Business Council for Sustainable Development (WBCSD) Global water tool

The World Business Council for Sustainable Development offers its Global Water Tool (GWT) as a free, publicly available Excel-based resource for identifying corporate water risks and opportunities. Launched in 2007, the GWT was developed by the global engineering company CH2M Hill and updated in 2011 and again in 2015. The Carbon Disclosure Project, Dow Jones Sustainability Initiative, and the Global Environmental Management Initiative were consulted to ensure compatibility.

The GWT uses public data on water, sanitation, population, and biodiversity for countries and watersheds around the world, plus 3 of the 12 indicators used in the WRI's Aqueduct water risk model (baseline water stress and seasonal and interannual variability in water supply), to answer the following questions for companies:[33]

- How many of your sites are in extremely water-scarce areas? Which sites are at greatest risk? How that will change in the future?
- How much of your total production is generated from your most at-risk sites?
- How many of your employees live in countries that lack access to improved water and sanitation?
- How many of your suppliers are in water scarce areas now and will be in 2025?

The firm-specific data required by the GWT are broken down by site: the volumes of freshwater withdrawn from rain, surface, groundwater, municipal, and wastewater sources, the volumes from nonfreshwater sources, water discharges broken down by the receiving body (ocean, surface, well, or offsite treatment), amounts recycled or reused, a size measure (production or sales) to calculate a water intensity ratio, and the number of site workers and their per capita water use.

The summary metrics reported by the GWT are water withdrawal (fresh and nonfresh), discharge, consumption, reuse/recycling, and intensity broken down by the water scarcity of the site in five levels: Abundant (4000+ m^3/p/y) and the four levels of the Falkenmark metric labeled Sufficient to Extreme Scarcity. Also reported are the number of the firm's locations broken down by the country's dependency ratio (percentage of total renewable water resources originating outside the country), by the country's industrial intensity of water usage, and by the country's percentage of population served by improved water and improved sanitation. Thus, the GWT does not calculate a water risk measure for a firm. It is left up to the reporter's analysts to compare the water usage data with the contextual data on local water scarcity.

The input data are aggregated to enable reporting on GRI indicators G4-EN8, total water withdrawal by source; G4-EN10, percentage and total volume of water recycled and reused; and G4-EN22, total water discharge by quality and destination. GWT does not report on G4-EN9, water sources significantly affected by withdrawal of water, because that would require data on local water supply, whereas the public data used by the GWT are at the national level.

GEMI's Local Water Tool™

The Global Environmental Management Initiative (GEMI) is a nonprofit organization "dedicated to fostering environmental, health and safety excellence and corporate citizenship worldwide."[34] Its Local Water Tool (LWT) was developed by GEMI staff with technical support from CH2MHill. The LWT was published in 2012. It is available free at the GEMI website.

The LWT was developed in cooperation with WBCSD and its Global Water Tool so that LWT can take data from the WBCSD GWT. Then, for a particular site, the GEMI LWT calculates specific impacts and water risks associated with physical supply, regulation, social forces, competition, and climate variability. The detailed information about a site permits analyses of the optimum water balance between process streams, monthly differences in water stress, and the share of local water resources (e.g., river flow) used in operations and helps a firm develop water management plans at the site level.

In its *Corporate Water Accounting* report, the CEO Water Mandate project of UNEP's Global Compact compared the GEMI Water Sustainability Tools to the WBCSD Global Water Tool and the Water Footprint Tool.[35] In general, UNEP found GEMI LWT to be useful for companies in the early stages of thinking about water stewardship, because it is inexpensive, fast, and does not require expertise to use. It concluded that both GEMI and WBCSD provided only rough or rudimentary assessments of risks.

Discussion

We have seen that the problem of water accounting is quite different from the problem of carbon accounting. Whereas global warming is a global problem, affected by every firm's emissions of greenhouse gases, the materiality of a firm's water use depends on the level of water scarcity in the regions where it operates and on the risks that derive from the social (governmental) control of water as a regional or national resource. Therefore, an analysis of water stress, or the derivation of data on local water stress, is the starting point for an assessment of the environmental and social impacts of water use.

In water accounting, the novice encounters many more new concepts than in carbon accounting. Carbon accounting boils down to an understanding of the *global warming potentials* of seven Kyoto gases (among which CO2 is the dominant member except in a few specialized industries) and of the *emission factors* of various fossil fuels that produce CO2 (for Scope 1 emissions), with a footnote that an electric power company also has an emission factor expressed as kgCO2 per water use, which is not only a matter of quantity but of quality due to the presence of water discharge in the basic volumetric water-balance equation:

Withdrawals = Consumption + Returns + Discharges

Withdrawals refer to a firm's volume of water withdrawn from all sources. Consumption refers only to water that is impounded in products or lost to evaporation. Returns are water given back to the local environment in an ecologically acceptable form. Discharges refer to the volume of polluted water put back into the environment.

Notice that "Recycled" does not appear in the water balance equation. Recycled water would include the amount of usable water recaptured from the outflow of business processes, as well as the quantity of purified wastewater. A firm's action to recycle water simply reduces the amount of water that it would otherwise have had to withdraw from the environment. A firm can improve the water-efficiency of its processes, or recycle some of the water it uses, with the same effect.

One might therefore wonder why firms are called on to report their amount of water recycled in the GRI (G4-EN10) and in all of the corporate rating and certification systems. All efforts at improving water efficiency, both through process improvements and through recycling, would be captured by a water productivity indicator (revenue per gallon withdrawn). In this respect, the parsimonious Global 100 corporate ranking, having only 12 indicators, one of which is water productivity, handles water better than the others that have individual indicators for water withdrawals and water recycling but that don't calculate the productivity ratio.

All the other corporate ratings and certifications focus on the three GRI indicators: withdrawals, recycling, and discharges, distinguished only by the amount of detail called for in each indicator, such as how many different sources of water must be accounted for and the types of pollution in discharges. In 2010, the United Nations Environment Program published the CEO Water Mandate, which stated, "Traditionally, quantitative water data disclosed has focused on indicators such as total water use, discharge, and/or recycling. This information alone is now widely considered inadequate as it does not address the local contexts in which the water is used." Only the DJSI explicitly uses a measure of water stress, the basic Falkenmark indicator. Even the GRI does not call for a measure of water stress as an indicator; its indicator G4-EN9 calls for reporting of any body of water from which the firm takes 5% of the volume per year, but that is a physical measure alone (water scarcity), not a measure that considers the demand on the resource (water stress). Only through the Disclosure on Management Approach in the GRI might a reporter think to give information about water stress, motivated by the principle of materiality.

A disturbing feature of the system of water accounting used in the GRI and the standards that follow its example is the separate treatment of water as a resource issue (G4-EN8 and EN10) and wastewater as a pollution issue (EN22). Water pollution is not like the atmospheric pollution that is accounted for through GHG methods and, as we will see in the next chapter, through measures for acidification, ozone depletion, and smog formation, which affect the quality of a "commons" resource. Water is bought and sold as a private resource, and it exists locally in a finite quantity. Discharges are not just another form of water to be footnoted by the type and concentration of pollutant. Discharges affect the quantity of useful water that is available to go around.

Put another way, the volumetric water balance equation gives the impression that a firm's pollution is a type of usage. Polluted water adds with Consumption and Returns to constitute total withdrawals. But can we just think of Discharges as another form of consumption? We cannot, and the reason is provided insightfully by the water footprint concept.

Grey water is water from households and commercial or light industrial use that is not generally usable (as freshwater or blue water) because it has been polluted by soaps, detergents, and other nonseptic sources but has some useful applications, such as in irrigation. (Septic water from toilets is called black water.) In the Water Footprint Assessment Manual, the *grey water footprint* of a firm is not the quantity of water discharged as polluted. The grey water footprint of a firm is the quantity of freshwater needed to dilute the grey water to an acceptable level for ecological use.

That concept—the dilution of grey water by freshwater—helps us to solve two important problems in water accounting. First, it integrates water consumption and water pollution, if we think that a firm that discharges grey water is thereby encumbering a specific amount of freshwater to effect the dilution to ecologically acceptable levels. Second, this gives us a concise summative measure for the ecological impact of water use by a business. The water footprint of a firm is equal to its Consumption plus the amount of freshwater it encumbers through discharge.

In carbon accounting, fuels have emission factors that determine how much CO2 is put into the environment per unit of fuel (gallon, kg, etc.). We shall see in the next chapter that the general concept for emission factor, referring more generally to the environmental effect of a human activity per unit of use, is a *characterization factor*. The grey water footprint concept directs our attention to the number of gallons of freshwater needed to dilute one gallon of a particular type of discharge. That is the characterization factor of the discharge.

In the field of toxicology, it is well known what maximum levels of various types of pollutants are acceptable in human water sources. Those levels are called the maximum safe concentration (MSC) and are typically expressed in parts per million (ppm) or parts per billion (ppb). As one milligram is one-millionth of a kilogram, and one liter of water weighs one kilogram, it is convenient to think of

The grey water footprint is expressed as a quantity of water. The concept behind it is that this amount of water is needed to dilute the pollutant to safe levels. There is another way to look at the grey water footprint, which draws not on the concept of dilution but on a concept of natural capital that is proxied by the quantity of water. The central idea is that nature does not just tolerate diluted pollutants. Nature detoxifies them. Ecological systems contain microbes that can detoxify pollutants such as organic compounds[36] and heavy metals[37] under the right conditions. When businesses pollute water, they implicitly rely on the detoxification services of those microbes. Thus, the microbes and the aqueous environment they live in constitute an important form of natural capital that businesses depend on when they pollute water. The grey water footprint of a business in this deeper sense would measure the amount of that natural capital that is tied up in the requirement to detoxify the amount of pollution in a firm's discharge. The amount of water needed to safely host the types and amounts of microbes required to detoxify in one year the quantity of pollutants discharged by a firm in one year would be a useful proxy measure for that natural capital requirement and could be interpreted as a grey water footprint.

This approach to accounting for the environmental effects of water usage would be consistent with the comprehensiveness principle promoted by the Global Initiative for Sustainability Ratings, under which metrics dealing with any aspect of sustainability "should systematically assess for impacts on human, intellectual, natural, and social capital."[38]

Regarding evaluative measures related to water, water accounting is replete with detail on the items that could be measured and reported, but it offers no simple, summative measures. The ultimate summative measure for a firm is water risk in each of the localities where it operates, but water risk is not a single quantitative concept. In theory, it could be expressed quantitatively in terms of the probabilities of business disruptions of various financial magnitudes resulting from natural, social, and political events that might flow from the firm's present water management practices. However, in common use, water risk will be assessed qualitatively based on a general reading and assimilation of the data.

In his introduction to KPMG's 2012 study of water reporting, Wim Bartels observed that water scarcity has risen to the top of the corporate agenda in light of predictions that global demand for freshwater will exceed supply by 40% by 2030. Governments have imposed taxes or higher prices when water became scarce, and corporate uses of water in water-scarce communities have threatened corporations' reputations or called into question their social license to operate. He argues that corporations must "demonstrate a robust response to water scarcity through their corporate reporting in order to convince investors of future growth and profitability."[39] The field of water accounting evolves to support that need for reporting as data sources become refined and extended and as researchers develop better measures of water use, water management practices, and business-related water risks.

Notes

1 Morrison, J., R. Schenck, and P. Schulte. 2010. *Corporate Water Accounting: An Analysis of Methods and Tools for Measuring Water Use and Its Impacts.* Oakland, CA: Pacific Institute. Available at <http://ceowatermandate.org/files/corporate_water_accounting_analysis.pdf> Accessed July 2015.
2 UN Global Compact. 2014. CEO Water Mandate Corporate Water Disclosure Guidelines: Toward a Common Approach to Reporting Water Issues. United Nations Global Compact. Available at <http://ceowatermandate.org/disclosure/> Accessed July 2015.
3 Brown, A., and M. D. Matlock. 2011. A Review of Water Scarcity Indices and Methodologies. The Sustainability Consortium White Paper #106 (April 2011). Available at <http://www.sustainabilityconsortium.org/wp-content/themes/sustainability/assets/pdf/whitepapers/2011_Brown_Matlock_Water-Availability-Assessment-Indices-and-Methodologies-Lit-Review.pdf>
4 Falkenmark, M., J. Lundquist, and C. Widstrand. 1989. Macro-Scale Water Scarcity Requires Micro-Scale Approaches: Aspects of Vulnerability in Semi-Arid Development. *Natural Resources Forum*, 13:4, 258–267.
5 White, C. 2012. Understanding Water Scarcity: Definitions and Measurements. UNESCO Global Water Forum. Available at <http://www.globalwaterforum.org/2012/05/07/understanding-water-scarcity-definitions-and-measurements/> Accessed July 2015.
6 Ohlsson, L. 2000. Water Conflicts and Social Resource Scarcity. *Physics and Chemistry of the Earth*, 25:3, 213–220.
7 Raskin, P., P. Gleick, P. Kirshen, G. Pontius, and K. Strzepek. 1997. *Water Futures: Assessment of Long-Range Patterns and Problems. Comprehensive Assessment of the Freshwater Resources of the World.* Stockholm, Sweden: Stockholm Environment Institute.
8 Alcamo, J., T. Henrichs, and T. Rosch. 2000. World Water in 2025: Global Modeling and Scenario Analysis for the World Commission on Water for the 21st Century. Kassel World Water Series Report No. 2, Center for Environmental Systems Research, Germany: University of Kassel, pp. 1–49.
9 Brown and Matlock. 2011. Op. cit.
10 Rijsberman, F. R. 2006. Water Scarcity: Fact or Fiction? *Agricultural Water Management*, 80, 5–22.
11 Seckler, D. W. 1998. *World Water Demand and Supply, 1990 to 2025: Scenarios and Issues* (Vol. 19). Colombo, Sri Lanka: International Water Management Institute.
12 Sullivan, C. 2002. Calculating a Water Poverty Index. *World Development*, 30:7, 1195–1210.
13 White, C. 2012. Understanding Water Scarcity: Definitions and Measurements. UNESCO Global Water Forum. Available at <http://www.globalwaterforum.org/2012/05/07/understanding-water-scarcity-definitions-and-measurements/> Accessed July 2015.
14 Brown and Matlock. 2011. Op. cit.

17 [illegible] Allocating [illegible] of Shared Water Resources (Scarcity Index): Case Study on Palestine-Israel. In H. Shuval and H. Dweik (eds.) *Water Resources in the Middle East.* Berlin Heidelberg: Springer, pp. 241–248.
18 Brown and Matlock. 2011. Op. cit.
19 Chaves, Henrique M. L., and S. Alipaz. 2007. An Integrated Indicator Based on Basin Hydrology, Environment, Life, and Policy: The Watershed Sustainability Index. *Water Resource Management*, 21, 883–895. Available at <www.clw.csiro.au/division/perth/seminars/documents/WSI_paper.pdf> Accessed July 2015.
20 Shi, D., N. Devineni, U. Lall, and E. Piñero. 2013. America's Water Risk: Water Stress and Climate Variability. Columbia University Water Center. Available at <http://water.columbia.edu/files/2013/09/GB_CWC_whitepaper_climate-water-stress_final.pdf> Accessed July 2015.
21 WRI. 2015. Aqueduct: Measuring and Mapping Water Risk.
22 Gassert, F., M. Luck, M. Landis, P. Reig, and T. Shiao. 2015. Aqueduct Global Maps 2.1.
23 CDP. 2015a. Guidance for Companies Reporting on Water on Behalf of Investors & Supply Chain Members 2015. Carbon Disclosure Project. Available at <www.cdp.net/en-US/Pages/guidance.aspx> Accessed July 2015.
24 CDP. 2015b. Water Program. Available at <www.cdp.net/water> Accessed July 2015.
25 CDP. 2015a. Op. cit.
26 UN Global Compact. 2014. CEO Water Mandate Corporate Water Disclosure Guidelines.
27 Hoekstra, A. Y., A. K. Chapagain, M. M. Aldaya, and M. M. Mekonnen. 2011. *The Water Footprint Assessment Manual.* London: Earthscan.
28 Ibid., p. 2.
29 ISO. 2014b. ISO 14046:2014 Environmental Management—Water Footprint—Principles, Requirements and Guidelines. Available at <www.iso.org/iso/catalogue_detail?csnumber=43263> Accessed July 2015.
30 RobecoSAM. 2015a. Corporate Sustainability Assessment, DJSI 2015—Test Companies SA. Available at <www.robecosam.com/images/sample-questionnaire-1.pdf> and <www.robecosam.com/images/sample-questionnaire-2.pdf> Accessed July 2015.
31 Thompson Reuters. 2015. ASSET4 ESG Data. Available at <http://thomsonreuters.com/content/dam/openweb/documents/pdf/tr-com-financial/fact-sheet/esg-data-fact-sheet.pdf> Accessed July 2015.
32 WBCSD. 2015. Global Water Tool. World Business Council for Sustainable Development. Available at <http://www.wbcsd.org/work-program/sector-projects/water/global-water-tool.aspx> Accessed July 2015.
33 Ibid.
34 GEMI. 2015. About the GEMI LWT. Global Environmental Management Initiative. Available at <www.gemi.org/localwatertool/about.html> Accessed August 2015.
35 Morrison, J., R. Schenck, and P. Schulte. 2010. *Corporate Water Accounting: An Analysis of Methods and Tools for Measuring Water Use and Its Impacts.* Oakland, CA: Pacific Institute and UNEP UN Global Compact. Available at <http://ceowatermandate.org/files/corporate_water_accounting_analysis.pdf> Accessed July 2015.

36 EPA. 2011a. Development of Specific Bacterial Detoxification Enzymes as Bioindicators and Biosensors of Environmental Pollution. U.S. Environmental Protection Agency. Available at <www.epa.ie/pubs/reports/research/waste/strivereport72.html#.VdfKJlaWsVo> Accessed August 2015.

37 Monachese, M., J. P. Burton, and G. Reid. 2012. Bioremediation and Tolerance of Humans to Heavy Metals Through Microbial Processes: A Potential Role for Probiotics. *Applied Environmental Microbiology*, 78:6397–6404. Available at <http://phys.org/news/2012–09-detoxifying-effect-microbes.html> Accessed August 2015.

38 GISR. 2015a. Global Initiative for Sustainability Ratings.

39 KPMG. 2012. Water Scarcity—A Dive Into Global Reporting Trends. KPMG Sustainable Insight. Available at <http://www.kpmg.com/Global/en/IssuesAndInsights/ArticlesPublications/sustainable-insight/Pages/water-scarcity.aspx> Accessed July 2015.

8
WASTE

The issue of waste is usually considered as a type of pollution problem. Toxic waste, of course, is a pollutant, and when it is released into a common or public resource such as the atmosphere or a river, a consequential ethic would call for the polluter either to internalize the pollution by disposing of it on private property or to compensate the victims of the pollution. By either of those solutions, the disposal of toxic waste becomes costly to the polluter.

For nontoxic solid waste, which is sent to landfills, the fees for disposal make it expensive to the emitter. Limitations on the amount of land suitable for waste disposal, especially in urban areas and where population is growing, will raise the cost of waste disposal and thus put emitters' investors at financial risk, which is a motivator of behavior even under a basic egoistic ethic.

Where waste is disposed in a common resource, such as the ocean, other stakeholders have a different set of ethical grounds for objection. It is not the finite carrying capacity of the resource that drives the objection. It is an ethical perspective on the relationship between humans and nature that objects either to the spoilage of that resource for use by other living beings (the biocentric perspective) or to the spoilage of the oceanic ecosystem itself (the ecocentric perspective).

The waste of nonrenewable abiotic resources, such as minerals and oil, raises additional ethical issues. These resources are finite, and some, such as the rare earths needed in computing equipment, are being depleted at an increasing rate.[1] Viewed as a common resource for humanity, these nonrenewable resources may be subject to ethical evaluations for their fair distribution among people in the present and the future. Such considerations drive stakeholders' attention toward methods for recycling nonrenewable resources. An ecocentric perspective on the naturohomic ethic leads to the same conclusion: we should seek closed-systems solutions to our use of natural capital, so that one business's waste is another business's "food."[2]

We begin this chapter with a review of the concepts that shape the ways that waste can be measured. Then we look at how waste is measured in the various standards for corporate disclosure, corporate ratings, and corporate certification for sustainability.

Types of Waste and Their Measurement

In sustainability reports, waste is typically accounted for by its type, not its contaminants. However, contaminants are what drive the ecological and social impacts of the waste. To respect both perspectives, we consider the measures of waste quantity and quality for four main types of waste: wastewater, biological waste, atmospheric emissions, and solid waste.

Three Ways to Report Environmental Pollution

Standards for the emission and treatment of waste may be expressed in one of three ways: as technology-based limits, as production-based loading limits, or as environmental quality limits. *Technology-based* limits indicate the percentage reduction of the pollutant from influent to effluent in a treatment process. They reflect governmental expectations about the capabilities of existing technology. *Production-based load* values are the metric used to quantify emissions from a source. Thus, production-based load limits state a maximum rate of emission of the pollutant from the source, expressed as a quantity of emissions per day or year. *Quality-based* limits express the concentration of the pollutant in the environment, expressed as an absolute level of the pollutant per unit such as milligrams per liter of water.

Wastewater

The CEO Water Mandate's *Corporate Water Disclosure Guidelines* distinguish four qualities of water: physical, chemical, biological, and organoleptic (taste-related) and thus of wastewater.[3] To that we add atomic to include radioactivity in our discussion of quality standards for water and wastewater.

The examples of wastewater quality in this chapter are generic, not related to a specific source or technology, so those examples will state quality-based limits. The corporate accounting for emissions, where the purpose is to describe a firm's total emissions during the accounting period, typically uses production-based load values, expressed in units like kilograms per year (kg/y). Corporate accounting may use quality-based values, expressed in units like milligrams per liter (mg/L), if the purpose is to indicate the quality of wastewater being emitted into the environment irrespective of the total amount of pollution.

The physical aspect of water pollution is expressed by the concept of turbidity ("hazy" or "muddy" water). Traditionally, it was measured as the mass of suspended solids, per liter of sampled water, that are too large to pass through a filter of a new units of measurement were introduced based on the technique of measuring turbidity in terms of the scattering of light by suspended solids.[6] The U.S. EPA standard for the TSS in drinking water is one nephelometric turbidity unit (NTU).[7]

In addition to solids suspended in water, there may be chemicals dissolved in the water. The concentration of dissolved chemicals is expressed as the total dissolved solids (TDS) and is measured, like the TSS, in milligrams per liter (mg/L). The total of TSS and TDS is the total solids, for which the WHO specifies 500 mg/L as "permissible," meaning generally accepted by consumers, and 1500 mg/L as "excessive," meaning that it markedly impairs the potability of the water.[8]

Chemical water pollution is measured differently for organic and inorganic pollutants. Inorganic pollution, which makes water unsafe for human use, is measured in terms of the concentration of the pollutant, expressed for example in grams, milligrams, or micrograms per liter. Standards exist for the acceptable levels of such chemicals in drinking water.[9] Another measure of chemical water pollution, focusing on chemicals that react in solution to form acids or bases, is the pH value of the water. A pH value of 7.0 is neutral. According to the WHO, expectation for permissible pH is between 7.0 and 8.5 (slightly basic), water is excessively acid with pH < 6.5 and excessively basic when pH > 9.2.[10] The U.S. EPA does not set a standard for pH, but it includes pH among the qualities of water that are subject to the voluntary National Secondary Drinking Water Regulations, where the acceptable range is 6.5 to 8.5.[11]

Organic chemical pollutants, in contrast to the inorganics, have a common effect: they promote the growth of biological organisms that break down the organic molecules. That decomposition process requires oxygen, so it depletes the oxygen dissolved in the water and thus makes the water less suitable for fish. One generic measure for the organic pollution of water is its five-day biochemical oxygen demand (BOD5), measured in milligrams of oxygen consumed per liter of sample during five days of incubation at 20°C. A common limit is for BOD5 in wastewater discharged to the environment is 30 mg/L as a monthly average and 45 mg/L as a 7-day average.[12]

Because almost all organic compounds can be oxidized into carbon dioxide, water, and ammonia, another generic measure of the presence of organic compounds is the chemical oxygen demand (COD), measured as the mass of oxygen needed to oxidize all organic compounds in one liter of a sample of water. COD is expressed in milligrams per liter (mg/L) and commonly reported as "parts per million" (ppm). It differs conceptually from biochemical oxygen demand in that there are also nonorganic compounds that can also be oxidized, but even so it presents an indicator of water pollution.

Biological pollution of wastewater is indicated by bacteria that are harmful to human health. There are many such types of bacteria, but the principal indicator of biological pollution focuses on bacteria that are often found in human and animal feces, such as *E. coli*. A coliform test measures the concentration of bacteria in a sample. The WHO standard for coliform bacteria is that 90% of 100 mL water samples tested in a year at a location should have a "most probable number" (MPN index) of less than 1.0 coliform organisms.[13] Values above a level known as the coliform index indicate a likelihood of fecal contamination.

Another form of water-based pollution is the emission of chemicals that result in eutrophication, which is the overstimulation of biological systems. The standard for measurement of eutrophication is phosphate (PO_4). Eutrophying chemicals are rated for *eutrophication potential* as multiples of the effect of phosphate, so the emission of eutrophying chemicals is measured in PO_4-equivalents, analogous to the measurement of greenhouse gas emissions using CO2-equivalents. A report of eutrophication in terms of PO_4-equivalents is a production-based load measure. The corresponding quality-based measure is a concentration of phosphate (PO_4) or of phosphorus (P) in water expressed in mg/L. According to the EPA, in the United States, most state water quality standards are expressed in terms of P, not PO_4, but the one measure can easily be converted into the other. The PO_4 molecule is three times as heavy as the P atom, so the PO_4 concentration is three times that of the P concentration.[14]

The final water-borne contaminant we consider here is radioactive waste. For radioactive substances that emit alpha particles, the U.S. EPA's maximum contaminant level in drinking water is 15 picocuries per liter.[15]

Biological Waste

Examples of concentrated biological waste are raw sewage from confined animal feeding operations and waste products from animal rendering operations. We do not discuss reporting on these in any detail, because these forms of waste can be reported in terms of chemical or biological load in the same manner as wastewater.

Atmospheric Pollutants

The emission of greenhouse gases is an example of atmospheric pollution, which we covered in Chapter 6. There, the principle of measurement was to establish a standard greenhouse gas (carbon dioxide) and measure all other greenhouse gas emissions in CO2-equivalents, using emission factors that relate the global warming potential of other greenhouse gases to carbon dioxide. We use a similar approach to measure and report on the emissions of other types of gas that have negative consequences for the environment. The environmental impacts that we consider in this chapter are the depletion of the ozone layer, the acidification of water bodies or water vapor, and the creation of smog.

(CFCs), which are a second category of atmospheric pollutant, in addition to the GHGs. The standard for measuring CFC emissions is CFC-11, trichlorofluoromethane, so the *ozone-depleting potentials* of other members of the CFC family are expressed as multiples of the CFC-11 potential. In the study of greenhouse gases, the global warming potentials of the Kyoto gases were described using emissions factors related to CO2. More generally, the environmental impacts of other members of a class are described using *characterization factors*. Ozone-depleting emissions are thus expressed in CFC-11-equivalents and reported as a mass, like pounds or kilograms, analogous to CO2e emissions.

A third form of atmospheric pollution is acid rain, caused by the presence of sulfur dioxide (SO2) in the atmosphere, which reacts with water molecules to form sulfuric acid. The *acidification potentials* (AP) of pollutants are expressed as a multiple of that of SO2, so the emission of pollutants that cause acidification is measured as the mass of SO2-equivalents.

Photochemical smog is a fourth type of atmospheric pollution. It is caused by oxides of nitrogen and volatile organic compounds (VOCs) from fossil-fuel combustion reacting with naturally occurring ozone in the lower atmosphere. The smog formation potential (SFP), also called photochemical oxidation potential (PCOP), of these compounds is expressed as multiples of the smog formation potential of ethylene (C2H4).[16] Also used as a standard for rating smog formation potential is 1-octene ($CH_2CHC_6H_{13}$), which is a derivative of ethylene.[17]

Solid Waste

Solid waste is distinguished as either hazardous or nonhazardous. The nonhazardous form is generally known as municipal solid waste (MSW), but it includes other forms of solid waste that may be discarded to a landfill, such as construction and demolition debris, nonhazardous industrial waste, and sludge from municipal wastewater treatment plants.

Nonhazardous Waste

Municipal solid waste (MSW) is nonhazardous waste from homes, schools, hospitals, and businesses. It includes compostable waste such as food scraps and yard clippings and more durable nonhazardous waste such as paper, wood, textiles, rubber, plastics, glass, rubber, and metal. It also includes items that may have a toxic impact on the environment but are not considered hazardous, such as paint, batteries, tires, appliances, and consumer electronics.[18]

In the cradle-to-grave system for waste, the total amount of municipal solid waste *generated* is reduced by the amount *composted* and the amount *recycled*, and the result is accounted for as "discards after recovery." Those discards are then either *combusted* in a waste-to-energy system or *discarded* in a landfill. The waste that is either composted or recycled is called "recovered." In 2013, a little more than half (52.8%) of America's municipal solid waste was discarded, 34.3% was recovered, and 12.9% was combusted for energy.[19]

Corporate accounting for solid waste follows the EPA's accounting for America's solid waste stream. Firms account for their total waste generated and its division into the four components: waste composted, waste recycled, waste combusted for energy, and waste directed to a landfill. Each of these destinations has different environmental impacts. Solid waste is reported preferably by weight, but sometimes it is reported by firms as a volume measure due to the ease of counting the number of full waste receptacles, of a standard volume, that are emptied by the firm's waste management service.

In the GRI's system for corporate waste accounting (G4-EN23), hazardous and nonhazardous wastes are accounted for separately. The nonhazardous forms of waste that are not considered MSW (including construction and demolition debris, nonhazardous industrial waste, and municipal wastewater sludge) may be added together with MSW in a report of waste generated and recycled.

In corporate sustainability reporting, the key summative metric for waste is waste productivity, defined as revenue per ton of waste. The waste in the denominator of that ratio should be waste directed to a landfill, because that has the most significant environmental and social effects. Thus, the percentage of solid waste that a firm recovers from its waste stream, and thus diverts from landfills, is a factor that improves higher waste productivity. Waste is diverted either by being composted or recycled. It is identified as "waste recovered" or "waste diverted from landfill," and is commonly reported as both an absolute measure (U.S. tons or metric tons) and as a percentage of total waste generated.

Corporate accounting for waste may also report the financial savings attributed to the recovery of waste from the waste stream.

Hazardous Waste

Hazardous waste is generally distinguished as household hazardous waste (HHW) and industrial hazardous waste. Household hazardous waste consists of products that contain corrosive, toxic, ignitable, or reactive ingredients. These include paints, cleaners, oils, batteries, and pesticides. Though they may be diverted to landfills, they require special care in disposal.[20]

In the same way that chemically loaded wastewater is reported in terms of the concentration of specific pollutants, when a firm has hazardous waste emissions, they tend to be reported as quantities of the specific substances. The EPA tracks hazardous waste in more than 630 chemicals and chemical categories, of and arsenic. These are generated primarily in zinc and gold mining (for lead) and steel manufacturing (for asbestos).

The PBT chemicals are lead, mercury, dioxin, and their compounds. Within such families, there may be many compounds having varying toxicities all produced from the same or similar types of production facilities. Firms report an aggregate measure of the toxicity of their emissions from such facilities using a concept similar to the characterization factor. Toxic equivalency factors (TEFs) describe the toxicity of each member of the family in terms of a standard member. In the dioxin family, the reference compound is the most toxic form of dioxin, 2,3,7,8-TCDD. The mass of each member of the family emitted by a facility is multiplied by its TEF to obtain a toxicity mass, which is summed over all members of the family to yield a total emission in toxicity equivalents (e.g., grams-TEQ).[23]

The total quantity of industrial hazardous waste generated annually in the United States is broken down into the quantities recycled, recovered for energy, treated, or disposed/released. Of the 25.63 billion pounds of production-related hazardous waste tracked in 2013 in the U.S., 36% was recycled, 11% was used in energy recovery, 37% was treated, and 16% was disposed or released.[24]

The measure of the number of pounds of toxic chemicals tracked in a year does not account for the differing toxicity of these chemicals. Following the logic of toxicity equivalents, the EPA publishes annually the results of its Risk Screening Environmental Indicators (RSEI) model, which accounts for the toxicity of different chemicals. The RSEI "hazard" estimate consists of the number of pounds of chemicals released multiplied by the toxicity weight of each chemical. RSEI also calculates an "RSEI risk score" for the nation, which accounts for the amount released, its toxicity, the location of the release (relative to populations), the pattern of the chemical's "transport" through the environment, and the human exposure by extent and route (ingestion, inhalation, skin).[25] The RSEI model could be used by a company to track and report its toxic emissions in an aggregate form.

In the European Union System for the Evaluation of Substances (EUSES), a standard toxic material used for a summative measure of the toxic effects on human life, terrestrial life, and aquatic life is 1,4-DCB (dichlorobenzene). The toxicity of a material is measured in relation to 1,4-DCB as a characterization factor, from which emissions can be reported in 1,4-DCB-equivalents. The summative measure of toxic emissions would be reported as mass (kilograms or pounds) of 1,4-DCB-equivalents emitted per year or per unit of product produced.[26]

Two quality-based summative indicators, used to describe the toxicity of the materials depending on their method of use, are the human toxicity potential by ingestion (HTPI) and the human toxicity potential by inhalation or dermal exposure (HTPE). HTPI is the dosage that is lethal to 50% of rats by oral ingestion, and HTPE is the

TABLE 8.1 HMIS Levels of Toxicity

4	Life-threatening, major, or permanent damage may result from single or repeated overexposures (e.g., hydrogen cyanide).
3	Major injury likely unless prompt action is taken and medical treatment is given.
2	Temporary or minor injury may occur.
1	Irritation or minor reversible injury possible.
0	No significant risk to health.

dosage that is lethal to 50% of flathead minnows.[27] Each of these measures expresses the concept of the median lethal dose, commonly denoted LD_{50}, which is quantified typically as milligrams of substance per kilogram of body mass.[28]

Underwriters Laboratories, in its UL 880 standard for the sustainability of manufacturing firms, has an indicator related to employee health and safety that calls for an inventory of chemicals based in part on the Acute Toxicity Rating of the Hazardous Materials Identification System (HMIS). In that rating system, chemicals are identified in four levels of hazard as shown in Table 8.1.[29]

Waste Metrics in the Standards for Disclosure

Regarding reports on waste, the corporate standards for disclosure and the metrics for corporate ratings and for certification on sustainability focus on wastewater and on the generation and recovery (composting and recycling) of nonhazardous solid waste. Some explicitly include measures of hazardous waste, but in the standards for disclosure and for certification, firms must decide what information is material to their stakeholders and report accordingly. Thus, even if a standard for disclosure or certification does not call on the reporter to provide details about hazardous wastes, those details are required implicitly when the reporter deems them to be material. In the rating systems, by contrast, the firm being rated is not involved in the determination of materiality; that is the responsibility of the rater and is reflected in industry-specific components of the rating system. The following accounts of the required reporting in various standards should therefore be taken as illustrative, not complete.

GRI

Among the indicators of the GRI-G4 guidelines for disclosure that relate to wastewater and other forms of waste, two ask for an account of materials used, broken down so that the percentage of materials recycled may be calculated:

- G4-EN2: materials used (weight or volume), by recycled, not recycled
- G4-EN10: Percentage and total volume of water recycled and reused.

- G4-EN1: materials used by renewable, nonrenewable.

What is missing in that item is an account of the recycling of the nonrenewable resources, for it is the disposal of nonrenewables, as opposed to their recycling, that constitutes a "waste" of the resource.

Of the four items related to solid waste, three focus on environmental impacts and one reveals efforts to design for recyclability:

- G4-EN23: Total weight of waste by type and disposal method
- G4-EN25: Weight of transported, imported, exported, or treated waste deemed hazardous under the terms of the Basel Convention Annex I, II, III, and VIII and percentage of transported waste shipped internationally
- G4-EN24: Total number and volume of significant spills
- G4-EN28: Percentage of products sold and their packaging materials that are reclaimed by category.

EN23 could have been combined with EN1 in a call for a complete accounting of materials used, broken down in three ways: by the amounts impounded in products, the amounts recovered, and the amounts discarded, the latter differentiated by disposal method as in EN23. Such an account of materials used, recovered, and discarded would be consistent with the EPA's current focus on sustainable materials management (SMM).[30] Firms will not generally know how the discarded waste is disposed of by a third party, whether by combustion for energy or by interment in a landfill, so it would not make sense to include combustion of waste as a disposal method for firm-level reporting.

Three items in GRI-G4 concern wastewater, one calling directly for the percentage of water recycled and reused, another calling for wastewater quality, and a third that is implicitly about the environmental impacts of wastewater:

- G4-EN10: Percentage and total volume of water recycled and reused
- G4-EN22: Total water discharge by quality and destination
- G4-EN26: Identity, size, protected status, and biodiversity value of water bodies and related habitats significantly affected by the organization's discharges of water and runoff.

Wastewater is only implicit in EN10 through the reference to recycling. This item may be motivated more by a concern for the equitable use of water in a water-stressed region. The total water withdrawal is called for in EN8. In contrast, EN22 calls directly for information about the quality of discharged water. The GRI-G4 *Implementation Manual* lists biochemical oxygen demand and total suspended solids as "standard effluent parameters" to be reported, while noting that the choice of water quality metrics will depend on the firm's industry and national or regional regulations.

Airborne emissions are reported in GRI-G4 under two items:

- G4-EN20: Emissions of ozone-depleting substances
- G4-EN21: NO_X, SO_X, and other significant air emissions.

EN20 calls for a report of ozone-depleting substances (ODSs) in metric tons of CFC-11-equivalent. Among the other types of air emissions called for under EN21 are persistent organic pollutants (POPs), volatile organic compounds (VOCs), hazardous air pollutants (HAPs), particulate matter, and other categories of air emissions for which the reporter is subject to regulation.

Sectoral disclosure requirements in the GRI prescribe more specific reporting for companies in waste-intensive industries. Examples include identifying types of sources for NO_x, SO_x, and other significant emissions and providing specific details on significant spills (mining); NO_x, SO_x, and other significant emissions as an intensity measure and separately reporting unusual cleanup activities, spills of even small quantities that reach the soil or water, and industry-specific types of waste (oil and gas); reporting ambient air quality levels and the use of de-icing fluids (airports); and specifying the types of materials used and the percentage recycled in each and reporting recycled grey water and black water (construction).

SASB

The Sustainability Accounting Standards Board's approach to disclosure is focused on materiality to investors. Across various industries, SASB calls for the familiar data on GHG emissions, water and waste management, and materials management. Where it seems appropriate, SASB probes for more detailed information specific to the industry, such as airborne emissions (Metals & Mining, Oil & Gas, Iron & Steel, Chemicals), hazardous materials (Metals & Mining, Oil & Gas Refining, Aerospace), ecosystem protection (Hotels & Lodging), wastewater and chemical discharges (Cruise Lines), fuel efficiency (Cable & Satellite, Health Care Distribution), and biodiversity impacts (Metals & Mining, Oil & Gas, Coal, Construction Materials).

For financial service firms, excepting insurance companies, and for several service industries including education, SASB does not even call for information about direct GHG emissions, water, or waste.

Waste Metrics in the Corporate Rating Systems

The corporate rating systems are involuntary, so they are based on publicly available [illegible] these ratings usually do so as a proprietary service to their clients, so there may be only limited public information about the details of the rating systems, particularly when a rater varies the set of indicators and weights for different industries. Even so, we observe interesting variations among the rating systems in how they treat the subject of waste.

DJSI

We observed previously that the indicators that constitute the DJSI's Total Sustainability Score depend on the reporting firm's industry. The Corporate Sustainability Assessment questionnaire consists of 80–120 indicators of sustainability, some of which pertain to subcategories for climate change governance and climate strategy, environmental footprint, and environmental reporting. However, in all cases a firm must identify its top three material issues pertaining to the environment and specify for each one a key performance indicator that the firm measures and communicates externally.

The DJSI metric includes many items that pertain not just to the firm's actions or performance measures on environmental impacts but to a firm's strategies, policies, and management systems. Examples are the presence and communication of an environmental policy, an environmental management system, and the management of environmental crises.

In one publicly available sample questionnaire, the only specifically waste-related indicator is total waste generated, from which a waste intensity measure can be calculated relative to sales revenues or production volume. In the second sample questionnaire, which appears to be for gold mining companies, reporters would reveal the percentage of gold produced from operations that are certified for using cyanide, the most widely used reagent for extracting gold, in addition to a measure of waste intensity.

FTSE4Good

In the Pollution & Resources theme (subcategory) of FTSE4Good, a firm gets points for having policies and targets to reduce pollution and waste and for making progress on those targets. Specific disclosures include emissions of ozone-depleting substances and the acidifying and smog forming emissions (NO_x, SO_x, and VOCs). Data on the firm's discharge of recycled and nonrecycled waste also contributes to the theme score.

ASSET4 ESG

The 226 key performance indicators computed from more than 500 data items in the ASSET4 ESG metric put substantial emphasis, in every aspect of sustainability, on policies, implementation, monitoring, and improvement, not just on environmental impacts. Emission reduction and reduction in resource utilization are important themes in ASSET4 ESG and are captured in absolute data, as well as intensity measures. Specific items call for data on emissions of fluorinated GHGs (F-gases), ozone-depleting substances, the acidifying and smog-forming emissions (NO_x, SO_x, and VOCs), hazardous waste, water discharges, waste recycling, and the impacts of spills.

Global 100 and Newsweek *Green Rankings*

The Global 100 is a simple metric, consisting of only 12 indicators. One of these, accounting for 8.3% of the Global 100 summary measure, provides the data needed to calculate waste productivity (the inverse of an efficiency or intensity measure) based on total waste generated. The Global 100 water measure is about water used, not wastewater.

Newsweek's Green Rankings use the Global 100 indicators for water and waste, but the Green Rankings give extra credit for a firm having externally audited environmental metrics.

Waste Metrics in the Certification Standards

Certification according to a sustainability standard is voluntary, so the standard setters tend to publish the details of their assessment methods in a technical manual available to applicants and to the public. The STARS and UL 880 standards are focused on specific industrial contexts, higher education, and manufacturing organizations, so their standards do not depend on other details of the applicant, but they should be expected to differ in ways that reflect these industrial contexts. The B-Corp standard is targeted to organizations of all types, including nonprofits, so its indicators and weights have been differentiated to recognize differences among organizations according to their industry and size. We base our review here on the standard that would apply to mid-sized universities to permit a direct comparison with STARS.

STARS 2.0

STARS is the sustainability certification program for colleges and universities in North America. STARS 2.0 awards 10 points (5%) out of approximately 200 for indicators related to waste. These are

- OP 22: Waste Minimization (5 points)
- OP 23: Waste Diversion (3 points)

- OP 24 Construction and Demolition Waste Diversion (1 point)
- OP 25 Hazardous Waste Management (1 point)

measure and an absolute performance measure. It gives half of its points (2.5 of 5) for a reduction of waste generation of up to 50% from a baseline year. The other half is awarded for an absolute waste generation amount that is up to 90% below a threshold of 0.45 U.S. tons (0.41 metric tons) of waste per year per average campus user.

The waste generated that does not get interred in a landfill, called "recovered" by the EPA, is called "diverted" in STARS. For STARS, it includes materials that are reused or resold as well as those composted or recycled as in the EPA's definition. A complication in the definitions is the treatment of incinerated waste. If the incineration is part of a waste-to-energy technology, it is not considered "discarded" by the EPA. Incinerated waste, and landfilled waste, is "disposed" in STARS.

For OP 23, STARS awards the maximum number of points to organizations that divert 100% of their municipal solid waste from landfills and incinerators. In OP 24, the maximum of 1 point is given to organizations that divert 100% of their construction and demolition waste from landfills.

In OP 25, organizations get half of the credit for having in place a strategy to safely dispose of hazardous, special, universal, and nonregulated chemical waste and to minimize their presence in the organization. The other half of the credit is given for having a program to reuse or recycle electronic waste in a responsible manner, e.g., by using certified recyclers.

Item OP 28 concerns wastewater, giving one point to universities that handle 100% of their discharged wastewater using natural wastewater systems (constructed treatment wetlands that mimic the biological, chemical, and physical processes occurring in natural wetlands), from which effluent is treated to secondary or tertiary standards prior to release to water bodies.

UL 880

In the Underwriters Laboratories standard for manufacturing companies, 48 points out of 1,005 (4.8%) are allocated to indicators related to solid waste management. Water and wastewater are addressed together in Section 19 of the standard, which was discussed in the previous chapter. In item 20.2, UL 880 gives 10 of the 48 points for having a waste inventory system that tracks solid waste by type (consumable versus durable materials as defined in the LEED:EBOM manual[31]) and discard method. In item 20.3, applicants earn up to 8 points for having a plan for waste reduction that includes waste prevention, recycling, and composting or reuse.

In item 20.4, applicants earn up to 25 points for demonstrating that they have met previous self-defined targets for waste reduction, have set targets for the future, and are making progress toward those; alternatively, reporters may have a zero-waste goal and earn points proportional to their achievement relative to a criterion of 95% reduction from a baseline year.

In item 20.5, organizations earn 5 points by disclosing their waste management performance publicly in an annual report. Required data are the materials stream disposal components (recycled, reused, recovered, incinerated, landfilled) identified by type (consumable or durable) and hazard level (nonhazardous, hazardous), with all data reported in absolute terms by weight and normalized by revenues to form intensity measures.

B-Corp

The B-Corp standard focuses on management systems. Applicants earn points by having programs or systems for environmental management, waste recovery and recycling, reduction of chemical use, and environmentally preferable purchasing (indicators EN2.04 to EN2.17) and hazardous waste (EN4.17). Data on waste generated and waste diverted (reused or recycled) are called for but are not weighted in the scoring system. There is no indicator that reports wastewater management specifically.

Integration of Waste Metrics in Life-Cycle Analysis

When a company wants to certify a product for general sustainability, it will typically be required by an evaluator to provide data from a life-cycle analysis (LCA) of the product. In the analysis of organizational sustainability, LCA provides both the concepts and methods needed to yield a summative measure of the environmental impact of an organization.

Life-cycle assessment identifies the environmental impacts of a product across its life cycle, from raw materials extraction through production, use, and disposal. The United Nations Environment Program sees LCA as a window into the "world behind the product."[32] The greenhouse gas emissions studied in Chapter 6 are one such impact, and we have seen some of the other environmental impacts in this chapter. Table 8.2 lists the 11 types of environmental impact that are commonly studied in life-cycle analysis.[33]

The last two rows of Table 8.2, for water use and other resource use, are stated in relation to the quantity of the resource that is left in reserve, as we saw in Chapter 7 on water accounting, because the use of a resource has less impact on human life if the resource is in abundant supply, but it should be recorded as a significant impact when the resource is locally scarce.[34]

According to the EPA's *Principles and Practice* document,[35] an LCA should result in a summative measure of the total environmental impact of the product or process under study, yet it is the most difficult step in the process:

Impact Category	Measurement Units	Environmental Results
[illegible] potential (GWP)	[illegible]	[illegible] longer seasons, forest loss/change, and change in wind and ocean patterns.
Ozone depletion potential (ODP)	CFC-11 equivalents	increased ultraviolet radiation
Acidification potential (AP)	Sulfur dioxide (SO_2) equivalents, or hydrogen (H^+) ion equivalents	building corrosion, water body acidification
Photochemical smog formation potential (SFP)	Ethane (C_2H_6) or ethylene (C_2H_4) equivalents	decreased visibility, eye irritation, respiratory tract and lung irritation, and vegetation damage
Eutrophication potential (EP) (overstimulation of biological systems)	Phosphate (PO_4) equivalents	nutrients (phosphorous and nitrogen) enter water bodies, causing excessive plant growth and oxygen depletion
Terrestrial toxicity potential (TTP)	Depends on the type of organism. LC50[i] can be converted to 1,4-DCB equivalents	decreased production and biodiversity and decreased wildlife
Aquatic toxicity potential (ATP)	Aquatic ecotoxicity potentials as 1,4-DCB equivalents	decreased aquatic plant and insect production and biodiversity and decreased fish populations
Human health (toxicity)	Human toxicity potentials as 1,4-DCB equivalents	increased illness and death
Energy use	Megajoules (MJ)	depletion of nonrenewable energy reserves
Land use	Solid waste: mass and volume	loss of terrestrial habitat for wildlife and decreased landfill space
Water use	Ratio of quantity of water used versus quantity of resource left in reserve	loss of available water
Other resource use	Ratio of quantity of resource used versus quantity of resource left in reserve.	decreased resources for future generations

[i] LC50, also called the median lethal concentration, is the concentration of a toxic substance in the surrounding medium that will kill 50% of a sample population of a specific test animal in a specific period of time through exposure via inhalation, expressed in mg/L or ppm.

The weighting step (also referred to as valuation) of a life cycle impact assessment assigns weights or relative values to the different impact categories based on their perceived importance or relevance. Weighting is important because the impact categories should also reflect study goals and stakeholder values. As stated earlier, harmful air emissions could be of relatively higher concern in an air non-attainment zone than the same emission level in an area with better air quality. Because weighting is not a scientific process, it is vital that the weighting methodology is clearly explained and documented.

Although weighting is widely used in LCAs, the weighting stage is the least developed of the impact assessment steps and also is the one most likely to be challenged for integrity. In general, weighting includes the following activities:

- Identifying the underlying values of stakeholders
- Determining weights to place on impacts
- Applying weights to impact indicators.

Weighted data could possibly be combined across impact categories, but the weighting procedure must be explicitly documented.

Several issues exist that make weighting a challenge. The first issue is subjectivity. According to ISO 14040:2006, Life Cycle Assessment, any judgment of preferability is a subjective judgment regarding the relative importance of one impact category over another. Additionally, these value judgments may change with location or time of year. For example, someone located in Los Angeles, CA, may place more importance on the values for photochemical smog than would a person located in Cheyenne, Wyoming. The second issue is derived from the first: how should users fairly and consistently make decisions based on environmental preferability, given the subjective nature of weighting? Developing a truly objective (or universally agreeable) set of weights or weighting methods is not feasible. However, several approaches to weighting do exist and are used successfully for decision-making, such as the Analytic Hierarchy Process, the Modified Delphi Technique, and decision analysis using multi-attribute theory.

Discussion

The two standards for disclosure, GRI and SASB, differ markedly in their treatment of environmental aspects of sustainability. We saw in Chapter 1 that the SASB standard for Media Production and Distribution did not call for any environmental indicators, while the GRI together with its Media Sectoral Disclosure had 34 environmental indicators, 5 of which pertain to waste. For the Metals and Mining industry, there was more balance between the two standards, with 6 indicators in the GRI for 3 in SASB.

Most of the rating and certification systems put substantial weight on reporting organizations having policies and management systems in place to deal effectively with waste. The DJSI and ASSET4 ESG ratings are like that, as are the UL 880 and the B-Corp certifications. Where quantitative data are required, it tends to be waste generated, reported both in absolute terms and as an intensity measure, had to be reported.

The specifics of the RobecoSAM corporate sustainability assessment vary across industries, but a section on Operational Eco-efficiency is common to all 59 industries for which RobecoSAM has developed versions of their Corporate Sustainability Assessment.[36] The CSA asks for data on total waste generated, not including waste sold for a positive price nor recycled internally. This total does not distinguish categories of waste as called for in GRI-G4 EN23, such as waste that is sent for recycling or composing or is used for energy recovery, as distinct from that which is sent to a landfill or incinerated.

The lack of data about recycled waste in those ratings and certifications is potentially confusing, because the material concern of investors, who see tipping fees (disposal fees) rising at landfills, should be with the waste generated *net of* waste recycled, reused, composted, or otherwise diverted from landfills and incinerators. Thus, investors should expect a firm to disclose the components of its waste stream, including the amounts recovered through recycling and composting and the amount used for energy production, not just the total.

Wastewater disclosure is also very limited in those metrics. Neither of the sample questionnaires for the DJSI has items related to wastewater. The Global 100 and *Newsweek* Green Rankings do not consider wastewater, nor does the B-Corp certification.

ASSET4 ESG and STARS call for some reporting on wastewater and extensive reporting of the components of the solid waste stream and the methods of disposal. ASSET4 ESG has indicators for wastewater, four types of airborne emissions, recycled solid waste, and hazardous waste. STARS gives credit for natural wastewater systems, waste diversion by various methods, and hazardous waste policies. In contrast to ASSET4 ESG, which gives a lot of credit for policies and management systems related to waste, in STARS only 0.5 points out of 10 related to policy; all others were directly for the achievement of performance criteria.

The example of STARS is also instructive, because it shows that, at least within a single industry sector, a group of industry peers (the STARS technical committee) could establish specific expectations for performance on waste generation at levels that were deemed reasonable (0.45 tons/user/year) and exemplary (90% below 0.45 tons/user/year).

The STARS 2.0 manual offers a useful suggestion for organizations that are trying to quantify their solid waste stream. It recognizes that many organizations cannot track all their quantities of waste by weight and that organizations therefore might want to record at least some parts of their material flow by volume. STARS recommends that reporters convert volumetric numbers to weights using standards given by the EPA[37] or UNEP.[38]

The brief presentation of life-cycle analysis in this chapter was a reminder that within a particular environmental aspect, the impact of any particular substance can be expressed as its "potential" to impact that aspect, and that potential can be measured in relation to a reference substance that has that impact. We saw in Chapter 6 that the global warming potentials of the seven Kyoto gases could all be expressed as factors relative to CO2 and thus stated as CO2-equivalents. The same principle was applied in this chapter to acidification (SO2-e), ozone depletion (CFC-11-e), smog formation ($C2H_4$-e), eutrophication (PO_4-e), and toxicity (1,4-DCB-e). Further, we saw that the concept of emission factor, used to calculate the greenhouse gas emissions from the use of a particular fuel, generalizes to the *characterization factor* of a substance for an impact, which is the amount of the environmental impact resulting from the use of a standard amount (mass or volume) of the substance.

The details of LCA are beyond the scope of this book, but the use of life-cycle analysis for products shows that there is a wide range of environmental impacts that can be studied in the assessment of sustainability and that scholars and practitioners do attempt to create summative metrics of total environmental impact. That work may influence the future development of organizational metrics for sustainability.

Notes

1 Cho, R. 2012. Rare Earth Metals: Will We Have Enough? State of the Planet. Columbia University Earth Institute. Available at <http://blogs.ei.columbia.edu/2012/09/19/rare-earth-metals-will-we-have-enough/> Accessed August 2015.

2 McDonough, W., and M. Braungart. 1998. The Next Industrial Revolution. *The Atlantic Monthly*, 282:4, 82–92.

3 Global Compact. 2014. Corporate Water Disclosure Guidelines: Toward a Common Approach to Reporting Water Issues. CEO Water Mandate. Available at <http://ceowatermandate.org/disclosure/> Accessed August 2015.

4 Standard pore sizes from 0.45 to 1.5 microns appear in the literature. For 0.45 microns, see Oram, B. 2015. Stream Water Quality—Importance of Total Suspended Solids / Turbidity. Available at <www.water-research.net/index.php/stream-water-quality-importance-of-total-suspended-solids-turbidity> For 1.5 microns, see StormwateRx. 2015. Total Suspended Solids. Available at <www.stormwaterx.com/Resources/Industrial Pollutants/TSS.aspx>

5 MDEQ. 2015. Total Suspended Solids. State of Michigan Department of Environmental Quality. Available at <www.michigan.gov/documents/deq/wb-npdes-TotalSuspended Solids_247238_7.pdf> Accessed July 2015.

6 USGS. 2015. Turbidity-Units of Measurement. Oregon Water Science Center. Available at <http://or.water.usgs.gov/grapher/fnu.html> Accessed July 2015.

7 U.S. EPA. 2015g. National Primary Drinking Water Regulations. Available at <http://water.epa.gov/drink/contaminants/upload/mcl-2.pdf> Accessed July 2015.

8 WHO. 1958. International Standards for Drinking Water. World Health Organization. Available at <http://apps.who.int/iris/bitstream/10665/43845/1/a91160.pdf> Accessed July 2015.

12 EPA. 2011b. *Principles of Design and Operations of Wastewater Treatment Pond Systems for Plant Operators, Engineers, and Managers*. U.S. Environmental Protection Agency. Report EPA/600/R-11/088 (August 2011). Available at <www2.epa.gov/sites/production/files/2014–09/documents/lagoon-pond-treatment-2011.pdf> Accessed July 2015.

13 WHO. 1958. Op. cit.

14 EPA. 2015j. Phosphorus. U.S. Environmental Protection Agency. Available at <http://water.epa.gov/type/rsl/monitoring/vms56.cfm> Accessed July 2015.

15 EPA. 2015g. National Primary Drinking Water Regulations. Op cit.

16 Fermeglia, M., L. Toma, and G. Longo. 2011. Process Sustainability Prediction: A Computer Aided Design Tool for Sustainable Industrial Development. *Ecosystems and Sustainable Development VIII*, 144, 165–176.

17 See Allen, D. T., and K. S. Rosselot. 1997. *Pollution Prevention for Chemical Processes*. Wiley-Interscience.

18 EPA. 2015a. Municipal Solid Waste. U.S. Environmental Protection Agency. Available at <http://www.epa.gov/epawaste/nonhaz/municipal/index.htm> Accessed July 2015.

19 EPA. 2013a. Advancing Sustainable Materials Management: Facts and Figures 2013. U.S. Environmental Protection Agency. Available at <www.epa.gov/epawaste/nonhaz/municipal/pubs/2013_advncng_smm_rpt.pdf> Accessed July 2015.

20 EPA. 2015b. Household Hazardous Waste. U.S. Environmental Protection Agency. Available at <www.epa.gov/epawaste/conserve/materials/hhw.htm> Accessed July 2015.

21 EPA. 2015c. TRI National Analysis 2013. U.S. Environmental Protection Agency. Available at <www2.epa.gov/toxics-release-inventory-tri-program/2013-toxics-release-inventory-national-analysis-supporting> Accessed July 2015.

22 EPA. 2015d. Release Chemical Report, 2013 Dataset Released March 2015. Available at <http://iaspub.epa.gov/triexplorer/tri_release.chemical> Accessed July 2015.

23 EPA. 2010. Recommended Toxicity Equivalence Factors (TEFs) for Human Health Risk Assessments of 2,3,7,8-Tetrachlorodibenzo-P-Dioxin and Dioxin-Like Compounds. U.S. Environmental Protection Agency IPA/100/R 10/005 December 2010. Available at <www.epa.gov/raf/files/tefs-for-dioxin-epa-00-r-10–005-final.pdf> Accessed August 2015.

24 EPA. 2015c. TRI National Analysis 2013.

25 Ibid.

26 BRE. 2015. Ecotoxicity. Available at <https://www.bre.co.uk/greenguide/page.jsp?id=2099> Accessed August 2015.

27 Fermeglia, M., L. Toma, and G. Longo. 2011. Process Sustainability Prediction: A Computer Aided Design Tool for Sustainable Industrial Development. *Ecosystems and Sustainable Development VIII*, 144, 165–176.

28 Wikipedia. 2015d. Median Lethal Dose. Last modified July 10, 2015. Available at <https://en.wikipedia.org/wiki/Median_lethal_dose> Accessed July 2015.

29 Wikipedia. 2015b. Hazardous Materials Identification System. Last modified February 16, 2015. Available at <https://en.wikipedia.org/wiki/Hazardous_Materials_Identification_System> Accessed August 2015.

30 EPA. 2015e. Sustainable Materials Management. U.S. Environmental Protection Agency. Available at <www.epa.gov/epawaste/conserve/smm/> Accessed July 2015.
31 USGBC. 2008. *LEED Existing Buildings: Operations and Maintenance Reference Guide*, 1st edition. MR credits 7.1 and 7.2. U.S. Green Building Council.
32 Fava, J. A. 2002. Life Cycle Initiative: A Joint UNEP/SETAC Partnership to Advance the Life-Cycle Economy. *The International Journal of Life Cycle Assessment*, 7:4, 196–198.
33 Scientific Applications International Corporation. 2006. Life Cycle Assessment: Principles and Practice. U.S. Environmental Protection Agency. Report # EPA/600/R-06/060, p. 49. Available at <www.epa.gov/nrmrl/std/lca/lca.html> Accessed August 2015.
34 Carre, A. S., and R. E. Horne. 2009. Will the Well Run Dry? Developments in Water Resource Planning and Impact Assessment. In R. Horne, T. Grant, & K. Verghese (eds.) *Life Cycle Assessment: Principles, Practice and Prospects.* Collingwood: CSIRO Publishing, pp. 93–106.
35 Scientific Applications International Corporation. 2006. Life Cycle Assessment.
36 RobecoSAM. 2015c. RobecoSAM's Corporate Sustainability Assessment Companion (April 2015). RobecoSAM. Available at <https://assessments.robecosam.com/documents/RobecoSAM_CSA_Companion.pdf>
37 EPA. 2015f. Standard Volume-to-Weight Conversion Factors. U.S. Environmental Protection Agency. Available at <www.epa.gov/osw/conserve/tools/recmeas/docs/guide_b.pdf> Accessed July 2015.
38 UNEP. 2009. Developing Integrated Solid Waste Management Plan Training Manual, Volume 1: Waste Characterization and Quantification with Projections for Future. United Nations Environment Program. Available at <www.unep.org/ietc/Portals/136/Publications/Waste%20Management/ISWMPlan_Vol1.pdf> Accessed July 2015.

9

SOCIAL IMPACTS

The environmental aspects of sustainability are the easy part, in the sense that environmental science has been a useful guide to understanding the sustainable relationship of humans to nature. Acid rain was recognizably associated with the production of oxides of sulfur and nitrogen in industrial atmospheric emissions. Climate change has now been recognized as the result of the increasing concentration of greenhouse gases. And, there is not much dispute about the actual and potential effects of these environmental changes on human society. The disputes about sustainability, which have implications for how sustainability should be reported, are focused on the characteristics of a "sustainable" society. Those in turn derive in large measure from the ethics and worldviews of various perspectives on social philosophy. Science is less of a guide here than it is for the environmental aspects of sustainability. A distinction between sustainable business and sustainable development may help us clarify the purpose of reporting social metrics, but even when the discussion is clearly about the one or the other, differences in the characterization of social sustainability are founded on different ethics concerning responsibility, equity, life, sovereignty, and identity.

The most basic ethic underlying the social element of sustainability is that, because the modern corporation is a legal form created by society, the corporation has a responsibility to conform to the laws of the society. In Chapter 4, we recognized this as an egoistic, legalistic ethic and called it the Law of the Concrete Jungle. Beyond that basic ethic, additional social responsibilities of business may be taken on by a firm or expected of a firm under the more comprehensive transactional ethics (relational, reactive, and consequential), distributional ethics, the duty ethic of forbearance, the humanitarian life ethic, and a broad appreciation of diversity under the identity ethic. These ethics push a corporation to be responsive to a range of stakeholders wider than the investors, consumers, and suppliers with whom it has a contractual relationship.[1]

In this chapter, we start with the concept of stakeholder as an organizing framework for the material aspects of social sustainability. Then we look at the variety of approaches taken to measuring social sustainability. As in the previous chapters, we review the indicators required in the various standards for disclosure, corporate ratings, and certification. Here, we will find more diversity of approach than we did in the study of environmental metrics.

Stakeholders for Corporate Social Responsibility

The stakeholder concept is so important to an understanding of corporate social responsibility and to the accounting for corporate social impacts that we begin the analysis of social indicators of sustainability with a review of the meaning of "stakeholder." In Chapter 1, we saw that the Global Reporting Initiative characterizes stakeholders as entities or individuals that the organization would reasonably expect to have the following characteristics:

- They are significantly affected by the organization's activities, and
- Their actions affect the ability of the organization to successfully implement its strategies.

As a special case of the above, the GRI mentions entities or individuals that have rights under law or international conventions that give them a legitimate claim vis-à-vis the organization.

Many corporate standards for sustainability recognize that planning a sustainability report begins with the identification of and engagement with the organization's stakeholders. To be clear, we should add a third element, making that task the "identification *and validation* of and engagement with" stakeholders. The validation is important, because it recognizes explicitly that an organization must choose the stakeholders to whom it will be responsive. For sustainability reporting, the stakeholder relationship is bilateral. The stakeholder must be significantly impacted by the corporation, and the corporation must view the stakeholder as having a legitimate claim to its attention. A unilateral expectation from an individual or entity does not establish its status as a stakeholder.

The organization has an obligation to report information that is "material" to these stakeholders. As the GRI-G4 guidelines remind readers, "Materiality is the threshold at which Aspects [of sustainability] become sufficiently important that they should be reported." Material topics relate to the "reasonable expectations and interests" of the stakeholders or substantively influence the "assessments and decisions" of stakeholders. With that in mind, we shall review the stakeholders whose interests represent a social obligation of the corporation and consider the impacts on these stakeholders that should be considered material for reporting on corporate social responsibility.

Customers as Stakeholders

[illegible] serves its customers well in order to make a profit for investors. A firm's relationship to its customers is therefore driven by financial, not social, considerations. That relationship is transactional. All firms make economic judgments about how they will conduct that relationship, for example, in the amount of resources they invest in product design or customer service. The proper conduct of business transactions is essential to the financial sustainability of the corporation. By this logic, customers should be analyzed as stakeholders under the economic or financial aspect of sustainability. The service of customers is not a social responsibility of business.

However, that logic assumes that businesses and their customers transact in markets with perfect information about price and quality. But not all markets are informationally efficient, and some markets are seriously inefficient. When information about products is limited, unreliable, or slow to get around, the interests of the customer may need to be supported by third-party oversight. That is why governments create and enforce laws about product safety and consumer health. Governments represent society as a whole, including people who may or actually do purchase specific products. Thus, with the nation-state (government) as the stakeholder, material indicators of social sustainability that relate to customers might include:

- The presence in a firm of policies and procedures to identify problems of customer health and safety and to respond to identified problems.
- The number and types of complaints filed by consumers on matters of product health or safety.

It would not be appropriate to include measures of the quality of customer service or of customer satisfaction as a social indicator. Those are strictly economic measures that drive revenues and profits.

Employees as Stakeholders

A sustainable business must be able to function effectively in its labor markets, as well as in its product markets. Thus, a firm must serve its employees well enough to make a competitive profit for investors. However, labor markets are notoriously inefficient, as most competent people discover when they try to change jobs. It is difficult for employers to assess job applicants correctly and completely for a particular job, while the applicants know well their own strengths and limitations. Thus, as in the used car market, the asymmetry of information between the seller of labor and the buyer of labor causes the market to function very inefficiently. Good people want to hold on to their jobs. The worse employees are the ones looking for work. This explains the typical employee's fear of being fired unjustly. Labor markets are also subject to a lock-in effect, where a person learns on the job what is needed by their employer, but that on-the-job knowledge may not be transferable to other employers, so the employee's best option is to stay with their employer, making the employee dependent on the employer and thus subject to exploitation.

The asymmetric information and lock-in effect in labor markets explain why employee rights and human resource management (HRM) practices are a social issue, not merely a transactional, economic issue. One social impact of a firm's HRM practices is therefore the level of dependency of employees on the firm and therefore the risk of exploitation. Those impacts, actual or potential, would affect existing employees' reasonable expectations and interests about their quality of work life and of their assessments and decisions about taking a job offer at the company. Those impacts would be moderated by an ethic of forbearance reflected in the management of the corporation. Indicators that may be material to existing and prospective employees include:

- Employee health and safety
- Training and promotion practices
- Policies for corrective feedback and progressive discipline
- Processes for handling complaints from employees
- Management–labor relations (practices and outcomes)
- Diversity of employees in relation to hiring and promotion
- Use of child labor, forced or compulsory labor
- Compensation policies (minimum wage versus living wage or maximum wage)

Local Communities as Stakeholders

If a standard for sustainability is to require a firm to disclose information about its impacts on the community where it is headquartered or where it operates, that requirement should be justified ethically and logically. The most difficult issues in corporate social responsibility center on a firm's relationship to the local community, because the ethics that underlie a community's expectations or interests may not be shared by the firm. Many such differences of expectation are due to differences of opinion about the respective roles of public and private organizations in community development, which determine the legitimacy of claims for corporate support or attention.

For example, citizens may want to have certain products or services available in their community. In the contemporary Western concept of the role of business in society, private enterprises are not obligated to provide specific products or services. If no enterprises do so, then it would be up to governmental organizations to determine if their provision is in the public interest and should be organized publicly.

Government at all levels has sovereign authority over some aspects of commerce. At the community level, that authority includes siting, permitting, and taxes and in worldviews about the relative dependence of the corporation and the community and their relative inclinations toward forbearance.

Differences among social metrics for sustainability may also reflect differences in the concept of sustainable business on which the metric is based. If sustainable business is taken to mean the long-term survival of the corporation, then obligations to local communities will be more limited than if sustainable business is assumed to mean a firm's contribution to sustainable development, because a firm can choose to avoid or leave communities that might compromise its financial performance. In the arena of sustainability metrics, there is a diversity of viewpoint on this matter. To SASB, sustainable business focuses on the creation of long-term value in a company:

> As it relates to corporate activities, and for the purpose of the SASB Standards, sustainability refers to *environmental*, *social* and *governance* [emphasis original] (ESG) dimensions of a company's operation and performance. More specifically, sustainability includes both the management of a corporation's environmental and social impacts, as well as the management of environmental and social capitals necessary to create long-term value.[2]

The Global Reporting Initiative has it both ways. In item G4-2, reporters are called on to report their impacts that affect "the long-term prospects and financial performance of the organization," but also to account for the "reasonable expectations and interests of the organization's stakeholders." ISO leans toward the other extreme. ISO intends its guidance in the ISO 26000 standard on social responsibility "to assist organizations in contributing to sustainable development."[3]

Considering the community as stakeholder, we understand calls for indicators that relate to the role of business in sustainable community development apart from the responsibilities of business to the natural environment and to investors, customers, and employees. An obvious example of good corporate citizenship relates to community health:

- Prevention of pollution and treatment of spills.

Other items that appear in some standards as evidence of good corporate citizenship rely on other ethical and logical justifications. These include:

- Local employment of workers and managers
- Local sourcing of materials (referring to the impact on local economic development as distinct from the reduction of GHG emissions)
- Local investment (not just "pulling profits" from the community)

- Use of locally constrained resources, such as water
- Treatment of indigenous people.

Nation-State as a Stakeholder

The nation-state as lawmaker is a stakeholder in every business. The lawmaking body sets forth the rules for competition in an industry and for corporate behavior in product and factor markets. The firm is obligated to obey these laws, to pay taxes, and not to bias the formation of public policy. The firm's obligations to the nation-state as stakeholder center on compliance with law. Indicators of compliance with law include:

- Number of lawsuits settled, and fines or penalties paid
- Taxes paid
- Money spent on lobbying and political contributions.

Standards Specific to Social Impacts

The primary standard that is uniquely social, and against which firms may be certified for their social impacts, is the SA8000 standard for social accountability, which we will focus on in this section. As the context for a more extensive discussion of the SA8000, we review a few other forms of code or standard for corporate social responsibility, which focus on working conditions.

The Business Social Compliance Initiative (BSCI) of the Foreign Trade Association offers a Code of Conduct that addresses labor issues in a firm's supply chain, however, they do not present the Code as a certification scheme, nor do they audit or accredit organizations against their Code, thought the requirements in the Code are auditable by third-party assessors. They refer their participants to the SA8000 for certification.[4]

The Electronic Industry Citizenship Coalition (EICC) publishes a Code of Conduct as a set of standards for social, environmental, and ethical issues in supply chain management. EICC version 5.0 was issued in April 2015. EICC offers a Validated Audit Process that guides external auditors in assessing performance against the Code.[5] The Code has sections that outline standards for labor, health and safety, environmental impacts, and business ethics. The labor components relate to forced labor, child labor, working hours, wages, humane treatment, nondiscrimination, and freedom of association. The health and safety aspects are occupational safety, emergency preparedness, occupational injury and illness, industrial hygiene, sanitation, and, where appropriate, food and housing. The ethics portion concerns bribery and corruption, disclosure of information required by law and industry practice, intellectual property rights, fair advertising and competition, whistleblowers' rights, privacy of personal information, and responsible sourcing of minerals.

The Ethical Trading Initiative offers its ETI Base Code as a standard to evaluate working conditions in global supply chains. Formed by a group of companies, trade required of corporate members. The Base Code is a set of 28 points of explanation for 9 general statements about free employment, freedom of association, safe and hygienic working conditions, no child labor, living wages, working hours, nondiscrimination, regular employment, and inhumane treatment.

The Fair Labor Association has its own FLA Code of Conduct consisting of nine Principles of Fair Labor and Responsible Sourcing covering the employment relationship, nondiscrimination, harassment, forced labor, child labor, freedom of association, health and safety, hours of work, and compensation. Its Compliance Benchmarks specify the requirements for meeting each standard in the Code,[7] and its Principles of Monitoring guide the assessment of compliance. Companies "affiliate" with the FLA by passing the FLA's audit of its Code.[8]

SA8000 Social Accountability

Social Accountability International launched its SA8000 standard in 2001 and updated it in 2004, 2008, and 2014. It is a voluntary, auditable standard against which firms may be certified to demonstrate publicly their commitment to the principles, practices, and management systems on which the standard is based.

The SA8000 Standard document summarizes the purpose of the standard:

> The intent of SA8000 is to provide an auditable, voluntary standard, based on the UN Declaration of Human Rights, ILO and other international human rights and labour norms and national labour laws, to empower and protect all personnel within an organisation's control and influence who provide products or services for that organisation, including personnel employed by the organisation itself and by its suppliers, sub-contractors, sub-suppliers and home workers. It is intended that an organisation shall comply with this Standard through an appropriate and effective Management System.[9]

Thus, the purpose of the SA8000 is to demonstrate an organization's protection of the basic human rights of workers. The SA8000 does not address the full range of social impacts of an organization. It is focused on employees as stakeholders. Table 9.1 lists the 8 categories of employment practice that are covered in the SA8000 through a total of 36 indicators and notes the number of indicators in each category.

In addition to these specific indicators, applicants are evaluated on the 26 attributes of the management system that supports human resource practices. The components and number of indicators for each are listed in Table 9.2.

Social Accountability International publishes a Performance Indicator Annex that provides details of how applicants may document their compliance with each indicator in the standard and how assurance organizations should audit applicants.[10]

TABLE 9.1 Categories of Indicators in the SA8000

- Child labor (4)
- Forced and compulsory labor (5)
- Health and safety (10)
- Freedom of association and collective bargaining (3)
- Discrimination (4)
- Disciplinary practices (1)
- Working hours (4)
- Remuneration (5)

TABLE 9.2 Components of the Management System in the SA8000

- Policies, procedures, and records (8)
- Social performance team (2)
- Identification and assessment of risks (2)
- Monitoring (3)
- Internal involvement and communication (1)
- Complaint management and resolution (3)
- External verification and stakeholder engagement (2)
- Corrective and preventive actions (2)
- Training and capacity building (1)
- Management of suppliers and contractors (2)

IFC Performance Standards on Social Sustainability

The International Finance Corporation of the World Bank Group published standards for environmental and social sustainability to ensure that their projects contribute to sustainable development.[11] These include a standard for the assessment and management of social risks and impacts, as well as for the aspects of social sustainability shown in Table 9.3, which reflect a focus on development projects. The IFC standard is sufficiently clear and precise that each indicator can be audited by the IFC, but the standard does not involve weights or points.

The standard for labor and working conditions reflects ILO criteria for employees' rights to information about the terms of employment including grievance mechanisms, rights of association and collective bargaining, avoidance of forced labor and child labor, and healthy and safe working conditions.

Indicators of community health and safety relate to the control of hazardous substances, the use of local ecosystem resources and services, community exposure to disease, and the provision of security services.

The standard for land acquisition and involuntary resettlement includes terms related to the compensation of displaced persons, resettlement and restoration

- Land acquisition and involuntary resettlement
- Indigenous peoples
- Cultural heritage

of livelihood, and grievance procedures. The standard on indigenous peoples is founded on the principles of "free, prior and informed consent" and "informed consultation and participation" in the engagement of indigenous peoples with development projects. Its terms reflect a focus on avoidance of adverse impact rather than minimization. The standard on cultural heritage addresses impacts on contemporary culture, as well as on sites of historical significance. It seeks to ensure adequate consultation and community access on the removal of replicable and nonreplicable cultural heritage.

ISO 26000:2010 Guidance on Social Responsibility

The International Organization for Standardization is known for its auditable standards and the certifications that those standards confer. In addition to those, ISO has developed and published "guidance" documents, which are not auditable and which do not confer certification. Among these is the *International Standard ISO 26000*, which is subtitled "Guidance on social responsibility" to reduce the potential confusion about the auditability of this program.[12]

ISO 26000:2010 is a detailed, 84-page exposition on the concepts, principles, background, trends, and core topics in social responsibility. It was developed over a five-year period through negotiations among representatives of several stakeholder groups: government, NGOs, industry, consumer groups, and labor organizations. Thus, the ISO presents this guidance as representing an international consensus on the topic of social responsibility.[13] In Chapter 10, we will look at the possible differences between sustainable business and sustainable development. On that point, it is noteworthy that the ISO intends the guidance "to assist organizations in contributing to sustainable development."[14]

As a guidance document, ISO 26000 publishes a set of principles by which organizations may formulate policies and management systems to promote social responsibility. It does not put forth a set of specific indicators against which performance may be assessed. It treats social responsibility in seven "core subjects," each of which is broken down into a number of specific topics for organizational attention (Table 9.4), and those 37 topics are further elaborated in a total of 289 "activities and expectations."

Like the GRI-G4 guidelines for disclosure, ISO 26000 does not yield a summative measure of sustainability. However, unlike the ISO 26000, each of the indicators

TABLE 9.4 ISO 26000 Core Subjects and Topics

- Governance (1)
- Human rights (8)
- Labor practices (5)
- Environment (4)
- Fair operating practices (5)
- Consumer issues (7)
- Community involvement and development (7)

in GRI-G4 is specified in sufficient detail that a third-party assurance firm could verify whether a reporting organization has correctly applied the standard for that indicator. Similarly, the SA8000:2010 social accountability standard is specified in sufficient detail, through its Performance Indicator Annex, that it can be audited. In contrast, ISO 26000 refers to the 37 topics of sustainability as "clauses" in the standard, not as requirement, though for each topic, its actions and expectations are sufficiently precise to provide clear and specific guidance to users. Those 289 activities and expectations covering 37 topics of sustainability make the standard comparable in scope and depth to the 350 or so items of information comprising the 91 indicators in the GRI-G4 guidelines for disclosure.

ISO 26000 social responsibility standard includes four topics related to the environment: the prevention of pollution; sustainable resource use; climate change mitigation and adaptation; and protection of the environment, biodiversity, and restoration of natural habitats. The 39 "activities and expectations" among these 4 topics cover the identification and measurement of aspects of each topic, the engagement with relevant stakeholders, and the implementation of activities, stated with more or less specificity, to improve organizational performance on each topic.

The coverage of human rights, labor practices, consumer issues, and community involvement is consistent with the characterization of social impacts in the GRI-G4. In fact, GRI publishes a crosswalk between ISO 26000 and the GRI-G4 framework that recognizes the comparability of coverage between the two standards, finding a difference primarily in the measurement of indicators quantifiably and the auditability of the G4.

Both ISO 26000 and the GRI Guidelines have a significant overlap and convergence in terms of the topics they cover. ISO 26000 offers a comprehensive guidance that provides a structure for companies to organize their activities, which can then be measured and presented in the organization's report by using the GRI Guidelines.[15]

Social Indicators in the GRI and SASB

The indicators on human rights include the screening of contracts and suppliers and assessment of operations, training of employees and security personnel, grievances filed, and violations of the rights of indigenous people. Other human rights

[illegible]	[illegible]	[illegible]
Human rights	[illegible]	[illegible]
Labor practices and decent work	16	67
Product responsibility	9	23
Society	11	30
Totals	**48**	**145**

indicators are incidents of discrimination, freedom of association and collective bargaining, child labor, and forced labor.

The social indicators in the GRI-G4 system are organized into four subcategories: human rights, labor practices and decent work, product responsibility, and society. The number of indicators and data points for each of these subcategories are shown in Table 9.5. Among the 16 indicators of labor practices addressed in the GRI-G4 are outcome measures such as employee turnover, retention after parental leave, workforce diversity, grievances filed, gender ratios in compensation, and rates of absenteeism, occupational illness, and injury; policy indicators such as benefits to full-time and part-time employees, representation on joint worker–management committees, minimum notice periods, and health and safety topics in union agreements; and activity measures such as hours of training and development per employee, percentage of employees getting regular performance reviews, and percentage of suppliers screened for labor practices.

Indicators of product responsibility include policies such as labeling practices and the assessment of health and safety impacts; activities such as noncompliance with regulations or sale of banned products; and outcome measures such as the results of customer satisfaction surveys, the numbers of substantiated complaints about breaches of customer privacy, and fines related to product use.

The "Society" subcategory in the GRI-G4 relates to local community engagement and matters related to corruption, supplier screening on social impacts, and fines for violation of laws and regulations. Charitable donations are categorized with economic indicators and are accounted for among the ways that the firm distributes the value it creates.

GRI Sectoral Disclosures give specific guidance on how to apply the standard disclosures in specific industries, and they call for additional indicators as appropriate to the industries. For example, in mining, the additional disclosures concern the reporter's experience with strikes and lockouts, consultations with unions, and engagement with local communities and indigenous peoples over land rights, mine closures, and resettlement practices.

All SASB standards are industry specific, but most industries have some indicators that SASB would classify as social. Table 9.6 lists the social indictors that may

TABLE 9.6 Select Subcategories of Social Disclosure Topics in SASB Standards

- Customer satisfaction
- Customer health and safety
- Customer privacy
- Disclosure and labeling
- Ethical marketing and advertising
- Communications and engagement
- Community development
- Impact from facilities
- Access to services

be required in SASB's standards.[16] SASB's five broad groupings for disclosure topics include the familiar sustainability categories of Environment, Social Capital, and Human Capital, the latter two covering the "S" in ESG, and Leadership and Governance providing the "G." The fifth category of SASB, Business Model and Innovation, could account for the financial component of a triple-bottom-line classification, but the element of governance may cut across a firm's obligations to stakeholders other than the owners and customers. In its standard for each industry, SASB does not classify disclosure topics by sustainability category, but they are tabulated by category in the Issues Tables provided as a summary of the SASB standard for each industry.[17]

In the example of Media, the only topic that is generically social is item SV0302-05, which calls for the classification of employees by type (executive, professional, other) and by gender and race/ethnicity. The Issues Table for Media classifies as Social item SV0302-04, the management approach to ensuring the journalistic integrity of news, and SV0302-06, policies and practices ensuring pluralism in news content. These two topics each relate to a media firm's social license to operate, as does item SV0302-03, revenue from embedded advertising (sponsored content). Item SV0302-01, fines for libel or slander, would be treated in other standards as social, because it relates to conformity to laws.

Social Indicators in the Corporate Ratings

The corporate ratings represent the contribution of Wall Street to the discussion of sustainable business, where that term is generally taken to mean the long-term ability of a firm to create value, not necessarily the firm's contribution to sustainable development. We have seen in previous chapters that the rating systems used as examples in this book break into two groups, those that require extensive amounts of data (DJSI, ASSET4 ESG, FTSE4Good) and those that are quite parsimonious (Global 100, *Newsweek* Green Rankings). Their treatment of the social impacts of business and the social responsibility of business makes for an interesting contrast with the GRI-G4 and the corporate certification standards.

for some industries. The DJSI publishes two examples for illustration, one for Mining & Metals and another for Diversified Consumer Services,[18] and it publishes a Companion document that gives guidance on answering questions that are common to all 59 industries for which the CSA is specialized.[19]

The preamble to the subsection of the CSA on Stakeholder Engagement sets a tone that highlights the importance of the social relationships of a business and the need for stakeholder engagement to preserve the "social license to operate."

> The rise of civil society and the resulting increase in availability of, and access to, information has increased awareness of the impact that corporate activities can have on societies at large. New communication technologies and social media have enabled stakeholders to better connect and coordinate, multiplying the impact of stakeholders on companies. These circumstances call for the implementation of adequate management strategies with a focus on the identification and management of relationships with stakeholders beyond the traditional boundaries of shareholders, employees and customers. By engaging with the relevant stakeholders, companies can minimize reputational risks (e.g. being the target of a high-profile activist campaign), improve operational efficiency via smooth collaboration with local communities and authorities, and strengthen their social license to operate by gaining greater respectability and credibility.

The DJSI is data intensive overall, and that is no less the case in the Social category. The extensive reporting in the subcategories of social impact for the services industry is shown in Table 9.7 and for mining in Table 9.8. The number of indicators is comparable to the GRI, despite the fact that in the DJSI, indicators related to product responsibility are placed under the "Economic" section of the CSA, not the "Social" section. The number of data points used in the DJSI Social category is greater than that of the GRI-G4, in part because the CSA questionnaire calls for four years of data on a few key indicators and asks respondents to indicate the details of some practices and policies from prespecified lists.

The Services and Mining standards of the DJSI differ substantially in their treatment of the common subcategory Occupational Health and Safety and differ in one respect in the common subcategory Stakeholder Engagement. The OHS category for services is focused almost entirely on employee health and well-being, having indicators dealing with stress management, fitness, flexible work schedules, child and elder care, the management of health programs, and incentives for healthy lifestyles. OHS in mining has none of those, but focuses on occupational illness, fatalities, recordable injuries, near misses, occupational diseases, and policies

TABLE 9.7 Social Subcategories, Indicators, and Data in the DJSI (Consumer Services)

Social Subcategories	*Indicators*	*Data Items*
3.1 Social Reporting	4	6
3.2 Labor Practice and Human Rights	7	24
3.3 Human Capital Development	5	25
3.4 Talent Attraction and Retention	5	23
3.5 Corporate Citizenship and Philanthropy	4	14
3.6 Occupational Health and Safety (Services)	4	28
3.7 Stakeholder Engagement	3	27
Totals	**32**	**147**

TABLE 9.8 Social Subcategories, Indicators, and Data in the DJSI (Mining)

Social Subcategories	*Indicators*	*Data Items*
3.1 Social reporting	4	6
3.2 Labor practice and human rights	7	24
3.3 Human capital development	5	25
3.4 Talent attraction and retention	5	23
3.5 Corporate citizenship and philanthropy	4	14
3.6 Occupational health and safety (mining)	8	52
3.7 Asset closure management (mining)	3	19
3.8 Social Impacts on Communities (Mining)	7	38
3.9 Stakeholder Engagement	3	35
Totals	**46**	**236**

regarding preventive care and treatment for HIV-AIDS, TB, and malaria. The Mining standard (Table 9.8) also has two subcategories not present for Services, namely 3.7 Asset Closure Management and 3.8 Social Impacts on Communities. Both focus on the social impacts of closing mines and the related management practices from the initial planning of a mine to its reclamation.

To compare the DJSI Social category to that of the GRI-G4, we remove GRI-G4's Product Responsibility subcategory, which was treated as economic in the DJSI, and we add the GRI-G4's indicators EC6–EC9 that pertain to local employment and economic impact, which the DJSI treats as social. We add the new indicators and Disclosure on Management Approach (DMA) that belong to designated subcategories in the GRI-G4 Mining & Metals Sector Disclosure, and we add a new subcategory "Sector Disclosures" for indicators and DMAs in the Sector Disclosure that were not classified in the existing subcategories. The result is Table 9.9, which shows that RobecoSAM's Corporate Sustainability Assessment,

TABLE 9.9 Social Subcategories, Indicators and Data in the GRI-G4 Guidelines and Sector Disclosures for Mining & Metals

[illegible]	[illegible]	[illegible]
Human rights	14	30
Labor practices and decent work	19	88
Society	14	45
Sector disclosures	5	19
Local economic impact	4	21
Totals	**56**	**203**

used for the DJSI, is comparable in volume of coverage to that of the GRI-G4 for the Social category of sustainability.

A detailed look at the two standards reveals other similarities. The GRI-G4 Sector Disclosures for mining include much of the content of the DJSI section 3.6 Occupational Safety and Health, which we noticed was quite different from that of the CSA example for the services sector. Also, the GRI-G4 Sector Disclosures on resettlement and closure planning are comparable in content, though less detailed, than the CSA sections 3.7 and 3.8 for mining companies.

The qualitative differences between the DJSI and GRI-G4 appear in the treatment of human resources. It is noteworthy that the DJSI treats investments in human capital not as an economic or financial indicator but as a social one, and the same is true for "talent attraction and retention." The indicators about human capital development pertain to investments in training, which is a benefit to employees as stakeholders but also benefits the firm's owners. Likewise, the indicators under Talent Attraction and Retention pertain to employee appraisals, employee turnover, and employee satisfaction, all of which relate well to the benefits received by employees as stakeholders of the corporation. The DJSI pushes reporters to identify the business case for key indicators of sustainability. In commenting on the Corporate Citizenship and Philanthropy subcategory of its Social category, the DJSI questionnaire notes, "The key focus of the criterion is on how companies assess the value of their corporate citizenship and philanthropy programs."[20]

The concept of sustainable business in the DJSI is clearly similar to that of SASB—focused on the creation of long-term value in the firm. That this is consistent with the approaches to sustainable development taken in the international community is evident from the inclusion of significant reporting in the DJSI on diversity, gender equity, human rights, freedom of association, corporate citizenship, occupational safety and health, and stakeholder engagement. We see these in both examples of the CSA questionnaire reviewed above, Mining and Services, and in the case of Mining alone, we see it in the reporting on corporate policies and actions in light of the rights and the reasonable expectations of the local communities where it is material to the company.

ASSET4 ESG

Thompson Reuters' ASSET4 ESG rating classifies indicators as universal (for all industries) or industry specific or region specific. The universal social indicators in ASSET4 ESG pertain to human rights. They include human rights policy, implementation, monitoring, and improvements, as well as supplier screening. Specific topics include freedom of association, child labor, and diversity and opportunity. All are measured as Boolean indicators, present/absent.

Among the social indicators that may be used, depending on the industry, are those related to product responsibility (19), health and safety (9), and training and development (10). Most of these are measured in Boolean form, yes/no. The quantitative indicators include measures of noncompliance with product laws, injuries and lost days, and training hours and training costs.

The region-specific subcategories are community engagement (14 indicators), diversity and opportunity (9), employment quality (17), and effective tax rate (1). Topics in community engagement relate to donations, indigenous people, public health, patent infringement, bribery, and corruption. Topics on diversity relate to the gender ratio in management, work–life balance, family-friendly policies, and compliance. Employment quality issues concern compensation, union representation, net employment creation, personnel turnover, and strikes.

FTSE4Good

FTSE4Good uses only publicly available information, so it may be expected to have a more limited array of indicators than DJSI or ASSET4 ESG. Even so, it has a substantial array of social indicators that are evaluated for all firms, irrespective of their industry and location. The social indicators are organized under the subcategories of health and safety, labor, human rights and community, customer responsibility, and supply chain. The numbers of indicators common to all industries and geographic locations are shown in Table 9.10, which distinguishes the strategy and policy indicators from those that are quantitative or performance related.

TABLE 9.10 Common Indicators in Social Subcategories of FTSE4Good

Social Subcategory	*S&P*	*Quant*
Health & safety	12	6
Labor standards	9	3
Human rights & community	10	5
Customer responsibility	7	1
Supply chain (social)	9	4
Totals	**47**	**19**

In FTSE4Good's governance category, there are indicators that might be classi- [illegible]

board of directors.

FTSE4Good in the whole has about 100 sector-specific or location-specific indicators, and these appear in several of the social subcategories, particularly in Health & Safety and in Customer Responsibility, where service and manufacturing industries differ.

The quantitative or performance-related social indicators in FTSE4Good are familiar from our examination of the GRI, DJSI, and ASSET4 ESG standards. For example, in Health & Safety, firms are rated on their fatality rates, lost-time incident rates, and number of unplanned plant shutdowns in the previous three years, all indicators well suited to manufacturing organizations. Under Labor Standards, the voluntary turnover rate among full-time employees is a familiar quantitative indicator of employee satisfaction, and the amount of time spent on employee training may be a proxy for employee engagement. However, FTSE4Good does not rate firms on quantitative labor-related indicators required by the GRI, such as workforce diversity, grievances filed, and rates of absenteeism.

FTSE4Good's treatment of Human Rights & Community is heavily weighted on policies rather than quantitative measures. Of the five "quantitative/performance" indicators, four merely indicate the presence of policies such as freedom of expression, data privacy, indigenous rights, and security guards, the remaining performance indicator being donations and community investments. Local employment, which is quantified by percentages for both employees and managers in the GRI, is treated as a strategy/policy variable in FTSE4Good. Similarly, a firm's scores for Customer Responsibility and Social Supply Chain are heavily weighted on policies and activities rather than quantitative measures of outcomes.

Global 100 and Newsweek *Green Rankings*

The Global 100 standard from Corporate Knights is one of the parsimonious standards of corporate sustainability, but 5 of its 12 indicators concern the social category of sustainability. These are presented in Table 9.11. All indicators scored as percentile rankings within the firm's industry. Pension fund status is used as an indicator only if the liability of the company is more than $50,000 per employee.

TABLE 9.11 Social Indicators in the Global 100

- CEO to average employee pay
- Pension fund status (unfunded liabilities divided by market cap)
- Safety performance (lost-time injury score and fatality score)
- Employee turnover
- Leadership diversity (board and senior executives)

These indicators reflect an ethical attention to issues of distributive justice, legal responsibility, reactive responsibility, and an inclusive perspective on identity. The measure of employee turnover, if it were adjusted for involuntary terminations, would be a direct outcome measure for employee engagement. Notably absent is an indicator about benefits to local communities, and there is no indicator about matters relating to customers.

The data for *Newsweek*'s Green Rankings are drawn in part from the Global 100 metrics, but *Newsweek* excluded all of the social indicators listed above. The closest that the Green Rankings get to a social indicator is the Sustainability Pay Link, but that rewards senior executives for environmental performance, not social performance.

Social Indicators in the Corporate Certifications

The corporate certifications can be more data intensive than the rating systems, because certifications are voluntary, and they may require the applying organization to report on any indicators deemed appropriate to sustainability. Even so, they tend not to be as extensive in their data requirements as the GRI, as the following examples show.

UL 880

As we saw in Chapter 3, the UL 880 standard from Underwriters Laboratories has a strong emphasis on management systems for each aspect of sustainability, and quantitative targets for indicators are usually selected by the reporting firm, not prescribed in the standard. Firms get points for having a policy, setting a target, and making progress toward the target.

The UL 880 has five major categories of indicators for which a total of 1008 points may be granted. Environment (45.7%) is the largest. Governance for Sustainability (10.6%) has elements of stakeholder engagement, which in other standards is treated as social, as well as more traditional governance aspects such as ethics, oversight, and incentives. The UL 880 does not have a "social" category. Instead, along with Environment and Governance it groups indicators as Workforce (13.9%), Customers and Suppliers (23.3%), and Community Engagement and Human Rights (6.4%). Here, we include all three categories in the discussion of social indicators, but in Chapter 10 we will have more to say about the classification of indicators about customers and suppliers.

These three UL 880 categories can be disaggregated into aspects that are individually more revealing of the social content in the standard, as shown in Table 9.12.

The UL 880 stands with the DJSI, STARS, and B-Corp by awarding points (here 3.4%) for measuring employee satisfaction, which is a direct *outcome* of employee

UL Social Subcategory	[illegible]	Points
Workforce	Diversity	20
Workforce	Employee engagement	26
Workforce	Employee satisfaction	34
Workforce	Health and safety	60
Customers and Suppliers	Customer satisfaction	22
Customers and Suppliers	Product information	10
Customers and Suppliers	Product safety	35
Customers and Suppliers	Supply chain	168
Community Engagement and Human Rights	Community	30
Community Engagement and Human Rights	Human rights	35
	Subtotal points (of 1008)	**440**

engagement, citing an appearance on the Great Place to Work Institute[21] list as one way to earn the points. The UL 880's inclusion of diversity and health & safety as workforce indicators presents a familiar picture in relation to the other standards featured in this book. Its use of employee training is a familiar indicator of employee engagement, but its inclusion of an indicator about employee performance evaluations sets it apart from the other standards, with the exception of the GRI, DJSI, and B-Corp.

The UL 880 award of 2.2% of its points for customer satisfaction is a direct outcome measure for another important stakeholder group. For those points, the UL 880 standard cites as a reference the ISO 10002 Quality Management—Customer Satisfaction standard.

STARS

The indicators and component scores in STARS 2.0 are not organized by ESG or PPP categories, but by the way that the university might practice sustainability: in operations, administration, academics, campus engagement, and public engagement. Among the recognizably social indicators, the familiar indicators are those related to employment: diversity, workplace health and safety, having a wellness program, payment of a living wage, and an assessment of employee satisfaction. Related to employee engagement, STARS has indicators for employee orientation and training, but it awards points only for education about sustainability, not orientation and training in general.

STARS gives points to universities that have policies to identify and engage their stakeholders in the community, and indicators reward community service by students (maximum points for 100% participation and for 20 hours per student), but not by staff or faculty. It also gives points for the affordability of education. Credits for community partnerships depend on the extent to which projects are merely supportive of community needs or are developed collaboratively or, at the highest level, "catalyze community resiliency . . . by simultaneously supporting social equity and wellbeing, economic prosperity, and ecological health on a community or regional scale." Credit for intercollegiate collaborations relate specifically to activities that build the campus sustainability community.

B-Corp

The B-Corp standard was designed to reward socially responsible business practices, so it has numerous indicators that take social responsibility beyond what the other standards call for. In health and safety, B-Corp asks whether data on illness, injury, and lost days are measured and reported, but it goes further than the other standards (except UL 880) by giving credit for wellness programs and employer-provided health insurance. Like other standards, it looks for a fair or living wage, but it stands only with the GRI in comparing part-time and full-time wages, and it goes along with the GRI, ASSET4 ESG, and Global 100 in examining the ratio of the highest to lowest compensations.

On employee engagement, like the others it calls for data about training, like the GRI, DJSI, and UL 880 it asks about performance evaluations of employees, and like ASSET 4 ESG and UL 880 it gives credit for family-friendly work policies, but it is alone among the standards in having indicators for internal hiring and employee stock ownership.

Discussion

The social indicators are the most difficult to roll up into subcategory and category measures of sustainability, because organization science has not developed to the point that there are clearly understood theories, established through empirical research, that demonstrate the relationships among all the factors of managing human resources and community relations as they impact a firm's long-term financial performance. The "business case for sustainability" is better understood for environmental impacts than for social impacts. Herb Blank, the leader of the team that developed the ASSET4 ESG metric, admitted these difficulties in general, not just specific to the Social pillar,

> There can be no definitive and universally accepted right or wrong way to weight and model the Key Performance Indicators, or KPIs, [subcategories] collected and measured by ASSET4. That said, hard decisions had to be

Blank's phrase "reconciliation of expectations" hints at the role of philosophies of sustainability in the formation of KPIs for the management of sustainability in a business. To some degree, perhaps to a large degree, the formulation of metrics for the social component of sustainability—the weighting of indicators in the calculation of subcategory scores—will be influenced by social norms and ethical sensibilities, not just social and economic science. Norms are "shoulds." They express the expectations and represent the values of different stakeholders, so they capture different philosophical perspectives that may be brought to bear on questions about the forms of business organization and types of business practice that will be appropriate in a sustainable economy and society.

The business world does not yet have a sufficiently complete science of social sustainability, and the methods for evaluating the impacts of social investments by businesses are still developing.[23] But as a summary of this chapter, we can review the indicators that have been used for various aspects of social sustainability to see which ones are common among the standards, meaning that they are considered basic to specific aspects of social sustainability, and which ones are atypical and thus represent extensions of the basic operationalization of the aspect. We will construct this analysis for subcategories of social sustainability defined in terms of the familiar stakeholder groups for the social component: employees, community and state, and customers and suppliers.

Indicators of Sustainable Employment Practices

Table 9.13 presents a summary of the analysis of the social aspects of sustainability related to employment across the two disclosure standards (GRI, SASB), the five corporate ratings (DJSI, FTSE4Good, ASSET4 ESG, Global 100, *Newsweek* Green Rankings) and the three corporate certification systems (STARS, UL 800, B-Corp) that have been featured throughout this book. "Common" indicators are not necessarily present in all standards, but they appear in most.

This table shows that employment-related social sustainability is represented heavily by process measures and only very lightly by outcome measures. Turnover, or its complement as retention, is the common measure of the satisfaction of employees as stakeholders to a business. Absenteeism is also used. Days lost to strike or lockout would be another, but it is not widely applicable across organizations. Direct measures of employee satisfaction, through surveys, are expensive and not uniform, so standards tend to give credit for their use rather than for their results, which reduces the indicator from an outcome measure to a process measure.

The DJSI is alone, among the standards featured here, in its use of metrics for human capital performance and return on human capital investments.

TABLE 9.13 Indicators for Social Aspects Related to Employment

Aspect	*Common*	*Extended*
Health and safety	Rates of work-related illness, accident, injury, and mortality	Employer's contribution to health insurance Employee participation in employer-sponsored health or wellness programs
Compensation and benefits	Living wage or wages in relation to minimum wage	Gender differences, full- and part-time differences, employee–contractor differences Ratio of highest to lowest paid
Employee engagement	Training	Regular performance evaluation Awards Family-friendly policies Grievance mechanisms and their use Whistleblowing protection Internal hiring Matched employee donations Employee bonus and stock ownership Long-term incentives Shared financial performance data
Direct measures of employee satisfaction	Retention or turnover Absenteeism	Surveys of employee satisfaction Days lost to strike or lockout
Human rights in the workplace	Core ILO standards: antidiscrimination, respect for diversity, freedom of association and collective bargaining, safe and sanitary working conditions Incidents of grievance about discrimination	Training of employees, e.g., security guards, in human rights

Indicators of Sustainable Community and State Relations

Indicators of sustainable community relations are best viewed in terms of the aspect of the community affected: economic, public health and safety, social, and cultural. The relationship of the business to the state is indicated by compliance with laws and regulations. Table 9.14 lists the common indicators for each of these aspects and shows their extension as evident in a few of the standards featured here.

Economic Impacts on the Community

Job creation and loss is an obvious aspect of the social impact of a business. It is commonly indicated by the number of employees in the business (full-time equivalent, FTE) or the total wage bill paid, but the trend in employment is often

TABLE 9.14 Indicators for Social Aspects Related to Community and State

Aspect	Common	Extended
Economic	Current employment as FTE or total wages paid Trend in FTE employed	Hires of disadvantaged populations (poor, young, minority, disabled, ex-con) Local purchasing Retraining or resettlement of displaced workers
Social	Employee diversity Anticorruption and antibribery policies and practices	Engagement with and rights of indigenous peoples, incidents of violations
Public health and safety	*(none)*	Impacts on air and water quality Emergency preparedness Expenditure on public health infrastructure
Sociocultural	Employee diversity Anticorruption and antibribery policies and practices Protection of sites of cultural significance	Engagement with and rights of indigenous peoples, incidents of violations Sponsorship of cultural events
Nation-state	Taxes paid, value and percent of profits (+) Fines and sanctions (–) Political activity (+/–)	Financial assistance received from government
Nonspecific	Donations of cash or goods Engagement with societal stakeholders	Employees' use of paid and unpaid time for community service as participation rate and percent of time. Formal grievance mechanisms for external stakeholders Community impact assessments

considered as well. Extended treatments of job creation examine who is getting the jobs, focusing on disadvantaged groups such as the poor, youth, minority, disabled, and previously incarcerated. A firm's treatment of plant closures and job loss, through job retraining or assistance in resettlement, appears in a few standards. The amount spent by the firm on purchases from local suppliers is another economic indicator.

A firm's policy and outcomes for employment of disadvantaged groups is classified here as a community impact, not an impact on workers, because the primary outcome of hiring disadvantaged groups is the engagement of those groups with their community, through economic empowerment, not the engagement of those groups with the firm as workers.

Social Impacts on the Community

Among the standards featured here, the common indicator of a firm's social impact on its community is employee diversity. Diversity among employees has two impacts. One is on the workers themselves, who may develop improved understanding through interaction on the job. The other impact is the effect that this improved understanding has within the community. As an indicator of social sustainability, workplace diversity may legitimately be classified under either or both subcategories. However, this point applies only to diversity in the workplace. The B-Corp standard has an indicator about diversity among the shareholders of a firm, but the shareholders do not need to interact with each other and do not do so regularly, so the impact of shareholder diversity on community relations will be very limited.

Also common as social indicators of community sustainability are data relating to the anticorruption and antibribery policies and practices of a firm. These policies are meant to uphold community values related to equal opportunity. The protection of sites having cultural value is recognized as an indicator of sustainability in several standards.

The rights of indigenous peoples are recognized in most standards to be industry specific, weighing most heavily on firms that extract natural resources. An indicator about a firm's expenditures on cultural events would be appropriate to the sociocultural impact of a firm, but it is not typical in the standards reviewed here.

Public Health and Safety Impacts on the Community

No items related to public health and safety are commonly used in the standards on sustainability. These indicators are typically industry specific, concentrating on firms that might pollute the air or water or transport hazardous materials as inputs or as products. Expenditures on public health infrastructure are appropriate to this impact on the community, but they are not common in the standards reviewed here.

Impacts on the Nation-State

The taxes paid by a firm, in monetary value and as a percentage of profits, are commonly taken to have a positive impact on a firm's relationship with the nation-state. Fines and sanctions are a negative indicator.

An account of political activity in the form of contributions to political parties is called for in the GRI guidelines for disclosure, the FTSE4Good rating, and the UL 880 certification. The GRI does not interpret its indicators in terms of polarity, because it does not result in an evaluation. The UL 880 gives points merely for disclosing political contributions, not for the amount, leaving the polarity of the indicator left ambiguous. FTSE4Good classifies its indicator under Anticorruption, so presumably it would assign a negative polarity to political contributions, though they do indicate an engagement of the firm with its nation-state and could have impacts either for

standards reviewed, but it was present in the GRI. Like political contributions, its polarity may depend on the details of the transactions.

Nonspecific Impacts on the Community

The indicators in most widespread use are charitable donations and policies and procedures for engagement with societal stakeholders, though these are not specific as to the type of impact on the community.

A few standards call for an accounting of employees' use of paid or unpaid time in community service, expressed as a participation rate (percentage of employees) or as an average amount of time per person. Relevant, but not typical in the standards reviewed, are also formal grievance mechanisms for external stakeholders and community impact assessments.

Indicators of Sustainable Relations With Customers and Suppliers

Customers and suppliers are an interesting stakeholder group to consider in the analysis of a company's sustainability. They are transactional partners with the reporting firm, and as such they are intimately related to the core of the business and directly impact the firm's profitability. In Chapter 10, we will consider whether indicators about Customers and Suppliers should be categorized as Economic/Financial, the third "P" in PPP, rather than as Social. Here, we set the stage for that discussion by considering what types of indicators appear in this subcategory commonly or atypically among the standards featured in the book.

Table 9.15 summarizes an analysis of the indicators about customer relations in the standards featured in this book. The standards commonly have indicators

TABLE 9.15 Indicators About Customer Relations

Aspect	*Common*	*Extended*
Consumer protection	Product information Product safety Fair marketing practices Data privacy	Warranties
Customer engagement	*(none)*	Public means to provide feedback, number of complaints Policy on vulnerable groups
Direct measures	*(none)*	Customer satisfaction
Legal and ethical	Fines paid	Sale of banned products

related to consumer protection: product information, product safety, and data privacy, and usually that includes fair marketing practices. An indicator under governance usually calls for information about fines or penalties paid for violations of consumer protection laws. As an extension, firms might be asked for details on their product warranties.

Methods for customer engagement are not typically requested. These include public means for customers to provide feedback to the firm, the number of complaints, or a policy for vulnerable groups. Only the DJSI expects extensive reporting about customer relationship management and brand management.

A Special Note About Suppliers as Stakeholders

With the exception of one indicator requested in one standard, there was no evidence that the standards view a firm's suppliers as a stakeholder group. Only the B-Corp's question about the tenure of a firm's significant suppliers gives evidence of how well the firm is meeting its suppliers' reasonable expectations and interests.

All other indicators about suppliers in the standards reviewed here concerned the *suppliers' impacts* on the reporting firm's stakeholders, the suppliers' practices related to aspects of sustainability that apply globally (e.g., human rights in labor practices), or about the business aspects of supply chain management that create risks for the firm.

Misclassification of Indicators in the Standards

Standards for rating or certification classify their indicators by subcategory and category to permit the calculation of subcategory and category scores for the evaluated firms, so the proper classification of indicators is essential. Systems for disclosure, such as the GRI-G4 and SASB, do not evaluate the data presented by reporting firms, but they do classify their indicators, and those classifications could be taken as models by firms that develop their own sustainability reports and even by the ratings and certifications when they update their standards. Consistency in such categorizations across rating systems will improve the acceptability of standards for sustainability.

Some indicators may have an impact on more than one category of sustainability, so they may well be placed in each one for the award of credits toward subcategory and category scores. Other indicators may be better located in a single category. As an illustration of the logic for classifying indicators by category and subcategory, we note here a few examples that appear to indicate a misclassification. We will return to some broader issues in the classification of indicators in Chapter 10.

Misclassification by Category

- In GRI-G4, charitable contributions are accounted for as an item in the distribution of generated economic value (EC1) under the Economic category, though the impact is on the community.
- In GRI-G4, the proportion of senior management hired from the local community at significant locations of operation (G4-EC6) is located in the subcategory Market Presence within the Economic category. The proportion of spending on local suppliers (EC8) is located in Procurement Practices under Economic, and the development and impact of infrastructure investments and services supported (EC7) is located in the Indirect Economic Impacts subcategory. The most immediate impact of local hiring, local purchasing, and infrastructure investments, however, is on the Community, not on the firm's shareholders, so if Economic is taken to mean the third P, these indicators are misclassified.

Misclassification by Subcategory Within Social

- In SASB, "fair wages" is listed as part of Community Relations (NR0302–13.70), whereas it concerns primarily employees' engagement with the business, not the community's engagement with the business, and thus belongs under Labor Relations.
- In FTSE4Good, the indicator "Policy on under-privileged and youth unemployment" is listed under the subcategory Labor Standards, but we noted in the commentary here that hiring from disadvantaged populations may be more usefully classified as impacting the community.
- In the B-Corp standard, employee attrition (CM2.03) and attrition rate (CM2.04a) are treated as indicators of Job Creation under the Community category (B-Corp does not use a Social category but has Community and Workers as two of its four primary Impact Areas). However, attrition does not affect the firm's employee count if a departing worker is replaced, and the attrition rate is a measure of employee dissatisfaction, not of job creation. Thus, these indicators are better classified under Workers.

Notes

1 The explanation of social responsibility here draws on a more expansive set of ethics than basic egoism. An egoistic response could be that the stakeholder perspective on business strategy also follows from a basic egoistic ethic along with the belief (worldview) that the support of this wider range of stakeholders will enable the firm to advance its business and to be more resilient against externally caused setbacks in its business. That may be called the "business case" for sustainability. The empirical evidence to support that worldview is building up, but until that evidence is solidly established, the debate will be driven more by the ethics than the worldview.

2 SASB. 2013. Conceptual Framework. Sustainability Accounting Standards Board.

3 ISO. 2014a. Discovering ISO 26000. International Organization for Standardization. Available at <www.iso.org/iso/discovering_iso_26000.pdf> Accessed July 2015.

4 FTA. 2015b. BSCI: What We Do. Available at <www.bsci-intl.org/content/what-we-do-0> Accessed July 2015.

5 EICC. 2015. Code of Conduct. Electronic Industry Citizenship Coalition. Available at <www.eiccoalition.org/standards/code-of-conduct/> Accessed July 2015.

6 ETI. 2015. What We Do. Ethical Trading Initiative. Available at <www.ethicaltrade.org/about-eti/what-we-do> Accessed July 2015.

7 FLA. 2011. FLA Workplace Code of Conduct and Compliance Benchmarks. Fair Labor Association. Available at <www.fairlabor.org/our-work/labor-standards> Accessed July 2015.

8 FLA. 2015a. Code of Conduct. Fair Labor Association. Available at <www.fairlabor.org/our-work/labor-standards> Accessed July 2015.

9 SAI. 2014a. Social Accountability 8000. Social Accountability International. Available at <www.sa-intl.org/index.cfm?fuseaction=Page.ViewPage&pageId=937> Accessed July 2015.

10 SAI. 2014b. SA8000:2014 Performance Indicator Annex. Social Accountability International. Available at <www.sa-intl.org/index.cfm?fuseaction=Page.ViewPage&pageId=937> Accessed July 2015.

11 IFC. 2012. IFC Performance Standards on Environmental and Social Sustainability. International Finance Corporation. Available at <www.ifc.org/wps/wcm/connect/c8f524004a73daeca09afdf998895a12/IFC_Performance_Standards.pdf?MOD=AJPERES> Accessed August 2015.

12 ISO. 2010. International Standard ISO 26000: Guidance on Social Responsibility. International Organization for Standardization. Available for purchase at <www.iso.org/iso/home/store/catalogue_tc/catalogue_detail.htm?csnumber=42546> Accessed July 2015.

13 ISO. 2015. ISO 26000—Social responsibility. International Organization for Standardization. Available at <www.iso.org/iso/home/standards/iso26000.htm> Accessed July 2015.

14 ISO. 2014a. Discovering ISO 26000. International Organization for Standardization.>

15 GRI. 2014a. GRI G4 Guidelines and ISO 26000:2010 How to use the GRI G4 Guidelines and ISO 26000 in conjunction. Available at <www.globalreporting.org/resourcelibrary/How-to-use-the-GRI-G4-Guidelines-and-ISO-26000-in-conjunction.pdf> Accessed July 2015.

16 SASB. 2013. Conceptual Framework. Sustainability Accounting Standards Board.

17 From the SASB home page www.sasb.org, select the industry from the Sectors drop-down menu and look for "Issues Table" among the documents for that industry.

18 RobecoSAM. 2015a. Corporate Sustainability Assessment, DJSI 2015—Test Companies SA

19 RobecoSAM. 2015c. RobecoSAM's Corporate Sustainability Assessment Companion.

20 RobecoSAM, 2015a, p. 87.

21 GPWI. 2015. About Us. Great Place to Work Institute. Available at <http://www.greatplacetowork.com/about-us> Accessed August 2015.

22 Blank, H. 2012. The ESG Decision Tree. Thompson Reuters Corporate Responsibility Ratings. Available at <www.trcri.com/images/TRCRI_Precis_Herb_Blank.pdf> Accessed August 2015.

23 KPMG. 2014. Unlocking the Value of Social Investment. KPMG International Cooperative. Available at <www.kpmg.com/global/en/issuesandinsights/articlespublications/sustainable-insight/pages/unlocking-value-social-investment.aspx> Accessed August 2015.

10

ISSUES IN THE ANALYSIS OF METRICS FOR SUSTAINABILITY

This book's review of standards for sustainability reporting, rating, and certification raises several issues that apply to the design of standards and to firms' formulation of their own sustainability reports. One gets at the definition of sustainable business in relation to the concept of sustainable development, and that leads us into a final look at the concept of materiality as it is used in financial accounting and in accounting for sustainability.

Another issue is the classification of indicators, which is very important when standards compute subcategory and category scores and when corporations use sustainability indicators to form aggregated performance measures for managerial decision-making. Under that heading, we compare the ESG framework to the triple bottom line (TBL or PPP) framework and we look specifically at how indicators relevant to governance, economic impacts, and social impacts should be classified.

The final issue we consider is the matter of data reduction. In view of the contrast between the "parsimonious" standards SASB and the Global 100 and the other, more voluminous, standards, we ask whether sustainability accounting—especially for small and medium-sized enterprises—would benefit from having a smaller set of key indicators.

Sustainable Business and Sustainable Development

A foundational issue in the field of sustainability metrics is the definition of "sustainability" as it applies to business. The heart of this issue is the difference, if there is one, between "sustainable business" and "sustainable development."

The definition of sustainability that is widely quoted in the literature on sustainable business comes from the 1987 Brundtland Report. It reads, "Sustainable development is development that meets the needs of the present without compromising the ability of future generations to meet their own needs."[1] Clearly, that is a definition of *sustainable development*, not of sustainability. How well does the Brundtland characterization of sustainable development carry over to sustainable business?

Different standards, and different scholars, give different answers to that question. Shrivastava and Hart, not long after the Brundtland report, examined "sustainable corporations" by examining "the basic concepts of sustainable development and their implications for corporations."[2] The ISO follows the Brundtland characterization closely, intending its guidance in the ISO 26000 standard on social responsibility "to assist organizations in contributing to sustainable development."[3] Schneider and Meins approached their analysis of corporate sustainability assessment from that perspective, reviewing approaches that "measure the contribution of firms to sustainable development."[4] Similarly, in their 2013 report *Carrots and Sticks*, the UNEP, GRI, KPMG, and the Center for Corporate Governance in Africa stated, "sustainability reporting plays a critical role, under the right conditions, in ensuring the private sector's contribution to sustainable development."[5]

However, to SASB, sustainable business focuses on the creation of long-term value in a company:

> sustainability includes both the management of a corporation's environmental and social impacts, as well as the management of environmental and social capitals necessary to create long-term value.[6]

Similarly, the Global Reporting Initiative emphasizes the business perspective in item G4-2, where reporters disclose the "impact of sustainability trends, risks, and opportunities on the long-term prospects and financial performance of the organization," concentrating specifically on information relevant to financial stakeholders. The business perspective is implicit in Lisa Newton's book *Ethics and Sustainability*, where an organization will have reached sustainability "when it can be maintained profitably and indefinitely, without degrading the systems on which it depends."[7] It is more explicit in the characterization of corporate sustainability by Sara Windolph and others as "an approach to systematically consider environmental and social issues and to integrate them into the economic management of a company."[8]

The distinction between a focus on long-term prospects and financial performance and a focus on the elements of sustainable development is seen most clearly in the differences between the SASB and STARS standards for the higher education industry. SASB standards have investors as their primary audience. In the United States, there are less than a dozen well-known investor-owned universities. As a group, their "social license to operate" is questioned, because there have been publicized incidents of hard sales tactics, unfavorable tuition policies, misrepresented job placement statistics, and low repayment of federal student loans,[9] as well as questionable academic practices known to regulators. SASB's standard has only nine indicators. The quantitative indicators largely illuminate the regulatory relating to governance, environmental, or human capital impacts, and there are none of the common Social indicators reviewed in Chapter 9.

Contrast that with the STARS 2.0 standard for universities, which has no indicators related to the financial performance or financial risk of an institution, despite the fact that higher education is undergoing disruptive change due to online technology.[10] STARS is strong on environmental metrics, having developed quantitative, industry-specific expectations for environmental performance that are not paralleled in any of the other standards reviewed in this book. STARS represents well the common indicators of the reasonable expectations and interests of employees and goes beyond the common in its indicators of service to the local community, two stakeholder groups that figure prominently in treatments of sustainable development. But STARS is only a double-bottom-line metric, reflecting a focus on a university's contribution to sustainable development rather than on its long-term performance. A Harvard business professor predicts that as many as half of the United States' 4,000 colleges and universities could fail by 2030 due to the disruptive change in the industry.[11] STARS has substantial penetration in its industry, with more than 700 colleges and universities registered to use the standard. So if the prediction of failures is correct, many of the failing institutions will have contributed to environmental and social sustainability in a world that was facing social and ecological challenges but without sustaining themselves.

Both SASB and STARS claim to be a standard for "sustainability" in higher education. It is obvious that their interpretations of sustainability differ, which highlights the need for attention to definition and the importance of transparency in the construction of metrics for corporate sustainability.

Materiality and the Stakeholder Concept

A debate about the definition of sustainable business can be avoided if the analysis of a standard focuses on the selection of indicators that reflect the organization's activities and their impacts on its stakeholders. This is the approach taken by the standards for sustainability reporting, the GRI and SASB, which require a report on indicators without prescribing weights on the indicators. It is also the first task for any organization that designs its own plan for sustainability reporting.

The widely recommended approach to the selection of indicators implements the concept of *materiality* that we discussed in Chapter 1. The classic definition of materiality, taken from financial accounting, takes the perspective of the "reasonable investor" and asks what financial information about a firm, if omitted, would alter the investor's evaluation of the firm. There, materiality is defined strictly by factors external to the firm.

The situation is different when a firm must assess the materiality of information about its activities and impacts on aspects of sustainability. The stakeholder principle establishes one feature of the generalized model of materiality: the replacement of the investor by "stakeholder." Another feature follows without controversy: the GRI-G4's replacement of the judgment or evaluation of the investor by the "reasonable expectations and interests" of the organization's stakeholders (in item G4-2).

The interpretation of "reasonable" is one point where materiality becomes controversial. The world of individuals to whom the corporation must be responsive seems to have expanded from the reasonable investor to anyone who has an expectation on or interest in the organization. Does "reasonable" constrain the scope of those individuals or of their expectations and interests? A standard would be unworkable if any person having a reason to lob a complaint at a corporation would qualify as a stakeholder and the topic of their complaint would be deemed material.

The GRI, in its description of indicator G4-2, offers one such constraint as "stakeholders' rights as defined by national laws and the expectations in internationally recognized standards and norms." This restricts idiosyncratic complaints and provides an objective standard for identifying material issues for a sustainability report.

In its statement of indicator G4-25, the GRI asks the reporting organization to give the basis for "identification and selection of stakeholders with whom to engage." The *selection* component of that statement is significant, because it recognizes the freedom that firms have to engage or not engage with various groups and interests. The GRI-G4 guidelines want reporting firms to be deliberate and systematic about their engagement with stakeholders and to document their reasons for engagement.

Engagement develops a relationship with a stakeholder group, and that relationship will necessarily focus on one or more topics, which in the context of standards would be called "aspects" of sustainability. The indicators in a standard or in a self-designed corporate sustainability report measure the impact of the firm on those aspects and thereby reflect the impact of the firm on the stakeholder group.

The GRI offered the example that reasons for engagement may relate to national laws and internationally recognized norms. SASB provides a longer list of the attributes they look for to identify topics for their industry-specific standards.[12] These include decision-usefulness to investors, having the potential to affect value creation, the benefits of information exceeding the cost of data collection, being actionable by the firm, and being reflective of the views of stakeholders.

The choice to engage or not engage a stakeholder group over a particular topic may also be driven by the firm's mission. This point distinguishes materiality in sustainability reporting from materiality in financial reporting. Statutory and case law have narrowed the limits of interpretation for what a reasonable investor deems actionable. Corporations have wide latitude in their choice of what business to be in and how to run the business. Those choices will be influenced by the values and worldviews of the leaders of the firm. The GRI calls on firms to be deliberate about that materiality in sustainability accounting is defined by factors within the firm as well as external to the firm. The GRI's prediction that companies in 2025 will tend to choose a particular sustainable development model (e.g., circular economy, collaborative economy, green economy)[13] could be an example of this expression of a philosophical orientation in their business.

The role of the firm in choosing which stakeholders to engage would be emphasized more clearly if firms, in their sustainability reports, describe how they "identify, *validate*, and engage with" stakeholders. Stakeholders may be identified by their potential impact on the firm or their public claims for attention, but it is in the validation step that a firm states the grounds for legitimating their claims, separating those it engages and those it does not. Legitimacy is a normative concept. It elicits the values and ethics behind a decision to engage or not, which may be as much a part of the decision as a rationalization around the type and magnitude of a stakeholder's impact on the firm.

ESG Does Not Represent Sustainability

Profits are not headlined in the standard ESG framework, nor are they adequately represented by Governance as a category of indicators. Should financial indicators be part of a standard for the sustainability of organizations? Underwriters Laboratories, in its UL 880 *Standard for Sustainability*: Manufacturing Organizations argued that they should not:

> UL 880 includes a comprehensive set of environmental, social, and governance sustainability indicators across five domains. This Standard does not include financial indicators, the third leg of the triple bottom line. Such issues are covered by sources of financial data that do not bear repeating in this Standard.[14]

An emerging trend in accounting is the integrated reporting of financial and "sustainability" data, which in almost all cases seems to mean ESG data. The trend toward integrated reporting got a boost in 2010 by the formation of what is now the International Integrated Reporting Council. Robert Eccles and Michael Krzus reviewed the state of integrated reporting in their 2010 book *One Report*,[15] and they surveyed the development of integrated reporting worldwide in their 2015 book *The Integrated Reporting Movement*.[16] Requirements now exist for integrated reporting in South Africa with developments forthcoming in Brazil, India, and the EU.[17]

The movement toward integrated reporting will make the stand-alone ESG framework obsolete. Sustainability for a business is the result of a comprehensive consideration of the reasonable expectations and interests of a firm's stakeholders. Schneider and Meins make this the primary point in their critique of corporate sustainability assessment, "Value creation, as a core condition for sustainability as well as for further contributions to economic sustainability, is often ignored in these assessments, suggesting that financial and non-financial organizational processes are separable."[18]

Owners' interests should not only be included alongside those of other stakeholders in assessing the long-term profitability of a firm (integrated reporting), but the relationships between the social and environmental aspects of sustainability and the financial aspect of sustainability need to be understood. The latter is the goal of the Connected Reporting Framework developed in the A4S project.[19]

To understand sustainability in business, it is necessary to know how the long-term profitability of a firm is related to environmental and social indicators. Those relationships establish the "business case" for ESG activities and measures. Connected reporting calls on firms to articulate those relationships in their annual reports. Only the integration of ESG measures with financial measures of performance and risk can genuinely be called sustainability reporting.

Categorizing Indicators: Refining ESG and PPP

John Elkington popularized the disaggregation of sustainability into three categories, the triple bottom line (TBL) of economic, environmental, and social aspects.[20] We have referred to that model here as PPP: people, planet, and profits. In his 1997 book *Cannibals With Forks*, Elkington saw the need for new indicators of sustainability and expressed hope that progress would be forthcoming:

> Ultimately, as Professor Rob Gray and his colleagues put it, sustainability reporting, "must consist of statements about the extent to which corporations are reducing (or increasing) the options available to future generations." This is an extremely complex task, but one which will probably look much easier once we have worked our way through a decade or two of experimentation in sustainability accounting, auditing and reporting.[21]

Nearly 20 years later, it seems that Elkington was overly optimistic. He hoped that progress would be made through new forms of full cost accounting, which would translate environmental and social indicators in financial terms. In the standards for sustainability reporting and certification, there is essentially no translation of environmental and social indicators into financial outcomes. The Dow Jones Sustainability Index stands out among the ones discussed here by having indicators such as "internal carbon pricing" and "human capital return on investment," but that is almost nothing in the full agenda of linking environmental and social outcomes to financial performance and risk.

A comprehensive translation of that type is, of course, the holy grail of the proprietary sustainability rating systems, which seek to advise their clients about how to invest for the long run. The rating systems do not generally reveal the weights

Elkington saw that progress would come most slowly in social accounting, but he now looks to have been optimistic about its future progress:

> Most medium-term progress, in fact, is likely to be made against the first and second bottom lines (economic and environmental), although the rate of progress in social accounting, auditing and reporting suggests that at least a core set of indicators could be available and in use within a matter of years. Meanwhile, the concept of the "sustainable corporation" is still evolving.[22]

Consistent Classification of Indicators by Category

Sarah Windolph cites the lack of standardization of measures and methodologies among rating systems as a significant weakness,[23] but our analysis in Chapter 9 suggests that standards do not even classify indicators consistently at the category level. Indicators do not need to be classified uniquely in a category within a standard; the effects of an indicator on multiple stakeholders or forms of capital can be reflected in a standard. But sustainability standards should be consistent at least in the primary classification of indicators and, we argue here, do so in a manner that reflects Elkington's triple bottom line and thereby permits a connection of environmental and social accounting with financial accounting.

From the literature on corporate social responsibility, the familiar disaggregation is environmental, social, and governance. Almost all standards for sustainability explicitly identify their indicators in a few primary categories and thereby either calculate, or permit others to calculate, category scores for reporting organizations. ESG is recognizable as an organizing framework in most but not all (Table 10.1).[24]

TABLE 10.1 Primary Categories of Indicators in Standards

Standard	*E*	*S*	*G*	*F*	*L*	*T*	*C*
GRI-G4	★	★	★	★			
SASB	★	★	★		★		
DJSI	★	★		★			
ASSET4 ESG	★	★	★	★			
FTSE4Good	★	★	★				
UL 880	★		★		★	★	★
B-Corp	★		★		★		★

Key: E = environmental. S = social. G = governance. F = financial or economic. L = labor, workers or human capital. T = transactional partners: customers and suppliers. C = community.

The evident inconsistency of these primary categories of sustainability across standards and the inconsistency in their components within a primary category, to be discussed shortly, are problematic because it means that category scores will not be comparable across standards. We take up this issue in its two parts, considering first the primary categorization.

ESG versus PPP

Is Elkington's triple bottom line substantively different from the traditional decomposition taken from the theory of social responsibility (ESG)? His environmental and social categories map clearly into ESG, so the question is whether Elkington's "economic" category equates with "governance."

One may well argue that it does not, or that it has become sufficiently different in practice that the Governance does not capture the Economic dimension of sustainability. The traditional problem of governance arises from the separation of ownership and control in an investor-owned corporation. Investors, possessing wealth, are not necessarily possessed of the expertise necessary to run a particular business, so they hire professional managers for that job. With their delegated authority, and in consideration of the opacity of information in organizations and the tendency of humans to opportunism, managers would run the business in their own interests, rather than those of the owners, unless the structure of authority and incentives is designed specifically to prevent that.

Thus, the classic problem of governance is one of designing structures for authority, reporting, and rewards.[25] The classic solutions, which safeguard the interests of the owners, include separating the positions of CEO and board chair, having independent (nonemployee) directors, having a simultaneous election of all directors (rather than staggered elections) with cumulative voting rather than straight voting, using proxy votes, having formal mechanisms for shareholders to submit resolutions to the board or for shareholder vote, using only nonexecutive board members on committees responsible for audit, nominations, and executive compensation, and aligning the interests of top managers with those of the shareholders through long-term incentive-based contracts.

Those policies on governance are meant to improve the economic performance of the firm, but there are many other factors internal to an organization that affect a firm's economic outcomes. Good governance is not sufficient for good economic performance. There are many other indicators of economic performance that would contribute to an understanding of a firm's sustainability, if by sustainability we continue to mean the "long-term prospects and financial performance of the organization," following the GRI.

The triple-bottom-line perspective explicitly focuses attention on the economic aspect of sustainability, which Elkington explicitly identified with the profitability of the company as driven by the firm's management of physical, financial, human, and intellectual capital.[26] In contrast, the ESG framework arose as a supplement

The same is true of SASB. It is a standard for "sustainability" that is meant to be complementary to, not inclusive of, financial reporting. SASB anticipates that the users of its standards will summarize their key sustainability data in a 10-K report's section on Management Discussion and Analysis, which focuses on events and uncertainties that would cause reported financial information not to be necessarily indicative of future operating results or of future financial condition. Thus, the sustainability data seem to be meant to modify the interpretations of the firm's performance that come out of financial reports.

FTSE4Good, in its Governance section, calls for several measures of financial risk (capital, leverage, and liquidity ratios), but it does not include any measures of financial performance.

Even the standards that explicitly categorize indicators as economic do not include traditional performance measures. DJSI includes risk analysis and stress testing as economic indicators, but not profitability ratios. The GRI includes economic value generated (G4-EC1), which is an indicator of economic performance. It acknowledges economic risks from climate change (G4-EC2), but its treatment is limited in comparison to that of the DJSI. The GRI's consideration of the reporter's coverage of financial obligations under defined-benefit plans (G4-EC3) is another measure of financial risk, but it is focused on employees as stakeholders rather than on total debt coverage, which would be more comprehensive.

Even the Global Initiative for Sustainability Ratings (GISR), founded in 2011 as an accreditor of sustainability ratings, rankings, and indices, equates sustainability with ESG:

> GISR's mission is to design and steward a global sustainability (i.e., Environmental, Social, and Governance–ESG) ratings standard to expand and accelerate the contribution of business and other organizations worldwide to sustainable development.[27]

If sustainability is meant to be inclusive of the long-term financial performance of a firm, and if integrated reporting is moving to evolve into connected reporting, demonstrating the relationships among the economic, environmental, and social performance of a firm, then standards for sustainability ratings and certifications should be extended beyond ESG to a proper triple bottom line.

A Stakeholder Perspective on the Triple Bottom Line

The approach advocated here is to use the stakeholder concept as an organizing framework for a TBL analysis of organizations. This is consistent with the stakeholder-based approach to materiality in sustainability reporting, which we discussed earlier in this chapter.

Where Is the G in PPP?

In view of the dominance of the ESG framework in sustainability reporting, we begin with a look at how Governance should be treated in a stakeholder-based conception of the triple bottom line.

We saw above that the purpose of good governance is essentially to hold a firm faithfully to its mission, which in the traditional concept of the firm is to maximize the wealth of its owners. Generalizing this by a stakeholder perspective, the role of good governance is to ensure that the organization is faithful to the reasonable (and we now add "validated") expectations and interests of all stakeholders. Thus, Governance is a concept that cuts across the stakeholders and thus across the categories of sustainability defined in the PPP framework. As it relates to investors and customers, good governance protects profits. As it relates to workers and the community, it protects people. As it relates to the environment, it protects the planet. Thus, indicators related to the governance of an organization belong in their respective categories of a standard for sustainability.

The GRI, DJSI, ASSET4 ESG, FTSE4Good, UL 880, and B-Corp standards each have an explicit category for indicators of Governance. Most contain the principal elements of the traditional approach to corporate governance. However, a brief review of the contents of those categories will show that some of the indicators on Governance in these standards reflect the expectations and interests of stakeholders other than owners and thus would benefit from inclusion in the appropriate stakeholder-defined category.

The GRI does not group its governance indicators with the "specific standard disclosures" that appear under economic, environmental, and social category headings but treats Governance as a category in "general standard disclosures." However, several of the GRI's indicators of governance can be classified in relation to the familiar stakeholder groups, such as the presence of executive-level positions with responsibility for environmental or social topics (G4-36), processes for consultation between stakeholders and the highest governance body on environmental and social topics (G4-37), competences related to environmental and social impacts among the governing board members (G4-38), whether the board's nomination and selection processes consider expertise relating to environmental and social topics (G4-40), measures taken to enhance the board's knowledge of environmental and social topics (G4-42), the board's role in identifying environmental and social issues and whether stakeholder consultation is involved (G4-45), whether the remuneration of senior executives is related to environmental and social objectives (G4-51), and other minor points along those lines.

The DJSI keeps Governance as a subcategory of its Economic dimension. Suitably, the great majority of its indicators are traditional. The exception is an item of information about the variable compensation of executives being linked to environmental or social metrics (1.1.7). A question about board committee using traditional words and phrases. Neither of these proprietary rating standards publishes a technical manual, so it is not possible to look further into these indicators to see if any of these indicators are broken down in ways that would permit reporting specific to the engagement with other types of stakeholder.

In its Governance section, UL 880 has separate indicators for shareholder engagement, employee engagement, and external stakeholder engagement (items 13.1–13.3). Each of those can be identified with a different stakeholder group and categorized accordingly.

The B-Corp standard is so strongly oriented toward social responsibility that its section on Governance has numerous questions related to the control of an organization's mission in relation to stakeholder groups. As a few examples, it asks whether the board reviews social and environmental performance, if there are key performance indicators related to social and environmental metrics or objectives, whether the CEO's variable compensation is related to the achievement of social or environmental goals, whether managers' written performance evaluations include social or environmental goals, and whether the board contains individuals elected specifically to represent the interests of listed stakeholder groups.

These examples show that the traditional elements of corporate governance serve the interests of owners, but standards for sustainability do have elements of governance that can be identified with responsiveness to other stakeholders and therefore, in a rating or certification program, should be accounted for as contributing to the environmental or social component of sustainable business.

What Belongs in "Economic" Sustainability?

The label "economic" for Elkington's first leg of the triple bottom line is unfortunate. "Profits" in PPP is much clearer, but Elkington's term is probably entrenched too deeply in the literature to be uprooted.

As examples of the confusion created by this term, consider GRI indicators G4-EC5 through EC8. EC5 is about wages relative to minimum wage and is justified in the *G4 Implementation Manual* as a measure of the "economic well-being of employees," which is a "factor in building strong community relations, employee loyalty, and strengthening an organization's social license to operate."[28] The stakeholders here are clearly employees and the community, not the owners. Likewise, EC6 is about local hiring of managers, which "can benefit the community." EC7 is about infrastructure investments, which are "one measure of an organization's capital contribution to the economy." EC8 is about other indirect economic impacts, which "include the additional impacts generated as money circulates through the economy" and which may expand "a social license to operate."

Under the stakeholder perspective, the "economic" leg of the triple bottom line is associated with the owners of the firm, who are the primary beneficiaries of profit. Indicators of financial performance and financial risk would reflect the expectations and interests of this group. For a nonprofit organization, the stakeholders corresponding to the Economic category of sustainability would be the primary beneficiaries of the stated mission of the organization.

Should "Social" Be Disbanded?

Table 10.1 revealed the interesting fact that the UL 880 and B-Corp certification standards did not use Elkington's "social" category. Instead, they reported its components at the highest level of their standard below the summative evaluation. No other standards did so. UL 880 organizes indicators directly under the three categories Workforce, Customers and Suppliers, and Community Engagement and Human Rights. The B-Corp standard uses the categories Workers and Community.

Implicitly, they raise the question of whether the Social category is sufficiently homogenous to warrant a position in the triple bottom line. Put another way, are the reasonable and legitimate expectations and interests of employees, the community, and customers/suppliers sufficiently different to warrant their own accounting in a multiple bottom line? Stated a third way, are human capital, social capital, and customer/supplier goodwill sufficiently different to warrant their own place at the top level of a sustainability accounting scheme, along with natural capital and financial/intellectual capital?

Does "social sustainability" have a meaning independent of its components? Is there a wholeness to social sustainability that is more than the sum of its parts? As one test, consider a concept that is often used to explain the presence of social indicators in a metric for sustainability, the "social license to operate." Does that license derive from all of the social stakeholders, or just some? The phrase evokes an image of the local community standing behind a beleaguered firm, or rallying at the gates of a controversial firm, so the concept draws from the community perspective. Worker dissatisfaction could also weaken the social license to operate, as when labor strife tarnishes the reputation of a firm. Customers' orientation toward a firm is usually described as goodwill, not as a social license, but a firm's violation of consumer protection laws would put its social license in jeopardy. This example suggests that the interests of employees, the community, and the nation-state may cohere in the form of a social license to operate. It is not clear whether customer goodwill is much of a factor.

Where Do Customers and Suppliers Belong?

The previous example brings up a related question about where customers and suppliers belong in a stakeholder-based formulation of the TBL concept.

The Dow Jones Sustainability Index, the ASSET4 ESG rating, and the GRI are [illegible]

[illegible] Performance "pillar" along with Shareholders Loyalty and (economic) Performance.[29] It puts Product Responsibility under its Social pillar, where issues of compliance would reflect responsibility to the nation-state, but Product Responsibility also includes attitudinal measures such as responsible marketing controversies and customer controversies. The DJSI has Customer Relationship Management and Supply Chain Management as distinct subcategories of its Economic dimension. The GRI places Product Responsibility as a subcategory of Social.

We noted previously that the UL 880 and B-Corp disaggregated the Social dimension of sustainability. UL 880 left Customers and Suppliers independent as a category. B-Corp does not appear to have indicators that concern customer relations. SASB has a category of Social Capital, but it put product quality and safety under a unique category, Business Model and Innovation, which includes integrated environmental and social impact analysis, so it does not correspond well to an Economic/Financial category.

FTSE4Good and ASSET4 ESG use an unalloyed ESG model for categorizing indicators. Not surprisingly, FTSE4Good puts its Customer Responsibility subcategory under Social, and ASSET4 ESG does the same with its Product Responsibility subcategory.

In Chapter 9's discussion of workers as a stakeholder group within the Social category, we justified the treatment of employee relations as social, rather than economic, by drawing on institutional economics, which recognizes that labor markets are so imperfect that classical contracting cannot govern the employment relationship efficiently, so the relationship gets internalized under relational contracting or hierarchical governance.[30] Does the same argument apply to the transactional relationship between a firm and its customers? No, because that relationship remains transactional under classical or neoclassical contracting. Thus, if we allow a firm's violations of consumer protection laws to be treated as indicators of the firm's relationship to the nation-state as a stakeholder, then what remains in the Customer Relations category are indicators of customer goodwill, which we have seen is not inherently social and may be better classified as having its primary impact on the financial capitals of the firm and on the owners as stakeholders.

The question about suppliers is answered simply. We noted in Chapter 9 that suppliers are not treated as a stakeholder group in any of the standards featured here, with the sole exception of the B-Corp, which has one question about the tenure of a firm's significant suppliers. All indicators about suppliers in the B-Corp and the other standards concern the management of ordinary supply-chain risks or the accounting for suppliers' impacts on aspects of sustainability. The latter indicators should be organized within each of the stakeholder-related categories advocated here. That would be consistent with the practice in FTSE4Good, which has subcategories Environmental Supply Chain and Social Supply Chain precisely for that purpose.

The Data-Reduction Problem

Using the extraordinary capacity of computers for storing and processing information, techniques for "data mining" are revolutionizing business intelligence.[31] To analysts, more data is better, but to the companies that have to generate sustainability reports, the standards that call for a hundred indicators, and many more hundreds of data items, create a substantial burden of time and expense.

In the sustainability standards featured here, we saw examples of some very parsimonious standards, SASB for sustainability disclosure and the Global 100 and *Newsweek* Green Rankings among the rating systems. We did not analyze whether they are as good as the other standards. That would be well beyond the scope of this book, but the answer is not simply a difference in the definition of materiality, that the parsimonious standards take the investor as the primary stakeholder while the voluminous standards serve a broader array of stakeholders. Like SASB, and in contrast with the GRI, the DJSI takes the investor as its primary stakeholder,[32] but the DJSI has about the same informational requirement as the GRI. So the question remains: Is there a reduced set of indicators that can capture a substantial portion of the story about the sustainability of a firm?

There probably is such a set of indicators. The number of major categories in which sustainability may be differentiated is relatively small. If categories are defined in terms of stakeholders, the categorical scores could be financial, environmental, workforce-related, community-related, socio-legal (nation-state), and perhaps customer-related, though that is up for debate. In each category, summative measures should reflect both performance and risk. That constitutes about a dozen summative measures. If these measures are correlated, the dimensionality of the categorical measures may be even less. When the GRI and RobecoSAM, provider of data for the DJSI rating standard, studied the materiality of sustainability issues as reported by companies and as perceived by investors, in the Technology Hardware & Equipment sector they found 13 financially material sustainability issues, at what we would call the subcategory level, that could be identified and prioritized.[33] Such prioritization might even lead to a summative measure. We noted in Chapter 8 that techniques have been developed in life-cycle analysis techniques to create a single, summative measure of the environmental impact of a product, cutting across nearly a dozen different environmental aspects. That gives hope for the derivation of useful summative measures in other categories and for "sustainable business" as a whole.

Within each category, there is likely to be correlation among the indicators, particularly in light of the common practice of simultaneously using policy and activity measures that are leading indicators of outcome measures. This presents further opportunities for data reduction.

The data reduction problem is important. Small and medium-sized enterprises (SMEs) are potentially burdened by the extensive data requirements of comprehensive models. The GRI would hold all organizations to the same requirements:

> G4 is designed to be universally applicable to all organizations, large and small, across the world. The features of G4—to make the Guidelines easier to use, both for experienced reporters and for those new to sustainability reporting from any sector—are supported by other GRI materials and services.[34]

Considerations of materiality, highlighted in the GRI, may reduce the amount of reporting required by SMEs, but only empirical research will tell us by how much.

For SMEs, sustainability reporting will largely be voluntary, but as sustainability reporting becomes mainstream, more SMEs will want to use it and will need guidance appropriate to their capacity. A more immediate concern for SMEs in business-to-business sales will likely be the widening adoption of sustainability reporting by large corporations, who will be required to include data about the sustainability of their supply-chain members. The suppliers will tend to be SMEs, and if the reporting requirements are anything close to what the corporations are reporting about themselves, the effect will be very burdensome.

Conclusions

John Elkington hoped that it would only take a decade or two of experimentation in sustainability accounting, auditing, and reporting to find easier ways to understand the extent to which corporations are reducing or increasing the options available to future generations. Those two decades have passed. Progress is evident in the increasing use worldwide of the Global Reporting Initiative's standard for reporting information relevant to sustainability, but a standard for disclosure does not provide summative measures about the options we are opening or closing. The parallel developments on that front have been promoted by the rating systems and the certification standards.

The rating systems offer the most hope for the development of mathematical models that translate economic and social activities and outcomes into measures of financial performance and risk. They have access to large amounts of data, because the objects of their rating are large corporations that do not want to be excluded from a rating and have the resources to collect the data needed for detailed analysis. The rating systems, however, are proprietary. They share with the public enough detail about their methods to maintain their credibility, and that lack of transparency has been a source of criticism from the academic community[35] and among commentators in the trade.[36] They cannot be fully transparent, of course, because they earn their revenue from the investment advice they can derive from the analysis of sustainability data. The analytic methods and results are the foundation of each rating system's competitive advantage, so the best scholarship on sustainable business will likely go unpublished or at least be delayed.

Or will it be? Will the rating systems actually produce the best scholarship to inform decisions that companies will make about how to manage their environmental and social activities comprehensively to assure long-term financial performance? The methodologies of the rating systems are based on ranking firms within a comparison group. They transform their indicators into percentile rankings and then weight the indicators to form subcategory and category scores (see the description of ASSET4 ESG in Chapter 2). The weights do reflect a strategic approach to managing stakeholder relations (e.g., the "relevance" to the industry or region and consistency with the academic literature) and an attention to the strength of impact (policy weighted less than action and action less than outcomes), and some methodological considerations are appropriate even for managerial decision-making (giving less weight individually to highly correlated indicators). But the raters' weights also reflect methodological considerations to enhance the stability of a rating, such as how widely reported an indicator is and whether its distribution is narrowly or widely scattered. And the ratings do not use the baselined data and progress scores apparent in the certification systems. One has to wonder if a firm that wants to use KPIs for management decision-making and can start with a blank slate would construct its KPIs in the same way as the rating systems. Might their approach be more like the certification standards?

The certification standards are an interesting experiment. They have their intellectual origins in the ISO 9001 standard for quality management systems introduced in 1987, which set the model for the ISO 14001 standard on environmental management systems in 1996. Like the ISO standards, Underwriters Laboratories' UL 880 standard for sustainability in manufacturing organizations gave a lot of points for policy making and for management systems, and it allowed applicants to set their own targets for performance measures. Its evaluation system, however, was different from that of the ISO 14001. It had some optional indicators and used a (compensatory) point system to award the certification. Its competitor, Green Seal's GS-C1 standard for product manufacturers,[37] used a tiered system of indicators to award certification at multiple levels (Bronze, Silver, and Gold) as the LEED system did for green buildings. Though each of these standards represented substantial intellectual effort in operationalizing the concept of sustainable business, neither of them received traction in the marketplace. The certification standards that took hold are the B-Corp, which appeals to companies that feel a very high degree of social responsibility, and the STARS standard that is meant as much for education about sustainability as it is for the measurement of sustainability. Each of these is a niche product.

It is doubtful that certification will become widespread in the business community. The two standards for manufacturing organizations, UL 880 and the GS-C1, all have practices to give third-party assurance on those reports.[38] Assurance does not validate the level of a firm's sustainability, as certification can, but it seems to add credibility to a firm's interpretation of their outcomes, and that is the main objective of certification. Sustainability reporting may even spread from the large corporations down to the SMEs, which might be a market for certification, particularly if the data-reduction problem can be solved to make reporting and certification less expensive. But having and reporting data on sustainability is just the first step for a company that needs or wants to manage itself effectively for the long run. Companies need formulas for the component and category measures of sustainability, their KPIs. The standards for certification, with their points system and publicly available technical manuals, offer a more comprehensible and intuitively sensible approach to the construction of KPIs than do the rating systems. To date, companies may not have seen enough value in the certification process, but some have emulated the UL 880 certification process internally.[39] That emulation, if not certification, may be the way of the future for management accounting in sustainability, but the development of KPIs as subcategory scores will need to be supported by scholarly research.

Let us renew the hope that significant progress on the conceptualization and measurement of sustainable business will be made in the next decade or two. Time is running out.

Notes

1 World Commission on Environment and Development. 1987. *Our Common Future.*

2 Shrivastava, P., and S. Hart. 1995. Creating Sustainable Corporations. *Business Strategy and the Environment* 4:3, 154–165.

3 ISO. 2014a. Discovering ISO 26000. International Organization for Standardization.

4 Schneider, A., and E. Meins. 2012. Two Dimensions of Corporate Sustainability Assessment: Towards a Comprehensive Framework. *Business Strategy and the Environment*, 21:4, 211–222.

5 KPMG, UNEP, GRI, and Center for Corporate Governance in Africa, 2013. Carrots and Sticks—Sustainability Reporting Policies Worldwide—Today's Best Practice, Tomorrow's Trends. Available at: <www.globalreporting.org/resourcelibrary/Carrots-and-Sticks.pdf> Accessed August 2015.

6 SASB. 2013. Conceptual Framework. Sustainability Accounting Standards Board.

7 Newton, L. 2003. *Ethics and Sustainability*, p. 5.

8 Windolph, S. E. 2013. Assessing Corporate Sustainability Through Ratings: Challenges and Their Causes. *Journal of Environmental Sustainability* 1:1, Article 5. Available at <http://scholarworks.rit.edu/jes/vol1/iss1/5> Accessed June 2015.

9 Detar, J. 2014. Are Publicly Traded, For-Profit Colleges Endangered? *Investor's Business Daily*, November 28, 2014. Available at <http://news.investors.com/

business-industry-snapshot/112814–728341-devry-grand-canyon-hybrid-education-model.htm#ixzz3jrC6QVkC> Accessed August 2015.

10 McDonald, M. 2014. Small U.S. Colleges Battle Death Spiral as Enrollment Drops. *Bloomberg Business*, Available at <www.bloomberg.com/news/articles/2014–04–14/small-u-s-colleges-battle-death-spiral-as-enrollment-drops> Accessed August 2015.

11 Ibid.

12 SASB. 2013. Conceptual Framework. Sustainability Accounting Standards Board, p. 12. Available at <www.sasb.org/wp-content/uploads/2013/10/SASB-Conceptual-Framework-Final-Formatted-10-22-13.pdf> Accessed August 2015.

13 GRI. 2015l. Sustainability and Reporting Trends in 2015—Preparing for the Future. May 2015. Global Reporting Initiative. Available at <www.globalreporting.org/resourcelibrary/Sustainability-and-Reporting-Trends-in-2025–1.pdf> Accessed August 2015.

14 UL Environment. 2011. UL 880 Standard for Sustainability: Manufacturing Organizations, 1st ed. (November 2, 2011), p. 9. Available at <http://ulstandards.ul.com/standard/?id=880&edition=1&doctype=ule> Accessed April 2015.

15 Eccles, R. G., and M. P. Krzus. 2010. *One Report*. Hoboken, NJ: Wiley.

16 Eccles, R. G., and M. P. Krzus. 2015. *The Integrated Reporting Movement*. Hoboken, NJ: Wiley.

17 Ibid.

18 Schneider, A., and E. Meins. 2012. Two Dimensions of Corporate Sustainability Assessment: Towards a Comprehensive Framework. *Business Strategy and the Environment*, 21:4, 211–222.

19 Hopwood, A., J. Unerman, and J. Fries, eds. 2010. *Accounting for Sustainability*. London: Earthscan.

20 Elkington, J. 1997. *Cannibals With Forks: The Triple Bottom Line of 21st Century Business*. Oxford: Capstone Publishing Ltd.

21 Ibid., p. 93.

22 Ibid., p. 94.

23 Windolph, S. E. 2013. Assessing Corporate Sustainability Through Ratings: Challenges and Their Causes. *Journal of Environmental Sustainability* 1:1, Article 5. Available at <http://scholarworks.rit.edu/jes/vol1/iss1/5> Accessed June 2015.

24 The Global 100 and STARS standards are not included in Table 10.1. Global 100 has only 12 indicators, and they are not disaggregated into categories. STARS uses categories that are specific to higher education: academics, engagement, operations, and administration.

25 Jensen, M. C., and W. H. Meckling. 1976. Theory of the Firm: Managerial Behavior, Agency Costs and Ownership Structure. *Journal of Financial Economics*, 3:4, 305–360.

26 Elkington, J. 1997. Op. cit., p. 74.

27 GISR. 2015b. About GISR: Vision and Mission. Global Initiative for Sustainability Ratings. Available at <http://ratesustainability.org/about/> Accessed August 2015.

28 GRI. 2013b. G4 Sustainability Reporting Guidelines.

29 Thompson Reuters. 2015. ASSET4 ESG Data.

30 Williamson, O. E. 1979. Transaction-Cost Economics: The Governance of Contractual Relations. *Journal of Law and Economics*, 233–261.

31 Maheshwari, A. 2015. *Business Intelligence and Data Mining*. New York: Business Expert Press.

32 GRI and RobecoSAM. 2015. Defining Materiality: What Matters to Reporters and Investors. Global Reporting Initiative and RobecoSAM. Available at <http://www.robecosam.com/images/Defining-Materiality-What-Matters-to-Reporters-and-Investors.pdf> Accessed August 2015.

and Their Causes. *Journal of Environmental Sustainability* 1:1, Article 5. Available at <http://scholarworks.rit.edu/jes/vol1/iss1/5> Accessed June 2015.

36 SustainAbility. 2011. *Rate the Raters Phase Four: The Necessary Future of Ratings.* July 2011. SustainAbility. Available at <www.sustainability.com/library/rate-the-raters-phase-four#.Vd04uVaWsVo> Accessed August 2015.

37 Green Seal. 2009. GS-C1 Pilot Sustainability Standard for Product Manufacturers, 1st ed. November 2, 2009. Available at <www.greenseal.org/Portals/0/Documents/Standards/GS-C1/green_seal_pilot_company_certification_gs-c1.pdf> Accessed August 2015.

38 KPMG. 2013. *The KPMG Survey of Corporate Responsibility Reporting 2013.*

39 Spence, C. 2013. Sustainability Assessment & Evaluations—How To Get Started & Pitfalls to Avoid. Presentation at the 2013 meeting of the Manufacturers Alliance for Productivity and Innovation (MAPI). Available at <www.mapi.net/events/sustainability-council-meeting-fall-2013> Accessed June 2015.

ABBREVIATIONS

A4S	Accounting for Sustainability
AASHE	Association for the Advancement of Sustainability in Higher Education
ACR	American Carbon Registry
AP	acidification potential
ARB	(California) Air Resources Board
ATP	aquatic toxicity potential
BICS	Bloomberg Industry Classification System; a system for classifying firms by industry, supported by Bloomberg L.P.
BOD5	five-day biochemical oxygen demand, a measure of organic pollution in water
BSCI	Business Social Compliance Initiative
BTU	British Thermal Unit, a unit of energy used in the United States but not in Great Britain
CAR	Climate Action Reserve
CARB	California Air Resources Board
CBEEX	China Beijing Environmental Exchange
CCFE	Chicago Climate Futures Exchange
CCX	Chicago Climate Exchange
CDM	Clean Development Mechanism (of the Kyoto Protocol)
CDP	originally Carbon Disclosure Project, but now used as a proper name
CER	Certified Emissions Reductions
CFC	chlorinated fluorocarbon, a chemical that destroys ozone
CH4	methane, also called natural gas (written chemically as CH_4)
CO2	carbon dioxide (written chemically as CO_2), the standard for measuring emissions of greenhouse gas (GHG)

COD	chemical oxygen demand, a measure of organic pollution in water
COGS	cost of goods sold
CSA	Corporate Sustainability Assessment, the questionnaire used by RobecoSAM to collect data for the DJSI
CSR	corporate social responsibility
CTX	Carbon Trade Exchange
DCB	dichlorobenzene, a standard for the measurement of toxic effects on life
DJSI	Dow Jones Sustainability Indices
DMA	disclosures on management approach; a phrase and acronym used by the GRI referring to narrative discussions pertaining to reported aspects of sustainability
EF	emission factor
EFTA	European Free Trade Association, having four members: Iceland, Liechtenstein, Norway, and Switzerland
EICC	Electronic Industry Citizenship Coalition
EMS	environmental management system
EPA	Environmental Protection Agency (U.S.)
ESG	environmental, social, and governance: three aspects of corporate social responsibility
ETI	Ethical Trading Initiative
ETS	Emissions Trading System
EUSES	European Union System for the Evaluation of Substances
FASB	Financial Accounting Standards Board
FLA	Fair Labor Association
FTE	full-time equivalent, a measure of total employment
FTSE4Good	not an acronym but a product name owned by the *Financial Times* and London Stock Exchange
GEMI	Global Environmental Management Initiative
GHG	greenhouse gas
GHGP	Greenhouse Gas Protocol
GICS	Global Industry Classification Standard; a system for classifying firms by industry, supported by Standard & Poors and used in the GRI, DJSI, and Global 100
GIIRS	Global Impact Investment Ratings System
GISR	Global Initiative for Sustainability Ratings
GRI	Global Reporting Initiative
GWP	global warming potential (of greenhouse gases)
GWT	Global Water Tool of the WBCSD
HAP	hazardous air pollutant
HDI	Human Development Index
HFC	hydrofluorocarbon, a family of GHGs

HMIS	Hazardous Materials Identification System
HRM	human resource management
HTPE	human toxicity potential by inhalation or dermal exposure
HTPI	human toxicity potential by ingestion
HVAC	heating, ventilating, and air conditioning
ICB	Industry Classification Benchmark; a system for classifying firms by industry, used in FTSE4Good standard
ICLEI	International Council for Local Environmental Initiatives, now operating as Local Governments for Sustainability
IIRC	International Integrated Reporting Council
IPCC	Intergovernmental Panel on Climate Change
ISIC	International Standard Industrial Classification, a standard method of classifying firms by industry, supported by the United Nations Statistics Division
ISO	International Organization for Standardization
kg	kilogram, 1000 grams, a measure of mass
KPI	key performance indicator
kWh	kilowatt-hour, a unit of electrical energy
L	liter, a measure of volume, approximately 0.264 U.S. gallons
LCA	life-cycle analysis
LEED	Leadership in Energy and Environmental Design, a standard for "green" buildings
LHV	lower heating value
LWT	Local Water Tool, a software program of GEMI
MCL	maximum contaminant level, a standard for water quality
mg	milligram, 0.001 grams, a measure of mass
mL	milliliter, 0.001 liters, a measure of volume, also called a "cubic centimeter" or cc
MPN	most probable number, a statistical result of a laboratory test for the existence of coliform bacteria in drinking water
MSC	maximum safe concentration (of a pollutant or toxin)
MSW	municipal solid waste
N2O	nitrous oxide, a GHG (written chemically as N_2O)
NACE	Nomenclature des Activités Économiques dans la Communauté Européenne, Nomenclature of Economic Activities in the European Community; a standard for classifying firms by industry, consistent with ISIC
NAICS	North American Industrial Classification System; a standard method of classifying firms by industry, supported by the United States Census Bureau

NGO	nongovernmental organization; usually referring to organizations that have a societal purpose but are neither governmental units nor for-profit businesses
NTU	nephelometric turbidity unit, a measure of the turbidiness (cloudiness) of water.
ODP	ozone depletion potential
ODS	ozone-depleting substance
OECD	Organization for Economic Cooperation and Development
OHS	occupational health and safety
PBT	persistent, bioaccumulative, and toxic (chemicals)
PCAOB	Public Company Accounting Oversight Board
PCOP	photochemical oxidation potential
PFC	perfluorocarbon, a family of GHGs
POP	persistent organic pollutant
ppm	parts per million, a measure of concentration
PPP	people, planet, and profits: a mnemonic for the components of the triple bottom line (TBL)
REC	renewable energy certificate
RSEI	Risk Screening Environmental Indicators (a model of chemical hazards)
SASB	Sustainability Accounting Standards Board
SCM	supply chain management
SF6	sulfur hexafluoride, a GHG (written chemically as SF_6)
SFP	smog formation potential
SICS	Sustainable Industry Classification System; a system for classifying firms by industry, supported by SASB
SME	small and medium-sized enterprises, in Europe meaning < 250 employees and in the U.S. meaning < 500.
SMM	sustainable materials management
STARS	Sustainability Tracking and Rating Systems, AASHE's standard for the sustainability of colleges and universities
TBL	triple bottom line, referring to the economic, environmental, and social evaluation of a firm
TDS	Total dissolved solids, a measure of chemical water pollution
TEF	toxic equivalency factor
TSS	Total Sustainability Score (in the Dow Jones Sustainability Index)
TSS	Total suspended solids, a measure of physical water pollution
TTP	terrestrial toxicity potential
UDHR	Universal Declaration of Human Rights, a 1948 publication of the United Nations
UNDP	United Nations Development Program
UNEP	United Nations Environment Program
UNFCCC	United Nations Framework Convention on Climate Change

UNGP	United Nations Guiding Principles on Business and Human Rights, also known as the Ruggie Framework
VCS	Verified Carbon Standard
VER	Verified Emission Reduction
VOC	volatile organic compound
WASH	water, sanitation, and hygiene; basic water-related services provided to employees
WBCSD	World Business Council for Sustainable Development
WHO	World Health Organization
WRI	World Resources Institute
WRM	water resource management
WTA	water-to-availability, a ratio used to indicate water stress
WWF	originally World Wildlife Foundation, but now used as a proper name

BIBLIOGRAPHY

AASHE. 2015. STARS 2.0 Technical Manual. Available at <https://stars.aashe.org/pages/about/technical-manual.html> Accessed June 2015.

Alcamo, J., T. Henrichs, and T. Rosch. 2000. World Water in 2025: Global Modeling and Scenario Analysis for the World Commission on Water for the 21st Century. Kassel World Water Series Report No. 2, Center for Environmental Systems Research, Germany: University of Kassel, pp. 1–49.

Allen, D. T., and K. S. Rosselot. 1997. *Pollution Prevention for Chemical Processes*. Hoboken, NJ: Wiley-Interscience.

Andrews, R. 1993. *Columbia Dictionary of Quotations*. New York: Columbia University Press, p. 392.

ARB. 2015a. Cap-and-Trade Program. California Environmental Protection Agency Air Resources Board. Available at <www.arb.ca.gov/cc/capandtrade/capandtrade.htm> Accessed August 2015.

ARB. 2015b. Mandatory Greenhouse Gas Reporting Regulation. California Environmental Protection Agency Air Resources Board. Available at <www.arb.ca.gov/cc/reporting/ghg-rep/regulation/mrr-regulation.htm> Accessed August 2015.

Asheesh, M. 2007. Allocating Gaps of Shared Water Resources (Scarcity Index): Case Study on Palestine-Israel. In H. Shuval and H. Dweik (eds.) *Water Resources in the Middle East*. Berlin Heidelberg: Springer, pp. 241–248.

Benson, L. 1970. That of God in Every Man–What Did George Fox Mean By It? *Quaker Religious Thought*, 12:2 (Spring). Available at <www.qhpress.org/essays/togiem.html> Accessed August 2015.

B Lab, Inc. 2015a. B Corporation. Available at <www.bcorporation.net> Accessed June 2015.

B Lab, Inc. 2015b. Corporation Legal Roadmap. Available at <http://www.bcorporation.net/become-a-b-corp/how-to-become-a-b-corp/legal-roadmap/corporation-legal-roadmap> Accessed June 2015.

Black, J., N. Hashimzade, and G. Myles. 2012. *Oxford Dictionary of Economics*. Oxford: Oxford University Press.

Blank, H. 2012. The ESG Decision Tree. Thompson Reuters Corporate Responsibility Ratings. Available at <www.trcri.com/images/TRCRI_Precis_Herb_Blank.pdf> Accessed August 2015.

Boylan, M. 2014a. Worldview and the Value-Duty Link to Environmental Ethics. In Michael Boylan (ed.) *Environmental Ethics*, 2nd ed. Chichester, West Sussex: Wiley Blackwell, pp. 95–109.

Boylan, M. 2014b. Ethical Reasoning. In Michael Boylan (ed.). *Environmental Ethics*, 2nd ed. Malden, MA: Wiley-Blackwell, pp. 3–13.

BRE. 2015. Ecotoxicity. Available at <https://www.bre.co.uk/greenguide/page.jsp?id=2099> Accessed August 2015.

Brown, A., and M. D. Matlock. 2011. A Review of Water Scarcity Indices and Methodologies. The Sustainability Consortium White Paper #106 (April 2011). Available at <http://www.sustainabilityconsortium.org/wp-content/themes/sustainability/assets/pdf/whitepapers/2011_Brown_Matlock_Water-Availability-Assessment-Indices-and-Methodologies-Lit-Review.pdf>

Carbon Catalog. 2015. Carbon Catalog. Available at <www.carboncatalog.org/> Accessed August 2015.

Carre, A. S., and R. E. Horne. 2009. Will the Well Run Dry? Developments in Water Resource Planning and Impact Assessment. In R. Horne, T. Grant, and K. Verghese (eds.) *Life Cycle Assessment: Principles, Practice and Prospects.* Collingwood: CSIRO Publishing, pp. 93–106.

CDP. 2015a. Guidance for Companies Reporting on Water on Behalf of Investors & Supply Chain Members 2015. Carbon Disclosure Project. Available at <www.cdp.net/en-US/Pages/guidance.aspx> Accessed July 2015.

CDP. 2015b. Water Program. Available at <www.cdp.net/water> Accessed July 2015.

CDP. 2015c. Climate Change Program Guidance. Carbon Disclosure Project. Available at <www.cdproject.net/en-US/Pages/guidance-climate-change.aspx> Accessed August 2015.

Chaves, Henrique M. L., and Suzana Alipaz. 2007. An Integrated Indicator Based on Basin Hydrology, Environment, Life, and Policy: The Watershed Sustainability Index. *Water Resource Management*, 21, 883–895. Available at <www.clw.csiro.au/division/perth/seminars/documents/WSI_paper.pdf> Accessed July 2015.

Cho, R. 2012. Rare Earth Metals: Will We Have Enough? State of the Planet. Columbia University Earth Institute. Available at <http://blogs.ei.columbia.edu/2012/09/19/rare-earth-metals-will-we-have-enough/> Accessed August 2015.

Corporate Knights Capital. 2014. Key Performance Indicators. Corporate Knights. Posted January 22, 2014. Available at <www.corporateknights.com/reports/2015-global-100/key-performance-indicators/> Accessed June 2015.

Corporate Knights Capital. 2015a. *Newsweek* Green Rankings Methodology 2015. Available at <www.newsweek.com/sites/www.newsweek.com/files/newsweek-green-rankings-final-methodology_2015.pdf> Accessed August 2015.

Corporate Knights. 2015b. 2015 Global 100 Methodology. Corporate Knights. Posted January 21, 2015. Available at <www.corporateknights.com/reports/global-100/methodology/overview.html/> Accessed June 2015.

CTX. 2015. How Are Carbon Credits Created? Carbon Trade Exchange. Available at <http://ctxglobal.com/faqs/how-are-carbon-credits-created/> Accessed August 2015.

Dash, E. 2009. If It's Too Big To Fail, Is It Too Big To Exist? *New York Times* (June 20, 2009). Available at <www.nytimes.com/2009/06/21/weekinreview/21dash.html?partner=rss&emc=rss> Accessed July 2015.

Documents/corporate-responsibility-reporting-survey-2013-exec-summary.pdf> Accessed August 2015.

Detar, J. 2014. Are Publicly Traded, For-Profit Colleges Endangered? Investor's Business Daily, November 28, 2014. Available at <http://news.investors.com/business-industry-snapshot/112814–728341-devry-grand-canyon-hybrid-education-model.htm#ixzz3jrC6QVkC> Accessed August 2015.

EC. 2010. Guidance on Interpretation of Annex I of the EU ETS Directive. European Commission, March 18, 2010. Available at <http://ec.europa.eu/clima/policies/ets/docs/guidance_interpretation_en.pdf> Accessed August 2015.

Eccles, R. G., and M. P. Krzus. 2010. *One Report.* Hoboken, NJ: Wiley.

Eccles, R. G., and M. P. Krzus. 2015. *The Integrated Reporting Movement.* Hoboken, NJ: Wiley.

EERE. 2015. Green Power Markets. U.S. Department of Energy, Office of Energy Efficiency and Renewable Energy. Available at <http://apps3.eere.energy.gov/greenpower/markets/carbon.shtml?page=0> Accessed August 2015.

EIA. 2015. Voluntary Reporting of Greenhouse Gases Program / Emissions Factors and Global Warming Potentials. U.S. Energy Information Administration. Available at <http://www.eia.gov/survey/form/eia_1605/emission_factors.html> Accessed August 2015.

EICC. 2015. Code of Conduct. Electronic Industry Citizenship Coalition. Available at <www.eiccoalition.org/standards/code-of-conduct/> Accessed July 2015.

Elkington, J. 1997. *Cannibals With Forks: The Triple Bottom Line of 21st Century Business.* Oxford: Capstone Publishing Ltd.

Elkington, J. 1998. Partnerships From *Cannibals With Forks: The Triple Bottom Line of 21st-Century Business. Environmental Quality Management*, 8:1, 37–51.

Engineering Toolbox. 2015a. Fossil Fuels-Energy Content. The Engineering Toolbox. Available at <www.engineeringtoolbox.com/fossil-fuels-energy-content-d_1298.html> Accessed July 2015.

Engineering Toolbox. 2015b. Fossil Fuels-Energy Content. The Engineering Toolbox. Available at <www.engineeringtoolbox.com/biofuel-energy-content-d_1356.html> Accessed July 2015.

EON. 2013. Buyer Liability Insurance Now Available for California's Cap-and-Trade Offset Program. Enhanced Online News. May 22, 2013. Available at <http://eon.businesswire.com/news/eon/20130522006404/en/Climate-Action-Reserve/cap-and-trade/carbon-offsets> Accessed August 2015.

EPA. 2010. Recommended Toxicity Equivalence Factors (TEFs) for Human Health Risk Assessments of 2,3,7,8-Tetrachlorodibenzo-P-Dioxin and Dioxin-Like Compounds. U.S. Environmental Protection Agency IPA/100/R 10/005 December 2010. Available at <www.epa.gov/raf/files/tefs-for-dioxin-epa-00-r-10–005-final.pdf> Accessed August 2015.

EPA. 2011a. Development of Specific Bacterial Detoxification Enzymes as Bioindicators and Biosensors of Environmental Pollution. U.S. Environmental Protection Agency. Available at <www.epa.ie/pubs/reports/research/waste/strivereport72.html#.VdfKJlaWsVo> Accessed August 2015.

EPA. 2011b. Principles of Design and Operations of Wastewater Treatment Pond Systems for Plant Operators, Engineers, and Managers. U.S. Environmental Protection Agency. Report EPA/600/R-11/088 (August 2011). Available at <www2.epa.gov/sites/production/files/2014–09/documents/lagoon-pond-treatment-2011.pdf> Accessed July 2015.

EPA. 2013a. Advancing Sustainable Materials Management: Facts and Figures 2013. U.S. Environmental Protection Agency. Available at <www.epa.gov/epawaste/nonhaz/municipal/pubs/2013_advncng_smm_rpt.pdf> Accessed July 2015.

EPA. 2013b. GHG Data and Publication. Q413. What Percentage of Total U.S. GHG Emissions is Covered in the GHG Reporting Program? (Updated February 6, 2013). U.S. Environmental Protection Agency. Available at <www.ccdsupport.com/confluence/pages/viewpage.action?pageId=141983792> Accessed August 2015.

EPA. 2014. Basic Information: GHG Reporting Program. U.S. Environmental Protection Agency. (Updated July 31, 2014). Available at <www.epa.gov/ghgreporting/basic-info/> Accessed May 2013.

EPA. 2015a. Municipal Solid Waste. U.S. Environmental Protection Agency. Available at <http://www.epa.gov/epawaste/nonhaz/municipal/index.htm> Accessed July 2015.

EPA. 2015b. Household Hazardous Waste. U.S. Environmental Protection Agency. Available at <www.epa.gov/epawaste/conserve/materials/hhw.htm> Accessed July 2015.

EPA. 2015c. TRI National Analysis 2013. U.S. Environmental Protection Agency. Available at <www2.epa.gov/toxics-release-inventory-tri-program/2013-toxics-release-inventory-national-analysis-supporting> Accessed July 2015.

EPA. 2015d. Release Chemical Report, 2013 Dataset Released March 2015. Available at <http://iaspub.epa.gov/triexplorer/tri_release.chemical> Accessed July 2015.

EPA. 2015e. Sustainable Materials Management. U.S. Environmental Protection Agency. Available at <www.epa.gov/epawaste/conserve/smm/> Accessed July 2015.

EPA. 2015f. Standard Volume-to-Weight Conversion Factors. U.S. Environmental Protection Agency. Available at <www.epa.gov/osw/conserve/tools/recmeas/docs/guide_b.pdf> Accessed July 2015.

EPA. 2015g. National Primary Drinking Water Regulations. U.S. Environmental Protection Agency. Available at <http://water.epa.gov/drink/contaminants/upload/mcl-2.pdf> Accessed July 2015.

EPA. 2015h. Renewable Energy Certificates. U.S. Environmental Protection Agency. Available at <http://www.epa.gov/greenpower/gpmarket/rec.htm> Accessed August 2015.

EPA. 2015i. Greenhouse Gas Equivalencies Calculator. U.S. Environmental Protection Agency. Available at <www.epa.gov/cleanenergy/energy-resources/calculator.html> Accessed August 2015.

EPA. 2015j. Phosphorus. U.S. Environmental Protection Agency. Available at <http://water.epa.gov/type/rsl/monitoring/vms56.cfm> Accessed July 2015.

ETI. 2015. What We Do. Ethical Trading Initiative. Available at <www.ethicaltrade.org/about-eti/what-we-do> Accessed July 2015.

Falkenmark, M., J. Lundquist, and C. Widstrand. 1989. Macro-Scale Water Scarcity Requires Micro-Scale Approaches: Aspects of Vulnerability in Semi-arid Development. *Natural Resources Forum*, 13:4, 258–267.

FASB. 2015. Statement of Financial Accounting Concepts No. 2: Qualitative Characteristics of Accounting Information, Paragraph 132. Available at <www.fasb.org/cs/BlobServer?blobcol=urldata&blobtable=MungoBlobs&blobkey=id&blobwhere=1175820900526&blobheader=application%2Fpdf> Accessed June 2015.

Fava, J. A. 2002. Life Cycle Initiative: A Joint UNEP/SETAC Partnership to Advance the Life-cycle Economy. *The International Journal of Life Cycle Assessment*, 7:4, 196–198.

Fermeglia, M., L. Toma, and G. Longo. 2011. Process Sustainability Prediction: A Computer Aided Design Tool for Sustainable Industrial Development. *Ecosystems and Sustainable Development*, VIII:144, 165–176.

FLA. 2015. Code of Conduct. Fair Labor Association. Available at <www.fairlabor.org/our-work/labor-standards> Accessed July 2015.

FTA. 2015. BSCI: What We Do. Available at <www.bsci-intl.org/content/what-we-do-0> Accessed July 2015.

FTSE. 2014a. FTSE ESG Ratings: Integrating ESG Into Investments and Stewardship. Available at <www.ftse.com/products/indices/F4G-ESG-Ratings> Accessed August 2015. A short summary is available at that site. With a free registration at <www.ftse.com/Analytics/ftse4good-esgratings/RegisterEmail.aspx>, users may log in to access resources such as the full summary referenced here.

FTSE. 2014b. FTSE ESG Ratings and FTSE4Good. Available at <www.ftse.com/products/indices/F4G-ESG-Ratings> Accessed August 2015. Access requires free registration at <www.ftse.com/Analytics/ftse4good-esgratings/RegisterEmail.aspx>

FTSE. 2015a. Index Inclusion Rules For The FTSE4Good Index Series, Version 1.6 June 2015. Available at <www.ftse.com/products/downloads/F4G-Index-Inclusion-Rules.pdf> Accessed July 2015.

FTSE. 2015b. Ground Rules for the FTSE4Good Index Series, Version 2.2, April 2015. Available at <www.ftse.com/products/downloads/FTSE4Good_Index_Series.pdf?95> Accessed July 2015.

Gassert, F., M. Luck, M. Landis, P. Reig, and T. Shiao. 2015. *Aqueduct Global Maps 2.1: Constructing Decision-Relevant Global Water Risk Indicators.* Working Paper. Washington, DC: World Resources Institute. Available at <http://www.wri.org/publication/aqueduct-global-maps-21-indicators> Accessed June 2015.

GEMI. 2015. About the GEMI LWT. Global Environmental Management Initiative. Available at <www.gemi.org/localwatertool/about.html> Accessed August 2015.

GHG Protocol. 2013. The Greenhouse Gas Protocol: A Corporate Accounting and Reporting Standard, Revised ed. Available at <www.ghgprotocol.org/files/ghgp/public/ghg-protocol-revised.pdf> Accessed August 2015.

GHG Protocol. 2015a. Project Protocol. Greenhouse Gas Protocol. Available at <http://www.ghgprotocol.org/standards/project-protocol> Accessed August 2015.

GHG Protocol. 2015b. GHG Protocol for Project Accounting. Greenhouse Gas Protocol. Available at <www.ghgprotocol.org/standards/project-protocol> Accessed August 2015.

GHG Protocol. 2015c. Global Warming Potentials (May 2015). Available at <http://ghgprotocol.org/sites/default/files/ghgp/Global-Warming-Potential-Values.pdf> Accessed August 2015.

GHG Protocol. 2015d. What is the GHG Protocol? GHG Protocol. Available at <www.ghgprotocol.org/about-ghgp> Accessed August 2015.

GISR. 2015a. Global Initiative for Sustainability Ratings: Principles Version 1.1, p. 15. Available at <http://ratesustainability.org/core/principles/> Accessed August 2015.

GISR. 2015b. About GISR: Vision and Mission. Global Initiative for Sustainability Ratings. Available at <http://ratesustainability.org/about/> Accessed August 2015.

Global Compact. 2014. Corporate Water Disclosure Guidelines: Toward a Common Approach to Reporting Water Issues. CEO Water Mandate. Available at <http://ceowatermandate.org/disclosure/> Accessed August 2015.

GPWI. 2015. About Us. Great Place to Work Institute. Available at <http://www.greatplacetowork.com/about-us> Accessed August 2015.

Green Seal. 2009. GS-C1 Pilot Sustainability Standard for Product Manufacturers, 1st ed. November 2, 2009. Available at <www.greenseal.org/Portals/0/Documents/Standards/GS-C1/green_seal_pilot_company_certification_gs-c1.pdf>

GRI. 2009. Rules and Procedures for the GRI Stakeholder Council. Available at <www.globalreporting.org/SiteCollectionDocuments/SC_RulesProcedures2009.pdf> Accessed August 2015.

GRI. 2012. Sector Guidance for G4. Available at <www.globalreporting.org/information/news-and-press-center/Pages/Sector-guidance-for-G4.aspx> Accessed July 2015.

GRI. 2013a. G4 Sustainability Reporting Guidelines: Reporting Principles and Standard Disclosures. Global Reporting Initiative. Available at <www.globalreporting.org/standards/g4/Pages/default.aspx> Accessed July 2015.

GRI. 2013b. G4 Sustainability Reporting Guidelines: Implementation Manual. Global Reporting Initiative, page 20. Available at <www.globalreporting.org/resourcelibrary/GRIG4-Part2-Implementation-Manual.pdf> Accessed June 2015.

GRI. 2013c. Sustainability Topics for Sectors: What Do Stakeholders Want to Know? Global Reporting Initiative. Available at <www.globalreporting.org/resourcelibrary/sustainability-topics.pdf> Accessed July 2015.

GRI. 2013d. Materiality Matters-GRI's New Check Service. December 11, 2013. Available at <www.globalreporting.org/information/news-and-press-center/Pages/Materiality-Matters-GRIs-new-check-service-.aspx> Accessed August 2015.

GRI. 2013e. Carrots and Sticks. Available at <www.globalreporting.org/reporting/reporting-support/publications/research-anddevelopment-publications/Pages/default.aspx> Accessed June 2015.

GRI. 2014a. GRI G4 Guidelines and ISO 26000:2010 How to use the GRI G4 Guidelines and ISO 26000 in Conjunction. <www.globalreporting.org/resourcelibrary/How-to-use-the-GRI-G4-Guidelines-and-ISO-26000-in-conjunction.pdf> Accessed July 2015.

GRI. 2014b. Linking CASS-CSR 3.0 and GRI's G4 Sustainability Reporting Guidelines. Available at <www.globalreporting.org/resourcelibrary/Linking-CASS-CSR-3.0-and-GRI's-G4-Sustainability Reporting-Guidelines.pdf> Accessed June 2015.

GRI. 2015a. Sustainability Disclosure Database. Global Reporting Initiative. Available at <http://database.globalreporting.org/> Accessed June 2015.

GRI. 2015b. GRI's Governance Bodies. Available at <www.globalreporting.org/network/network-structure/governance-bodies/Pages/default.aspx> Accessed June 2015.

GRI. 2015c. An Introduction to GRI's New Governance Structure. Available at <www.globalreporting.org/SiteCollectionDocuments/2014/GRIs-new-governance-structure.pdf> Accessed August 2015.

GRI. 2015d. Stakeholder Council. Available at <www.globalreporting.org/network/network-structure/stakeholder-council/Pages/default.aspx> Accessed August 2015.

GRI. 2015e. Organizational Stakeholders. Available at <www.globalreporting.org/network/organizational-stakeholders/Pages/default.aspx> Accessed June 2015.

GRI. 2015f. GRI Secretariat. Available at <www.globalreporting.org/network/network-structure/secretariat/Pages/default.aspx> Accessed June 2015.

GRI. 2015g. Governmental Advisory Group. <www.globalreporting.org/network/network-structure/governmental-advisory-group/Pages/default.aspx> Accessed June 2015.

GRI. 2015h. National Annexes. Global Reporting Initiative. Available at <www.globalreporting.org/standards/reporting-framework-overview/national-annexes/Pages/default.aspx> Accessed June 2015.

GRI. 2015i. Content Index Service. Available at <www.globalreporting.org/services/alignment/Content_Index_Service/Pages/default.aspx> Accessed August 2015.

GRI. 2015j. Become a Certified Training Partner. Global Reporting Initiative. Available at [illegible] training-program/Pages/default.aspx> Accessed June 2015.

GRI. 2015k. G4 Exam. Global Reporting Initiative. Available at <www.globalreporting.org/reporting/Pages/GRI-G4-Exam.aspx> Accessed June 2015.

GRI. 2015l. Sustainability and Reporting Trends in 2015—Preparing for the Future. May 2015. Global Reporting Initiative. Available at <www.globalreporting.org/resource library/Sustainability-and-Reporting-Trends-in-2025–1.pdf> Accessed August 2015.

GRI and RobecoSAM. 2015. Defining Materiality: What Matters to Reporters and Investors. Global Reporting Initiative and RobecoSAM. Available at <http://www.robecosam.com/images/Defining-Materiality-What-Matters-to-Reporters-and-Investors.pdf> Accessed August 2015.

Herrera, T. 2011. LG, Intuit, Igefa Pilot New UL 880 Sustainability Standard. GreenBiz.com (December 6, 2011). Available at <http://www.greenbiz.com/blog/2011/12/06/lg-intuit-igefa-pilot-new-ul-sustainability-standard> Accessed June 2015.

Hoekstra, A. Y., A. K. Chapagain, M. M. Aldaya, and M. M. Mekonnen. 2011. *The Water Footprint Assessment Manual*. London: Earthscan.

Hopwood, A., J. Unerman, and J. Fries, eds. 2010. *Accounting for Sustainability*. London: Earthscan.

Huang, A., and S. Herriott. 2013. Relational Governance: The Normative Element in Technology Licensing Contracts. *Journal of Management Policy and Practice*, 14:4, 137–151.

ICB. 2015. Industry Classification Benchmark. Available at <www.icbenchmark.com> Accessed July 2015.

IFC. 2012. IFC Performance Standards on Environmental and Social Sustainability. International Finance Corporation. Available at <www.ifc.org/wps/wcm/connect/c8f524004a-73daeca09afdf998895a12/IFC_Performance_Standards.pdf?MOD=AJPERES> Accessed August 2015.

ISO. 2004. ISO 14001:2004 Requirements with Guidance for Use. International Organization for Standardization. Available at <www.iso.org/iso/iso_catalogue/catalogue_tc/catalogue_detail.htm%3Fcsnumber=31807> Accessed June 2015.

ISO. 2010. International Standard ISO 26000: Guidance on Social Responsibility. International Organization for Standardization. Available for purchase at <www.iso.org/iso/home/store/catalogue_tc/catalogue_detail.htm?csnumber=42546> Accessed July 2015.

ISO. 2014a. Discovering ISO 26000. International Organization for Standardization. Available at <www.iso.org/iso/discovering_iso_26000.pdf> Accessed July 2015.

ISO. 2014b. ISO 14046:2014 Environmental Management—Water Footprint—Principles, Requirements and Guidelines. Available at <www.iso.org/iso/catalogue_detail?csnumber=43263> Accessed July 2015.

ISO. 2015. ISO 26000—Social Responsibility. International Organization for Standardization. Available at <www.iso.org/iso/home/standards/iso26000.htm> Accessed July 2015.

Jensen, M. C., and W. H. Meckling. 1976. Theory of the Firm: Managerial Behavior, Agency Costs and Ownership Structure. *Journal of Financial Economics*, 3:4, 305–360.

Kolk. A. 1999. Evaluating Corporate Environmental Reporting. *Business Strategy and the Environment*, 8, 225–237.

KPMG. 2012. Water Scarcity—A Dive Into Global Reporting Trends. KPMG Sustainable Insight. Available at <http://www.kpmg.com/Global/en/IssuesAndInsights/Articles Publications/sustainable-insight/Pages/water-scarcity.aspx> Accessed July 2015.

KPMG. 2013. The KPMG Survey of Corporate Responsibility Reporting 2013. KPMG International. Available at <www.kpmg.com/Global/en/IssuesAndInsights/Articles Publications/corporate-responsibility/Documents/corporate-responsibility-reporting-survey-2013-exec-summary.pdf> Accessed August 2015.

KPMG. 2014. Unlocking the Value of Social Investment. KPMG International Cooperative. Available at <www.kpmg.com/global/en/issuesandinsights/articlespublications/sustainable-insight/pages/unlocking-value-social-investment.aspx> Accessed August 2015.

KPMG, UNEP, GRI and Center for Corporate Governance in Africa. 2013. Carrots and Sticks—Sustainability Reporting Policies Worldwide—Today's Best Practice, Tomorrow's Trends. Available at: <www.globalreporting.org/resourcelibrary/Carrots-and-Sticks.pdf> Accessed August 2015.

Leopold, A. 1949. *A Sand County Almanac and Sketches Here and There*. New York: Oxford University Press.

Macaulay, S. 1963. Non-Contractual Relations in Business: A Preliminary Study. *American Sociological Review*, 28:1, 55–67.

Macneil, I. R. 1974. The Many Futures of Contracts. *Southern California Law Review*, 147: 691–816.

Maheshwari, A. 2015. *Business Intelligence and Data Mining*. New York: Business Expert Press.

March, J. G., and J. P. Olsen. 1998. The Institutional Dynamics of International Political Orders. *International Organization*, 52:4, 943–969.

March, J. G., and H. A. Simon. 1958. *Organizations*. New York: Wiley.

McDonald, M. 2014. Small U.S. Colleges Battle Death Spiral as Enrollment Drops. Bloomberg Business. Available at <www.bloomberg.com/news/articles/2014–04–14/small-u-s-colleges-battle-death-spiral-as-enrollment-drops> Accessed August 2015.

McDonough, W., and M. Braungart. 1998. The Next Industrial Revolution. *The Atlantic Monthly*, 282:4, 82–92.

MDEQ. 2015. Total Suspended Solids. State of Michigan Department of Environmental Quality. Available at <www.michigan.gov/documents/deq/wb-npdes-TotalSuspended Solids_247238_7.pdf> Accessed July 2015.

Monachese, M., J. P. Burton, and G. Reid. 2012. Bioremediation and Tolerance of Humans to Heavy Metals Through Microbial Processes: A Potential Role for Probiotics. *Applied and Environmental Microbiology*, 78, 6397–6404. Available at <http://phys.org/news/2012–09-detoxifying-effect-microbes.html> Accessed August 2015.

Morhardt, J. E. 2010. Corporate Social Responsibility and Sustainability Reporting on the Internet. *Business Strategy and the Environment*, 19:7, 436–452.

Morrison, J., R. Schenck, and P. Schulte. 2010. *Corporate Water Accounting: An Analysis of Methods and Tools for Measuring Water Use and Its Impacts*. Oakland, CA: Pacific Institute and UNEP UN Global Compact. Available at <http://ceowatermandate.org/files/corporate_water_accounting_analysis.pdf> Accessed July 2015.

Newton, L. H. 2003. *Ethics and Sustainability*. Upper Saddle River, NJ: Addison-Wesley.

Ohlsson, L. 2000. Water Conflicts and Social Resource Scarcity. *Physics and Chemistry of the Earth*, 25:3, 213–220.

Oram, B. 2015. Stream Water Quality—Importance of Total Suspended Solids/Turbidity. Available at <www.water-research.net/index.php/stream-water-quality-importance-of-total-suspended-solids-turbidity> Accessed August 2015.

Park, D. 2015. Putting the 'A' Back in MD&A. Sustainability Accounting Standards Board. Available at <www.sasb.org/putting-a-mda/> Accessed June 2015.

[illegible] publications&eod=1> Accessed August 2015.

Phrase Finder. 2015. Power Corrupts; Absolute Power Corrupts Absolutely. Available at <www.phrases.org.uk/meanings/absolute-power-corrupts-absolutely.html> Accessed July 2015.

Putt del Pino, S., and P. Bhatia. 2002. Working 9 to 5 on Climate Change: An Office Guide. World Resources Institute. Available at <http://www.wri.org/publication/working-9-to-5-on-climate-change> Accessed August 2015.

Raskin, P., P. Gleick, P. Kirshen, G. Pontius, and K. Strzepek. 1997. *Water Futures: Assessment of Long-Range Patterns and Problems. Comprehensive Assessment of the Freshwater Resources of the World.* Stockholm, Sweden: Stockholm Environment Institute.

RGGI. 2015a. Regional Greenhouse Gas Initiative. Available at <http://www.rggi.org> Accessed August 2015.

RGGI. 2015b. Program Design. Regional Greenhouse Gas Initiative. Available at <www.rggi.org/design> Accessed August 2015.

Rijsberman, F. R. 2006. Water Scarcity: Fact or Fiction? *Agricultural Water Management*, 80, 5–22.

RobecoSAM. 2014. Measuring Intangibles: RobecoSAM's Corporate Sustainability Assessment Methodology. (March 2014) Available at <www.robecosam.com/images/CSA_methodology_en.pdf> Accessed July 2015.

RobecoSAM. 2015a. Corporate Sustainability Assessment, CSV Test Company. Available at <www.robecosam.com/images/sample-questionnaire-1.pdf> Accessed July 2015.

RobecoSAM. 2015b. Corporate Sustainability Assessment, MNX Test Company. Available at <www.robecosam.com/images/sample-questionnaire-2.pdf> Accessed July 2015.

RobecoSAM. 2015c. RobecoSAM's Corporate Sustainability Assessment Companion (April 2015). RobecoSAM. Available at <https://assessments.robecosam.com/documents/RobecoSAM_CSA_Companion.pdf> Accessed August 2015.

Ruggie, J. 2008. Protect, Respect and Remedy: A Framework for Business and Human Rights. Innovations, 3:2, 189–212, paragraphs 6 and 52. Available at <www.reports-and-materials.org/sites/default/files/reports-and-materials/Ruggie-report-7-Apr-2008.pdf> Accessed July 2015.

S&P Dow Jones Indices. 2015. Dow Jones Sustainability Indices Methodology (June 2015). Click on "Methodology" at <http://eu.spindices.com/indices/equity/dow-jones-sustainability-world-index> Accessed July 2015.

SAI. 2014a. Social Accountability 8000. Social Accountability International. Available at <www.sa-intl.org/index.cfm?fuseaction=Page.ViewPage&pageId=937> Accessed July 2015.

SAI. 2014b. SA8000:2014 Performance Indicator Annex. Social Accountability International. Available at <www.sa-intl.org/index.cfm?fuseaction=Page.ViewPage&pageId=937> Accessed July 2015.

SASB. 2013. Conceptual Framework. Sustainability Accounting Standards Board. Available at <www.sasb.org/wp-content/uploads/2013/10/SASB-Conceptual-Framework-Final-Formatted-10-22-13.pdf> Accessed August 2015.

SASB. 2014. Media Production & Distribution: Provisional Standard. Sustainability Accounting Standards Board. Available at <www.sasb.org/standards/download/services/> Accessed July 2015.

SASB. 2015a. Vision and Mission. Sustainability Accounting Standards Board. Available at <http://www.sasb.org/sasb/vision-mission/> Accessed July 2015.

SASB. 2015b. Standards Council. Sustainability Accounting Standards Board. Available at <http://www.sasb.org/sasb/standards-council/> Accessed June 2015.

SASB. 2015c. Industry Briefs. Available at <www.sasb.org/approach/our-process/industry-briefs/> Accessed July 2015.

Schneider, A., and E. Meins. 2012. Two Dimensions of Corporate Sustainability Assessment: Towards a Comprehensive Framework. *Business Strategy and the Environment*, 21:4, 211–222.

Scientific Applications International Corporation. 2006. Life Cycle Assessment: Principles and Practice. U.S. Environmental Protection Agency. Report # EPA/600/R-06/060, p. 49. Available at <www.epa.gov/nrmrl/std/lca/lca.html> Accessed August 2015.

Seckler, D. W. 1998. *World Water Demand and Supply, 1990 to 2025: Scenarios and Issues* (Vol. 19). Colombo, Sri Lanka: International Water Management Institute.

Shi, D., N. Devineni, U. Lall, and E. Piñero. 2013. America's Water Risk: Water Stress and Climate Variability. Columbia University Water Center. Available at <http://water.columbia.edu/files/2013/09/GB_CWC_whitepaper_climate-water-stress_final.pdf> Accessed July 2015.

Shrivastava, P., and S. Hart. 1995. Creating Sustainable Corporations. *Business Strategy and the Environment*, 4:3, 154–165.

Smakhtin, V. Y., C. Revenga, and P. Döll. 2004. Taking Into Account Environmental Water Requirements in Global-Scale Water Resources Assessments (Vol. 2). IWMI. Available at <https://books.google.com/books?isbn=9290905425>

Spence, C. 2013. Sustainability Assessment & Evaluations—How To Get Started & Pitfalls To Avoid. Presentation at the 2013 Meeting of the Manufacturers Alliance for Productivity and Innovation (MAPI). Available at <www.mapi.net/events/sustainability-council-meeting-fall-2013> Accessed June 2015.

Standard and Poors. 2015. Global Industry Classification Standard Methodology. Available at <www.spindices.com/documents/index-policies/methodology-gics.pdf> Accessed June 2015.

StormwateRx. 2015. Total Suspended Solids. Available at <www.stormwaterx.com/Resources/IndustrialPollutants/TSS.aspx> Accessed December 2015.

Sullivan, C. 2002. Calculating a Water Poverty Index. *World Development*, 30:7, 1195–1210.

SustainAbility. 2010. Rate the Raters Phase Two: Taking Inventory of the Ratings Universe. Available at <www.sustainability.com/library/rate-the-raters-phase-two#.VYmUr1aWsVo> Accessed June 2015.

SustainAbility. 2011. Rate the Raters Phase Four: The Necessary Future of Ratings. July 2011. SustainAbility. Available at <www.sustainability.com/library/rate-the-raters-phase-four#.Vd04uVaWsVo> Accessed August 2015.

Taylor, P. W. 1986. *Respect For Nature: A Theory of Environmental Ethics*. Princeton, NJ: Princeton University Press.

The Climate Registry. 2015. 2015 Default Emissions Factors. Available at <www.theclimateregistry.org/wp-content/uploads/2015/04/2015-TCR-Default-EF-April-2015-FINAL.pdf> Accessed August 2015.

Thomson Reuters. 2014. Thomson Reuters Corporate Responsibility Ratings: Rating and Ranking Rules and Methodologies (August 2014). Available at <www.trcri.com/images/pdf/TRCRR_Rule_Book_8–14–2014.pdf> Accessed July 2015.

Thompson Reuters. 2015. ASSET4 ESG Data. Available as the "Thompson Reuters ESG Data Fact Sheet" at <http://thomsonreuters.com/content/dam/openweb/documents/pdf/tr-com-financial/fact-sheet/esg-data-fact-sheet.pdf> Accessed August 2015.

1st ed. (November 2, 2011). Available at <http://ulstandards.ul.com/standard/?id=880 &edition=1&doctype=ule> Accessed April 2015.

Underwriters Laboratories. 2015. UL 880 Standard for Sustainability for Manufacturing Organizations. Available at <http://ulstandards.ul.com/standard/?id=880&edition=1& doctype=ule> Accessed June 2015.

UNEP DTU. 2015. CDM Projects by Type. Centre on Energy, Climate and Sustainable Development. Available at <http://cdmpipeline.org/cdm-projects-type.htm> Accessed August 2015.

UNEP. 2009. Developing Integrated Solid Waste Management Plan Training Manual, Volume 1: Waste Characterization and Quantification with Projections for Future. United Nations Environment Program. Available at <www.unep.org/ietc/Portals/136/Publications/Waste%20Management/ISWMPlan_Vol1.pdf> Accessed July 2015.

UN Global Compact. 2014. CEO Water Mandate Corporate Water Disclosure Guidelines: Toward a Common Approach to Reporting Water Issues. United Nations Global Compact. Available at <http://ceowatermandate.org/disclosure/> Accessed July 2015.

United Nations. 1948. Universal Declaration of Human Rights. Available at <www.ohchr.org/EN/UDHR/Pages/UDHRIndex.aspx> Accessed July 2015.

U.S. Code of Federal Regulations 17 CFR 229.303(a)(3) (Item 303).

U.S. Energy Information Administration. 2015. Voluntary Reporting of Greenhouse Gases Program / Emissions Factors and Global Warming Potentials. Available at <http://www.eia.gov/survey/form/eia_1605/emission_factors.html> Accessed August 2015.

U.S. Forest Service. 2005. Summary of Requirements for ISO 14001:2004 <www.fs.fed.us/ems/includes/sum_ems_elements.pdf> Accessed June 2015.

USGBC. 2008. LEED Existing Buildings: Operations and Maintenance Reference Guide, 1st edition. MR credits 7.1 and 7.2. U.S. Green Building Council.

USGS. 2015. Turbidity-Units of Measurement. Oregon Water Science Center. Available at <http://or.water.usgs.gov/grapher/fnu.html> Accessed July 2015.

WBCSD. 2015. Global Water Tool. World Business Council for Sustainable Development. Available at <http://www.wbcsd.org/work-program/sector-projects/water/global-water-tool.aspx> Accessed July 2015.

White, C. 2012. Understanding Water Scarcity: Definitions and Measurements. UNESCO Global Water Forum. Available at <http://www.globalwaterforum.org/2012/05/07/understanding-water-scarcity-definitions-and-measurements/> Accessed July 2015.

White, L. 1967. The Historical Roots of Our Ecological Crisis. *Science*, 155, 1203–1207.

WHO. 1958. International Standards for Drinking Water. World Health Organization. Available at <http://apps.who.int/iris/bitstream/10665/43845/1/a91160.pdf> Accessed July 2015.

Wikipedia. 2015a. Carbon Offsets. Available at <http://en.wikipedia.org/wiki/Carbon_offset> Accessed August 2015.

Wikipedia. 2015b. Hazardous Materials Identification System. Last modified February 16, 2015. Available at <https://en.wikipedia.org/wiki/Hazardous_Materials_Identification_System> Accessed August 2015.

Wikipedia. 2015c. Sulphur hexafluoride. Available at <http://en.wikipedia.org/wiki/Sulphur_hexafluoride#Greenhouse_gas> Accessed July 2015.

Wikipedia. 2015d. Median Lethal Dose. Last modified July 10, 2015. Available at <https://en.wikipedia.org/wiki/Median_lethal_dose> Accessed July 2015.

Wikipedia. 2015e. Nitrous Oxide. Available at <http://en.wikipedia.org/wiki/Nitrous_oxide> Accessed July 2015.

Williamson, O. E. 1979. Transaction-Cost Economics: The Governance of Contractual Relations. *Journal of Law and Economics*, 22:2, 233–261.

Windolph, S. E. 2013. Assessing Corporate Sustainability Through Ratings: Challenges and Their Causes. *Journal of Environmental Sustainability*, 1:1, Article 5. Available at <http://scholarworks.rit.edu/jes/vol1/iss1/5> Accessed June 2015.

World Commission on Environment and Development. 1987. *Our Common Future*. Oxford: Oxford University Press.

WRI. 2015. Aqueduct: Measuring and Mapping Water Risk. World Resources Institute. Available at <www.wri.org/our-work/project/aqueduct> Accessed July 2015.

INDEX

Jyuroku Naihanchi Goju-ryu Seison Gojushiho Seiuchin
Wankan Tensh ... Fukyugata Bunkai
Heian Kun ... Passai-Dai Kata
Naihanchi ... Wanshu Unsu
Sankaku ... Seiryu Kanku-
dai Tek ... ngetsu Bunkai
Seienchin ... ken Naifanchin
Wado-ryu ... Unshu Gankaku
Martial Arts ... ensei-ryu Sanseiru
Jiin Kururunfu ... Bunkai Naihanchen

Bunkai Press

Nipaipo Sanzhan Taikyoku Seisan Kata Ananku Wansu Seishan Annan Naifanchi Bunaki Chinto Annanko Meikyo Jitte Kusanku Isshin-ryu Seiunchin Niseishi Seipai Chatanyara Kushanku Shito-ryu Ninjutsu Sanchin Bassai-Sho Sunsu Kempo Jyuroku Naihanchi Goju-ryu Seison Gojushiho Seiuchin Wankan Tensho Enpi Jion Rohai Fukyugata Bunkai Heian Kung Fu Saifa Ryuko Sesan Passai-Dai Kata Naihanchin Shotokan Suparinpei Wanshu Unsu Sankakutobi Shorin-ryu Karate Chinte Seiryu Kanku-dai Tekki Shuri-ryu Pinan Sochin Hangetsu Bunkai Seienchin Jusan Seiyunchin Kata Happiken Naifanchin Wado-ryu Shimpa Tae Kwon Do Empi Unshu Gankaku Martial Arts Shisochin Kushanku Gensei-ryu Sanseiru Jiin Kururunfu Sanseru Pechurin Bunkai Naihanchen Nipaipo Sanzhan Taikyoku Seisan Kata Ananku Wansu Seishan Annan Naifanchi Bunaki Chinto Annanko Meikyo Jitte Kusanku Isshin-ryu Seiunchin Niseishi Jiin Seiuchin Wankan Tensho Enpi Jion Rohai Fukyugata Bunkai Heian Kung Fu Saifa Ryuko Sesan Passai-Dai Kata Naihanchin Shotokan Suparinpei Wanshu Unsu Sankakutobi Shorin-ryu Karate Chinte Seiryu Kanku-dai Tekki Shuri-ryu Pinan Sochin Hangetsu Bunkai Seienchin Jusan Seiyunchin Kata Happiken Naifanchin Wado-ryu Shimpa Tae Kwon Do Empi Unshu Gankaku Martial Arts Shisochin Kushanku Gensei-ryu Sanseiru Jiin Kururunfu Sanseru Pechurin Bunkai Naihanchen Nipaipo Sanzhan Taikyoku Seisan Kata Ananku Wansu Seishan Annan Naifanchi Bunaki

Suruchin

Flexible Weapon of Okinawan Kobudo

By

Leo Scott Britt III

Suruchin: Flexible Weapon of Okinawan Kobudo

Cover design by Leo Scott Britt III

Editing by Dr. Olivia Susan Fritts

ISBN-13: 978-0-578-91258-5

Bunkai Press

Printed in the U.S.A.

Note: this book was corrected July 2021 with earlier references to the Meteor Hammer as brought to the authors' attention by fellow author Christian Russo; many thanks for the additional information!

Table of Contents

Acknowledgments

My thanks to those that helped me get this book together – to my wife Mindy, my mother Laurie, my karate students for their constant encouragement and proofreading, and to my aunt Dr. Olivia Susan Fritts for her professional editing services – this would not have been possible without your help. My thanks also go to those that inspired me to create this book through their dedication to the traditional martial arts and the teaching of Bunkai. First and foremost, I want to thank my teacher Keith Cofer for planting a lifelong passion for karate in me, and for serving as a role model and father to me. My thanks also go to those that have served to spread the study of Bunkai to so many – in particular, Pete Mills, Michael Garner, and Ian Abernathy. A special thanks is in order for fellow instructor Jeff Poore (who appears as Uke several places in this book); you have been a great source of help and encouragement, both for this book and for every single class of our martial arts school. This book would not be possible without those who shared with me their time and knowledge of the suruchin weapon during my research for this book, and permission to use various materials (in alphabetical order):

- Andrea Guarelli, 6th dan Matayoshi Kobudo, of the International Matayoshi Kobudō Association
- Angie Spencer, 7th dan Isshinryu, of Spencer's Isshinryu Karate, Virginia
- Bernard Edwards, Chief Master Instructor of the US Karate-Do Hakua Kai Association
- Chris Willson, photographer, of www.travel67.com
- Christian Russo, Jūtaijutsu martial artist and author
- Emile van Heerden, 7th dan Ryukyu Kobudo, Basingstoke England
- Franco Sanguinetti, 8th dan Matayoshi Kobudo, www.bushikan.com
- Hiroshi Akamine, 8th dan Ryukyu Kobudo and 3rd president of Ryukyu Kobudo Hozon Shinkokai

- Juga Paazmaya, photographer, of www.flickr.com/photos/paazio
- Julian Mead, 7th dan Ryukyu Kobudo and Chief instructor and chairman of Ryukyu Kobujutsu Association G.B
- Ken Jack, 2nd dan Ryukyu Kobudo, Indianapolis Dokokai
- Kevin Gurganus, 5th dan Ryukyu Kobudo, Carolina Martial Arts Center
- Kisho Inoue, Ryukyu Kobjutsu Hozon Shinko Kai
- Kuniyoshi Yukio sensei, 8th dan and President of Ryukyu Kobudo Hozon Shiko Kai
- Mario McKenna, 6th dan Ryukyu Kobudo, instructor Vancouver Kowakan school
- Mark D. Bishop, prolific Okinawan karate and kobudo author
- Michael Clayton, president Matayoshi Kobudo Ass. Of Great Britain
- Miguel Da Luz, Okinawa Karate Information Center (http://okic.okinawa)
- Murray Simpson, 8th dan new Zealand under Kiichi Nakamoto Hanshi of Ufuchiku Kobujutsu
- Neil Anderson, of www.antiquechinesesword.com and zhongyimartialarts.org
- Paul Brennan, of brennantranslation.wordpress.com
- Tomohiro Arashiro, 8th dan Ryuei Ryu
- Victor Donald Smith, master rank Isshinryu, prolific writer
- Yasushi Matayoshi, son of Shinpo Matayoshi, of Matayoshi Kobudo
- Yoshimura Hiroshi, 7th dan Ryukyu Kobudo, chairman of Ryukyu Kobudo Shinkokai

Lastly, a dedication to my grandmother, Lovelle V. Atkisson, who passed in 2020; your influence and love continue to show in my life, and I wish that I could have shown you this completed work. You are very, very missed.

About the Author

At the time of this writing, Scott Britt was a 6th degree black belt in Isshinryu karate, and held rank in Shotokan, Agedo, and Kendo as well. In 2004, he was inducted into the United States Martial Arts Hall of Fame as "Bunkai Instructor of The Year." He has been an avid competitor, with one of his most notable accomplishments being serving on the U.S. team in the 2004 world games in Athens, Greece, where he brought home several medals in various divisions. He was also the 2004 and 2005 U.S. National Martial Arts team Alliance "National Points Champion." In 2012, he was honored to join a team of martial artists going on a mission trip to the Ukraine, where they used their skills and talents to reach others for God.

Scott teaches karate in Oak Ridge, TN, and has a day job as an Instrumentation technician. He, his wife Mindy, and their three sons live in Knoxville, TN. He views karate not as a hobby or as a part-time job, but as a calling and a ministry to help those who are weak become better able to defend themselves, and to introduce Christ and Christian values to those that otherwise may have never had the opportunity to know Him.

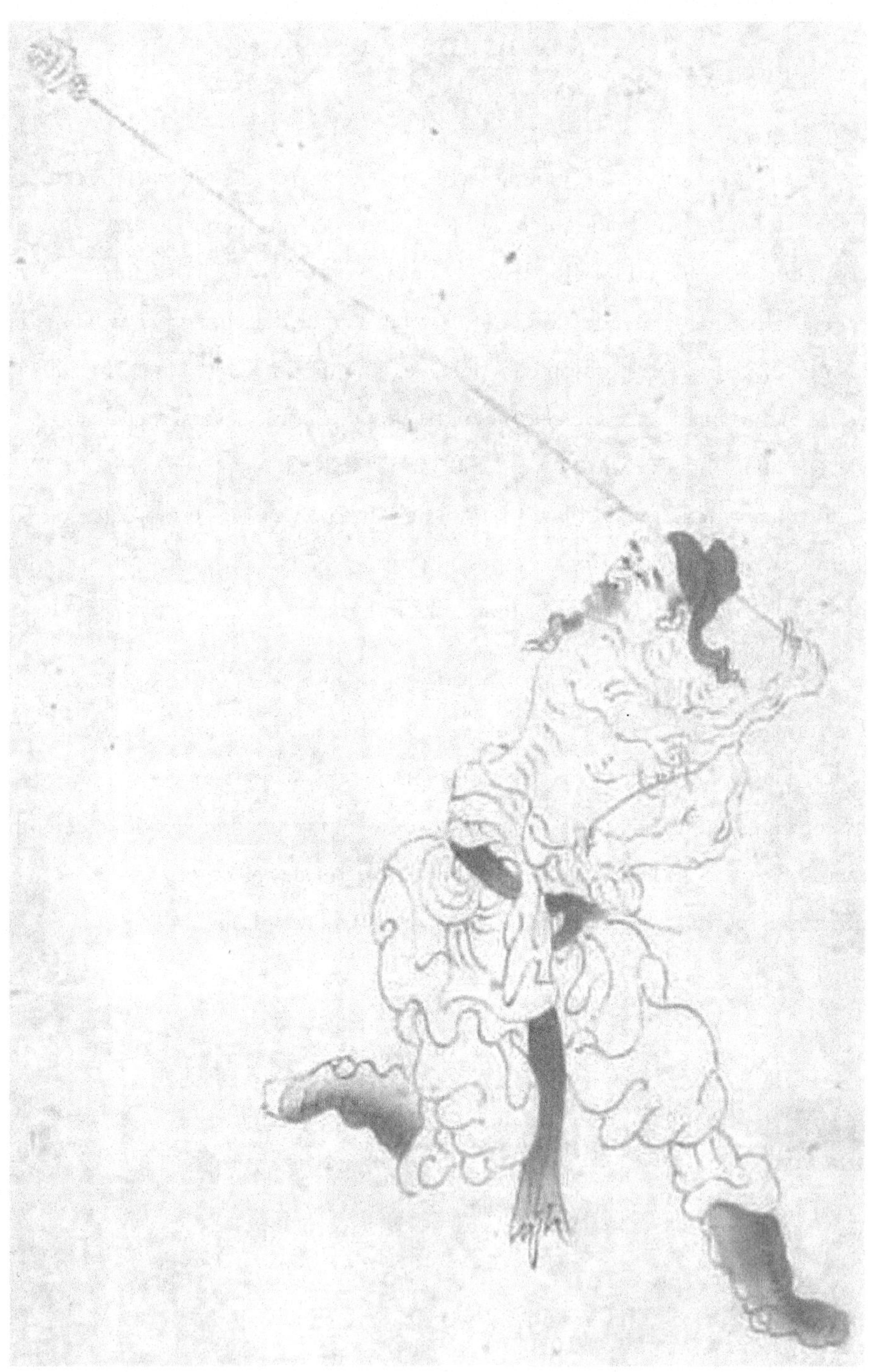

Figure 1 1800's Illustration from Water Margin; story written late 14th century.
http://gmzm.org/gudaizihua/shuihurenwu/index.asp?page=15

Introduction

This book is the result of countless hours of study and research, during which I sought and compiled information from people across the globe, as well as from out of print and foreign language books. This search crossed multiple styles and lineages. My hope in creating this book is that other martial artists learning the suruchin will have a succinct, single source for all the knowledge and katas I have pieced together from dozens of sources.

Figure 2 Tiara Shinken

The suruchin is a fascinating weapon. It is a lesser-known weapon in the category of flexible weapons. Unlike other traditional Kobudo weapons it can be hidden or concealed; it can also be improvised from such things as power cords and tow straps and is highly portable. These qualities make it an excellent candidate for study in modern times.

I also hope to further the art of suruchin in a practical sense, adding in what I have developed through the careful study of the three main styles that utilize the suruchin. These additions to the global suruchin knowledge base (Miichiryu suruchin kata, modern construction techniques, etc.) are clearly labeled as such in this book and should give the reader additional grist for the mill.

I hope the reader enjoys this content and finds it easily understandable and relevant. I have striven to be both accurate and comprehensive; however, should the reader discover any inaccuracies or know of additional information not provided in this book, please contact me at isshin-ryu@hotmail.com and I will gladly incorporate these comments into any future editions.

History of the Suruchin (スルチン)

Origins

As with most topics related to martial arts, there is only so far back the written record goes before events are lost to history. It is believed that the suruchin (also spelled Surujin, or less commonly Surichin) in some form started in the ancient past as a hunting weapon, possibly thrown in a similar manner to the South American Bolas used by the gauchos (Argentinian cowboys). While maintaining hold of one end, it basically becomes a way of hunting small animals by casting a weight which can then be quickly recovered to be recast. From there, it was used through the centuries by various armies under different names, in part because of its effectiveness for and against mounted soldiers.

As far as the Okinawan history of the weapon, Mikio Nishiuchi of Matayoshi Kobudo presents several possible origins for the suruchin and its name [13]:

a) Surukaa = bark/hemp rope, chin = weights used to hold paper down while brush writing
b) Surukaa = bark/hemp = rope, chin = to make peaceful
c) Weighted ropes used to hold down shingles on a roof
d) Weighted rope added to fishing net for fishing in deep waters

Meanwhile, Mark Bishop [2] suggests that the origin was often claimed to be the balance/weights used by Okinawan shopkeepers and merchants, though he points out that there is not a perfect carryover in size/weight to the suruchin. However, this is also the version heard by Kuniyoshi Yukio of Ryukyu Kobudo.

Lastly, the Meteor hammer section of this book describes the possibility that the Okinawan practitioners of the suruchin may have been inspired by the Shaolin weapons of China.

Figure 3 Boys with Suruchin, from nanto zatsuwa (1880)

There are two primary martial art styles that use the suruchin: Ryukyu Kobudo (through Taira Shinken) and Matayoshi Kobudo (through Shinpo Matayoshi). There is a third style to be counted, Shaolin kung Fu, whose double-sided meteor hammer is mostly different in name only. These three styles have surprisingly little overlap in techniques and kata, each offering a different perspective on the weapon.

In addition to these main styles for suruchin, another deserves mention. Ryūei-ryū was originally the family style of the Nakaima family of Naha. It was founded by Norisato Nakaima (1819-1879) and passed down to his son Nakaima Kenchu (1856-1953). While there are references to the suruchin being included in the weapons list, the official stance is that the suruchin is not practiced in the style in modern times. No known suruchin katas exist in Ryūei-ryū.

Lastly, some sources mention other styles such as Matsumura Orthadox Shorin-ryu, Koryu Kobudo, and Ufuchiku kobudo practicing suruchin [2,3,12]. However, research has been unable to find examples of the weapon in use in modern times in these styles.

Figure 4 Ufuchiku, who reportedly practiced suruchin [12]

Figure 5 Taira Shinken, Motokatsu Inoue, Higa Seiko, and Matayoshi Shinpo (1960)

Ryukyu Kobudo

Sometimes called the father of Okinawan Kobudo, Taira Shinken carefully studied and cataloged the traditional weapon katas of the Ryukyu islands, while also at times creating katas to document techniques when no traditional katas were in existence. He is credited with preserving 42 weapons katas, covering Bo, Sai, Tonfa, Nunchaku, Kama, Tekko, Tinbe-rochin, Eku, and Suruchin. Taira had the given name Shinken Maezato (he took his mother's name Taira later), so in accordance with the tradition of naming katas after their originator, some katas connected with Taira are called Maezato no Tekko or the like.

Much of Taira Shinken's kobudo was learned under Moden Yabiku, founder of the Ryukyu Kobujutsu Kenkyu Kai (Ryukyu Kobujutsu Research Association). However, it is Taira Shinken's grandfather Kanegawa Gimu (or Gibu) who is credited with introducing him to the suruchin weapon. Not much is known about Kanegawa Gimu, other than that he was a high-ranking official in the Ryuku kingdom government. After the Riuki's affiliation with Japan, he lost his job and had to survive from farming and fishing. He was a master of nichou kama (double kama), tekko, suruchin, and tinbe [6]. Contradicting this is an account [9] that states Tatsuo was taught by Master Yafuso (no full name known), a disciple of Taira's grandfather. However, this being said, it is impossible to fully isolate Taira Shinken's suruchin influences as he spent his lifetime learning the techniques and katas of countless people across Okinawa.

In 1940, shortly before the death of Yabiku Sensei in 1941, Taira established the Ryukyu Kobudo Hozon Shinko-Kai, the association for the preservation and promotion of Ryukyu Kobudo based in Naha, built on the organization of Yabiku Sensei's Ryukyu Kobujutsu Kenkyu Kai [9]. While Taira hoped to write several books, the only book produced before his death in 1970 was Ryukyu Kobudo Taikan in 1964 (translated into English [14,18]).

This brief book unfortunately only has an introductory paragraph for the suruchin.

Upon Taira's passing, Eisuke Akamine took over the style in Okinawa, followed by Akamine Hiroshi. The current head of the Ryukyu Kobudo Hozon Shinko Kai is Yukio Kuniyoshi. Meanwhile, Motokatsu Inoue was the head in Japan after Taira's death. Motokatsu published several books to document the katas of Ryukyu Kobudo [10,11]. The first volume of his Ryukyu Kobujutsu trilogy has the Long suruchin kata documented, while the third (as well as his English book Ryukyu Kobujutsu [Chi no maki]) has the short suruchin kata. His son Kisho Inoue is the current head of the Ryukyu Kobujutsu Hozon Shinko Kai and Yuishinkai organization in Tokyo. The following lineage is restricted to suruchin history and does not include all influences on the style.

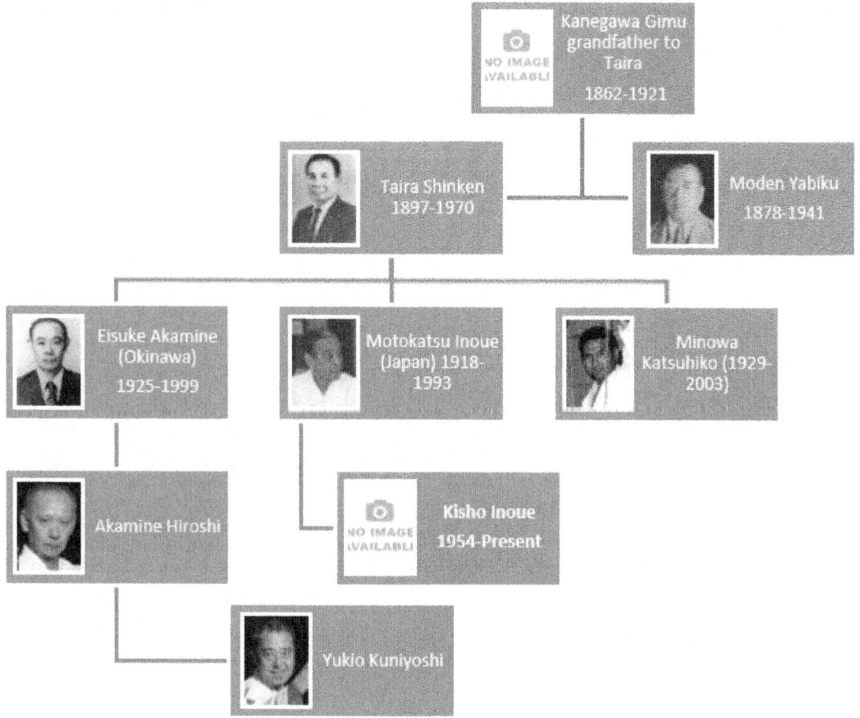

Figure 6 Ryukyu Kobudo lineage

There is some controversy around the exact origin of the two suruchin katas, Naga (long) suruchin and Tan (short) suruchin. Some people interviewed have stated that Taira only practiced Waza (techniques) and did not do any kata. Written sources [21] have Naga suruchin created by Taira Shinken himself, while the Tan suruchin kata was created by Minowa Katsuhiko (called Maezato no suruchin and Minowa no suruchin). However, in interviews for research for this book, 7th dan Yoshimura Hiroshi of Ryukyu Kobudo Shinko Kai (student of Minowa) states that both katas are the creation of Motokatsu Inoue, and that Maezato Suruchin is a separate kata (no example found of a different kata). Meanwhile, Kisho Inoue, the current head of Ryukyu Kobujutsu Hozon Shinko Kai, states that both kata are handed down from Taira Shinken's grandfather, Kanegawa Gimu. It is the author's theory that the long kata was created by Taira, and the short by one of his students, either Motokatsu (since it is highlighted in his books over the long kata and is the only kata with video of himself performing it) or Katsuhiko. This was likely done with the blessing of Taira himself (and possibly his guidance), and then incorporated into the style. However, with no written record from Taira himself, this is only a theory.

Figure 7 Taira Shinken

Figure 8 Eisuke Akamine

Figure 9 Motokatsu Inoue

Figure 10 Akamine Hiroshi

Figure 11 Yukio Kuniyoshi

Permission not received to include photo of master Inoue in lineage.

Figure 12 Kisho Inoue

Figure 13 Moden Yabiku

Figure 14 Minowa Katsuhiko

Matayoshi Kobudo

The other main style of Kobudo in Okinawa to practice suruchin is Matayoshi Kobudo. The founder, Shinko Matayoshi, was ancestor to the well known Okinawan lord Shinjo Gima, and learned Kobudo weapons from his father Matayoshi Shinchin, as well as Agena Chokubo and Ire Okina. However, it was on a trip to China that he became acquainted with the suruchin. In 1905 at the age of 17, he left Okinawa on his way to China. He ended up stopping in the Manchuria area for 2-3 years and living with a band of mounted nomads/bandits. After moving on, he ended up in Fuchow city, in Fujian province, where he trained under Kingai Roshi, who taught him the Kingai-ryu style [7,8].

It is here that sources start to disagree regarding the suruchin; some state that he learned the Bola (suruchin-like weapon) from the nomads, along with the lasso and Shuriken. Other sources say that he learned suruchin along with tinbei, and nunti from Kingai Roshi [5]. Whichever is accurate, there was no kata for the suruchin at this point, but a collection of techniques.

Shinko's son, Shinpo Matayoshi, carried on the tradition of Kobudo. It was Shinpo that created the suruchin kata of Matayoshi Kobudo, "Suruchin no Toseki" (throwing the stone). It is also of interest that some students of the 1960s have known Shinpo Matayoshi to use a single-ended suruchin (similar to the single-ended meteor hammer of today). A good example of the suruchin kata can be seen in the film "Matayoshi Shinpo's Traditional Okinawan Kobudo" [19].

The current descendant of Matayoshi Kobudo is Yasushi Matayoshi. Several direct students of Shinpo Matayoshi have branched out with their own organizations; of note are Kenishi Yamashiro and Andrea Guarelli, (next page) who have modified versions of the suruchin kata. The following lineage is restricted to suruchin history and does not include all influences on the style.

Figure 15 Kenichi Yamashiro

Figure 16 Andrea Guarelli

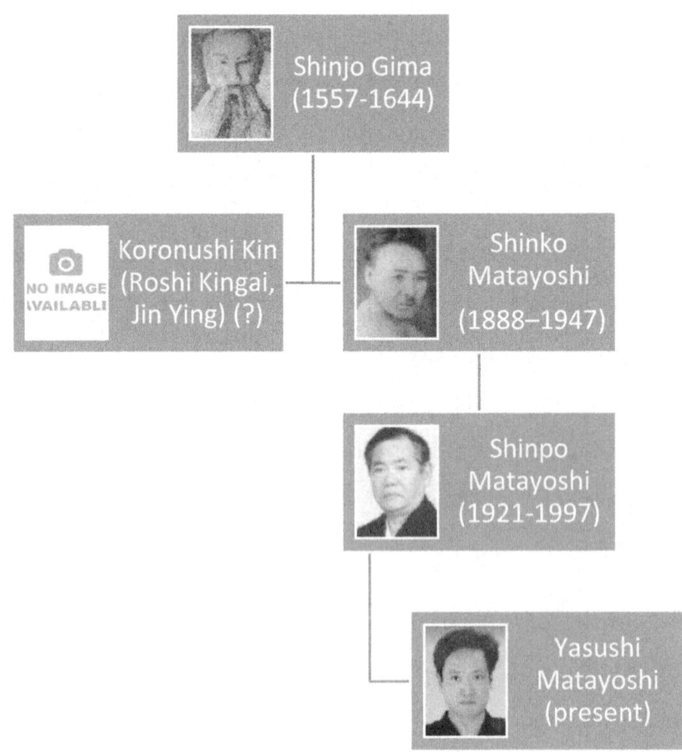

Figure 17 Matayoshi Kobudo lineage

Figure 18 Shinko Matayoshi

Figure 19 Shinpo Matayoshi

Figure 20 Shinjo Gima Portrait

Figure 21 Yasushi Matayoshi

Meteor Hammer

Found in Shaolin Kung Fu and Wushu, the meteor hammer (also called dai chui, flying hammer, or dragon's fist) is close kin to the suruchin.

There are two kinds of meteor hammer: the single-ended version, usually about 5 meters in length, and the double-ended version which is about two meters in length (which most closely resembles the traditional suruchin). While the single-ended version is the more popular one today, the double meteor hammer has one of the oldest references of any suruchin-like weapon.

Figure 22 Meteor Hammer - By Samuraiantiqueworld - Own work, CC BY-SA 3.0, https://commons.wikimedia.org/w/index.php?curid=12682113

The following page is from volume 104 of the Wubei Zhi ("Records of Military Training"), also called the Bubishi, written in 1621 [20]; it reads:

> Flying hammers, also called "meteor hammers," are used in pairs. The one held in the front hand is the "direct hammer" and the other held lifted in the rear hand is the "emergency hammer" (translation courtesy of Paul Brennan, brennantranslation.wordpress.com).

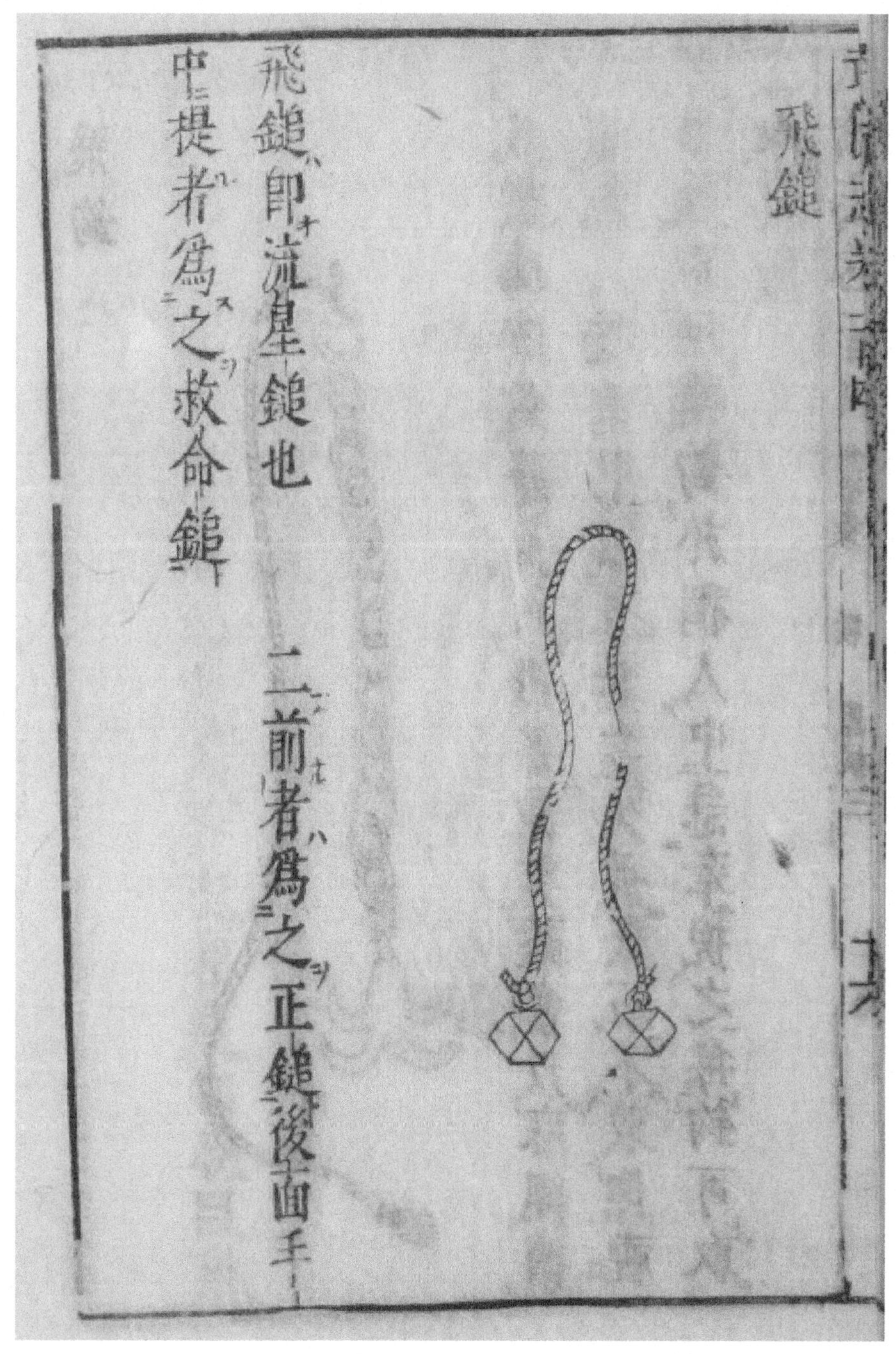

飛鎚

飛鎚即流星鎚也

二前者為之正鎚後面手

中提者為之救命鎚

Figure 23 Wubei Zhi 1621 - meteor hammers

The weights for antique meteor hammers have several designs: gourd, garlic head, and tetradechahedron shapes, made of copper, brass, brass-studded wood, and iron. Weights average around 1lb, up to 2lb (much heavier than modern remakes). See below for a representative sample of end weights. The Shaolin meteor hammer, like several other schools of soft weapons, do not have a strict kata or form (like some schools of Manriki fundo), but rather a collection of techniques.

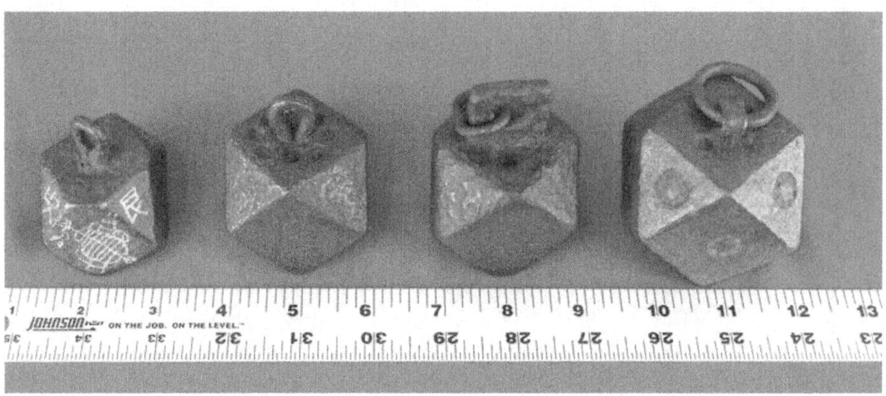

Figure 24 Example of various Chinese meteor hammer end weights, later Qing era. Courtesy of the Neil Anderson Collection, of antiquechinesesword.com

Figure 25 Later Qing era garlic head mace, brass 14.1oz. Courtesy of the Neil Anderson Collection, of antiquechinesesword.com

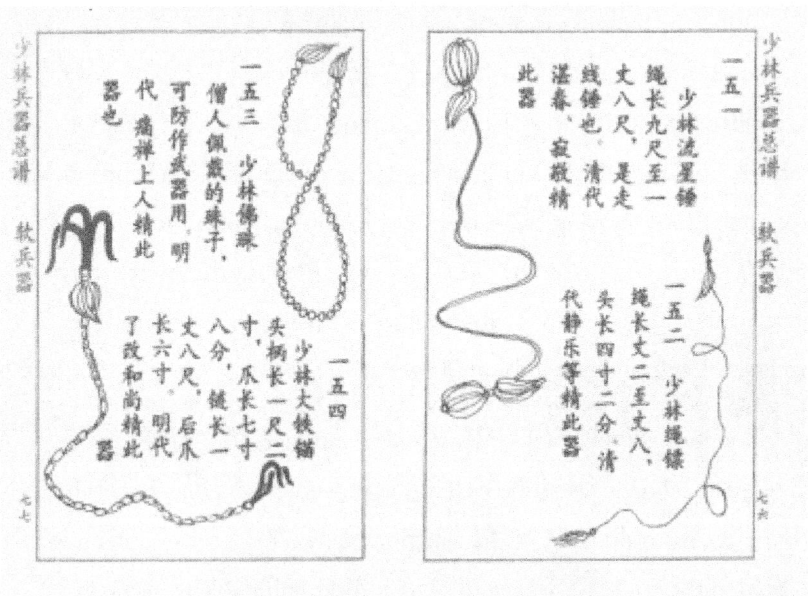

少林兵器总谱　软兵器

一五一　少林流星锤
绳长九尺至一丈八尺，是走线锤也。清代湛春、寂嶶精此器

一五二　少林绳镖
绳长丈二至丈八，头长四寸二分。清代静乐等精此器

七六

少林兵器总谱　软兵器

一五三　少林佛珠
僧人佩戴的珠子，可防作武器用。明代痴禅上人精此器也

一五四　少林大铁锚
头柄长一尺二寸，爪长七寸八分，链长一丈八尺，后爪长六寸。明代了改和尚精此器

七七

Figure 26 Engraving describing Shaolin 8-9ft meteor hammer of Qing dynasty.

The double-ended meteor hammer has also seen use for street performance, both in modern times and in times past, as can be seen by this early 19th century painting:

Figure 27 Meteor hammer painting. Courtesy of the Neil Anderson Collection, of antiquechineseswords.com

The meteor hammer is mentioned in the Water Margin story (late 14th century) as well as Romance of the Three Kingdoms (circa 1322), two of four novels considered to be the four great classical novels of Chinese literature. However, the origin of the meteor hammer likely stretches back significantly further, with author Dr. Yang [22] suggesting it may have been developed as early as the Tang dynasty (618-907 A.D.). Of note in these stories are the description of its use, including a mounted soldier using a meteor hammer to strike backwards at a pursuing mounted enemy.

As mentioned, the single-sided meteor hammer is by far the most common meteor hammer used today. The single-ended version can be up to 20 feet in length, with one end of the rope including a loop for the practitioner to place around the wrist. Of interest is Yugen Budo Shinkokai, a style in France founded in 1986 that has applied suruchin techniques to the single-ended meteor hammer (http://oudekrijgskunsten.nl/), complete with the katas O-kusari kata and Ishiguro no suruchin.

Lastly, while there is no definitive proof or record, it is the author's strong belief that the meteor hammer was the precursor and inspiration for the Okinawan suruchin. While it is possible that they were developed independently of each other, the fact that Okinawa was a major shipping hub and a melting pot due to the constant stream of travelers, combined with Shinko Matayoshi's travels through China, lends credence to the idea that the Okinawans saw the meteor hammer, and adopted/adapted it to their Kobudo weapons list. This would be no more than what happened constantly with the open hand katas of martial arts; for instance, several Okinawan katas have roots in white crane kung fu, though they have been modified to the point of becoming their own entity. A perfect example of this development in action is the Rante; the Chinese-inspired weapon of Delima Silat, an Indonesian martial art [4]. A light chain with 2oz weights added to ends, this weapon is like the suruchin in that it is basically a double ended meteor hammer with a local name applied.

Figure 28 Rante of Indonesia [4], Copyright © 1972 by Charles E Tuttle Publishing Co., Inc.

Figure 29 (Left) Illustration from the Water Margin story, Shui hu ren wu quan tu by Du Jin, 1467-1487 (Right) Illustration from History of the Three Kingdoms, 1368-1644, World Digital Library

The Future of the Suruchin

Due to several likely factors, such as focusing on the more common weapons (e.g., Bo) and lack of dojo space, the suruchin in most schools is not learned until black belt, and in many schools (Ryukyu Kobudo and Matayoshi Kobudo both included) it is reserved for after Go-Dan (5th degree black belt), or as an optional kata. One of the given reasons for this is that suruchin is a more difficult weapon to master; unfortunately, this policy has resulted in the suruchin becoming in danger of going extinct. In researching for this book for example, many of the "ambassador instructors" for a style to other countries did not know their style's suruchin kata. Even the head of one of the branches of Ryukyu Kobudo could not provide an example of the long suruchin kata (Naga Suruchin) being run, effectively making it a dead kata in that branch. While the suruchin is a more difficult weapon to master than say, the Bo, this weapon can still be easily learned by practitioners of all ages and ranks as has been proven in the author's dojo.

It is the author's opinion that the suruchin needs to move to an earlier point in the curriculum of Kobudo schools to prevent it from eventually going extinct altogether as masters pass away. Some of these Kobudo styles have 11 kata just for Bo; surely the suruchin, this fascinating and unique weapon, can be moved up the list for posterity's sake. With this in mind be sure to read the introduction to the Mini kata section provided later in this book.

Construction of Suruchin

Length

There are a large variety of lengths used traditionally. Ryukyu Kobudo with the handle-style suruchin will usually use 5 shaku (150-152cm) for a short suruchin (from end of weight to start of handle, excluding handle) and eight shaku (230-240cm) for a long suruchin (again, excluding the handle). Matayoshi Kobudo has been known to use three, five, six, and eight shaku length suruchins (90.9cm, 151cm, 181cm, and 240cm).

However, especially due to the differing sizes of karate students, the author prefers the method of measuring set out by Mikio Nishiuchi of Matayoshi Kobudo. This involves measuring the weapon specific to the user, at 1.5x arm span. See below for example. This is a similar length and method of measurement to the Shaolin meteor hammer.

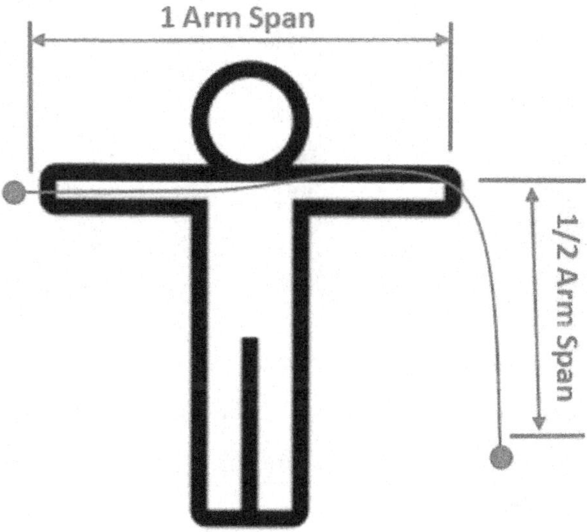

Figure 30 Suruchin length

Rope Suruchin

Rope suruchins are the type more commonly used in Matayoshi Kobudo. They are made from hemp rope (which has a much higher breaking strength than a jute rope of the same diameter), with two river rocks serving as the weights. The rocks should be flat, preferably teardrop shaped, and approximately 6-10oz and 2-2.5" x 2.5-3.5". The rocks require a diamond drill bit to make the holes. The rope is then threaded through the rocks and spliced back into itself and whipped at the end. Note that splicing retains the full strength of the rope, while any type of knot will create a weak spot in the rope.

Additional examples of rope suruchin:

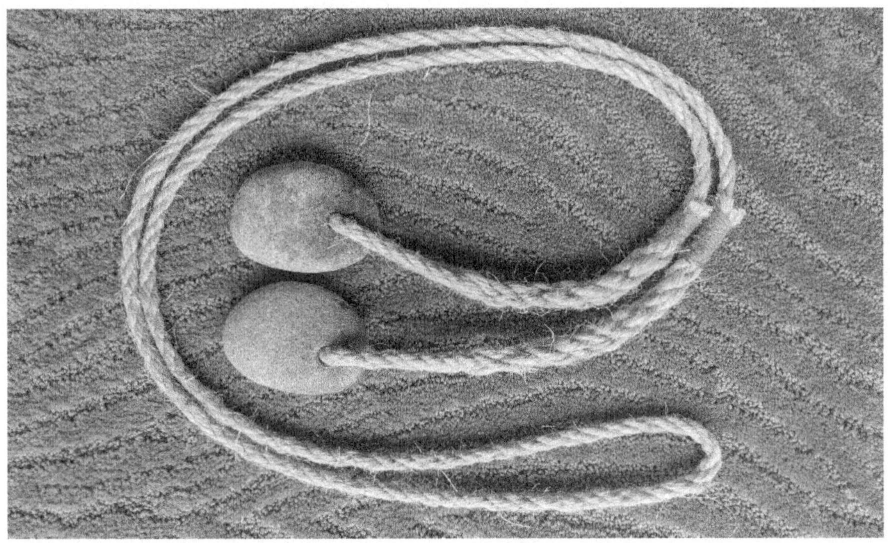

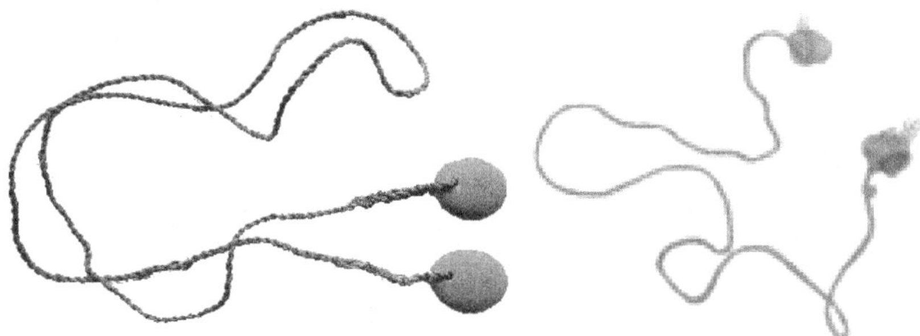

Figure 31 Additional examples of rope suruchins

Chain Suruchin

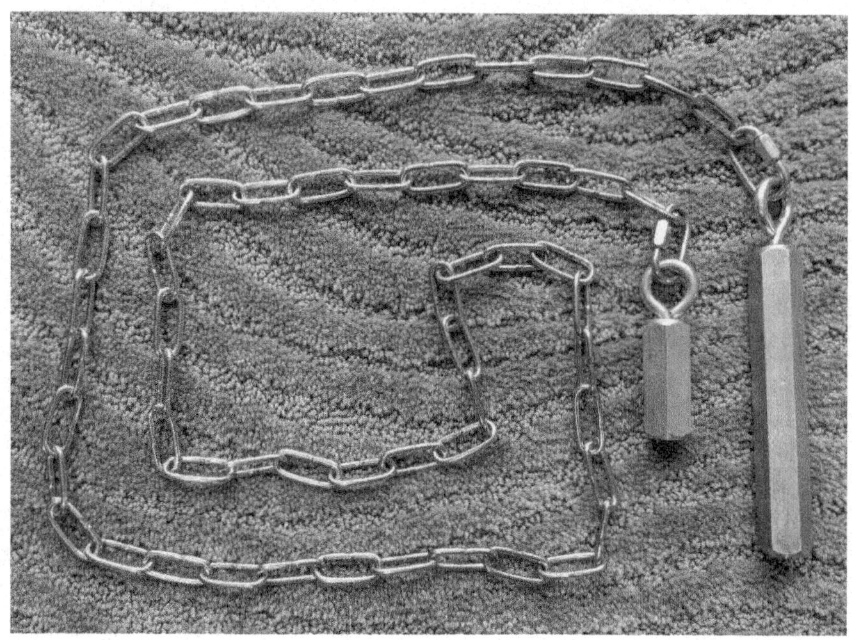

The chain suruchin, usually with a handle on one end, is typically used by the Ryukyu Kobudo style. It can be manufactured several different ways, with the original ones being hand forged. As can be seen in next image, they were also occasionally made with backward spikes on the end, allowing the weight to grip and hold when wrapping around a target. A consideration if making a chain suruchin: the chain must be significantly lighter than the weight at the end. Otherwise, the suruchin will handle like a single long heavy chain and will not behave properly on casting techniques.

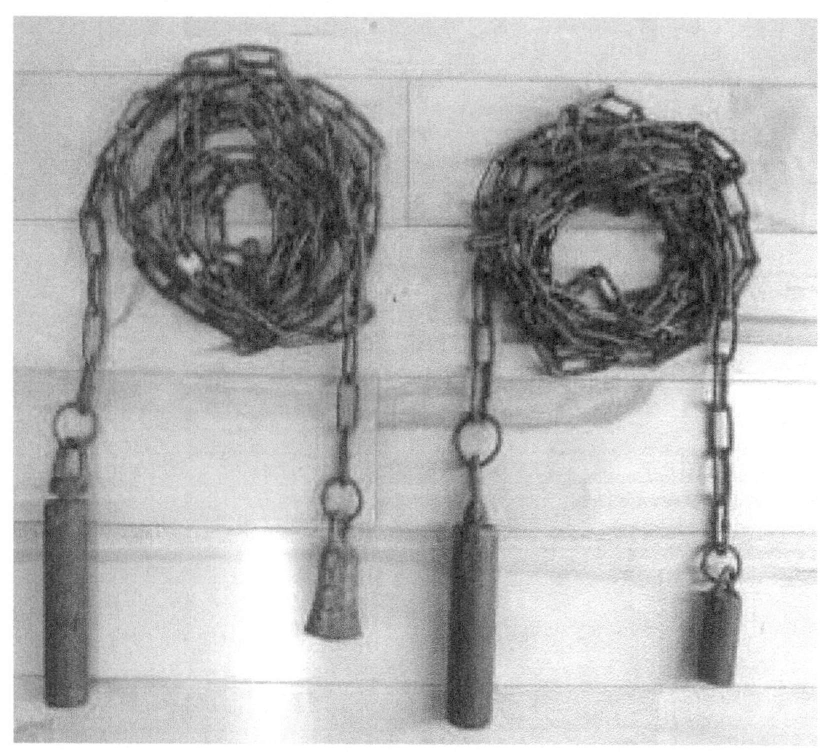

Figure 32 Traditional chain suruchins of karatekobudopalau.com

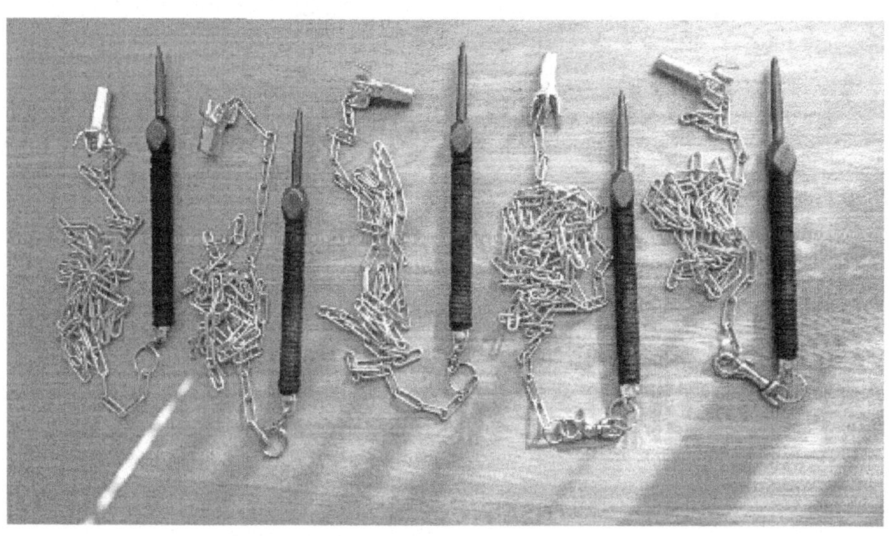

Figure 33 Suruchin with barbs, courtesy of http://bushukan.wp.xdomain.jp/

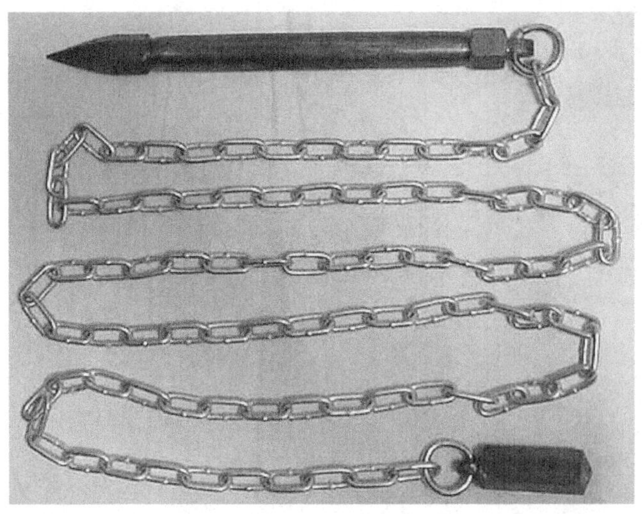

Figure 34 suruchin from jin-1.juttemaster.gozaru.jp

Figure 35 Taira lineage suruchins, of ryukyukobujutsuhozonshinkokai.org

Figure 36 Chain Suruchin Photo: paazio / flickr

The photo above (courtesy of Juga Paazmaya of Flickr, www.flickr.com/photos/paazio) shows an example of a handle that tapers to a point. While this adds a dimension to using the handle in the manner of a Yawara or Kubaton, it also opens up the possibility of reversing the grip on the suruchin and utilizing Rope Dart techniques.

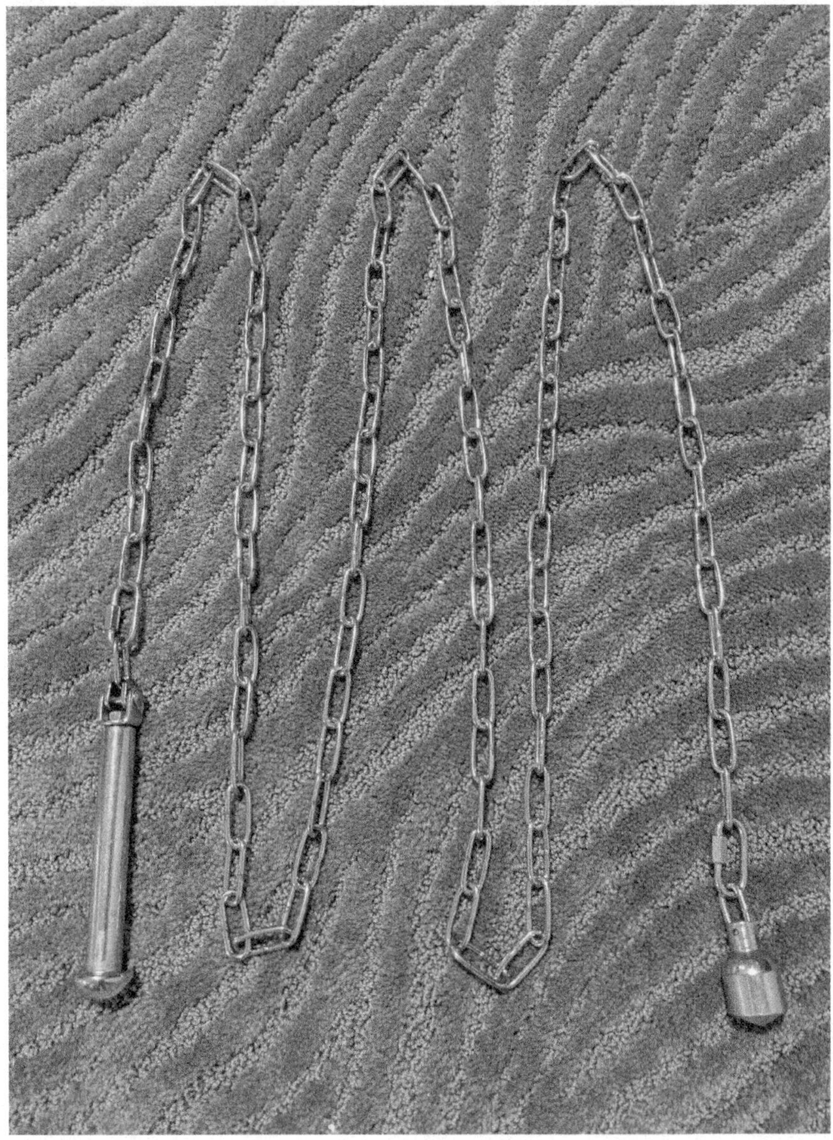

Figure 37 Suruchin made from Manriki

The photo above shows a suruchin made from commercially available Manriki weapons cut apart (one handle version, one ball version) with 1/8 inch chain added with steel quick links.

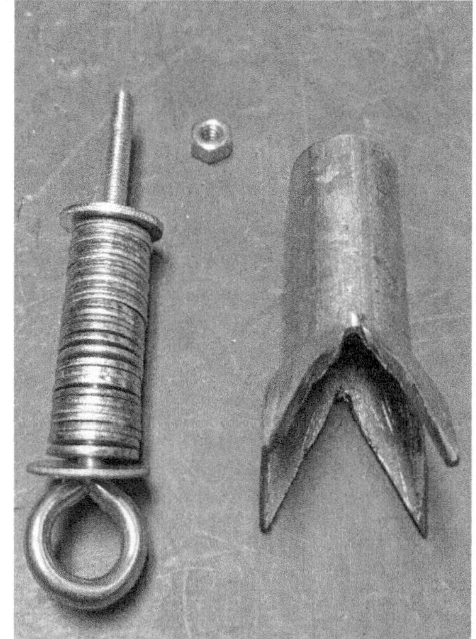

Figure 38 Barbed suruchin, with details of construction

Barbed suruchin using metal pipe, eyelet bolt, and washers. Excess bolt removed with grinder. Nut epoxied in place.

Modern versions

Figure 39 Modern monkey fist suruchin

The photo above shows a rope suruchin constructed using 1.5" steel ball bearings wrapped in a monkey fist knot (ABoK #2202). The rope is 5.6mm Atwood "Battle Cord" rope, with a tensile strength of 2,650lbs. The remaining end of rope from each knot is tied back into the standing end using a Celtic button knot (ABoK #545). A drop of epoxy on the Celtic button knots helps ensure it never comes unraveled. Below is a youth sized suruchin, using traditional hemp rope and 3/4" steel ball bearings in a monkey fist:

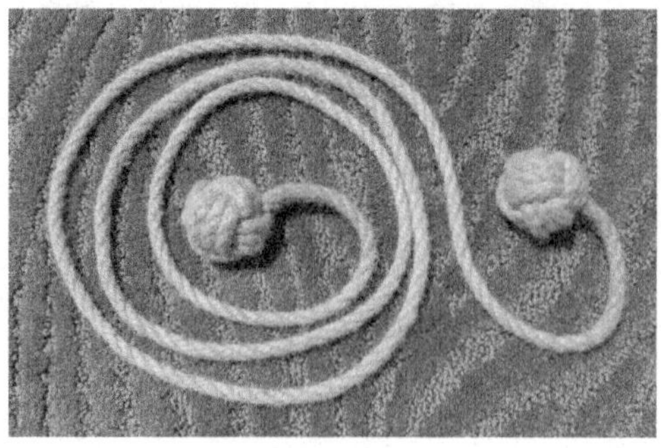

Figure 40 Youth Hemp suruchin

Practice Suruchin

The following photos depict five different styles of practice suruchin (a very wise investment when starting out):

1. A monkey fist suruchin using 750 paracord and ¾" steel ball bearings. Weights are too small for use as a weapon, but very compact for travel.
2. A tennis ball suruchin using 550 paracord and 2" tennis balls (such as those used for pet toys). Holes are drilled in the tennis balls, and the rope pushed through with a "paracord needle." The rope is finished with an Ashley stopper knot (ABoK #526). This is by far the best kind of practice suruchin for the beginning practitioner.
3. A child-size monkey fist suruchin using soft cotton rope and a wooden bead as the core.
4. A full-size tennis ball connected to cotton 3/8" rope. A PVC pipe with drilled & glued caps is added for a handle (stained for appearance).
5. A fishing weight (south bend bank sinkers) wrapped with tape, attached to 550 paracord; good for full-contact practice against a Kobudo dummy (wooden post wrapped in rope)

Figure 41 3/4" ball bearing suruchin

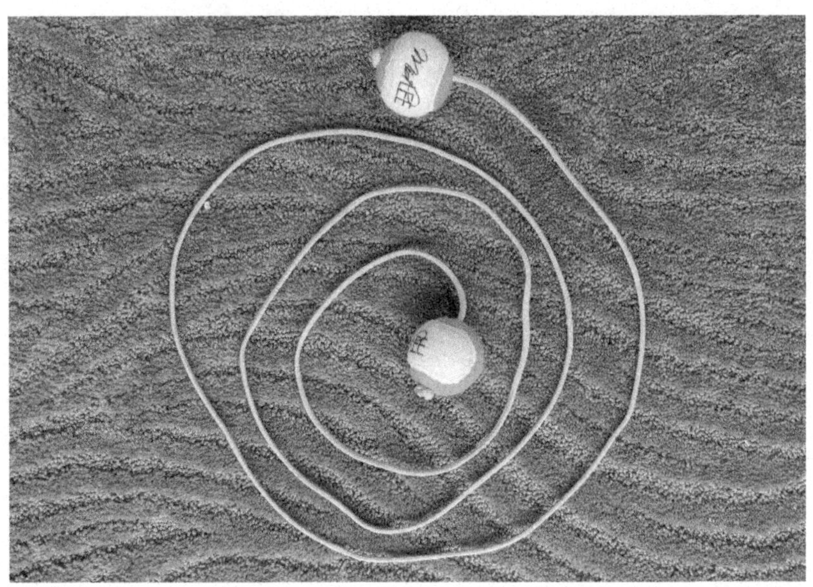

Figure 42 Tennis ball suruchin

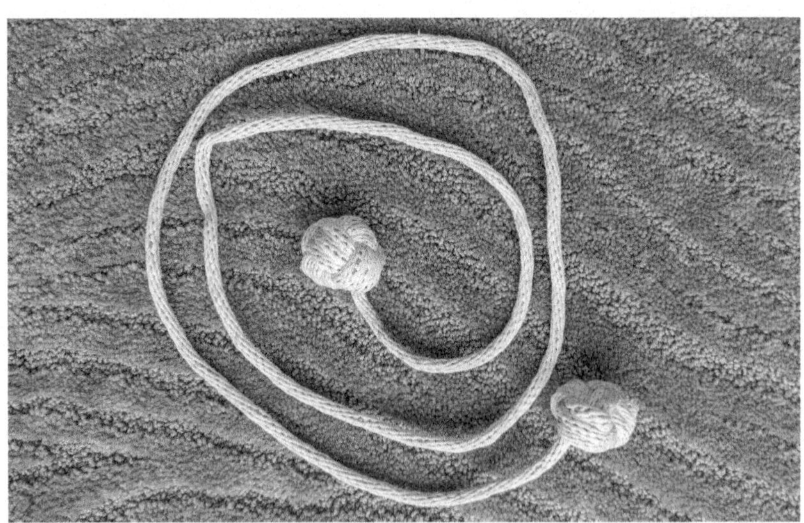

Figure 43 Cotton rope/wooden bead suruchin

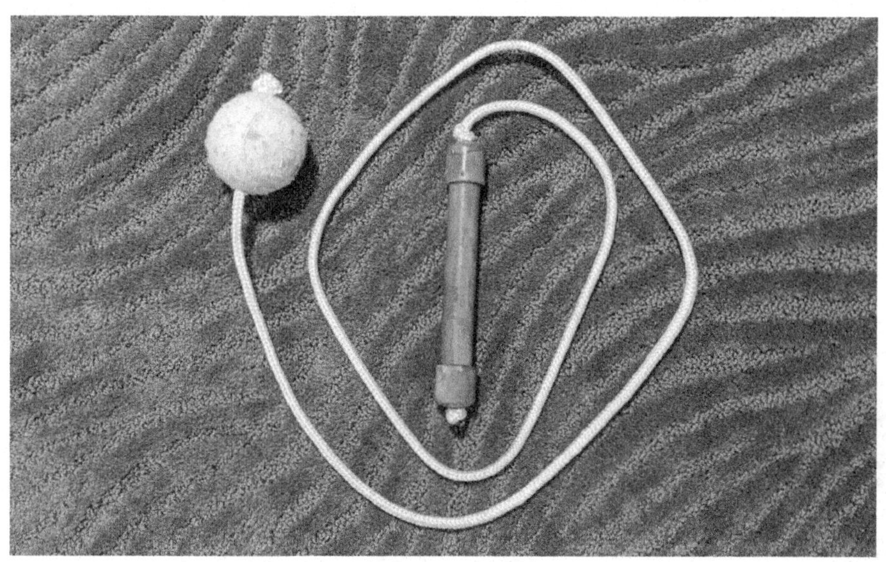

Figure 44 Handle-type practice short suruchin

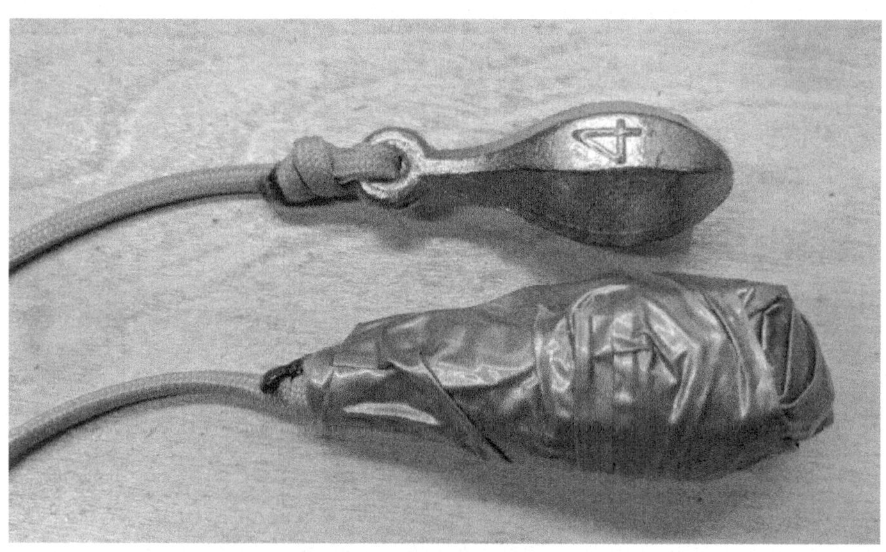

Figure 45 Fishing weight suruchin

Constructing a Pocket Suruchin

Figure 46 Pocket Suruchin (collapsed)

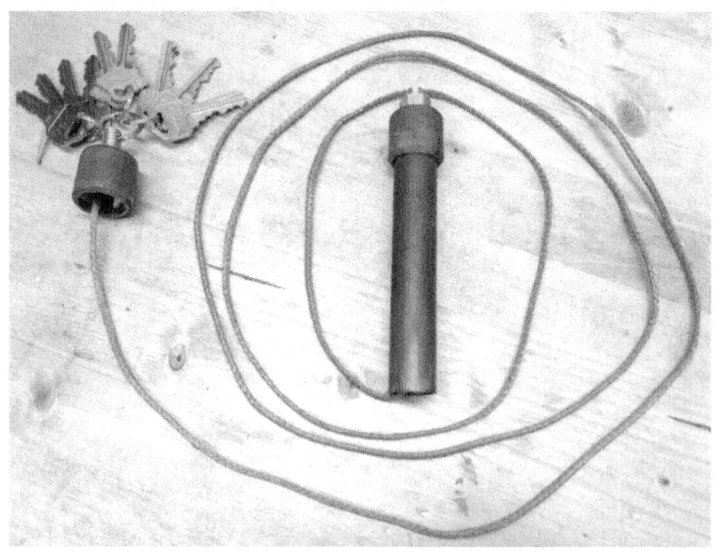

Figure 47 Pocket suruchin (expanded)

This section will discuss the construction of a concealed pocket suruchin, the invention of the author. This suruchin has the advantage that, in its concealed form, it can double as a Yawara or Kubaton weapon before being deployed.

IMPORTANT NOTE ON ROPE STRENGTH:

Manufacturers will commonly list a rope's breaking (or tensile) strength. This value is very different from a rope's safe working load; a rope's breaking strength is tested under ideal conditions in a laboratory on brand new rope with no wear, with the ropes wrapped around drums and subjected to slowly increasing stress until breaking point is reached. Knots will typically introduce a weak point, reducing rope strength by 10-40%. In addition, a 100lb load on a rope that is jerked around will put a stress on the rope far higher than 100lb. A general rule of thumb is that the safe working load for a rope is 20% of the breaking strength. So, to swing a rope with a 1/2lb weight on the end (without hitting anything) would produce around 2.5lb of force on the rope, so you would need a rope with at least 12.5lbs breaking strength. However, to wrap/trap and throw a 200lb opponent, you would want a rope with at least 1,000lbs breaking strength. Case in point, a length of 550lb of paracord will snap in half if attempting to use as a climbing rope for a 100lb child (personal experience from the author's childhood). Ideally, even for a practice suruchin with tennis balls the author would not use a rope with less than 50lb breaking strength for safety.

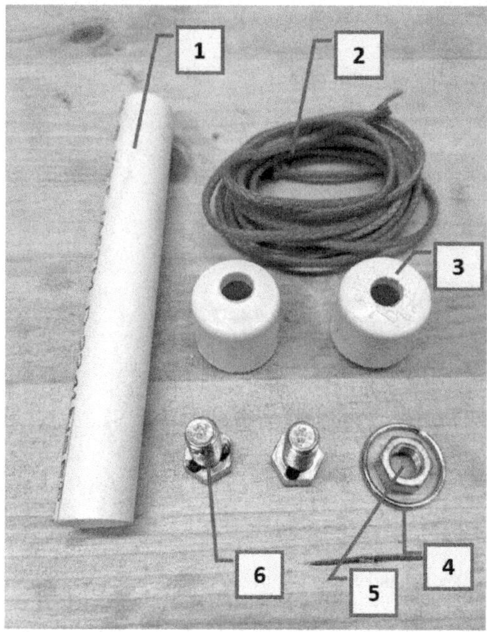

Figure 48 Pocket suruchin parts list

Parts list:

1. 5" long ½" SDR-13.5, 315PSI PVC pipe or equivalent (note: it is important to get this and not schedule 40 PVC pipe, which due to the thicker wall has too little space inside for the rope)

2. Appropriate length rope (1.5 times arm span; see suruchin measurement section). The rope used here was 3/32" HTS-99 from mapleleafropes.com, with a breaking strength of 2000lb (material: Dyneema® SK99).

3. 2x ½" PVC pie caps, with 3/8" holes drilled in the ends

4. 1x Keyring; there are titanium ones available that are much more durable that standard keyrings

5. 1x 3/8" nut

6. 2x 3/8"x1/2" bolts. These are modified; each bolt has two 5/32" holes drilled at a 45-degree angle just under the bolt head, with the holes meeting in a single exit hole in the center of the top of the bolt (see photos). In addition, one of the bolts has an extra 1/8" hole drilled in the end of the bolt. A vise and drill press are ideal for modifying these bolts.

Construction:

After all parts are modified as described in the parts' list, you can color the PVC as desired by using 1mL of solvent (or petroleum dye such as Rekhaoil Red HF, etc.) in a 4oz can of PVC clear cleaner.

First thread the rope through the middle of the head of the bolt, wrap halfway around, back down the other hole, and tie a stopper knot (such as the Ashley Stopper, ABoK #526) as shown in the photo. Repeat on the other end of the rope.

For the back end ("A"), insert the bolt without the additional hole and tighten the nut on the other end. A drop of glue/epoxy will help ensure this nut never comes off. Then slide the 5" PVC pipe over the rope and use PVC cement to permanently lock it into the cap.

For the front end ("B"), insert the second bolt through the other cap. Secure bolt by placing keyring through hole in end of bolt. This cap end WILL NOT be glued in place.

Finish off with a handful of keys for weight. About a dozen does well. For practice suruchins, sometimes hardware stores or locksmiths will have a box of mis-cut or throwaway keys you can get for free. If keys are not providing enough weight, the "Bank Sinkers" fishing weights (available form 2-8oz) can be easily added.

Lastly, it works well to wrap the rope around your hand as shown in the photo, then take the rope off your hand and slide into the tube as a bundle. This helps avoid snagging.

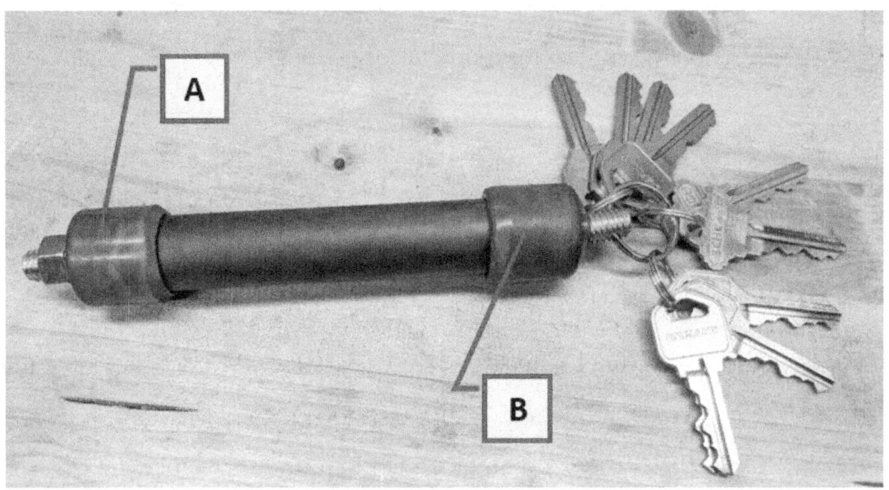

Figure 49 Construction of pocket suruchin

Figure 50 Wrapping for storage

Hojōjutsu (Tying and Binding)

The techniques of Hojōjutsu, or the Japanese martial art of tying and restraining opponents with rope, are not traditional to the suruchin weapon. However, it is so closely related to the suruchin, and the techniques lend themselves so well to the weapon, that a section is included in this book to help the practitioner realize the full potential of the suruchin in training. This is a full martial art in and of itself, so this section does not attempt to fully explore all possibilities. A few representative techniques are shown; there are excellent resources [15,16,17] available to the student who wishes to learn more.

Figure 51 Captive prisoner before magistrate, 1870 by Shimooka Renjō

Figure 52 Japanese prisoner, late 1800's

Brief History of Hojōjutsu

While tying up an enemy with rope goes as far back in history as rope itself, the first recording of Japanese Hojōjutsu techniques dates to approximately 1467. Originally for the Bushi class, this art became one of the "18 Warrior's Skills" (along with archery, horseback riding, etc.). However, it was during the Edo period (1603-1868) that the art truly came into its own.

The rope was used by police officers before the advent of modern handcuffs to detain and transport criminals. They would hold down a criminal using joint locks, and then dispense rope from a small bundle held in the hand as they wrapped limbs and neck. The actual workings of the techniques of various schools were kept secret as much as possible (in part to help keep criminals from circumventing the knots). There are literally hundreds of techniques, and separate knots were used to denote both the type of prisoner (Samurai, Monk, farmer, women, children, etc.) as well as whether the crime committed was a minor or major offense. In addition, the color of the rope had significance; white, yellow, red, blue or black could signify the Guardians of Chinese Taoism (as a talisman against negative energies), the elements, the seasons, or (later) the precinct that made the arrest.

Figure 53 Seiko Fujita, Zukai Torinawajutsu author 1898 – 1966

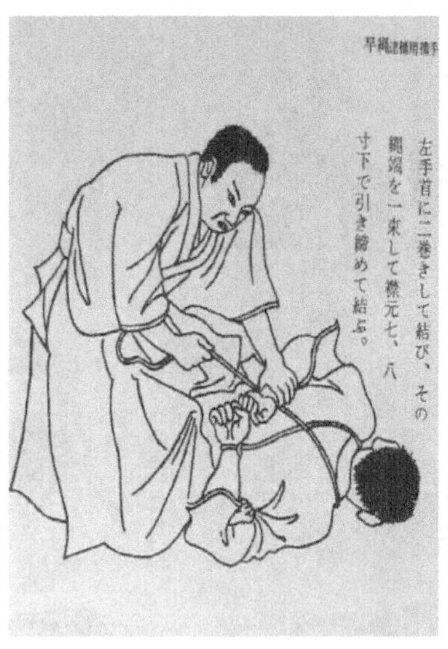

Figure 54 Capturing technique, from Zukai Torinawajutsu

The Techniques of Hojōjutsu

Hojōjutsu has two main categories of techniques; first is Hayanawa (fast rope), which is for the initial arrest of a criminal. It uses simpler, straightforward, and fast techniques using a slender (3-4mm) rope of approximately 4.5-6.5 meters in length (though sometimes 2 meters, depending on the school) with a small loop in one end, and was meant for a resisting opponent. The techniques on the following pages using the suruchin are Hayanawa techniques.

The second category uses Honnawa (main rope) techniques. These would typically be used in the transportation of prisoners, and would be far more elaborate and detailed, and customized to the category of prisoner. The ropes used would be 6-8mm thick, and anywhere from 6.5-20 meters long.

Rope coil

This small rope bundle (or Hojōmaki) allowed rope to be dispensed from one end without tangling during an arrest. It also allows for a method of storing a suruchin so that it can be carried in a gear bag without becoming tangled throughout the bag and allows for rapid deployment of the suruchin when ready. A slight modification is made from the original method since there is a weight on both ends; it ends in a slip knot instead of going completely through the loop.

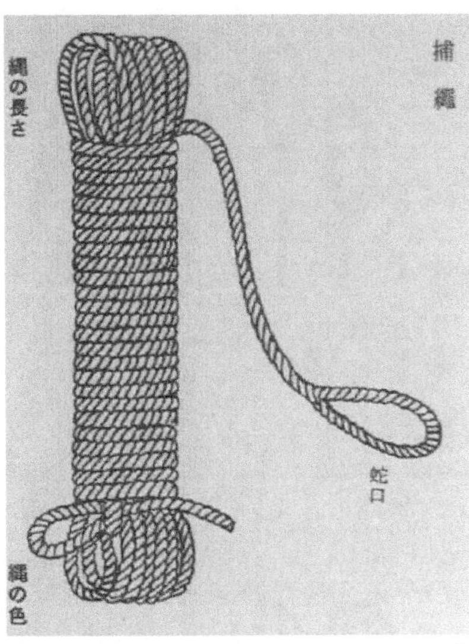

Figure 55 Rope coil, from Zukai Torinawajutsu

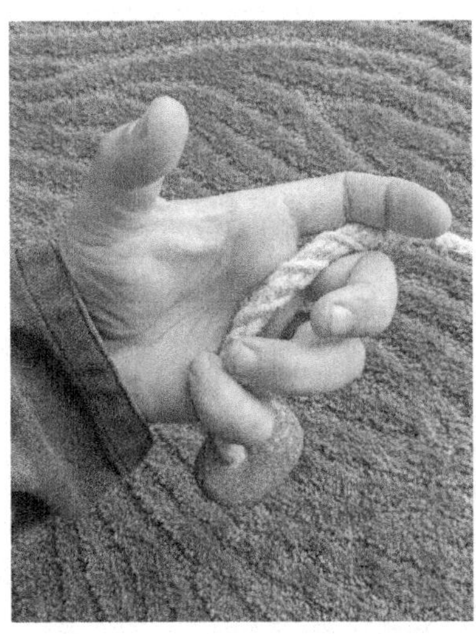
1. Hold one end in hand, with thumb and forefinger extended

2. Wrap rope around fingers in figure 8 pattern, leaving about 16”

3. Wrap coil with remaining rope, finish with slipped loop (pull bottom weight to secure slipped loop)

4 Knots

The four simple knots detailed on the following pages are a tiny sampling of what is possible with the suruchin.

Jaguchi (end loop) slip knot, for the initial loop around wrist or neck; pinch rope through splice and pull through

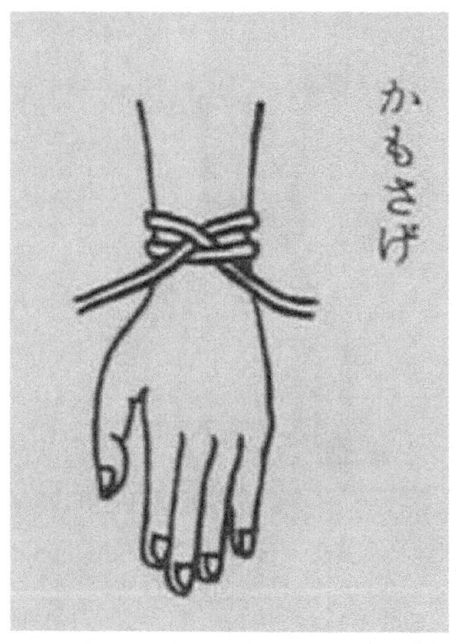

Figure 56 Kamagakushi, from Zukai Torinawajutsu

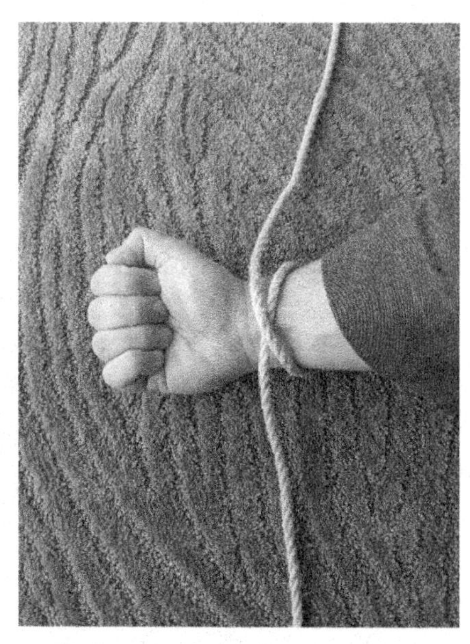

1. Wrap around wrist (or wrists)

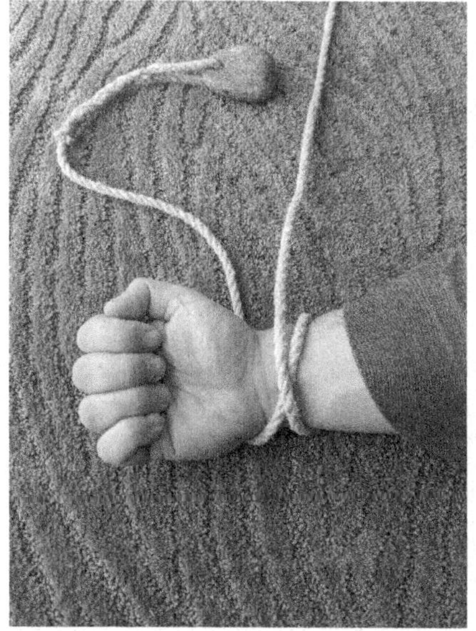

2. Continue wrapping

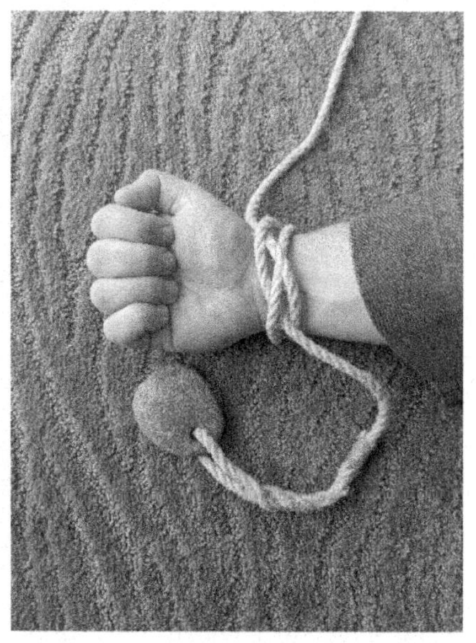

3. Pass on same side of standing end as loop, pass under first loop

Kamagakushi (or Sack knot, ABoK #1243) Good for binding wrists together.

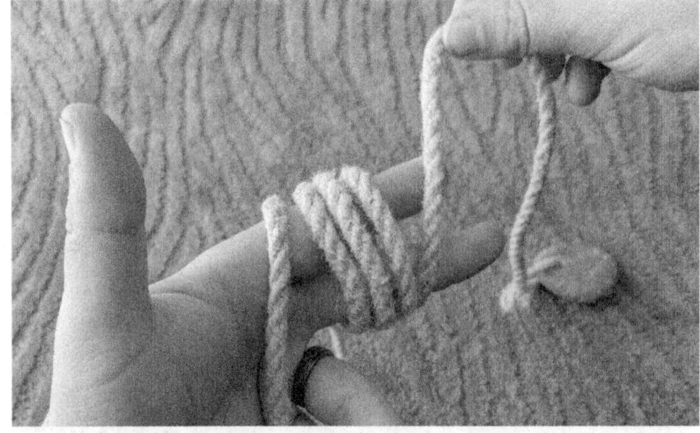

1. Wrap around first two fingers (spread out) 3 times

2. Feed both ends back through the 3 loops

3. Pull loops tight; tighten on wrists by pulling loose ends

Tejo Nawa (or Handcuff knot, or Commercial Cord Curtain Holdback, ABoK #1113) There is a slightly simpler handcuff knot (Kake-musubi, or ABoK #1134), but this one is more secure.

1. With rope draped over wrist, grab one side (can be either side)

2. Bend hand down and pinch other side with 1st and 2nd fingers

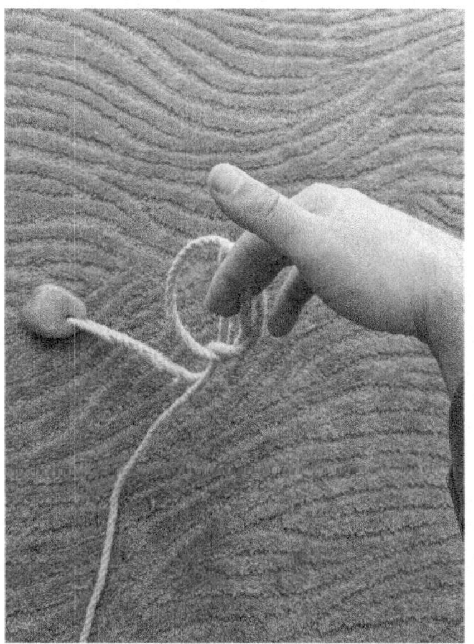

3. Allow loop around wrist to fall off over fingers

4. Pull/shake to enlarge loop

Kata-Musubi (Or Slip knot, ABoK #529) A fast one-handed slipping loop that can be formed while the other hand is holding the rest of the line tight.

Hayanawa technique – Variant 1

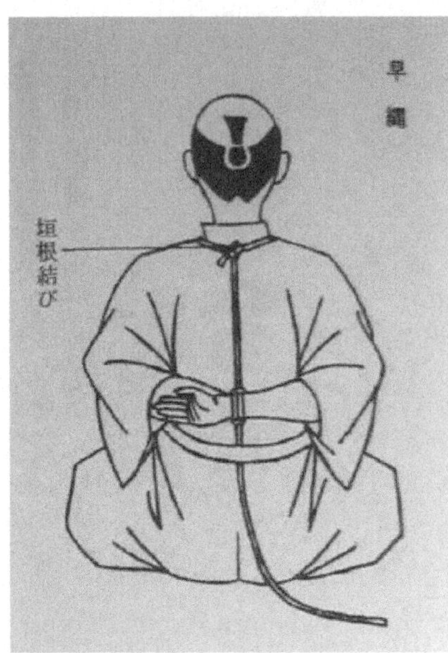

Figure 57 Hayanawa technique 1, from Zukai Torinawajutsu [16]

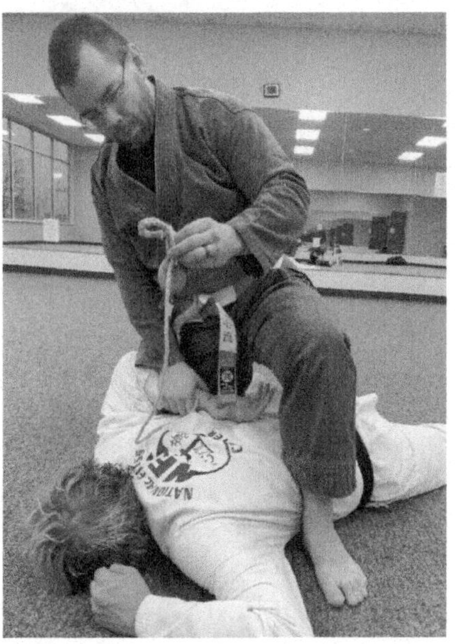

1. Pinch rope through splice and pull through to make slip knot

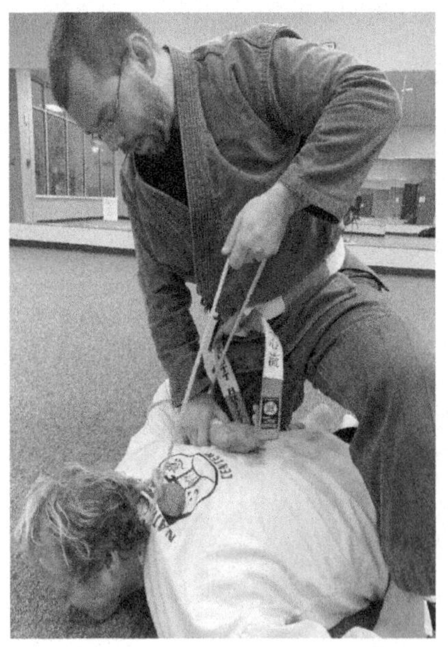

2. Loop slip knot around neck

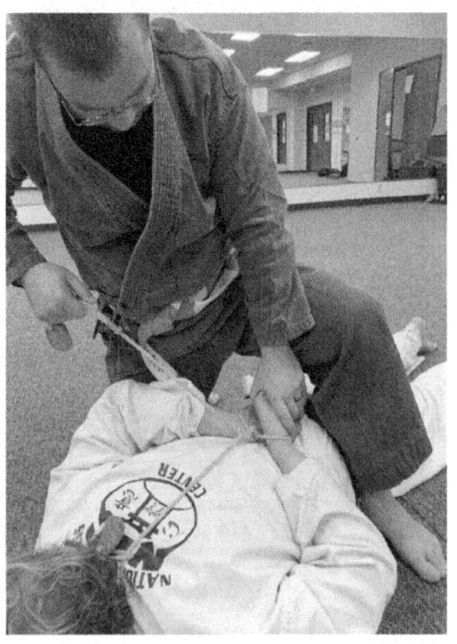

3. Bind both wrists with Tejo Nawa (shown) or Kamagakushi; finish with overhand knot as desired

Hayanawa technique – Variant 2

Figure 58 Hayanawa technique 2, from Zukai Torinawajutsu [16]

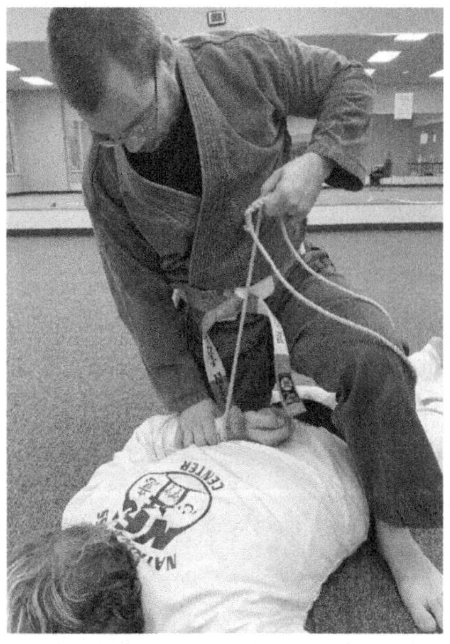

1. Make slip knot similar to step 1 of Hayanawa 1 technique; bind R wrist

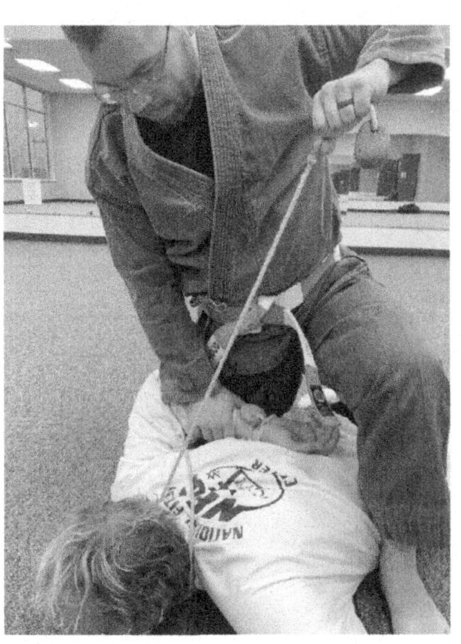

2. Thread rope around opposite side of neck

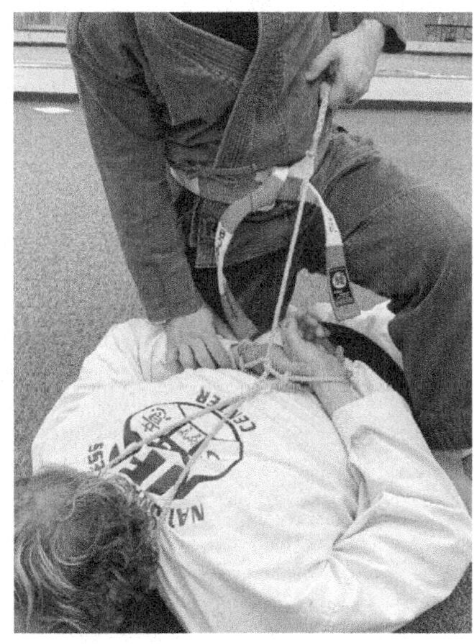

3. Bind left wrist with Kata-Musubi, overhand knot to right wrist, or bind both wrists with Kamagakushi

Suruchin Techniques

Techniques key

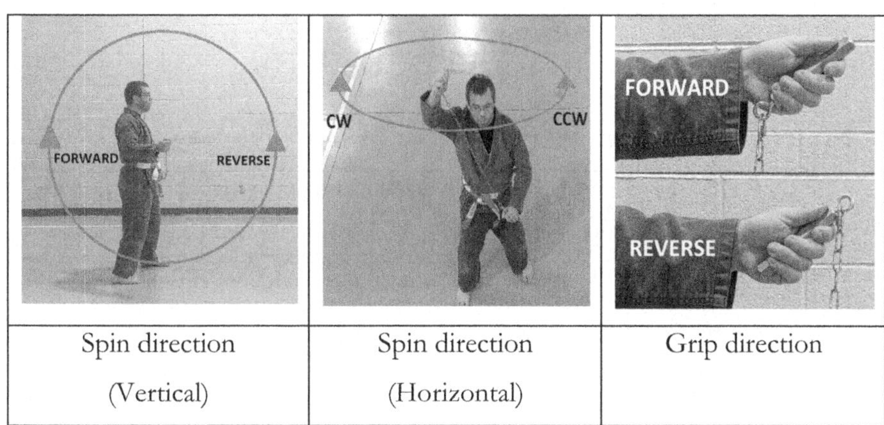

Spin direction (Vertical)	Spin direction (Horizontal)	Grip direction

General suruchin abbreviations:

FW =	Forward	H =	Holds	B =	Blocks
RV =	Reverse	S =	Swings	ST =	Stretch
CW =	Clockwise	C =	Cast/Strike	SH =	Shorten
CC =	Counterclockwise				

Movement Abbreviations:

RFF =	Right foot forward	LFF =	Left foot forward
RFB =	Right foot back	LFB =	Left foot back
RS =	Right Side	LS =	Left Side
ST =	Straight		

The following techniques list is in alphabetical order by abbreviation.

#	Abbreviation	Description	Page
Holds			
1	H.BLT.RS	Wear suruchin as belt, weights to right side	64
2	H.CHG.LH	Change hands, handle in left hand, weight in right	64
3	H.CHG.RH	Change hands, handle in right hand, weight in left	65
4	H.DBF.FW	Double hand hold, chain folded, handle forward	66
5	H.DBF.RV	Double hand hold, chain folded, handle reversed	66
6	H.FLD.DB	Folded in thirds in both hands, manriki length	67
7	H.GTH.LH	Gathered in left hand, weight in right hand	68
8	H.GTH.RH	Gathered hold in right hand	68
9	H.LHE.FW	Left hand extended hold, handle forward	68
10	H.LHE.RV	Left hand extended hold, handle reversed	69
11	H.LHG.FW	Left hand gathered hold, handle forward	69
12	H.LHG.RV	Left hand gathered hold, handle reversed	69
13	H.RHG.FW	Right hand grip (chain only over hand)	70
14	H.STD.FW	Standard hold (handle in left hand, middle of chain in right hand), chain forward	70
15	H.STD.RV	Standard hold (handle in left hand, middle of chain in right hand), chain reversed	70
16	H.SWH.FW	Switch handle direction to forwards	71
17	H.SWH.RV	Switch handle direction to reverse	71
18	H.WDB.RH	Wrap doubled Chain/rope around right hand	71
19	H.WRP.RH	Wrap Chain/rope around right hand to shorten	72

Swings			
20	S.BCK.CW	Transfer suruchin around back, clockwise	73
21	S.CAT.LH	Catch swinging weight with left hand, ending with doubled hold	74
22	S.CHG.HT	Change direction by letting weight hit ground	74
23	S.CHG.ST	Change direction by stalling in air	75
24	S.DBL.F8	Figure 8 pattern with both weights at once	76
25	S.DBL.FW	Swing both weights forwards	76
26	S.DBL.RV	Swing both weights in opposite directions	77
27	S.ELB.FW	Catch on elbow (change direction), forward swing	77
28	S.ELB.RV	Catch on elbow (change direction), reverse swing	78
29	S.EXT.CC	Fully extended overhead swing, counterclockwise	79
30	S.EXT.CW	Fully extended overhead swing, clockwise	79
31	S.EXT.F8	Fully extended figure 8 swing	80
32	S.FG8.FW	Swing figure of 8, forward direction	80
33	S.FG8.RV	Swing figure of 8, reverse direction	80
34	S.FRT.CC	Swing in front, counterclockwise direction	81
35	S.FRT.CW	Swing in front, clockwise direction	81
36	S.HD8.FW	Figure-8 swing with suruchin handle, forwards	81
37	S.HD8.RV	Figure-8 swing with suruchin handle, reverse	82
38	S.LSD.FW	Swing at left side, forward direction	82
39	S.LSD.RV	Swing at left side, reverse direction	82
40	S.OVH.CC	Swing overhead, counterclockwise direction	83
41	S.OVH.CW	Swing overhead, clockwise direction	83
42	S.RSD.FW	Swing at right side, forward direction	83
43	S.RSD.RV	Swing at right side, reverse direction	84

Casting / Strikes			
44	C.DBL.LS	Double strike (both weights) to left side	85
45	C.DBL.RS	Double strike (both weights) to right side	85
46	C.DBS.LS	Double weight swing to left side	87
47	C.DBS.RS	Double weight swing to right side	87
48	C.DNC.LS	Downward cast, 45 degrees from left side	87
49	C.DNC.RS	Downward cast, 45 degrees from right side	88
50	C.DNC.ST	Downward cast, straight down	88
51	C.DNS.LS	Downward strike, 45 degrees from left side	88
52	C.DNS.RS	Downward strike, 45 degrees from right side	89
53	C.DNS.ST	Downward strike, straight down	89
54	C.ELB.LS	Elbow cast, left side	89
55	C.ELB.RS	Elbow cast, right side	90
56	C.FOT.FW	Cast with right foot forward direction	90
57	C.FOT.LS	Cast with right foot to the left	91
58	C.FOT.MD	Cast with right foot forward, modified (looping)	91
59	C.HDL.FW	Strike with handle, forward grip	92
60	C.HDL.RV	Strike with handle, reverse grip	92
61	C.HKN.RS	Horizontal swing at right side while kneeling	93
62	C.HZC.LS	Horizontal cast at left side	93
63	C.HZC.RS	Horizontal cast at right side	93
64	C.HZS.LS	Horizontal swing at left side	94
65	C.HZS.RS	Horizontal swing at right side	94
66	C.KNE.LS	Knee cast, left side	94
67	C.KNE.RS	Knee cast, right side	95
68	C.ROP.DB	Strike with both weights in 1 hand, rope end	95
69	C.UP4.LS	Upward cast, 45 degrees from left side	95
70	C.UP4.RS	Upward cast, 45 degrees from right side	96

Holds

1. H.BLT.RS Belt hold

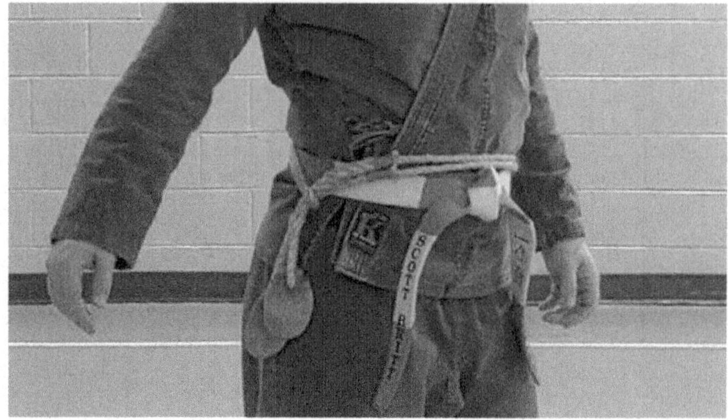

Wear suruchin as belt, weights to right side

2.a H.CHG.LH Change hands (left)

Handle in right hand, weight in left

2.b

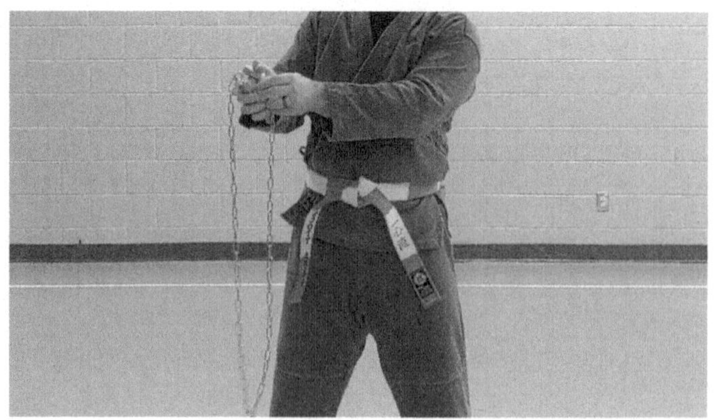

Move first finger of right hand to other side of handle, pinch weight

2.c

Take handle in left hand

3.a H.CHG.RH Change hands (right)

Handle in left hand, weight in right

3.b

Move first finger of left hand to other side of handle, pinch weight

3.c

Take handle in right hand

4. H.DBF.FW Doubled hold (forward)

Double hand hold, chain folded, handle forward

5. H.DBF.RV Doubled hold (reverse)

Double hand hold, chain folded, handle reversed

6.a H.FLD.DB Folded in thirds

Hold both ends in reverse hold

6.b

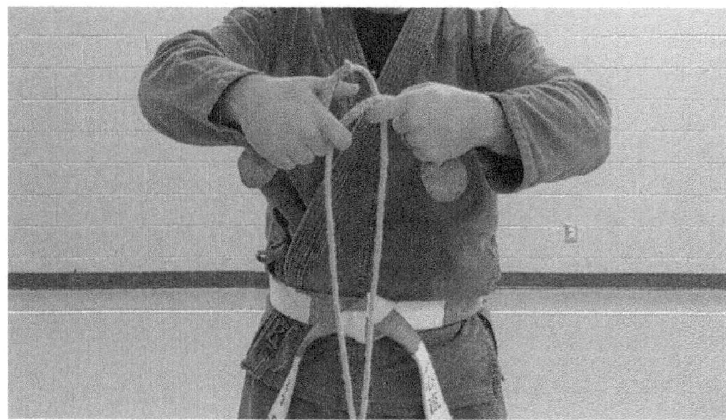

Hook first finger of both hands on opposite side's rope

6.c

Pull out to create a three-strand rope

7. H.GTH.LH   Gathered (left)

Gathered hold in left hand, with weight in right hand (4-8" out)

8. H.GTH.RH   Gathered (right)

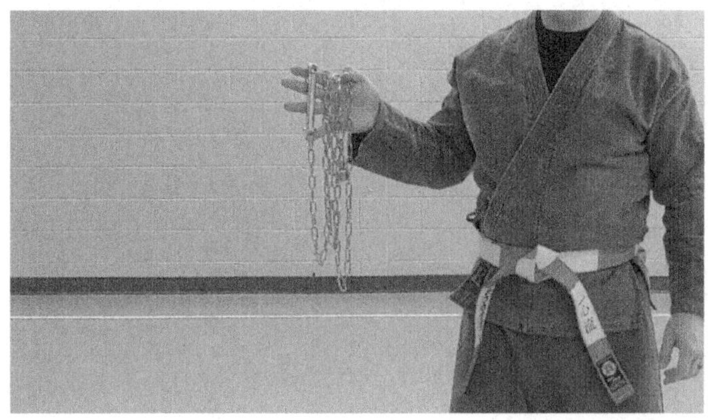

Gathered hold in right hand (usually transferred from gathered in left hand, before bowing out)

9. H.LHE.FW   Left hand extended (forward)

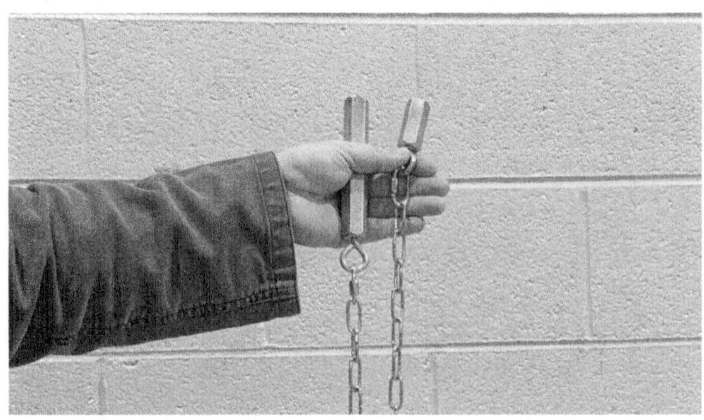

Left hand extended hold, handle forward

10. H.LHE.RV Left hand extended (reverse)

Left hand extended hold, handle reversed

11. H.LHG.FW Left hand gathered (forward)

Left hand gathered hold, handle forward

12. H.LHG.RV Left hand gathered (reverse)

Left hand gathered hold, handle reversed

13. H.RHG.FW   Right hand grip

Right hand grip (chain only over hand)

14. H.STD.FW   Standard hold (forward)

Standard hold (handle in left hand, middle of chain in right hand), chain forward (away from thumb)

15. H.STD.RV   Standard hold (reverse)

Standard hold (handle in left hand, middle of chain in right hand), chain reversed (towards thumb)

16. H.SWH.FW Switch handle (forward)

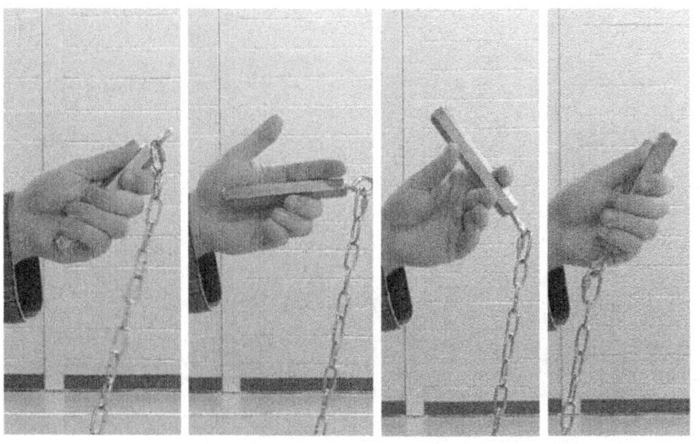

Switch handle from reverse to forwards grip

17. H.SWH.RV Switch handle (reverse)

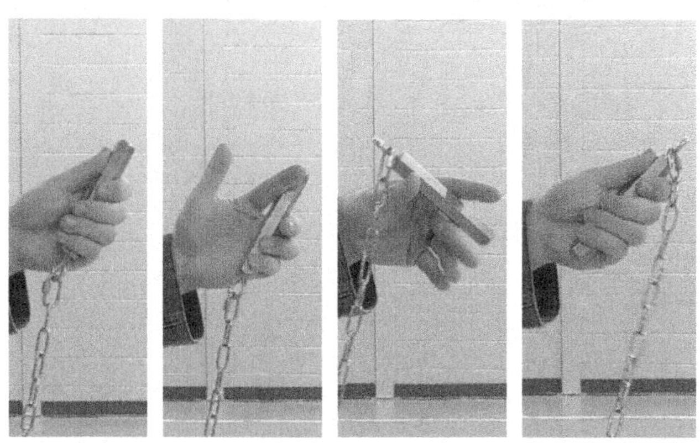

Switch handle from forwards to reverse grip

18. H.WDB.RH Wrap doubled chain

Wrap middle of rope around right hand (stick pinky in midpoint of loop)

19. H.WRP.RH Wrap chain

Wrap Chain/rope around right hand to shorten

Swings

20.a S.BCK.CW Transfer around back

Transfer suruchin around back, clockwise; start with extended swing

20.b

Pass behind back, transfer handle to left hand

20.c

Continue swing and catch middle of rope with right hand

21. S.CAT.LH Catch weight

Catch swinging weight (counter-clockwise) in left hand

22.a S.CHG.HT Change direction; hit

Change directions by allowing weight to hit ground; start with forward swing

22.b

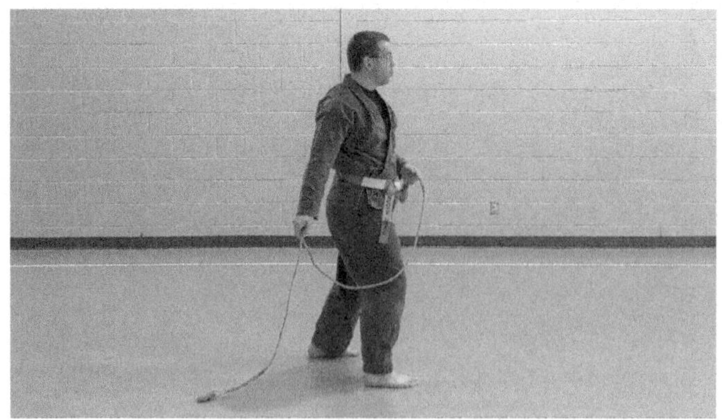

Allow weight to hit ground to stop

22.c

Pull and start swing in opposite direction

23.a S.CHG.ST Change direction; stall

Change directions by stalling in mid-air; applicable to all swing directions

23.b

Suddenly extend hand in direction of taught rope to stall circular motion

23.c

Pull and start swing in opposite direction

24. S.DBL.F8 Double figure 8

Figure 8 pattern with both weights at once

25. S.DBL.FW Double forwards

Swing both weights forwards

26. S.DBL.RV Double swing, opposite

Swing both weights in opposite directions

27.a S.ELB.FW Change direction on elbow; FW

Catch on elbow (change direction), forward swing.
Swing at right side, forwards

27.b

Extend right elbow out to catch chain

27.c

Pivot feet to turn other direction, using elbow to move trajectory of suruchin to other side

28.a S.ELB.RV Change direction on elbow; RV

Catch on elbow (change direction), reverse swing. Extend right elbow out to catch chain

28.b

Move elbow to the right (behind) to move trajectory to other side while…

28.c

...Pivoting feet to face other direction

29. S.EXT.CC Extended overhead, CC

Fully extended swing overheard, counter-clockwise direction

30. S.EXT.CW Extended overhead, CW

Fully extended swing overheard, clockwise direction

31. S.EXT.F8 Extended figure 8

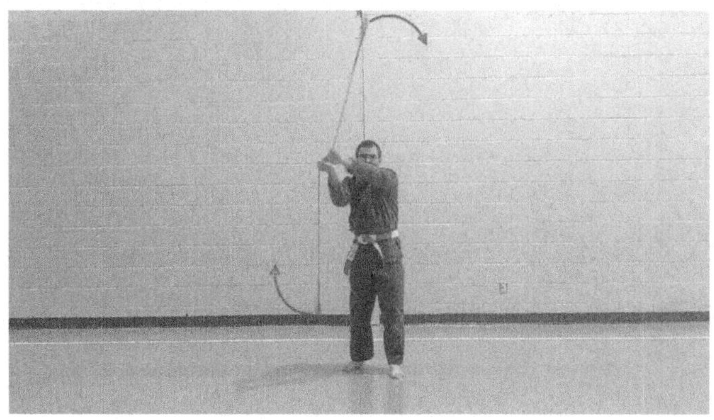

Fully extended figure 8 swing (start with S.DBL.F8 and slowly bring hands together)

32. S.FG8.FW Figure 8 (forward)

Swing figure of 8, forward direction

33. S.FG8.RV Figure 8 (reverse)

Swing figure of 8, reverse direction

34. S.FRT.CC Circle at front CC

Swing in front, counterclockwise direction

35. S.FRT.CW Circle at front CW

Swing in front, clockwise direction

36. S.HD8.FW Figure 8 with handle (forward)

Figurc-8 swing with suruchin handle, forwards

37. S.HD8.RV Figure 8 with handle (reverse)

Figure-8 swing with suruchin handle, reverse

38. S.LSD.FW Left side (forward)

Swing at left side, forward direction

39. S.LSD.RV Left side (reverse)

Swing at left side, reverse direction

40. S.OVH.CC Overhead, CC

Swing overhead, counter-clockwise direction

41. S.OVH.CW Overhead, CW

Swing overhead, clockwise direction

42. S.RSD.FW Right side (forward)

Swing at right side, forward direction

43. S.RSD.RV Right side (reverse)

Swing at right side, reverse direction

Casting/Strikes

44. C.DBL.LS Double strike, left

Double strike (both weights) to left side. Reverse steps of C.DBL.RS, from Part e to Part a

45.a C.DBL.RS Double strike, right

Double strike (both weights) to right side. Starting with weights wrapped from left side swing.

45.b

Swing both weights horizontally towards front

45.c

Continue swing around and over head

45.d

Continue swing down to right side (weight in right hand is now on top)

45.e

Allow swing to wrap around body

46. C.DBS.LS Doubled swing, left

Holding middle of doubled rope H.WDB.RH swing to left side

47. C.DBS.RS Doubled swing, right

Holding middle of doubled rope H.WDB.RH swing to right side

48. C.DNC.LS Downward cast, left

Downward cast, 45 degrees from left side

49. C.DNC.RS Downward cast, right

Downward cast, 45 degrees from right side

50. C.DNC.ST Downward cast, straight

Downward cast, straight down

51. C.DNS.LS Downward swing, left

Downward strike, 45 degrees from left side

52. C.DNS.RS Downward swing, right

Downward strike, 45 degrees from right side

53. C.DNS.ST Downward swing, straight

Downward strike, straight down

54. C.ELB.LS Elbow cast, left

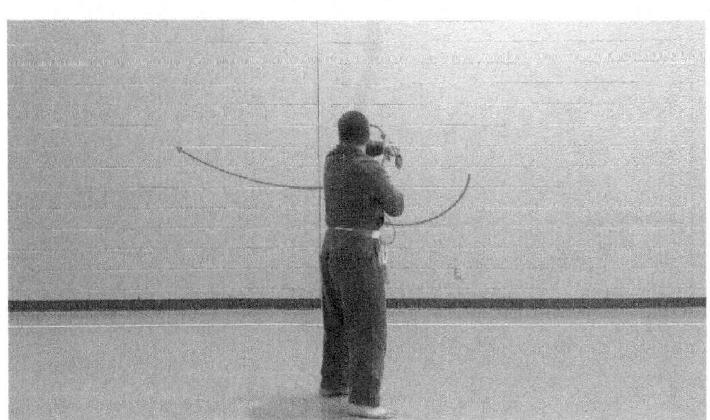

Swing forwards at left side, allow to wrap left elbow and slip off to cast backward (see C.ELB.RS)

55. C.ELB.RS Elbow cast, right

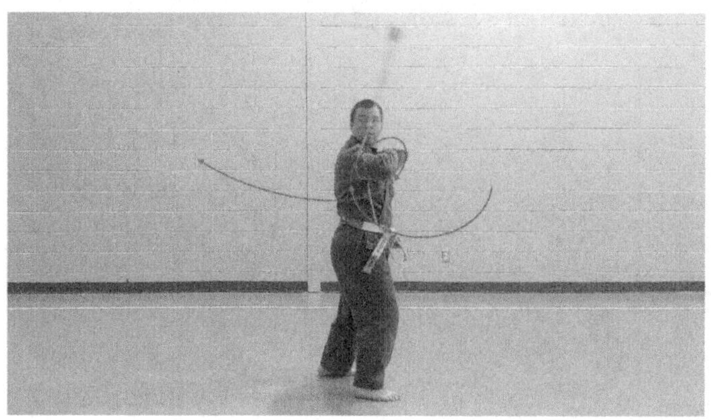

Swing forwards at right side, allow to wrap right elbow and slip off to cast backward

56.a C.FOT.FW Foot cast, foward

Cast with right foot forward direction. Forward swing…

56.b

Catch last 3-4 inches on outward turned right foot

56.c

Kick out with right foot, sending weight forward (side view)

57. C.FOT.LS Foot cast, left

Cast with right foot to the left. Same as C.FOT.FW except in Part c, kick to left

58.a C.FOT.MD Modified foot cast

Cast with right foot forward, modified (looping). Forward swing

58.b

Catch last 1-1.5ft of rope on outturned right foot, allow to swing in tight loop outside of leg to cast

59. C.HDL.FW   Handle thrust, forward

Forward thrusting strike with butt of handle

60. C.HDL.RV   Handle thrust, reverse

Thrusting strike with chain end of handle, or hammer fist strike with butt of handle

61. C.HKN.RS Horizontal kneeling strike

Horizontal cast at right side while kneeling

62. C.HZC.LS Horizontal cast, left

Horizontal cast at left side

63. C.HZC.RS Horizontal cast, right

Horizontal cast at right side

64. C.HZS.LS Horizontal swing, left

Horizontal swing at left side

65. C.HZS.RS Horizontal swing, right

Horizontal swing at right side

66. C.KNE.LS Knee cast, left

Left side knee cast; forward swing; allow to wrap right knee and slip off to cast forwards

67. C.KNE.RS Knee cast, right

Right side knee cast; forward swing; allow to wrap right knee and slip off to cast forwards

68. C.ROP.DB Strike with doubled rope

From H.WDB.RH, strike with rope-wrapped right hand

69. C.UP4.LS Upward cast, left 45

Upward cast, 45 degrees from left side

70. C.UP4.RS Upward cast, right 45

Upward cast, 45 degrees from right side

71. C.UPC.BK Upward cast, back

Upward cast to the back, starting with forward swing at right side

72. C.UPC.LS Upward cast, left side

Starting with front circle S.FRT.CW, cast to left side

73. C.UPC.RS Upward cast, right side

Starting with front circle S.FRT.CC, cast to right side

74. C.UPC.ST Upward cast, straight

Upward cast, straight up

75. C.UPS.LS Upward strike, left 45

Upward strike, 45 degrees from left side

76. C.UPS.RS Upward strike, right 45

Upward strike, 45 degrees from right side

77. C.UPS.ST Upward strike, straight

Upward strike, straight up

78. C.WGT.1W Strike with weight

Thrusting strike with weight held in thumb/ forefinger grip

79. C.WGT.DB Strike with both weights

From H.WDB.RH, strike with double weights

80. C.WRP.RS Cast wrapped weight

With rope around right hand (H.WRP.RH) upward cast, right fingers extended

Blocks

81. B.CHN.LS   Chain parry, left

Check (parry) with doubled chain to left side

82. B.CHN.RS   Chain parry, right

Check (parry) with doubled chain to right side

83. B.DBH.LS   Double block, left

Doubled block to the left, right hand high

84. B.DBH.RS Double block, right

Doubled block to the right, left hand high

85. B.DBL.RH Double high block, right

Doubled high block to the right side

86. B.DBL.LH Double high block, left

Doubled high block to the left side

87. B.DBR.LW Double block, low

Double block

Low

88. B.DBR.OH Double block, overhead

Double block

overhead

89. B.LCH.LS Leg check, left

Leg check (swing weight down) to the left side (use handle)

90. B.LCH.RS Leg check, right

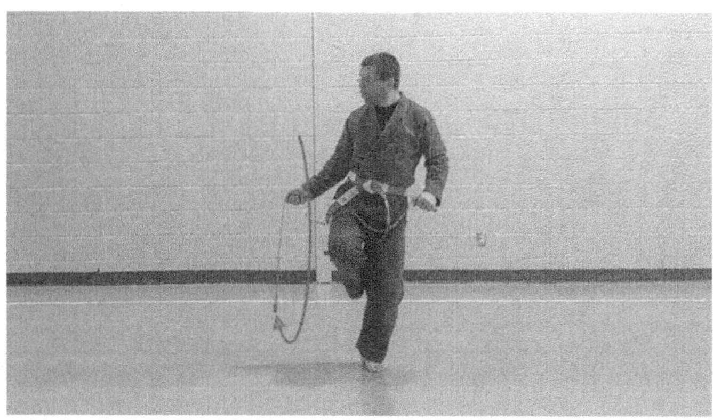

Leg check (swing weight down) to the right side

91. B.NCH.LS Nunchuck block, left

Nunchuck block, left side with suruchin doubled

92. B.NCH.RS Nunchuck block, right

Nunchuck block, right side with suruchin doubled

93. B.VTL.RH Vertical block, right

Single vertical block to right side

94. B.VTR.LH Vertical block, left

Single vertical block to left side

Suruchin Katas

This book includes all known katas for the suruchin; three traditional katas, and one created by the author (plus a basic exercise):

Tan (Short) Suruchin Kata – Originating from Ryukyu Kobudo (founded by Taira Shinken), this is the most common suruchin kata in the style. The kata is characterized by simple swinging techniques, done in repetitive sets. This kata shows the influence of the other weapons in Kobudo.

Naga (Long) Suruchin Kata – Also originating from Ryukyu Kobudo, this kata is nearly extinct; few in Ryukyu Kobudo practice the kata.

Suruchin no Toseki – This kata originates from Matayoshi Kobudo. It includes some of the more dramatic suruchin techniques, possibly showing an influence of the Shaolin meteor hammer (especially considering the founder of Matayoshi Kobudo learned the weapon in mainland China)

Miichiryu Suruchin Kata – This kata was created by the author to combine the more practical techniques of Ryukyu Kobudo, Matayoshi Kobudo, and Shaolin meteor hammer. The full description / history is included prior to the kata.

Suruchin Mini-Kata – This "kata" is a set of introductory techniques that can be used as an introduction to the suruchin for students. See description prior to kata for suggested applications of the kata.

Tan (Short) Suruchin Kata

Also called Mijikai Suruchin or Tan kusari no kata. This kata originates from Ryukyu Kobudo by way of Taira Shinken, and traditionally uses a metal (chain) suruchin with a handle on one end of approximately 150-152cm, or about 60 inches (not including the handle).

Figure 59 Taira Shinken with suruchin

1. Stand at attention; chain in gathered hold in left hand; handle reversed; bow H.LHG.RV

2. Left foot back; grab middle of loop with right hand, overhead block B.DBR.OH

3. Step up with left foot; double block right hand high. B.DBH.LS

4. Step up with right foot; double block left hand high. B.DBH.RS

5. Step up with left foot; double block right hand high. B.DBH.LS

6. Step up with right foot; figure 8 swing forward direction S.FG8.FW

7. Stall at lower right, reverse direction. Figure 8 reverse direction S.FG8.RV

8. Swing at right side, reverse direction S.RSD.RV

9. Stall in front; begin swinging in forward direction S.RSD.FW

10. Continue swinging and move to the left side, forward direction S.LSD.FW

11. Stall at back; begin swinging in reverse direction at left side S.LSD.RV

12. Transfer to swinging overhead, clockwise direction S.OVH.CW

13. Allow to wrap around back to change directions

14. Swing overhead in counter-clockwise direction S.OVH.CC

15. Right foot back & raise left foot; swing downward for leg check B.LCH.LS

16. Step back with left foot & raise right foot; swing downward for leg check B.LCH.RS

17. Right foot back & raise left foot; swing downward for leg check B.LCH.LS

18. Step up with left foot then right foot; figure 8 swing forwards S.FG8.FW

19. Stall at right back; figure 8 swing in reverse direction S.FG8.RV

20. Continue swinging reverse direction at right side S.RSD.RV

21. Stall in front; start swinging forward direction S.RSD.FW

22. Continue to swing; move to left side, forward direction S.LSD.FW

23. Stall at back; swing reverse direction S.LSD.RV

24. Transfer to overhead swing, clockwise direction S.OVH.CW

25. Allow to wrap around back to change directions

26. Overhead swing, counter-clockwise S.OVH.CC

27. Bring left hand to right hand to swing full-length counter clockwise S.EXT.CC

28. Pull left hand back to shorten swing S.OVH.CC

29. Draw up with right foot; leg check to the right B.LCH.RS

30. Continue swing into figure 8 pattern, forward direction S.FG8.FW

31. Draw up with left foot; leg check to left side
B.LCH.LS

32. Set left foot down forwards; forward direction figure 8 swing with handle
S.HD8.FW

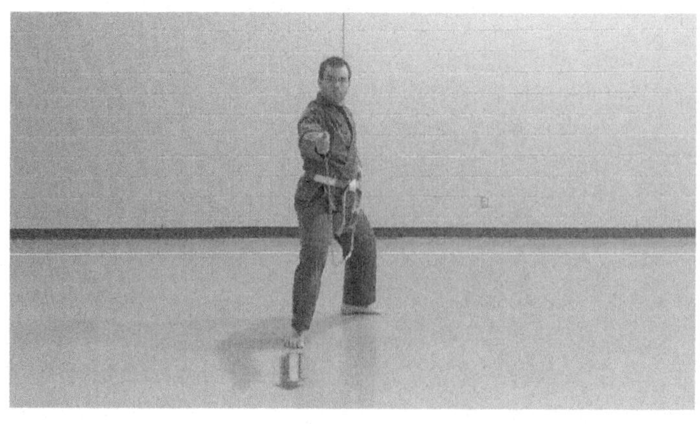

33. Step up with right foot; thrust with weight in right hand
C.WGT.1W

34. Left foot up as changing hands; thrust with weight in left hand H.CHG. RH C.WGT.1W

35. Right foot up as changing hands; thrust with weight in right hand H.CHG. LH C.WGT.1W

36. Step back with right foot; swing reverse direction at right side S.RSD.RV

37. Upwards cast forward; shuffle forwards C.UPC.ST

38. Step backwards with left foot; swing reverse direction at left side S.LSD.RV

39. Upwards cast forwards; shuffle forward C.UPC.ST

40. Change handle direction to forwards; up with left foot, thrust with handle H.SWH.FW C.HDL.FW

41. Right foot up; figure 8 swing forwards; switch handle back H.SWH.RV S.FG8.FW

42. Catch weight in left hand, ending with doubled hold S.CAT.LH

43. Step back with right foot; nunchuck style block to left side. B.NCH.LS

44. Step back with left foot; nunchuck style block to right side. B.NCH.RS

45. Shuffle forward; doubled high block B.DBR.OH

46.
Gathered hold in right hand; stand at attention
H.GTH.RH

47. Bow.
End of kata

Tan (Short) Suruchin Kata Summary

 1. Gathered hold; bow H.LHG.RV	 2. Left foot back B.DBR.OH	 3. Left foot forward B.DBH.LS
 4. Right foot forward B.DBH.RS	 5. Left foot forward B.DBH.LS	 6. Right foot forward S.FG8.FW
 7. Stall; reverse swing S.FG8.RV	 8. Swing right side S.RSD.RV	 9. Stall; reverse swing S.RSD.FW
 10. Left side swing S.LSD.FW	 11. Stall; reverse swing S.LSD.RV	 12. Overhead CW S.OVH.CW
 13. Wrap around body to reverse	 14. Overhead CCW S.OVH.CC	 15. Right foot back B.LCH.LS

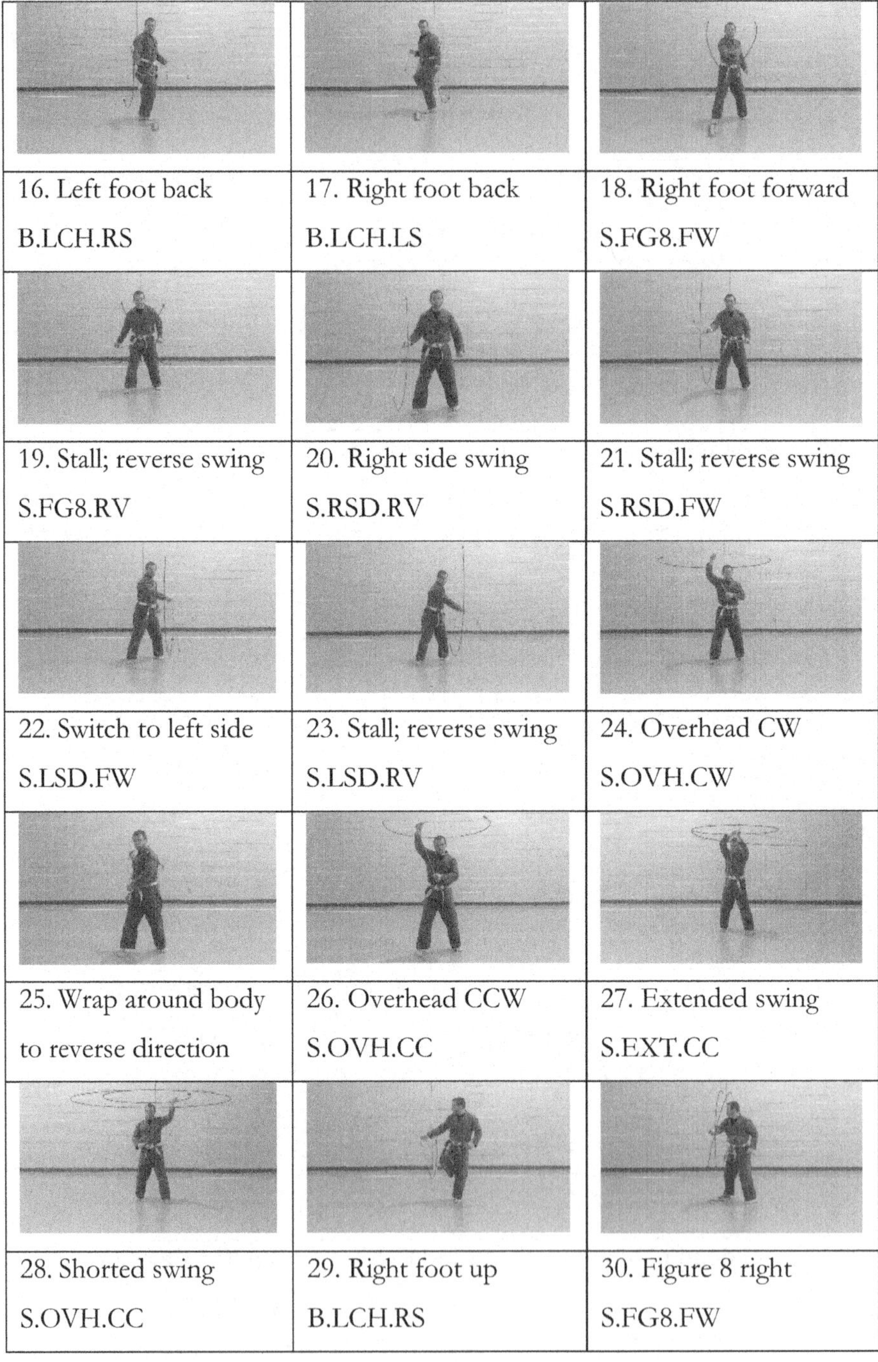

16. Left foot back B.LCH.RS	17. Right foot back B.LCH.LS	18. Right foot forward S.FG8.FW
19. Stall; reverse swing S.FG8.RV	20. Right side swing S.RSD.RV	21. Stall; reverse swing S.RSD.FW
22. Switch to left side S.LSD.FW	23. Stall; reverse swing S.LSD.RV	24. Overhead CW S.OVH.CW
25. Wrap around body to reverse direction	26. Overhead CCW S.OVH.CC	27. Extended swing S.EXT.CC
28. Shorted swing S.OVH.CC	29. Right foot up B.LCH.RS	30. Figure 8 right S.FG8.FW

31. Left foot up B.LCH.LS	32. Figure 8 with handle S.HD8.FW	33. Right foot forward C.WGT.1W

34. Left foot forward; switch grip C.WGT.1W	35. Right foot forward; switch grip C.WGT.1W	36. Right foot back S.RSD.RV

37. Shuffle forward C.UPC.ST	38. Left foot back S.LSD.RV	39. Shuffle forward C.UPC.ST

40. Left foot forward; switch grip C.HDL.FW	41. Right foot forward; switch grip S.FG8.FW	42. Catch in left hand S.CAT.LH

43. Right foot back B.NCH.LS	44. Left foot back B.NCH.RS	45. B.DBR.OH Bow out (not shown)

Naga (Long) Suruchin Kata

Alternative names are Cho Kusari no kata, Maezato no suruchin, or Kanegawa no Suruchin. This kata is from Ryukyu Kobudo and is the rarest suruchin kata to find performed today. It traditionally uses a metal (chain) suruchin with a handle on one end of approximately 230-240cm, or about 92-94 inches (not including the handle).

Note: In preparing this book for publication, influence from other weapon katas was noted in the author's performance of this kata; notably, holding the upper hand at shoulder height throughout vs. the traditional chin/ear height.

Figure 60 Motokatsu Inoue demonstrating bunkai, courtesy of Victor Smith.

1. Stand at attention, suruchin in left hand (gathered hold) H.LHG.RV

2. Bow

3. Pull left foot back, raise right foot; hold chain horizontally H.GTH.LH

4. Lower right foot forwards

5. Pivot both feet to the left; vertical block left hand high B.VTR.LH

6. Bring left foot up to right foot; right hand high

7. Step up with right foot; right hand forward

8. Step up with left foot; left hand forward

9. Step up with right foot; right hand forward

10. Pivot on right foot, moving left foot CCW; vertical block B.VTL.RH

11. Bring right foot next to left foot; vertical block B.VTR.LH

12. Slide right foot to the right

13. Bring left foot to right foot; vertical block B.VTL.RH

14. Step forward with right foot, right hand forward

15. Step forward with left foot, left hand forward

16. Step forward with right foot; right hand forward

17. Pivot on right foot, moving left foot CCW; vertical block B.VTL.RH

18. Draw right foot up; vertical block B.VTR.LH

19. Set right foot down; look left

20. Raise left foot; vertical block B.VTL.RH

21. Lower left foot parallel with right foot

22. Step up with right foot; right hand forward

23. Step up with left foot; left hand forward

24. Extend chain to midpoint; forward swing S.RSD.FW

25. Step forward with right foot; stop swinging

26. swing in overhead counter-clockwise circle S.OVH.CC

27. Continue swinging overhead; pivot on right foot to face back

28. Continue swinging; pivot on right foot forwards; extend chain S.EXT.CC

29. Shorten chain by pulling in with left hand

30. Stop swinging

31. Draw right foot back to left foot; swing in forwards figure 8 pattern S.FG8.FW

32. Swing in forwards direction at right side S.RSD.FW

33. Swing at left side, forwards direction S.LSD.FW

34. Horizontal swing to right C.HZC.LS

35. Horizontal swing to left side C.HZC.RS

36. Step forwards with right foot; stop swinging

37. Bring right foot parallel to left foot; hold chain horizontally

38. Kneel on right knee; hold chain right hand up, left hand down

*Note: translation tells to "pull left foot back to kneel" – believed to be typo in original text

39. Stand back up; hold chain horizontally

40. Gather chain in right hand; attention stance H.GTH.RH

41. Bow

42. End

Naga (Long) Suruchin Kata Summary

 1. At attention H.LHG.RV	 2. Bow	 3. Left foot back, raise right H.GTH.LH
 4. Right foot forwards	 5. Pivot left; vertical block B.VTR.LH	 6. Left foot up to right foot; right hand high
 7. Right foot and hand forward	 8. Left foot and hand forward	 9. Right foot and hand forward
 10. Pivot CCW on right foot B.VTL.RH	 11. Right foot to left foot B.VTR.LH	 12. Right foot to right
 13. Left foot to right foot B.VTL.RH	 14. Right foot and hand forward	 15. Left foot and hand forward

 16. Right foot and hand forward	 17. Pivot CCW on right foot B.VTL.RH	 18. Right foot raised B.VTL.LH
 19. Set right foot down look left	 20. Left foot raised B.VTL.RH	 21. Lower left foot parallel with right
 22. Right foot and hand forward	 23. Left foot and hand forward	 24. Forward swing S.RSD.FW
 25. Right foot forward; stop swinging	 26. Swing overhead CCW S.OVH.CC	 27. Continue swing; pivot on R foot CCW
 28. pivot on R foot CCW; extend chain	 29. Shorten chain	 30. Stop swinging

31. Right foot back S.FG8.FW	32. Forward swing S.RSD.FW	33. Left side forward swing S.LSD.FW

34. Horizontal swing to right C.HZC.LS	35. Horizontal swing to left side C.HZC.RS	36. Right foot forward; stop swinging

37. Right foot parallel with left	38. Kneel on right knee, chain vertical	39. Stand up, chain horizontal

40. At attention H.GTH.RH	41. Bow	42. End

Suruchin no Toseki

Also called Suruchin No Kata, this kata originates form Matayoshi Kobudo. It traditionally uses a rope and rock suruchin, measured to 1.5x the arm span of the practitioner (Image below of Matayoshi Shinpo courtesy of www.bushikan.com).

Note that some schools have developed variations of the kata (such as Sensei Andrea Guarelli's and Sensei Yamashiro Kenichi's versions); what follows is the version as documented in Matayoshi Shinpo's 1990's film [19].

Figure 61 Matayoshi Shinpo demonstrating suruchin technique, courtesy of www.bushikan.com

1. Stand at attention; suruchin gathered in thirds H.FLD.DB

2. Bow

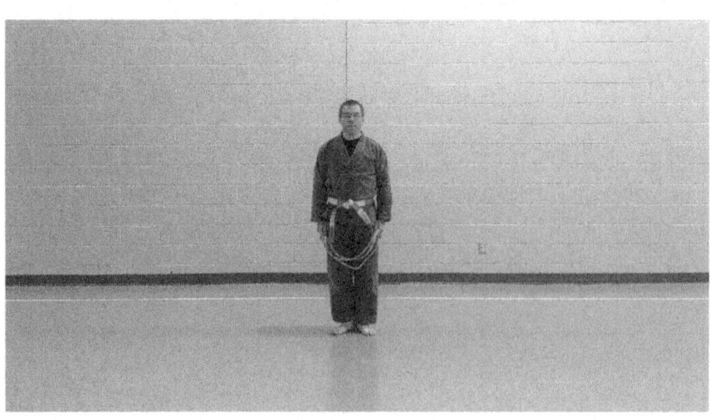

3. Back to attention

4. Right foot forward; left hand up high block B.DBH.RS

5. Left foot forward, right hand up high block B.DBH.LS

6. Release with right hand, swing in left hand to cast forward horizontally C.HZC.LS

7. Continue fully extended swing counter-clockwise S.EXT.CC

8. Shorten swing by drawing through right hand S.OVH.CC

9. Continue swing; pivot on left foot counter-clockwise to rear (180)

10. Continue pivot 90 degrees counter-clockwise

11. Continue pivot 90 degrees counter-clockwise to face front

12. Step up with right foot during forward horizontal cast…. C.HZC.LS

13. … step up with left foot; forward cast again C.HZC.LS

14. Stay stationary; forward cast a third time C.HZC.LS

15. From overhead CCW swing, begin wrapping around right hand H.WRP.RH

16. Continue wrapping, step back CCW with left foot

17. Continue wrapping, step 180 degrees CCW with right foot

18. Finish wrapping, step back CCW with left foot, horizontal strike C.HZS.LS

19. Switch feet (up then back), swing CW overhead; horizontal strike C.HZS.RS

20. Step CCW with right foot, swing CCW overhead to prepare for…

21. …strike horizontally while drawing left foot back to kneel C.HZS.LS

22. Step up with left foot; swing overhead and strike horizontally C.HZS.RS

23. Swing CCW overhead as stepping CCW with right foot…

24. …step back with left foot, horizontal strike C.HZS.LS

25. Switch feet (left up, right back); swing overhead & horizontal strike C.HZS.RS

26. Switch feet (up then back); swing overhead & horizontal strike C.HZS.LS

27. Switch feet (left up, right back); swing overhead, horizontal strike C.HZS.RS

28. Step forward with right foot to kneeling, horizontal strike C.HZS.LS

29. Swing overhead and horizontal strike C.HZS.RS

30. Horizontal strike to left side C.HZS.LS

31. Stand up; swing overhead and horizontal strike C.HZS.RS

32. Swing overhead and horizontal strike C.HZS.LS

33. Swing overhead clockwise to unwind suruchin from hand

34. Swing forward direction at right side 2x S.RSD.FW

35. Swing forward direction at left side 1x S.LSD.FW

36. Swing forward direction at right side 2x S.RSD.FW

37. Swing forward direction at left side 1x S.LSD.FW

38. Swing forward direction at right side 2x S.RSD.FW

39. Extend rope in left hand, double forwards swing S.DBL.FW

40. Step back with left foot; double weight swing to left C.DBL.LS

41. Switch feet (up then back); circle overhead and double strike to right C.DBL.RS

Note: overhead rotation path of both weights not shown with arrows for clarity's sake; same through step #48

42. Step CCW with right foot while swinging weights CCW…

43. …circle both weights overhead and side strike; left foot back C.DBL.LS

44. Step up with left foot, circle both weight overhead and side strike C.DBL.RS

45. Step CCW with right foot, start swinging weights CCW…

46. … step back with left foot; circle weights overhead and side strike C.DBL.LS

47. Switch feet (left up, right back), circle weights overhead and side strike C.DBL.RS

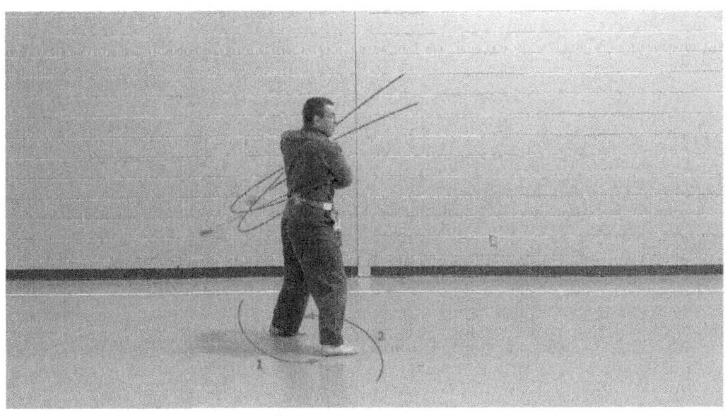

48. Step CCW with right then left foot to face side, circle overhead & side strike C.DBL.LS

49. Turn CW (left then right foot); adjust to standard hold, forward swing S.RSD.FW

50. Step up with right foot; figure 8 swing in forwards direction S.FG8.FW

51. Double figure 8 S.DBL.F8

52. Spin CCW while transitioning to standard hold; overhead CCW swing S.OVH.CC

53. Continue turn to face forward; continue overhead CCW swing S.OVH.CC

54. Shuffle forward and horizontal cast right to left C.HZC.LS

55. Open right hand to wrap suruchin H.WRP.RH

56. Catch swinging weight with left hand S.CAT.LH Step up with right foot and…

57. Strike with right hand

58. Bring left foot up parallel with right foot

59. Bring left foot next to right, attention stance; suruchin in right hand

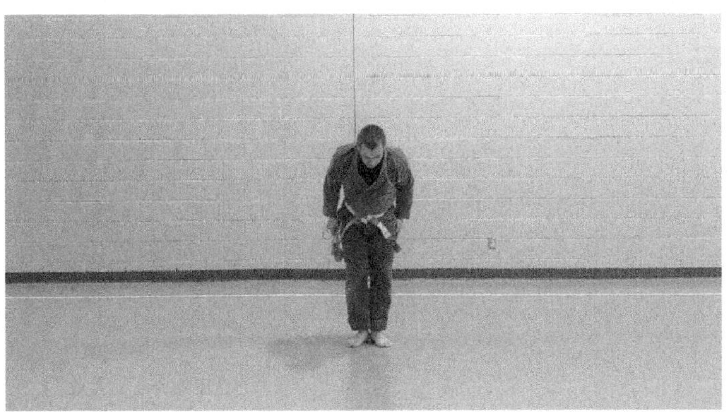

60. Bow (end)

Suruchin No Toseki Kata Summary

 1. Attention H.FLD.DB	 2. Bow	 3. Attention
 4. Right foot forward B.DBH.RS	 5. Left foot forward B.DBH.LS	 6. Release right hand C.HZC.RS
 7. Overhead CCW swing S.EXT.CC	 8. Overhead swing S.OVH.CC	 9. Pivot CCW on left foot 180 degrees
 10. Pivot CCW on left foot 90 degrees	 11. Pivot CCW on left foot 90 degrees to front	 12. Right foot forward C.HZC.LS
 13. Left foot forward C.HZC.LS	 14. Forward cast C.HZC.LS	 15. Wrap around hand H.WDB.RH

 16. Step back 180 with left foot (wrap)	 17. Step back 180 with right foot (wrap)	 18. Left foot back 180 C.HZS.LS
 19. Switch feet, over-head C.HZS.RS	 20. Right foot CCW 180, overhead…	 21. Left foot back; kneel C.HZS.LS
 22. Left foot forward, overhead C.HZS.RS	 23. Right foot CCW 180, overhead…	 24. Left foot back C.HZS.LS
 25. Switch feet; over-head C.HZS.RS	 26. Switch feet; over-head C.HZS.LS	 27. Switch feet; over-head C.HZS.RS
 28. Right foot forward; kneel C.HZS.LS	 29. Overhead C.HZS.RS	 30. C.HZS.LS

31. Stand, overhead C.HZS.RS	32. Overhead C.HZS.LS	33. CW swing to unwrap

34. Forward swing 2x S.RSD.FW	35. Left side swing 1x S.LSD.FW	36. Forward swing 2x S.RSD.FW

37. Left side swing 1x S.LSD.FW	38. Forward swing 2x S.RSD.FW	39. Double forward swing S.DBL.FW

40. Left foot back C.DBL.LS	41. Switch feet; over-head C.DBL.RS	42. Right foot CCW 180; overhead…

43. Left foot back C.DBL.LS	44. Left foot forward, overhead C.DBL.RS	45. Right foot CCW 180; overhead…

 46. Left foot back C.DBL.LS	 47. Switch feet, over- head C.DBL.RS	 48. Turn 90 CCW; overhead C.DBL.LS
 49. Turn 90 CW S.RSD.FW	 50. Right foot forward S.FG8.FW	 51. Double figure 8 S.DBL.F8
 52. Spin 180 CCW…	 53. turn 180 CCW S.OVH.CC	 54. Shuffle forward C.HZC.LS
 55. Wrap suruchin H.WRP.RH	 56. Catch in left hand S.CAT.LH	 57. Right foot forward, strike right hand
 58. Left foot forward	 59. Left foot to right foot; rope in right hand	 60. Bow (end)

Miichiryu Suruchin Kata

Introduction to Miichiryu Suruchin kata

In the world of martial arts, it is rare to get an insight into the mind of the creator of a kata, to know the exact thought process that went into the kata's creation. It is with that in mind that the author includes the following description of Miichiryu (me-che-roo) kata:

Authors Note:

This kata was designed to combine the movements of Ryukyu Kobudo, Matayoshi Kobudo, and Meteor Hammer. This is reflected in the name, which translates to "Three Styles suruchin." No single style included the full range of potent suruchin techniques. As far as the footwork, this kata uses the Naihunchin kata pattern. This was done for three reasons; first, the pattern works well with several of the techniques (leg check, foot casting, etc.). Second, this pattern does not roam around much. Considering how much room is needed to swing a suruchin, conserving space was a priority for practicality in the dojo. Third, the pattern is already known to the students of my dojo, being Isshinryu, making one less thing to learn. As far as techniques go, while there are some fantastic and powerful techniques available, I restricted some categories for practicality's sake. I tried to avoid movements that overly wrapped around the body, since an attacker rushing forward and interrupting a movement would leave you at a severe disadvantage. I also avoided techniques that took several seconds to prepare (wrapping/spinning getting ready for a cast) for the same reason. Lastly, there are two forms of casting with the foot; letting the weight rest on the lower half of the foot and then casting the weight with a kick or hitting higher up the rope and letting the weight make a tight circle past the foot to cast. While the second method generates significant centrifugal force, the first method is less susceptible to failing if positioning is not perfect and allows casting in directions other than the initial swing direction. Lastly, this kata is not intended to be the last word in all the best techniques for suruchin, but a starting place that a student can then add additional katas and techniques to as they progress.

Regards,

Leo Scott Britt III

1. Stand at attention; suruchin in gathered hold in left hand handle reversed H.LHG.RV

2. Bow

3. Salutation (right hand flat over left hand)

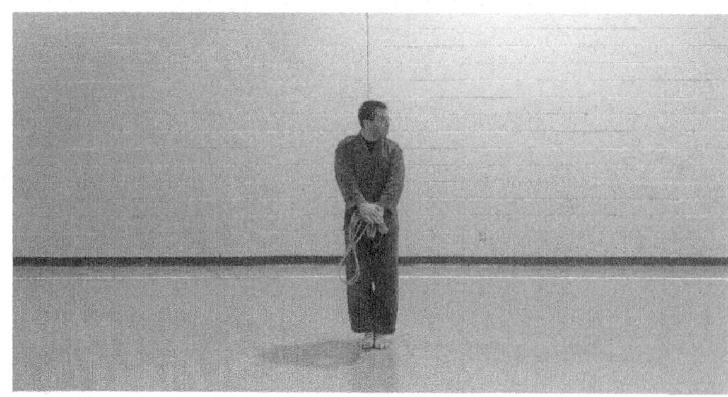

4. Look to left; feet come together

5. Step across with right foot, while grabbing middle of rope with right hand

6. Step out to left with left foot, block to left side B.DBL.LS

7. Release weight with left hand; swing at side in forward direction S.RSD.FW

8. Continue swinging and step across to the right with left foot

9. Bring right foot up (toes out) and catch suruchin 3-4" up rope

10. Kick out with right foot to cast weight forward at head height C.FOT.FW

11. Return to forward swing at side, look back over right shoulder S.RSD.FW

12. Upward cast to the back C.UPC.BK

13. Return to side spin, this time in the reverse direction S.RSD.RV

14. Upward cast in the forward direction at head height C.UPC.ST

15. Resume spinning at side, forward direction S.RSD.FW

16. Extend right foot, toes out and catch suruchin 3-4" up rope

17. Kick right foot to the left to cast weight to left C.FOT.LS

18. Recover rope and swing in a circle in front, CCW S.FRT.CC

19. Cast to right side C.UPC.RS

20. Pivot 45 degrees; swing in figure 8 pattern forwards direction S.FG8.FW

21. Swing at right side in forwards direction; look left S.RSD.FW

22. Extend right elbow into path of rope so suruchin swings up into it

23. Pivot feet to other 45; at same time move elbow to front of body S.ELB.FW

24. Look right, extend elbow into path of rope so it comes down on it

25. As weight comes up, lean back slightly, and move elbow out while…

26. …Pivoting feet to other 45, continue forward swing S.ELB.RV

27. Pivot feet to front and swing overhead clockwise S.OVH.CW

28. Bring the left hand to the right hand for a full-length overhead swing S.EXT.CW

29. Release with left hand; continue swing lower…

30. …Continue swing around back, reach to catch with left hand

31.
Transfer to left hand, bring right hand to front to catch rope
S.BCK.CW

32.
Continue movement into overhead clockwise swing
S.OVH.CW

33.
Swinging strike to front, left to right
C.HZS.RS

34. Allow weight to wrap body and be stopped by arm to change directions

35. Swing back around and over-head, counter-clockwise S.OVH.CC

36. Look to the left

37. Cast to the left with right-to-left horizontal swing C.HZC.LS

38. Shorten up rope; continue swinging overhead; look right S.OVH.CC

39. Kneel on left knee; cast to right (right-to-left swing) C.HCZ.LS

40. Stand back up; continue swing overhead counter-clockwise S.OVH.CC

41. Swing weight down to meet left hand, catch S.CAT.LH

42. Doubled high block to the right; left hand high B.DBL.RS

43. Stack both hands on the right hip; look left

44. Release weight to allow it to hang down about 1 foot

45. Step across to the left with the right foot

46. Bring left foot up; swing weight down in block B.LCH.LS

47. Set left foot down; doubled rope high block B.DBR.OH

48. Catch right pinky finger in loop; look left

49. Wrap doubled rope around right hand one time H.WDB.RH

50. High block to the left, right hand high B.DBL.LS (modified)

51. Release weights with left hand; swing clockwise to left side C.DBS.LS (modified)

52. Allow weights to wrap around body to change directions

53. Swing weights back in clockwise direction over head

54. Swing left to right; wrap around body C.DBS.RS (modified)

55. Swing back overhead, & strike right - left; weights wrap C.DBS.LS (modified)

56. Left hand regains control of weights

57. Double high block; rope still wrapped around right hand B.DBR.OH (modified)

58. Loop rope forward in catching movement

59. Wrap rope around right elbow, look left B.NCH.RS

60. Sweep up with left foot

61. Set left foot down; strike to left with weights in left hand. **Kiai (yell)** C.WGT.DB

62. Bring feet together, release wrapped rope and gather, right hand open over left

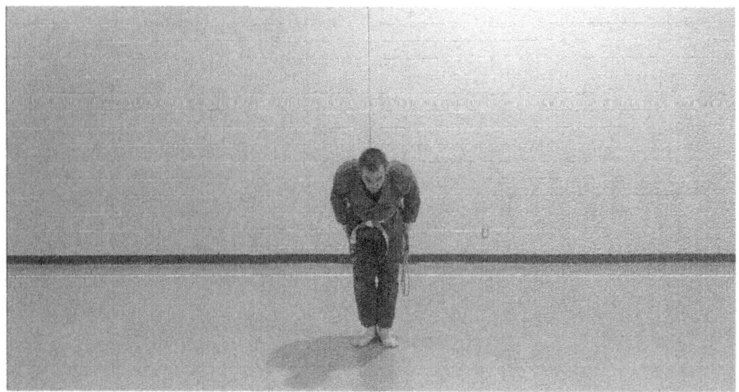

63. Bow. End of kata

Miichiryu Summary

 2. Bow H.LHG.RV	 3. Salutation	 4. Look left; feet together

5. Right foot step across	6. Left foot step out B.DBH.RS	7. Look right; spin forward S.RSD.FW

8. Left foot step across	9. Catch rope on right foot	10. Cast forward C.FOT.FW

11. Look over right shoulder S.RSD.FW	12. Cast backwards C.UPC.BK	13. Spin in reverse direction S.RSD.RV

14. Upward cast, forward C.UPC.ST	15. Spin forwards S.RSD.FW	16. Catch rope on right foot; look left

 17. Kicking cast to left C.FOT.LS	 18. Circle in front, clockwise S.FRT.CW	 19. Upward cast to right C.UPC.RS
 20. Fig. 8 swing, right 45 S.FG8.FW	 21. Look left; forward swing S.RSD.FW	 22. Extend right elbow to catch rope
 23. Pivot to left 45 S.ELB.FW	 24. Look right; extend right elbow	 25. Lean back; move elbow around…
 26. Pivot to right 45 S.ELB.RV	 27. Feet to front; swing overhead S.OVH.CW	 28. Extended overhead swing S.EXT.CW
 29. Release with left hand	 30. Swing behind back; switch to left hand	 31. Swing to front; catch rope right hand

 32. Overhead clockwise swing S.OVH.CW	 33. Left to right strike C.HZS.RS	 34. Weight wrap around body
 35. Overhead counter-clockwise S.OVH.CC	 36. Look left	 37. Right to left strike C.HZC.LS
 38. Overhead counter-clockwise S.OVH.CC	 39. Kneeling right to left strike C.KNE.RS	 40. Overhead counter-clockwise S.OVH.CC
 41. Catch weight in left hand H.LHG.RV	 42. Double block to right B.DBH.LS	 43. Stack hand on right hip, look right
 44. Lower weight 1 foot	 45. Step across with right foot	 46. Leg block (left foot up) B.LCH.LS

 47. Doubled high block B.DBR.OH	 48. Catch right pinky in loop, look left	 49. Wrap once around right hand H.WDB.RH
 50. High block left B.DBH.RH	 51. Release left hand; swing left C.DBS.LS	 52. Wrap around body
 53. Swing clockwise overhead	 54. Swing left to right; wrap C.DBS.RS	 55. Swing right to left; wrap C.DBS.LS
 56. Left hand grab weights	 57. Overhead block B.DBR.OH	 58. Looping forward
 59. Wrap around right elbow B.NCH.RS	 60. Sweep up left foot	 61. Strike with weights Bow out (not shown)

Suruchin Mini-Kata

About Mini Katas

The concept of mini katas came about from students who joined karate with the hopes of working on a particular weapon they had dreamed of learning. However, in the author's Isshinryu school a student does not traditionally start on weapons until at least green belt. This could be discouraging for some students. However, the rank requirements already included an "extra credit" requirement for many ranks that could be fulfilled by attending a seminar, attending a tournament, writing a paper, etc. So "mini-katas" were created for all weapons as an option for extra credit. These katas were designed to be 12 moves or less, could be learned in a single class, and would serve as an introduction to the weapon with some of the basic blocks and strikes for that weapon. This gives students an option to learn about what interests them at an earlier stage and whets the appetite for the full katas that come further down the road.

While the dynamics of the suruchin make it a more difficult weapon to master than, say, the Bo, it is by no means beyond the reach of students who wish to apply themselves. To prove this point, the photos in this kata are of Ian, a six-year-old student who took an interest in the suruchin and took it upon himself to learn it and become proficient at it (in addition to his normal curriculum).

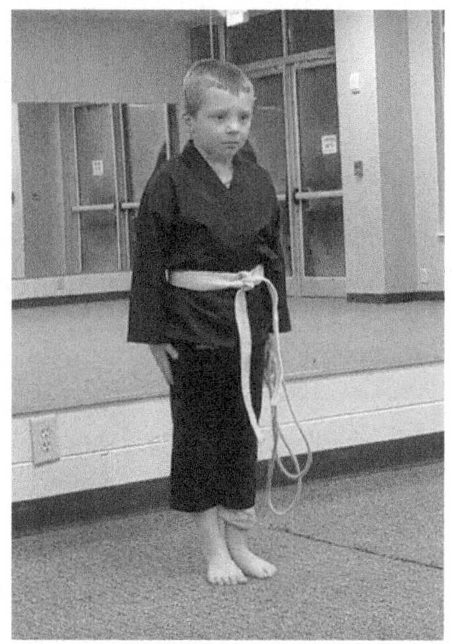

1. Bow in

2. Step back with left foot; overhead block

3. Swing in forward figure of 8 (2x)

4. Reverse direction, reverse swing at side 2x

5. Cast forward

6. Swing counterclockwise overhead 2x

7. Cast forward

8. Swing forward at side 2x

9. Cast forward with right foot

10. Resume swinging forward at side

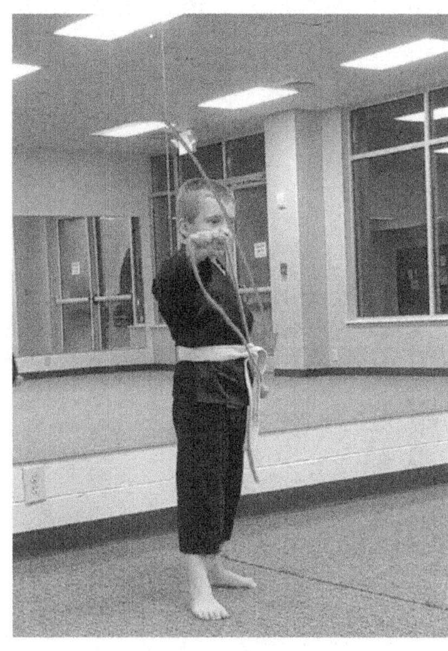

11. Catch weight with left hand

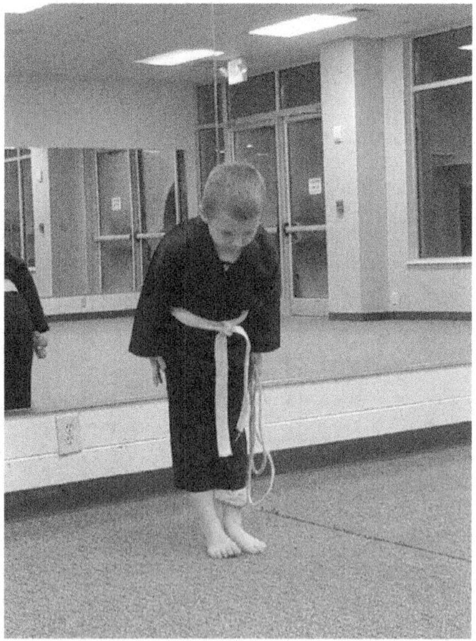

12. Bow out

Kumite

The following section demonstrates example applications (Bunkai) for the suruchin techniques, inclusive of various styles and suruchin types. It is in no way intended to be comprehensive of all the ways to use a suruchin.

Technique 1: Forward figure 8 against bo, to outside

1. Figure 8 swing; strike head/collar bone as suruchin is at right side

2. Opponent raises bo to try to guard

3. Step up; strike with weight to midsection

Technique 2: Forward figure 8 against bo, to inside

1. Figure 8 swing; strike head/collar bone as suruchin is at right side

2. Opponent raises bo to try to guard

3. Step up and to side; strike with weight to kidney area

Technique 3: Double block to outside against bo

1. Double block (parry) bo to right

2. Release one weight and swing forwards to head/ collar bone

3. Step to side; strike to kidney area

Technique 4: Double block to inside against bo

1. Double block bo to left side

2. Release one weight and swing forwards strike head/ collar bone

3. Step up; strike with other weight to midsection

Technique 5: Single block to inside against bo

1. Single bock (parry) bo to left side

2. Swing free end down on head/ collar bone

3. Step up; strike with other weight to midsection

Technique 6: Single block to outside against bo

1. Single block bo (parry) to right side

2. Swing free end down on head/ collar bone

3. Step to side; strike with other weight to kidney area

Technique 7: Single leg block against bo

1. Hold rope 8-12" from end in right hand

2. Parry bo with right leg raised

3. Step forward and strike with weight in right hand

Technique 8: Double neck wrap to throw

1. Holding suruchin in 3rds (manriki length), head block

2. Force forwards; trapping hand as wrap around back of neck

3. Pivot body (hip-to-hip); throw opponent

Technique 9: Trap weapon, switch and strike

1. Swing and wrap weapon

2. Maintain tension, step forward and grab rope with left hand (let go of left weight)

3. Step forward and strike with weight using right hand

Technique 10: Entangle leg and throw

1. Horizontal swing to wrap lead leg

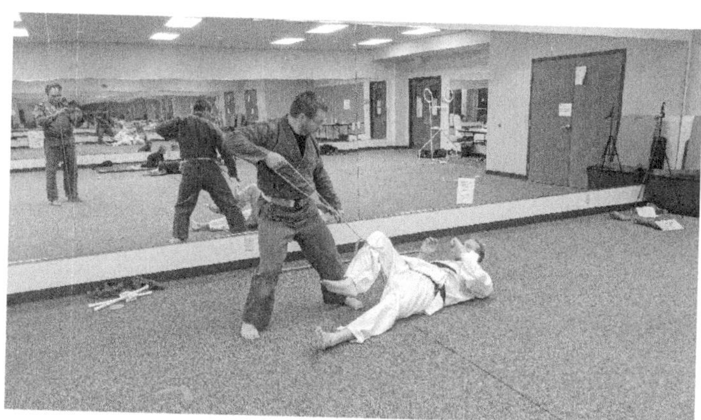

2. Pull to take down opponent

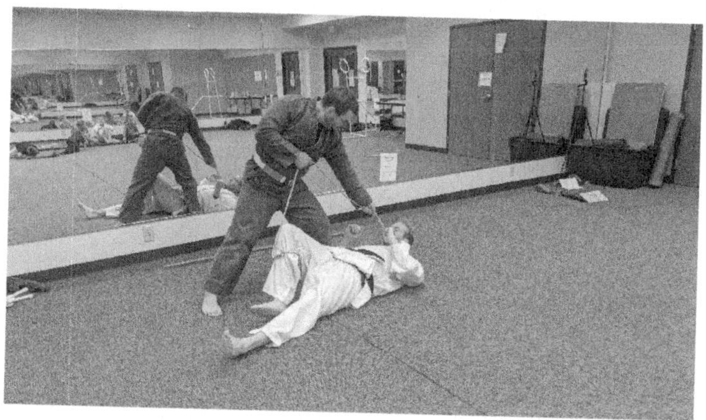

3. Step forward; strike with other weight to head

Training Methods

Below are a few ideas for training with the suruchin, both solo and in the dojo. For most methods of practice other than solo kata, some form of practice suruchin is suggested. See the "Construction" section of this book for ideas on making a practice suruchin.

1. **Kobudo Dummy**. A relatively inexpensive Kobudo dummy can by formed using 2x4 lumber made into a cross shape with a short crosspiece, which is then wrapped in rope. This is good for both light and full contact practice (once the student is capable enough to use a heavy suruchin without hurting themselves). The dummy below was made with 2x4 and 2x10 lumber and wrapped in carpet, and includes a hole at head height for target practice with casting techniques.

Figure 62 Kobudo Dummy

2. **Floor targets.** These inexpensive rubber/poly discs (sometimes called Spot Markers or Carpet Spots) can provide safe targets for younger/more inexperienced students, especially with the tennis ball type suruchin.

Figure 63 Spot markers

3. **"Ladder ball" PVC pipe.** This configuration of ¾" PVC pipe which is similar to the game Ladder Ball can be used by two students at once to cast and wrap around various parts, or to cast through various openings for target practice.

Figure 64 PVC Target

Resources

[1] Alexander, George (director), Motokatsu Inoue (performer) (2007). *Ryukyu Kobujutsu*. DVD.

[2] Bishop, Mark (2017). *Okinawan Weaponry: Hidden Methods, Ancient Myths of Kobudo & Te.* ISBN-13 : 978-1326916749

[3] Clarke, Christopher M. (2013). *Okinawan Kobudo: A history of weaponry styles and masters.* Clarke's Canyon Press, Huntingtown MD. ISBN-13: 978-1480264366

[4] Draeger, Donn F. (1972). *The Weapons and Fighting Arts of Indonesia.* Tuttle Martial Arts. ISBN-13 : 0-8048-1716-2.

[5] Guarelli, Andrea (2016). *Okinawan Kobudo: The History, Tools and Techniques of the Ancient Martial Art.* Skyhorse. ISBN-13 : 978-1634504843

[6] Heinze, Thomas (2009). *The Meister des Karate und Kobudo. Teil 1: before 1900.* Norderstedt, Germany: Books on Demand GmbH. EAN 9783839117859

[7] Lohse, Frederick W. (2014). *The Matayoshi Family and Kingai-ryu.* Meibukan Magazine.
https://kodokanboston.files.wordpress.com/2014/02/kingairyuarticle.pdf

[8] Lohse, Frederick W. (2014). *Matayoshi Kobudo: A Brief History and Overview.* https://kodokanboston.files.wordpress.com/2014/02/meibukanmagazine-no-9_matayoshi.pdf

[9] Masahiro Nakamoto (1983). *Okinawa dentō kobudō: sono rekishi to tamashii.* Naha-shi, Bunbukan.

[10] Motokatsu Inoue (1972). Ryukyu Kobujutsu (Jou kan, Chu kan, & Ge kan) (Japanese only)

[11] Motokatsu Inoue (1989). Ryukyu Kobujutsu (Ten no maki & Chi no maki) (English and Japanese)

[12] Nail, Jim. "The Forbidden Art." *Black Belt Magazine*, Nov. 1982, pp. 76-80.

[13] Nishiuchi's Traditional Okinawan Kobudo Weaponry Series: Vol 11 - Mastering the Suruchin (Whip Rope). Century. (DVD)

[14] Patrick McCarthy (1999). *Ancient Okinawan Martial Arts: Koryu Uchinadi, Vol. 1*. Tuttle Martial Arts. ISBN-13 : 978-0804820936.

[15] Russo, Christian (2019). *Hojojutsu: The Warrior's Art of the Rope*. Yoshin Ryu Editions, Turin (Italy). ISBN-13: 978-8894232820

[16] Seiko, Fujita (1964). *Zuki Torinawajutsu*. http://www.freepdf.info/index.php?post/Fujita-Seiko-Zukai-Torinawajutsu

[17] Seiko, Fujita & Shahan, Eric Michael (2020), *Samurai Bondage*.. ISBN-13: 978-1950959112

[18] Shinken, Taira (2009 translated). *Encyclopedia of Okinawan Weapons*. ISBN-10 : 0920129242

[19] Shinpo, Matayoshi (2008). *Matayoshi Shinpo's Traditional Okinawan Kobudo*. Rising Sun Productions. DVD.

[20] Wubei Zhi (section with meteor hammer; page 560 of PDF). http://www.freepdf.info/index.php?post/Yuanyi-Mao-Wubei-Zhi-31-40

[21] https://ryukyukobudoshinkokai.wordpress.com/ryukyu-kobudo-weapons/ (*…The Ryukyu Kobudo Shinkokai inherited the long suruchin kata developed by Taira Shinken sensei (Maezato no suruchin) and the short suruchin kata developed by Minowa Katsuhiko sensei (Minowa no suruchin).*) Retrieved 3-13-2021.

[22] Dr. Yang, Jwing-Ming (1999). *Ancient Chinese Weapons: A Martial Artist's Guide*. ISBN-13: 9781886969674

Index of Figures

Made in the USA
Columbia, SC
15 February 2022